Everyday Life in the Early Republic

EDITED BY

Catherine E. Hutchins

Henry Francis du Pont Winterthur Museum
Winterthur, Delaware

The text of this book is composed in Electra.

Library of Congress Cataloging-in-Publication Data

Everyday life in the early republic / edited by Catherine E. Hutchins.
— 1st ed.
   "Published for Henry Francis du Pont Winterthur Museum."
   Includes bibliographical references.
   ISBN 0-912724-28-5 pb
   ISBN 0-912724-31-5 cb
   1. United States—Social life and customs—1783–1865.
I. Hutchins, Catherine E.   II. Henry Francis du Pont Winterthur
Museum.
E164.E94   1994   94–22568
973.4—dc20   CIP

Contents

Contents

Contents

Introduction
Catherine E. Hutchins

We often describe the forty years between the ratification of the Constitution in 1789 and the inauguration of President Andrew Jackson in 1829 as a period of political unification and economic growth. These years were also ones of great social and cultural change, even upheaval. While the federal government was implementing theories of republicanism and nationalism that had been set forth at the Constitutional Convention of 1787, the nation doubled in physical size, and its population swelled from just under 4 million to more than 12 million. Technological developments in printing made newspapers, periodicals, and books widely affordable. An improved turnpike system connected cities, towns, villages, and farms, rich and poor, while steam engines and canals facilitated the production and transportation of durable and perishable goods. New reform movements took root; older ones flourished. The importation of slaves ceased. Some merchants became immensely wealthy; others went bankrupt. A list of political and economic changes such as this one, however, reveals little of the reality of life for the vast majority of people—the "middling" and "lesser sort."

Our lack of knowledge about the ordinary people of this period is perplexing. An abundance of documentary and artifactual evidence survives. Perhaps too much. To limit their studies to manageable bodies of evidence, scholars have tended to focus on data related to the "better sort," have traced the growth of political parties and nationalism, or have examined labor unrest and economic crises. In consequence, when pressed to talk about what life was like for most people, we have generalized forward or back from a number of outstanding studies written about eighteenth-century life or antebellum life.

Recent preliminary work by a handful of scholars using the daunting amount of material surviving from the federal period indicates that options available to—and choices made by—middle- and lower-class Americans resulted in life-styles that were considerably different from those of the elite, a suggestion that raises questions about whether they were indeed interested in emulating the life-styles of wealthier Americans. We can now say with some surety that most people had discretionary income or at the very least a choice about which essential goods to purchase or where to buy them. This ability to choose changed the quality of people's lives. These early conclusions, however, prompt us to question the suitability of our continuing to use hypotheses and models formulated to fit conditions and evidence from earlier or later periods of study.

The twelve papers in this book address issues of theory and model and explore specific facets of life. They are focused on four major themes: the changing physical and perceptual landscape; the immediate environment of house and home; patterns of consumerism; and the impact of art, science, and literature. Their authors, drawn from five different disciplines, employ a variety of techniques to read both documentary and artifactual evidence. The diversity of this evidence allows them to pose a number of questions. They ask us to reassess our assumptions about the quality of everyday life and how it was achieved by the vast majority of Americans during the early years of the republic.

Political Dimensions of Everyday Life in the Early Republic

Noble E. Cunningham, Jr.

Visiting the United States in 1831, Alexis de Tocqueville observed that politics was the "biggest concern and, so to speak, the only pleasure an American knows. . . . Even the women frequently attend public meetings and listen to political harangues as a recreation from their household labors."[1] The national obsession with politics that de Tocqueville noticed was not new to Jacksonian America. It had been growing for decades, and it gave an important dimension to everyday life in the early republic.

Isaac Weld, Jr., an English traveler touring America in the 1790s, sensed the popular political involvement. After stops at numerous crowded taverns, he recorded that it was scarcely possible for a dozen Americans to sit together without quarreling about politics. In another observation Weld declared that Americans were always complaining about some public measure. "Something or other is always wrong, and they never appear perfectly satisfied. If any great measure is before congress for discussion, seemingly distrustful of the abilities or the integrity of the men they have elected, they meet together in their towns or districts, canvass the matter themselves, and then send forward instructions to their representatives how to act."[2]

Weld here pointed to an activity in which many ordinary Americans were at one time or another engaged: sending petitions to Congress. Popular petitioning of legislative bodies, both on the national and state levels, is only beginning to receive the attention of historians that it merits, and it is a practice that can throw considerable light on the everyday life of Americans in the early republic.[3] On matters that people today might write to a legislator, Americans in the young nation appealed directly to Congress, commonly by sending a petition to a representative or senator to introduce on the floor of Congress.

Because petitions—except for private claims—frequently originated from groups of people sharing some special interest, they provide invaluable sources of information about the concerns of large numbers of Americans. Numerous artisans and craftsmen, for instance, petitioned for tariff protection for the products of their labor. Some petitions were handwritten. Many were printed and had multiple pages of signatures attached. A few signers penned only an "X." On a petition from hatters of Dauphin County, Pennsylvania, in 1802, each hatter listed beside his name the number of hats manufactured in one year. Such examples offer numerous insights into the everyday lives of Americans, not the least of which is that ordinary people kept up with what was happening in Congress and exerted direct pressures on the legislative process. Petitioning provided access to government by people of all circumstances, including aliens. One petition in 1802 from aliens in Philadelphia was signed in four columns across a sheet of paper eight feet in length; another from Baltimore in 1803 had four feet of signatures attached.[4]

An understanding of the relationship of people to their government is important to any assessment of the society in which they live and work. If we exclude the years of the War of 1812, the daily life of Americans in the new republic was not much intruded upon by government. In the 1790s the collection of the federal excise tax passed by the First Congress constituted the greatest intrusion. As revenue collectors roamed the countryside looking for unregistered stills, resentment against the tax on whiskey mounted in western areas, and increasing violence led President George Washington to send troops to enforce the law. Following Thomas Jefferson's election to the presidency, however, all excise taxes were repealed, and the entire internal revenue service of some five hundred collectors and other officials was disbanded. Jefferson boasted in his second inaugural address that the federal government was supported by revenue from taxes on the consumption of foreign goods, paid by those who could afford to buy luxuries, declaring: "It may be the pleasure and pride of an American to ask, what farmer, what mechanic, what laborer, ever sees a tax-gatherer of the United States?"[5]

During John Adams's administration, the alien and sedition laws produced intrusions on individual liberties greater than any other legislation during the federal era. With the advent of Jefferson's administration, these encroachments also ended. Jefferson reaffirmed his commitment not only to civil liberties but also to a government of simplicity that would not interfere in people's lives, promising "a wise and frugal government, which shall restrain men from injuring one another but leave them otherwise free to regulate their own pursuits of industry and improvement and shall not take from the mouth of labor the bread it has earned."[6]

Before his second term ended, Jefferson himself was wrestling with the problem of governmental intervention in the economic life of his countrymen. The Embargo Act of 1807, an effort to force Great Britain to respect American neutrality by prohibiting all exports from the United States, soon required a host of government regulations and enforcement procedures that were contrary to Jeffersonian restraint and simplicity. Once more, an intrusive measure of government was short lived. The embargo was repealed before Jefferson left office.

The department of the national government most directly touching the everyday lives of Americans in all parts of the country was the post office. It was the one real service agency of the federal government, and its importance in daily life was evident. As settlement spread westward and new communities formed, one of the first things people did was petition for the establishment of post roads, and Congress was responsive. The growth of the country, indeed, is strikingly apparent in the reports of the General Post Office to Congress. In 1790 there were only 75 post offices and fewer than 2,000 miles of post roads in the United States. When Jefferson became president in 1801, 957 post offices served 21,000 miles of post roads. By the end of his eight years in office, the number of post offices had more than doubled, to nearly 2,000; post roads totaled over 34,000 miles; and post riders and other conveyances of mail covered about 12,000 miles daily. Two decades later there were over 8,000 post offices and 115,000 miles of post roads.[7]

Figure 1.   Broadside, "*A Geographical View of All the Post Towns in the United States of America and Their Distances from Each Other*," Anderston Printfield, Scotland, 1815. Printed textile; H. 20 ¼″, W. 26″. (Winterthur.) Miniature portraits of President Washington, John Adams, Thomas Jefferson, and James Madison adorn the borders, embellished also with eagles, Liberty, and the seal of the United States.

"A Geographical View of All the Post Towns in the United States of America and Their Distances from Each Other," a broadside printed on textile in 1815, was apparently designed for popular usage (fig. 1). In the same style as modern-day mileage charts found on highway maps and in atlases, it showed the distance between towns. It also provided the schedule of postage rates, which, according to distance, ranged from 6¢ for distances less than 30 miles to 25¢ for distances over 450 miles.

Post offices, as important as they were in private and business correspondence, were also vital to the circulation of news and information. Congress early adopted a policy of aiding newspaper circulation through low postal rates. The post office act of 1792 fixed newspaper rates at 1¢ for distances not more than 100 miles and 1¹/₂¢ for any greater distance. The act also permitted newspapers exchanged between editors to be carried free. The low rate meant that the cost for delivery of a weekly newspaper published in the capital at Philadelphia to any post office in the United States was 75¢ a year. One congressman wrote to his constituents hailing the measure: "A lower rate could not be required and if the people hereafter remain uninformed it must be their own fault, for in this particular government has acted liberally." He also added "that the diffusion of knowledge is productive of virtue and the best security for our civil rights are incontrovertible truths which cannot be too frequently, or too forcibly inculcated."[8]

The low postal rate was but one factor in the success of newspapers. Although many were short lived, the number of papers in the United States steadily increased, growing from about 100 in 1790 to over 300 by 1810. In proportion to population, the extent of newspapers was unprecedented. When Noah Webster started his New York *Minerva* in 1793, he observed that newspapers were eagerly sought after and generally diffused. "In no other country on earth, not even in Great Britain," he wrote, "are Newspapers so generally circulated among the body of the people as in America." Pierre Samuel du Pont de Nemours observed in 1800 that "in America, a great number of people read the Bible, and all the people read a newspaper," noting that many fathers read aloud to their children while breakfast was being prepared.[9]

It was obviously an exaggeration to say that *all* the people read a newspaper, but contemporary commentators agreed that newspapers circulated widely and that a single copy was commonly shared by more than one family. A traveler visiting Lexington, Kentucky, in 1807 reported that a coffeehouse with a reading room offered the files of 42 different newspapers from throughout the United States. Though open to "subscribers and strangers," it was supported by sixty subscribers paying $6 per year. After traveling for more than a year in the United States, Frances Wright wrote in 1820 that "it would be impossible for a country to be more completely deluged with newspapers than is this; they are to be had not only in the English but in the French and Dutch languages, and some will probably soon appear in the Spanish. It is here not the amusement but the duty of every man to know what his public functionaries are doing."[10]

Members of Congress also played a role in seeing that newspapers—which were the principal recorders of congressional debates—circulated in their districts, especially in areas far from cities where major newspapers were published. Congressional rules allowed each representative and senator to receive at government expense subscriptions to three daily papers. This rule came to be interpreted to permit subscriptions to as many weekly papers as equaled the price of three dailies. In the House debate that sanctioned this interpretation, it was indicated that the newspapers were secured by members "to be sent to their constituents, in order that those who live at a distance from presses may be informed of the proceedings of the National Councils."[11] Members also mailed copies of laws and other government documents for circulation in their districts, along with printed copies of some of their speeches. A number of congressmen, particularly in the southern and western states, sent periodic circular letters reporting on the proceedings of Congress. These practices indicate that people in their everyday lives were not so remote from the affairs of the national government as they have sometimes been depicted.

Newspapers were not equally distributed through all sections of the country, and most papers were highly partisan in politics. Indeed, many editors scorned the idea of political impartiality. In launching the Baltimore *American* in 1799, the editor insisted that impartiality of newspapers in politics was a delusion. "Every party will have its *printer*, as well as every sect its *preacher*," he declared.[12]

Officers in the government were not always pleased with the newspapers people were reading, but their observations confirm that they saw newspapers as playing an important role in the everyday life of large numbers of Americans. Postmaster general Gideon Granger, traveling from Washington, D.C., to Philadelphia along back roads in 1802, reported to President Jefferson that he had found on the road a very general circulation of Federalist papers. "They were to be seen at most of the Public houses," he observed, noting unhappily that he had run across but one Republican paper along his circuitous route of some 190 miles. "This was not altogether pleasing to one who believes that public opinion will in a great measure be governed by that Vehicle of Intelligence," he mused.[13]

A democratization of politics was already under way in the United States in the 1790s and gained momentum as the new century opened.

With the broadening of white male suffrage and the more open and direct campaigning fostered by the development of parties, politics became increasingly a common—if not an everyday—part of the life of ordinary Americans. Terms of office of legislators and governors in all the states were shorter than they generally are today, requiring frequent elections, though governors were not elected by direct popular vote everywhere. Political practices varied from state to state, influenced by regional attitudes and habits, but political participation nationwide was broadening.

By 1800 stump-speaking was already common in political campaigning in a few states. In Maryland, for example, one contemporary observed that wherever there is a large gathering—"at a horse race—a cock fight—or a Methodist quarterly meeting"—candidates for political office assemble with their partisans, "mount the rostrum, made out of an empty barrel or hogshead, [and] harangue the sovereign people." Another commentator described this as candidates condescending "to collect dissolute and ignorant mobs of hundreds of individuals, to whom they make long speeches in the open air." A visitor in South Carolina at election time in 1806 reported candidates stationing themselves outside church doors after Sunday services to greet worshipers. Contemporary accounts reveal something of the social dimension of political campaigns. Based on the account of a participant, British diplomat Sir Augustus John Foster described a Maryland barbecue at which two competing candidates for Congress spoke. "Married ladies and girls were of the party," he wrote, "and the candidates delivered their orations sometimes mounted on the stump of a tree and sometimes on a beer barrel." When the candidates finished speaking, according to Foster's report, "they joked and flirted and danced till one o'clock in the morning."[14]

Some observers objected to such mixing of politics and frivolity. Others deplored the free drinks with which candidates in some states courted voters. One unsuccessful candidate for Congress from Kentucky complained in 1806: "A pack of cards, a keg of whisky, and a game cock, have on some occasions (it is said) been a good electioneering apparatus, for a man, who if elected, was to assist in making laws for a nation. But this is not all," he continued. "The candidate according to the present mode of electioneering, if he wishes to succeed, must, for at least a year before the election, totally neglect his private affairs . . . [and] if elected, he has perpetually to take the rounds, through the district with

Figure 2.   John Lewis Krimmel, *Election Day in Philadelphia*, Philadelphia, 1815. Oil on canvas; H. 25 5/8″, W. 16 3/8″. (Winterthur.)

the velocity of a race rider. If he does not do this, there are not wanting men to accuse him of neglect and pride."[15]

These contemporary observations vividly portray a society in which politics had become a common aspect of many people's lives—in cities and towns, at the county seats on court days, and in the countryside. However much some contemporaries deplored the campaign barbecues, treating for votes, and direct solicitation of voters, politics was an important part of the social fabric of the early republic. Frequent elections brought people out to vote, to watch the election-day activities, and to share in the excitement of close races. John Lewis Krimmel, who painted a number of scenes of everyday life in the early republic, caught something of the spirit of public involvement in an 1815 election in his painting *Election Day in Philadelphia* (fig. 2). The street scene shows activity and excitement and a mingling of all classes of society. Flags wave as a parade moves through the crowd; couples stroll, children run, and groups of women and of men (among them former mayor John Barker) gather to debate the politics of the day.[16] A voter arriving in a carriage posted with electioneering broadsides draws no notice from a worker, wearing his shop apron, engaged in animated discussion with a small circle of men nearby. The painting portrays the sense of popular involvement of Americans in politics that de Tocqueville, Weld, and other visitors to the United States so frequently noticed.

Hezekiah Niles, who published election returns from throughout the country in *Niles' Weekly Register*, also recognized the wide public interest in politics when he wrote: "To a people so much interested in the business of elections as (blessed be God for it!) the people of the United States are, it is important to the public instruction, as well as to gratify a laudable curiosity, that exact accounts of the returns of votes, showing the strength and progress of parties, in the several states, should be published and preserved."[17]

Politics permeated popular culture through channels other than election campaigns and political parties. Independence Day, the nation's most celebrated holiday, was commemorated with wide popular participation. Krimmel painted at least two works depicting Centre Square in Philadelphia on the Fourth of July. The earliest, exhibited at the second annual exhibition of the Society of Artists of the United States and the Pennsylvania Academy in 1812, depicts a rather sedate scene. The second, completed in 1819, pictures a lively scene, recording the increasingly boisterous nature of the celebrations.[18]

New York City was often the scene of elaborate pageantry on the Fourth of July. In 1804 a pageant entitled "The Glory of Columbia, Her Yeomanry" offered an elaborate recreation of the American infantry charging a British battery at the battle of Yorktown. The effect was created by employing artificial figures in perspective and using "boys completely equipped, and of a size to correspond in perspective with the Machinery and Scenery." During the finale, a large transparency descended, showing an eagle holding a laurel crown over the head of Washington.[19]

Transparent paintings of the president then in office frequently accompanied portraits of the first president or were displayed alone. At the first Fourth of July celebration after Jefferson's inauguration, Waldron's Museum in New York illuminated an eight-by-five-foot transparent painting of Jefferson that was so popular that the exhibition was repeated on the following Christmas and New Year's evenings. The illumination of Charles Willson Peale's museum in Philadelphia on March 3, 1805, the eve of Jefferson's second inaugural, featured a large transparency of President Jefferson by Rembrandt Peale. The artist's recently completed oil portrait of Jefferson was also on display in the museum, affording visitors a rare public opportunity to view a likeness of the president taken from life.[20]

Political parties also held special celebrations. Federalists commemorated Washington's birthday. Although Republicans criticized the practice as resembling monarchical custom, after Jefferson's election they began holding annual celebrations on March 4, the anniversary of his inauguration. Notable events also offered opportunities to involve large numbers of people in political celebrations. The acquisition of Louisiana was one such occasion. An unsympathetic Federalist congressman reported from Washington in January 1804 that a jubilee had been proclaimed by the Republicans. "There is to be such a feast, it is said, as was never known in America, on account of taking possession of *Louisiana*," he wrote. "There are to be dinners—suppers—balls—assemblies, dances, and I know not what. . . . The *Jubilee* is to begin here—but they expect it will run—like *wildfire*, to every dark and benighted corner of America." That expectation was fulfilled. Republican newspapers throughout the country called for a national festival, and Jefferson's supporters responded by organizing public celebrations. If Philadelphia newspapers are any indication of the extent of activity, the celebration must have dominated the life of the city for days before the festival on May 12, 1804, altering the daily routines of large numbers of people of all ranks.[21]

Another event of the federal era that inspired public involvement of a magnitude sufficient to disrupt everyday life was the death of Washington in the waning days of 1799. Across the nation memorial services, solemn processions, and glowing eulogies began a period of national mourning rarely, if ever, equaled. Theaters in New York draped their stages in black and gave memorial performances. Printers hurried through their presses new editions of Washington's farewell address, while engravers labored to produce ornamented memorial prints. Perhaps the best example of popular involvement in the national grief was the proliferation of needlework mourning pictures. Numerous American women filled many hours with careful needlework to complete one of the mourning designs offered in outline on white satin (fig. 3). In the process they started a trend that made such needlework a distinctive art form in the early decades of the nineteenth century.[22] It is a striking ex-

Figure 3. E. S. Sefford, "*Sacred to the Memory of the Truly Illustrious George Washington*," 1800–1810. Silk and watercolor on satin; H. 15 1/4", W. 16 3/4". (Winterthur.)

ample of the influence of a political event on the everyday lives of large numbers of American women.

Samuel Miller, a New York Presbyterian minister and social commentator, wrote in 1803 that "the *love of gain* peculiarly characterizes the inhabitants of the United States." That was certainly observable in the marketing of various prints, memorial medals, rings, and lockets to mourn Washington's death, not to mention Mason Locke Weems's biographical sketch of Washington rushed into print within weeks of the president's death. Perhaps the most unusual product from the everyday work-world of federal America was the handiwork of a New York confectioner who offered for sale at his store on Broadway "a Monument in Sugar" to the memory of Washington. The design included a portrait of the late president, two figures of a weeping Columbia, and other embellishments, which the confectioner advertised would "scarcely fail to excite the admiration of the curious."[23]

Folk art also provides examples reflecting the political context in which Americans lived out their lives. An unknown artist in a painting of *Liberty and Washington* portrayed the evolving figure of Liberty, flag in hand, crowning a bust of Washington on a pedestal with the popular laudation "First in War, First in Peace, and First in the Hearts of His Countrymen" (fig. 4). A textile banner that may have been waved to celebrate Thomas Jefferson's victory over John Adams in 1801 presented a crude portrait of Jefferson framed by stars representing the sixteen states of the Union (fig. 5). The portrait is held in the talons of the national eagle, which carries in its beak streamers proclaiming "T. Jefferson President of the United States of America" and "John Adams Is No More." In the 1820s a wooden pastry board used in Pennsylvania was carved with the figure of John Quincy Adams and the slogans "Peece and Liberty" and "Home Industry" (fig. 6). Tavern signs with portraits of Washington, eagles, and other patriotic symbols also reflected the broad parameters of politics.[24]

Life-size figures of political leaders, especially presidents, were common in popular exhibitions of waxworks, some of which were moved from city to city. After Aaron Burr mortally wounded Alexander Hamilton in their famous duel in 1804, a New York City exhibitor quickly added a wax reproduction of that deadly scene.[25]

Many people spent some of their discretionary income to visit such waxworks and other exhibitions with strong political content. They also used a portion of their income to buy material objects of a patriotic and political character. Sets of brass buttons were offered for sale for Washington's first inauguration in 1789 (fig. 7). Indeed, some fifty varieties have been identified as being produced in association with that event. A number of political objects for the American market were produced in Great Britain. During Jefferson's presidency, his Republican supporters could buy Sheffield razors elegantly burnished on one side of the blade with the words "a true Jeffersonian," while Federalists could purchase razors adorned with "a true Washingtonian." As the presidential election of 1808 approached, senator Samuel Latham Mitchill of New York re-

Figure 4. *Liberty and Washington*, 1800–1810. Oil on canvas; H. 6′2″, W. 3′8″. (New York State Historical Association, Cooperstown.)

Figure 5.   Election banner, 1801. Linen; H. 20″, W. 37″.
(National Museum of American History, Smithsonian
Institution.)

ported from Washington that "razors are sold here in great Numbers
with the Words 'a true Madisonian' superbly legible on the steel."[26]

Pieces of Liverpool pottery were decorated with transfer designs
depicting American heroes, presidents, ships, and eagles (fig. 8). The
arms or seal of the United States was common as a secondary embellishment on many pieces. While some of the larger pieces, especially jugs
or pitchers, were elaborately decorated and sometimes purchased as expensive presentation pieces, there were also less ornately decorated mugs
that could be purchased by the ordinary person and used in everyday life.
Potteries produced mugs with the portraits of most of the early presidents
and other political figures such as John Hancock and Benjamin
Franklin. That both pitchers and mugs were produced for the mass
market rather than for the connoisseur is indicated by the lack of attention given by British manufacturers to the likenesses offered as portraits
of American presidents. The same likeness, derived from a poor engraving of Jefferson, was employed on different pieces identified as both President Jefferson and President Madison. Another image, identified on
some Liverpool pieces as a portrait of Jefferson and on others as being
President Monroe, was neither man.[27]

Figure 6.   Pastry board, 1820–28. Wood; H. 10⅛″, W. 5¾″. (Abby Aldrich Rockefeller Folk Art Center, Williamsburg, Va.)

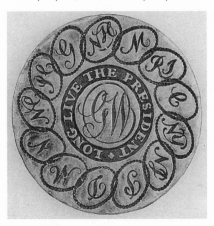

Figure 7.   Commemorative button, Philadelphia, 1789. Brass; Diam. 1⁵/₁₆″. (National Museum of American History, Smithsonian Institution.)

While consumers did not always get reliable likenesses of their presidents, the embellishments promoted patriotism and nationalism. Portraits of presidents on Liverpool pottery pieces were commonly framed by a border containing the names of the states, sometimes on a ribbon with stars for each state and at other times in a symbolically important interlocking chain. The representation of the arms of the United States was often striking. Pieces honoring Washington were filled with symbols of liberty and independence. After his death, prints of the apotheosis of Washington were also transferred to Liverpool creamware pitchers and were even reproduced in China as reverse paintings on glass. One would assume that the American market for these products was large enough to encourage such enterprises.

A Russian traveling in the United States between 1811 and 1813 observed that the country was "glutted with bust portraits of Washington" from the brush of Gilbert Stuart and wrote that "every American considers it his sacred duty to have a likeness of Washington in his home, just as we have images of God's saints . . . Washington's portrait is the finest and sometimes the sole decoration of American homes." In his 1813 painting the *Quilting Frolic*, genre artist Krimmel depicted a

Figure 8.   Pitcher, Liverpool, Eng., ca. 1800. Earthenware, transfer print; H. 8½". (National Museum of American History, Smithsonian Institution, gift of Robert H. McCauley.)

common scene in a modest dwelling (fig. 9). On the wall above the fireplace mantel he painted a framed portrait of Washington. Some two decades later an American magazine editor wrote about the "prints of Washington dark with smoke . . . pasted over the hearths of so many American homes."[28]

Washington's was not the only presidential portrait displayed in American homes. After Jefferson's election to the presidency, numerous engraved portraits of him were offered for sale. Although information on the number of such prints is scant, the account books of Philadelphia publisher Mathew Carey provide rare data. Between March and June 1801, Carey had 800 impressions made from the Jefferson plate that he had had engraved to celebrate Jefferson's inauguration (fig. 10). The prints sold for $2 unframed, $5 framed. Carey himself had 268 of the 800 prints framed before offering them for sale.[29] Although there were several

Figure 9.　John Lewis Krimmel, *Quilting Frolic*, Philadelphia, 1813. Oil on canvas; H. 167/8" W. 223/8". (Winterthur.)

other competing prints of Jefferson being sold at the same time, Carey's sales appear to have been brisk.

Portraits of Jefferson never gained the popularity of Washington, but they did find a ready market. A superior engraving by Robert Field of Gilbert Stuart's 1805 presidential portrait of Jefferson was offered for sale in Boston in 1807 for $1, a price low enough for it to be widely purchased.[30] In contrast to some earlier engravings of Jefferson that showed little artistic skill, Field's well-executed piece demonstrated the advancement of the art in the early republic and made available to ordinary Americans a work of artistic merit.

Some Americans also adorned the walls of their homes with a broadside facsimile of the Declaration of Independence (fig. 11), and by the 1820s they could add an engraved print of John Trumbull's famous painting of its signing, demand for which was stimulated by the original painting's display in leading cities. Broadside prints of presidential inaugural addresses also became wall decorations. Some were printed on

Figure 10.   Cornelius Tiebout after Rembrandt Peale, *Thomas Jefferson: President of the United States*, 1801. Engraving; H. 11″, W. 8³/₄″. (National Portrait Gallery, Smithsonian Institution.)

satin and framed. A daybook of the early 1800s kept by John Doggett, a Roxbury, Massachusetts, merchant, glass importer, and picture framer, contains entries for framing portraits of Washington and the second in-

Figure 11. Declaration of Independence, ca. 1820. Printed cotton; H. 32¼″, W. 27″. (Winterthur.)

augural address of President Jefferson (fig. 12). Doggett charged $6.67 for framing Jefferson's speech and $4.00 for the frame and glass only. In a time when a middle-level clerk in a government office earned about $20.00 a week, framed prints probably hung mainly in the homes or businesses of the more affluent.[31] The prints themselves, however, were not as expensive as the frames, and the high quality paper on which they were commonly printed permitted wall display without framing. In whatever manner exhibited, a broadside of a presidential address, printed and designed for display, acquired importance beyond its con-

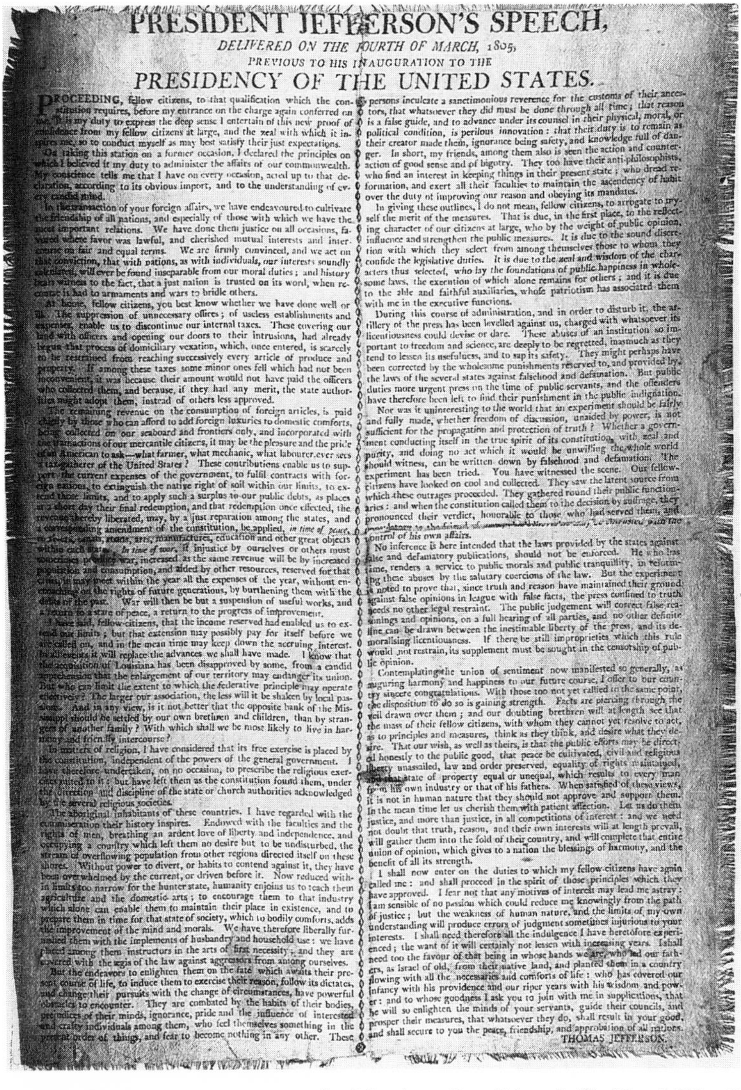

PRESIDENT JEFFERSON'S SPEECH,

DELIVERED ON THE FOURTH OF MARCH, 1805,

PREVIOUS TO HIS INAUGURATION TO THE

PRESIDENCY OF THE UNITED STATES.

Figure 12.   Commemorative textile, March 4, 1805. Printed silk; H. 17″, W. 12″. (American Antiquarian Society.)

tent. It became a material object that revealed something of the political culture of American society.

Less costly than prints were silhouettes, which provided Americans with inexpensive images of themselves, their families, and friends. Silhouettes of political figures offered images that admirers could keep or display. Those based on Jean-Antoine Houdon's bust of President Jefferson were given away at Peale's museum in Philadelphia as an inducement for visitors to have their own silhouettes cut with the aid of the physiognotrace, which inventor John I. Hawkins had given to the museum. In 1804 Raphaelle Peale, who traveled around the country cutting profiles, advertised that with the purchase of a 25¢ frame he would give away the choice of a profile of any of "our three illustrious Presidents," Washington, John Adams, or Jefferson.[32]

Among the works of art available to the public at inexpensive prices, none reflected higher artistic merit than commemorative medals. Such medals, however, were relatively scarce in the early republic. In 1790 a medallic portrait of Washington executed by Samuel Brooks, a Philadelphia goldsmith and seal engraver, was struck by Jacques Manly—the first medal with Washington's likeness to be made in the United States. It was available in gold, priced according to weight, and was produced in silver for $4, in bronze for $2, and in white metal (pewter) for $1.[33]

The earliest presidential inaugural medal celebrated Jefferson's installment in office in 1801 (fig. 13). Engraved by John Reich, who also executed the die for the Indian peace medal with Jefferson's likeness, the portrait was taken from Houdon's bust of Jefferson and won the approval of Jefferson and his daughter Martha Jefferson Randolph. The artistic merit of the medal was enhanced by a classical design on the reverse, depicting Liberty holding the Declaration of Independence in her hand and standing by a rock inscribed "Constitution." This medal, which both Mrs. Randolph and Senator Mitchill described as elegant, sold for $4.25 in solid silver, but only $1.25 in pewter, making it widely affordable. Jefferson himself commented that "it sells the more readily as the prints which have been offered the public are such miserable caracatures."[34] The pewter medal could be purchased for less than many engravings. Although Reich's offering appears to have been a material object of considerable interest to Jefferson's admirers, the striking of inaugural medals was a tradition that only slowly developed.

Figure 13. John Reich, Thomas
Jefferson inaugural medal, Philadel-
phia, 1802. Silver; Diam. 1³/₄".
(American Numismatic Society.)

Meanwhile, other political mementos requiring less artistic skill
were offered to the public. Americans could buy scarves printed with the
text of the Declaration of Independence, snuff boxes adorned with
Jefferson's portrait, and sewing boxes with the portrait of John Quincy
Adams.[35] These and other examples show how much politics permeated

the everyday world, inviting Americans to spend money on political objects of interest or to decorate their homes with political icons.

Political figures were also frequent subjects of popular reading matter. They were prominent in James Hardie's *New Universal Biographical Dictionary, and American Remembrancer of Departed Merit*, which began publication in 1801. This is a work of particular interest because it was available to the average person who might be unwilling or unable to pay for a leather-bound volume of biographical sketches. Hardie issued his work in 64-page signatures that could later be bound into a four-volume reference work, if the reader desired. Each section, published fortnightly, was offered for sale for 25¢. The second section, published in June 1801, offered a short biography of Jefferson and included a small, although not very accurate, engraved portrait of the recently inaugurated president of the United States.[36]

In 1804 the *Literary Magazine and American Register*, published in Philadelphia, began a series of sketches of "eminent and illustrious men" in America by publishing brief biographies and engravings of the portraits of the presidents of the United States. This early example of collective biographies of presidents would be much imitated. As soon as the list of presidents was long enough, books containing the accounts of their lives appeared, along with the biographies of the signers of the Declaration of Independence and other sketches of famous Americans.[37] Such works, designed for a broad market, offer another dimension revealing the common political culture of Americans in the early republic.

Few events illustrate so strikingly the broad dimensions of political influences on early nineteenth-century American life as the visit of Lafayette to the United States in 1824–25. Arriving in New York in August 1824 at the invitation of Congress, the revolutionary hero began a triumphal farewell tour that in thirteen months carried him to every one of the twenty-four states of the Union. He visited all the major cities and numerous smaller places, south as far as New Orleans, north to Portland, and west to St. Louis. Crowds estimated at 50,000 in Baltimore and 70,000 in Boston turned out to cheer the general. At every stop he was accorded innumerable honors, lauded with endless glowing speeches, and celebrated with elaborate festivities. Not since the death of Washington in 1799 had so many Americans of all ranks been so involved in honoring a single man. And never before in the United States had there been produced for any occasion so many mementos. Ribbons, buttons,

Figure 14. Handkerchief, Philadelphia, 1824–25. Printed linen; H. 14″, W. 15″. (Winterthur.)

medallions, fans, handkerchiefs, gloves, plates, bowls, pitchers, and other souvenirs were advertised and sold throughout the nation. A linen handkerchief produced by the Germantown Print Works offered engraved scenes of Lafayette's arrival in New York and at Independence Hall in Philadelphia, where the prospect of his visit had inspired the renovation and refurbishing of that historic hall (fig. 14). The elaborate parade in Philadelphia included not only the traditional military units and civic dignitaries but also contingents of trade groups and other associations involving an estimated 20,000 people—the majority of them common citizens—marching in the parade, carrying banners, and pulling floats.[38] Among many souvenirs produced for the American market in England, one impressive example was a Staffordshire pitcher elaborately

Figure 15. Pitcher, Staffordshire, Eng., 1824–25. Earthenware; H. 9¹⁄₈″. (Larsen Collection, National Museum of American History, Smithsonian Institution.) Lafayette was in America for the opening of the Erie Canal, which Clinton had avidly supported.

adorned with portraits of Lafayette, Washington, Jefferson, and New York governor DeWitt Clinton (fig. 15). Other surviving relics of the celebration include a pair of gloves with the portraits of Washington and Lafayette (fig. 16).

    Lafayette arrived in the United States in the midst of a warmly contested presidential election campaign in which the candidate most

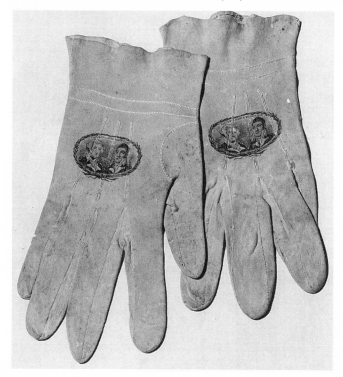

Figure 16. Gloves, New England, 1825. Kid, transfer printed. (Winterthur.) The inscription at the top of the oval is "Imperishable Their Fame."

likely to benefit from the visit of the revolutionary hero was Gen. Andrew Jackson, the hero of the War of 1812. That Jackson's supporters sought to portray him in the mold of Washington and Lafayette and picture him with those heroes can be seen in a tortoiseshell comb with a miniature portrait of Jackson flanked by smaller portraits of Washington on his left and Lafayette on his right. "New Orleans" is inscribed on a banner above Jackson's portrait (fig. 17). Thus were history and politics intertwined in the everyday life of Americans in the early republic.

National politics, the focus of this essay, gave an important commonalty to American political life, but the impact of local and state

Figure 17. Comb, 1824–25. Tortoiseshell. (National Museum of American History, Smithsonian Institution.) Jackson's likeness is after a portrait by Joseph Wood.

politics, in which American were actively involved, was also pervasive. With the role of the national government limited, the actions of state and local governments often more immediately affected their daily lives. Whether in town meetings in New England, at county court days in Virginia, or in new communities in Ohio, there was a wide political consciousness. Only a people with a political culture mature enough to incorporate politics into everyday life could have expanded so rapidly and successfully from a confederation along the Atlantic coast into a nation that by 1820 stretched beyond the Mississippi River. Had there not been a vital political component in the lives of Americans in the early republic, the success of the American experiment would surely have been less certain.

---

[1] Alexis de Tocqueville, *Democracy in America*, ed. Phillips Bradley, 2 vols. (1945; reprint, New York: Vintage Books, 1963), 1:259–60, see also pp. 252–53.

[2] Isaac Weld, Jr., *Travels through the States of North America, and the Provinces of Upper and Lower Canada, during the Years 1795, 1796, and 1797*, 2 vols. (3d ed., London: John Stockdale, 1800), 1:102, 124–25.

[3] An example of recent scholarship is Ruth Bogin, "Petitioning and the New Moral Economy of Post-Revolutionary America," *William and Mary Quarterly*, 3d ser., 45, no. 3 (July 1988): 391–425.

[4] Petitions in House Records, Record Group 233, National Archives; Noble E. Cunningham, Jr., *The Process of Government under Jefferson* (Princeton: Princeton University Press, 1978), pp. 294–315.

[5] Thomas Jefferson, second inaugural address, March 4, 1805, *The Works of Thomas Jefferson*, ed. Paul L. Ford, 12 vols. (New York: G. P. Putnam's Sons, 1904), 10:130. On the repeal of excise taxes, see Cunningham, *Process of Government*, p. 98.

[6] Thomas Jefferson, inaugural address, March 4, 1801, transcribed from Jefferson's final manuscript copy, Thomas Jefferson Papers, Library of Congress, Washington, D.C.

[7] Cunningham, *Process of Government*, pp. 147–48; Leonard D. White, *The Jeffersonians: A Study in Administrative History, 1801–1829* (New York: Macmillan Co., 1951), p. 303.

[8] John Steele, circular letter to his constituents, January 15, 1792, *Circular Letters of Congressmen to Their Constituents, 1789–1829*, ed. Noble E. Cunningham, Jr., 3 vols. (Chapel Hill: University of North Carolina Press, 1978), 1:9. On the 1792 post office act, see *Annals of Congress*, 2d Cong., 1st sess., pp. 63–64, 1339.

[9] Noah Webster, *American Minerva* (New York), December 9, 1793, quoted in Donald H. Stewart, *The Opposition Press of the Federalist Period* (Albany: State University of New York Press, 1969), p. 20; Pierre Samuel du Pont de Nemours, *National Education in the United States of America*, trans. B. G. du Pont (Newark: University of Delaware Press, 1923), p. 4; Stewart, *Opposition Press*, pp. 16, 652.

[10] Fortescue Cuming, *Sketches of a Tour to the Western Country* (Pittsburg, 1810), pp. 166–67; Frances Wright, *Views of Society and Manners in America*, ed. Paul R. Baker (1821; Cambridge: Harvard University Press, 1963), p. 212.

[11] *Annals of Congress*, 7th Cong., 2d sess., pp. 275, 282–85; *Senate Journal*, 4:106.

[12] *American and Daily Advertiser* (Baltimore), May 16, 1799.

[13] Granger to Jefferson, September 5, 1802, Jefferson Papers.

[14] *Maryland Gazette* (Annapolis), September 25, 1800; Oliver Wolcott to Fisher Ames, August 10, 1800, *Memoirs of the Administrations of Washington and John Adams, Edited from the Papers of Oliver Wolcott, Secretary of the Treasury*, ed. George Gibbs, 2 vols. (New York: W. Van Norden, 1846), 2:404; J. Franklin Jameson, ed., "Diary of Edward Hooker, 1805–1808," in *Annual Report, 1896*, 2 vols. (Washington, D.C.: American Historical Association, 1897), 1:900. Augustus John Foster, *Jeffersonian America: Notes on the United States of America Collected in the Years 1805–6–7*

and 11–12, ed. Richard Beale Davis (San Marino, Calif.: Huntington Library, 1954), pp. 203–4.

[15] Robert H. Grayson, broadside, June 5, 1806, Filson Club, Louisville, Ky.; Noble E. Cunningham, Jr., *The Jeffersonian Republicans in Power: Party Operations, 1801–1809* (Chapel Hill: University of North Carolina Press, 1963), pp. 278–79.

[16] Milo M. Naeve, *John Lewis Krimmel: An Artist in Federal America* (Newark: University of Delaware Press, 1987), p. 77.

[17] *Niles' Weekly Register* (Baltimore), June 28, 1816.

[18] Naeve, *John Lewis Krimmel*, pp. 67–68, 101–2.

[19] *American Citizen* (New York), June 30, 1804, in Rita Susswein Gottesman, *The Arts and Crafts in New York, 1800–1804: Advertisements from New York City Newspapers* (New York: New-York Historical Society, 1965), pp. 457–58.

[20] Noble E. Cunningham, Jr., *The Image of Thomas Jefferson in the Public Eye: Portraits for the People, 1800–1809* (Charlottesville: University Press of Virginia, 1981), p. 131; Charles Coleman Sellers, *Charles Willson Peale*, 2 vols. (Philadelphia: American Philosophical Society, 1947), 2:190.

[21] Manasseh Cutler to Francis Low, January 21, 1804, "Seven Letters Written by Manasseh Cutler while Representing the Essex District," *Essex Institute Historical Collections* 39, no. 4 (October 1903): 325. On the newspaper reports of the Philadelphia celebration, see *Aurora* (Philadelphia), March 29, April 6, 20, 26, May 10, 14, 1804; Cunningham, *Jeffersonian Republicans in Power*, p. 286.

[22] For more on mourning pictures, see *Commercial Advertiser* (New York), January 7, 1800, in Gottesman, *Arts and Crafts*, p. 456; *Aurora* (Philadelphia), December 31, 1799; Davida Tenenbaum Deutsch, "Washington Memorial Prints," *Antiques* 111, no. 2 (February 1977): 324–31; Anita Schorsch, "A Key to the Kingdom: The Iconography of a Mourning Picture," *Winterthur Portfolio* 14, no. 1 (Spring 1979): 41–42, 47, 51–54.

[23] Samuel Miller, *A Brief Retrospect of the Eighteenth Century*, 2 vols. (New York: T. and J. Swords, 1803), 2:406–7. *Mercantile Advertiser* (New York), February 24, 1800, in Gottesman, *Arts and Crafts*, p. 388.

[24] Weld, *Travels*, 1:17.

[25] *Mercantile Advertiser* (New York), November 6, 1804, in Gottesman, *Arts and Crafts*, p. 92.

[26] Mitchill as quoted in Roger A. Fischer, *Tippecanoe and Trinkets Too: The Material Culture of American Presidential Campaigns, 1828–1984* (Urbana: University of Illinois Press, 1988), p. 6. For more on political memorabilia, see Fischer, *Tippecanoe and Trinkets*, pp. 2–3; Edmund B. Sullivan, *American Political Badges and Medalets, 1789–1892* (Lawrence, Mass.: Quarterman Publications, 1981), pp. 1–7; Margaret Brown Klapthor and Howard Alexander Morrison, *George Washington: A Figure upon the Stage* (Washington, D.C.: Smithsonian Institution, 1982), p. 191.

[27] Cunningham, *Image of Thomas Jefferson*, pp. 102–5; Mariam Klamkin, *American Patriotic and Political China* (New York: Charles Scribner's Sons, 1973), pp. 77–78.

[28] Avraham Yarmolinsky, *Picturesque United States of America, 1811, 1812, 1813; Being a Memoir on Paul Svinin, Russian Diplomatic Officer, Artist, and Author, Containing Copious Excerpts from His Account of His Travels in America* (New York: W. E. Rudge, 1930), p. 34. The Krimmel painting is discussed in Edgar P. Richardson, *American Paintings and Related Pictures in the Henry Francis du Pont Winterthur Museum* (Charlottesville: University Press of Virginia, 1986), pp. 106–7. *American Magazine of Useful and Entertaining Knowledge* 2, no. 7 (March 1836): 266.

[29] Mathew Carey account books, Carey Papers, American Antiquarian Society, Worcester, Mass.; Cunningham, *Image of Thomas Jefferson*, pp. 49–50.

[30] Cunningham, *Image of Thomas Jefferson*, pp. 88–89.

[31] *Aurora* (Philadelphia), January 22, 1819; *Union* (Philadelphia), January 14, February 20, 1819; John Doggett daybook, 1802–9, Joseph Downs Collection of Manuscripts and Printed Ephemera, Winterthur; Cunningham, *Process of Government*, pp. 156–57.

[32] Raphaelle Peale as quoted in *Aurora* (Philadelphia), November 19, 1804; Cunningham, *Image of Thomas Jefferson*, pp. 123–34; Charles Coleman Sellers, *Mr. Peale's Museum: Charles Willson Peale and the First Popular Museum of Natural Science and Art* (New York: W. W. Norton, 1980), pp. 163, 169, 197–99, 220.

[33] Neil MacNeil, *The President's Medal, 1789–1977* (New York: Clarkson N. Potter, 1977), p. 16.

[34] Jefferson to Martha Jefferson Randolph, April 3, 1802; Martha Jefferson Randolph to Jefferson, April 16, 1802, *The Family Letters of Thomas Jefferson*, ed. Edwin Morris Betts and James A. Bear, Jr. (Columbia: University of Missouri Press, 1966), pp. 221–22; Samuel L. Mitchill to Catherine Mitchill, March 3, April 1, 1802, Samuel Latham Mitchill Papers, Museum of the City of New York; Cunningham, *Image of Thomas Jefferson*, pp. 71–73.

[35] Noble E. Cunningham, Jr., *Popular Images of the Presidency: From Washington to Lincoln* (Columbia: University of Missouri Press, 1991), pp. 241–44.

[36] *American Citizen* (New York), June 30, 1801; Cunningham, *Image of Thomas Jefferson*, pp. 9–10.

[37] *Literary Magazine, and American Register* 2, no. 10 (July 1804): 243. Washington's portrait appeared in July; Adams's, in August; and Jefferson's, in September. Robert W. Lincoln, *Lives of the Presidents of the United States; with Biographical Notices of the Signers of the Declaration of Independence; Sketches of the Most Remarkable Events in History of the Country . . .* (New York: N. Watson, 1833).

[38] Stanley J. Idzerda, Anne C. Loveland, and Marc H. Miller, *Lafayette, Hero of Two Worlds: The Art and Pageantry of His Farewell Tour of America, 1824–1825* (Hanover, N.H.: Queens Museum and University Press of New England, 1989), pp. 63–72, 116, 125–31.

The Model Farmer and the Organization of the Countryside

Bernard L. Herman

The American countryside of the early national period was a landscape in the process of transformation. At the close of the eighteenth century Americans were reconsidering and rearranging the rural world in ways reflecting the florescence of regional tradition, emerging sensibilities about agricultural life and work, rural industrialization, and the economic intricacies of the urban marketplace. To landlords and tenants, residents and travelers, free people and slaves, the appearance of the countryside articulated a vast and complex array of social and economic relationships. Ordinary objects of the rural world—road systems, field patterns, livestock and crops, towns and villages, and buildings from mansion houses to wagon sheds—were made and remade to signify ideas about property, progress, class, and authority. A significant component in the creation of a symbolic landscape was the personification of the model farmer and his material world. The image of the model farmer espoused in the politically charged agricultural literature of the day provides a measure for the evaluation of the broader, grittier realities of the early American countryside.

Benjamin Rush, writing in 1786 to the *Columbian Magazine*, described the people and countryside of Pennsylvania and the Delaware Valley through an extended metaphor based on a progression of three "species" of settlers. The three species represented the rise of an established and civilized landscape. At the bottom of his hierarchy Rush portrayed the frontiersman residing in a rough log cabin in the wilderness, avoiding governance, living in an undomesticated state close to that of native Americans. At the top of Rush's model stood the enlightened agriculturalist with his productive farm and commitment to improving the land. The middle settler existed somewhere between the two, building on the initiative of the first settler but unable to attain the material success and landed stability of the third. In keeping with his investment in the improvement of property, the third settler valued "the protection of laws," supported schools and churches "as a means of promoting order and happiness in society," and possessed a benevolent "public spirit." Visually expressing the cultural values associated with each generation of the settled landscape were houses, farm buildings, field patterns, fences, and livestock. While Rush's model of three settlers suggests much about the way in which early American writers constructed a doctrine of progress, the following discussion focuses on the image and reality of Rush's culminating settler—the model farmer. Rush's image of the model farmer's world persists in the popular imagination. The symbolic stature of his presence expressed in his organization of the countryside continues to influence the growing literature on gentility and rural life in early America.[1] The idyll of the model farmer's material world disguises the substance of economic privilege and social hierarchy that undergird the paradox of early American republican culture.

The actions of the model farmer (Rush's "third settler") marked the completion of "the progress from the savage to civilized life." It was his task to conclude the transformation of untamed landscape into cultured countryside. The third settler alone deserved the title "farmer" and was engaged in "a new species of war," one waged "in the mode of extending population and agriculture." This conquering settler bore "the implements of husbandry" as armament and took the virtues of "industry and economy" as his guide. The goal of the American warrior-farmer, as later agricultural writers baldly stated, was "to realize an estate" and his final achievement "an almost total revolution in the agriculture of the United States."[2]

On the metaphorical field of battle, the model farmer pursued a specific strategy to marshal and control the resources of the countryside. His first actions improved the land—clearing, enclosing, and manuring fields and meadows. Unlike the first and second settlers, who exploited the land, the third settler strove to improve and husband his property. He built a large stone barn "very compact, so as to shut out the cold winter; for . . . horses and cattle, when kept warm, do not require near as much food." To save firewood and labor in cutting and hauling fuel, he heated his house and cooked with stoves. The third settler's dedication to ordering the rural landscape extended from fields to garden to the construction of new farm buildings and culminated with the improvement of the dwelling. The house is "generally built of stone . . . it is large, convenient, and filled with useful furniture . . . It sometimes adjoins the house of the second settler, but is frequently placed at a little distance from it."[3]

Rush promoted the third settler as the embodiment of a specific type of cultural process expressed through the visual regulation and political economy of the material world. To illustrate that achievement Rush developed a rhetoric of ordinary objects—fields, fences, barns, and farmhouses—that conveyed the substance of his agrarian world view. Who was the third settler, and what was his relationship to the larger organization of the federal-era countryside? The third settler profiled in the *Columbian Magazine* was a property owner who managed his lands to produce their greatest possible yield. He plowed his land with efficient horses instead of plodding oxen, cultivated a variety of grains for milling and export, and kept dairy cows for the production of butter marketed in nearby towns and cities. The third settler's farm was further improved with a stone barn, sturdy fences, milk or springhouse, and a one- to two-acre vegetable garden and orchard. The crowning measure of his success was "building a commodious dwelling-house, suited to the improvements and value of the plantation."[4]

Did such farmers exist? How did the reality of the countryside match the metaphor of the model farmer's estate? What are the gaps between prescribed and enacted behaviors?

We can discern the presence and actions of farmers in the Delaware Valley at the close of the eighteenth century in a number of ways, among which are the statistical and descriptive analysis of tax and probate records and surviving structures.[5] Following Rush's lead, we profit most from examining the organization of the countryside with special reference to the landscape features Rush valued in the third settler— improved land, farm buildings, houses, and livestock. As we shall discover, the lionized farmer of the *Columbian Magazine* was an influential rarity in the late eighteenth-century Delaware Valley.

At the close of the eighteenth century, Chester County, Pennsylvania, had been settled for a century and was one of the most intensively developed agricultural landscapes in the United States. A local tax list compiled in 1799 for West Bradford Township, located just west of the county seat at West Chester, enumerated amounts and values of acreage, buildings, and livestock. The list distinguished among landholders (rateables owning land and tenants liable for the taxes on the land they rented), inmates (householders who were non-landholders), and single men, or freemen (generally lodgers residing in landholders' and inmates' houses)(table 1). The average farmstead contained 126 acres, nearly all of which was in production as cultivated fields, pasture, and maintained woodlots.[6] Little land was identified as nonproductive waste. Rush's hallmarks of improvement—the stone house, barn, and springhouse—were the property of a distinctive minority, four-fifths of whom lived on their farms (table 2).

TABLE 1. Rateables, 1799, West Bradford Township, Chester County, Pennsylvania

Classification	Number	Percentage
Landholder	82	42
Inmate	42	22
Freeman	46	24
Tenant	6	3
Nonresident landholder	18	9

TABLE 2. Frequency of Building Materials, West Bradford Township, Chester County, Pennsylvania, 1798

	Dwellings		Barns	
	Number	Percentage	Number	Percentage
Log	75	65	32	53
Frame	3	2	22	29
Stone	36	31	3	7
Brick	2	2	0	0

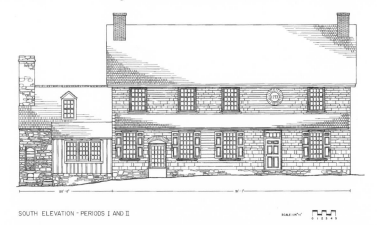

SOUTH ELEVATION - PERIODS I AND II

Figure 1.   Humphry Marshall house, Marshallton, Chester Co., Pa., 1990.
(Drawing, Gabrielle M. Lanier.)

Of the 194 rateables only 2 owned the stone house, stone barn, and
stone springhouse complement associated with Rush's model farmer;
only 26 possessed two of the three architectural components. With key
exceptions, such as Humphry Marshall's elaborate residence, which had
a conservatory and a botanical specimen room, the houses were culturally conservative (figs. 1, 2). In central Chester County, the rural elite inhabited two-story and one- and two-room houses. The best of these were
of stone with a kitchen wing of log or frame. Masonry houses had been
preferred by the rural elite as early as the first decade of the eighteenth
century, but as increasing numbers of farmers in Chester County began
replacing wood houses with stone ones, the elite social status of stone
dwellings diminished (fig. 3).[7]

Mill Creek Hundred, situated in the northwestern corner of
Delaware approximately twelve miles south of West Bradford Township,
reveals much the same pattern of ownership and architecture. In this
piedmont region, where just over one-third of the rateables owned more
than 25 acres, the average farm of roughly 140 acres was two-thirds improved with the remainder left in timber. In the architectural landscape
just over one-third of the houses were designated as stone or partly of
stone construction; and only 5 of 119 barns were stone. Because spring-
houses were not enumerated by the local assessors, we cannot know what

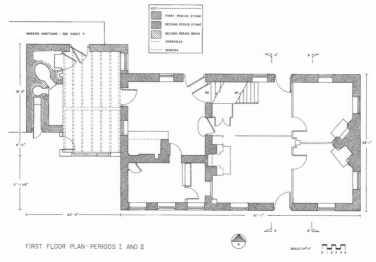

FIRST FLOOR PLAN - PERIODS I AND II

Fig. 2. Humphry Marshall house, Marshallton, Chester Co., Pa., 1990. (Drawing, Gabrielle M. Lanier.)

proportion of Mill Creek Hundred's rateables attained the full array of the model farmer's buildings.

The returns of the orphan's court further establishes the position of the Mill Creek Hundred's model farmers in the rural elite. Compared to the range of farms described in the documentary record, William Wilson's estate of 1793 describes the architectural standard for middling landed farmers.[9] Wilson's "Middle size Log House" was typically out of repair, requiring "several glass windows, a garret floor, and [partition] across the second story." Associated with the house was a "midling Log Barn," which the court was informed was in need of an encircling pent eve, and a stone springhouse that required a new door jamb and wall repairs. The entire farm contained 70 acres, of which nearly 80 percent was improved land. Wilson's farm and nearly two-thirds of his neighbors' farms also fell beneath the 144-acre average for the community.

Owners of stone houses and stone barns represented the wealthiest segment of the Mill Creek Hundred population. Closest to the ideal was Harrison and Hannah Wells's 180-acre farm (72 percent improved), which had a two-story stone house, large stone barn, and corn crib —

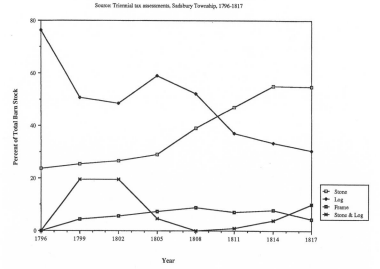

Building Material for Barns, Sadsbury Township, 1796-1817

Source: Triennial tax assessments, Sadsbury Township, 1796-1817

Figure 3. Rate of improvement in building materials. (Graph, Gabrielle M. Lanier.)

all in good repair—and "an old Log Spring House not in repair." The Wellses' 130 improved acres were divided into a series of small fields, lots, and pastures. Approximately one-third of the improved land was dedicated to grain culture with oats, wheat, and corn predominating in 1- to 15-acre fields. The remaining two-thirds of the farm was dedicated to hay fields and pasturage for the livestock, which included oxen and horses for plowing, beef cattle, dairy cows, sheep, and hogs. The Wellses' neighbors, Ephraim Yarnell and John Dixon, had architecturally similar estates and followed the same pattern of diversified crops and extensive livestock holdings.[10] Ephraim Yarnell had "a Stone Dwelling House being the Mansion House with a log Kitchen, also a Barn built of part Stone and the other parts logs, also a log tenement" and a 240-acre tract of which two-thirds was improved. Dixon stored hay in the ends of the barn along with harvested wheat, rye, oats, barley, and sheaves of flax; kept corn "in the crib" and "in the garrett"; and had three additional stacks of hay and fodder in the farmyard. The Wells, Dixon, and Yarnell

Figure 4.   Cadwalader house, Chester Co., Pa., ca. 1985. (Photo, Bernard L. Herman.)

farms of Mill Creek Hundred exhibited some or all of the landscape features associated with the ideal of the model farmer's estate. As representatives of the model farmer personified, they, like their West Bradford
counterparts, were a distinct minority even among affluent property
owners.

Generally in Mill Creek Hundred, as in West Bradford Township,
the late eighteenth-century countryside was dominated by an aging
dwelling stock. Mansion houses of an early eighteenth-century origin remained mansions, or at least farmhouses of superior size and finish, in
the 1790s. These older houses were, however, being improved with the
addition of new service wings and fashionable upgrading of earlier decorative finishes. The Cadwalader House, a log structure built around
1730 as one-and-a-half story, hall-parlor dwelling with a single chimney
stack, had by 1810 been raised to two stories, subdivided into a three-room
arrangement, and enlarged with a new brick kitchen wing (fig. 4). Mov-

ing southward in the Delaware Valley and out of the stone building areas, we find the same pattern of land ownership and architectural improvement that existed in the Pennsylvania and Delaware piedmont. Salem County, New Jersey, an area in which stone was little used for construction, shows analogous development. The county had been the scene of intensive rural settlement since the 1670s, when English Quakers led by John Fenwick began to encroach on the remnants of older Swedish and Dutch settlements. By the 1720s an Anglo-American pattern was firmly established in the monumental domestic architecture of a native-born elite.[11] At the close of the century the organization of the countryside was in the control of a minority of landowners and was characterized by the extensive improvement of land; housing stock was aged. Two tax lists—one a general assessment of land, livestock, slaves, and personal wealth; the other an accounting of houses and barns, compiled in 1797 and 1798 for Mannington and Lower Alloways Creek townships—provide a detailed view of landholding and social order.

In 1797 the typical agricultural holding above 50 acres contained 150 acres, nearly all of which was in some state of production, from the tidal meadows to well-drained, stone-free upland soils. Unimproved acreage was generally represented by large undeveloped tracts rather than scattered forest lots. Inequality in the distribution of property extended beyond land. While just over 90 percent of the landowners possessed hogs, horses, and cattle, a meager 5 percent of the landless owned any livestock. The same pattern of land and livestock holding characterizes Lower Alloways Creek Township. Landholders represented almost 60 percent of the rateable population. The 1798 schedules focused on the value of houses, outbuildings, and farm structures. In both Mannington and Lower Alloways Creek the total rateable population listed in 1798 is identical to the landholder class of 1797. The 1798 list, however, distinguishes between owner-occupied and tenant-occupied houses, revealing that 55 percent of the landholding class was composed of nonlandowners. Thus, only a quarter of the rateable population might be classified as Rush's third settler and potentially worthy of the title farmer. The society they controlled through land ownership was complex and embraced tenants including renters taxed for lands they worked, householders occupying small tenements, and single men living with relatives or lodging in their employers' households.

Largely absent from Rush's world of the model farmer were free African Americans, slaves, landless white tenants and laborers, women, and children. What was their place in the landscape of the Delaware Valley? St. George's Hundred, New Castle County, in the grain-rich, large-farm district of central Delaware, had 71 free black men out of a total rateable population of 567 individuals. Of this 12 percent, a mere 33 percent owned livestock and only 2 individuals were assessed for land. Alexander Lee had 93 acres, and Timothy Scott was assessed for 3. The inequity of a total landholding population of only 36 percent is demonstrably the product of black and white opportunities for the acquisition of real property. Representing nearly 20 percent of the landless labor force (as opposed to 1 percent of the landholders), free blacks in St. George's Hundred found their livelihoods generally limited to day labor and agricultural tenancy.

Alexander Lee's "93 acres improved with a small log house barn & stables &c" and other rateable assets placed him in the top 25 percent of the general taxable population, but those same assets still left him well below the community average of 144 acres. More significant is Lee's position as a free black landholder possibly obligated for taxes on land he did not own. The household objects and farm tools listed in Lee's 1822 probate inventory identified him with the more well-to-do ranks of tenant farmers and minor landholders in his neighborhood.[12] He owned sufficient tools for his family and hired hands and a wagon, cart, and plows. Lee's farm implements and draft animals, like those of white farmers, represented a potential source of additional income. They could be rented to neighbors as well as turned to the cultivation of his own ground. His oxen were ideal for hauling and other heavy work and required minimal care in terms of feed and shelter. His 4 horses required stabling and more expensive feeds such as oats, but they could plow twice the daily acreage covered by the oxen. Lee also kept cattle (12 milk cows, 7 heifers, 10 calves, and 1 bull) along with sheep and hogs. At the time of his midwinter inventory, Lee's crops included corn, oats, barley, tobacco, potatoes, and flax stored in his house and outbuildings. He had also planted 30 acres with winter wheat and rye. Like the model farmer, Alexander Lee found agricultural prosperity through a strategy of mixed farming dominated by cereal cultivation and dairying. As a black farmer, though, he had attained a degree of prosperity at once envied and unattainable by the majority of his neighbors—black or white.

Two other freedmen tenant farmers—Cato Dickinson of Kent County, Delaware, and Jupiter Sesar of Salem County, New Jersey—pursued the difficult careers of African American agricultural tenants. Neither individual appears to have been a property owner, but both men possessed an interest in the land. Dickinson, a tenant on John Dickinson's plantation in St. Jones Hundred, owned "a loged House" on which he paid ground rent and had the "liberty of Moving [it] agreeable to Lease."[13] Dickinson furnished his one-room, one-story dwelling with a bed, pine chest, spinning wheel, three "old" chairs, and two "old" tables. The one room served as kitchen, dining room, parlor, sleeping chamber, and shop. Like Lee, Dickinson owned livestock, including a heifer, hog, and ox, and implements including a cart, several axes, pick, and spade. Cato Dickinson's cart—most likely a tall, two-wheeled wain—and ox distinguished him as an individual with the assets to contract his services to others for tasks involving heavy plowing and hauling. Although he was not a wealthy man, Cato Dickinson had the means to occupy a small (and vulnerable) entrepreneurial place in the interstices of the model farmer's economic authority.

Jupiter Sesar occupied a similar position in a neighborhood across the Delaware River. Sesar's house most likely contained a kitchen or common room and a sleeping chamber. In it he had the same range of furniture, hand tools, and kitchen utensils found in Cato Dickinson's house. More important for understanding Sesar's position in the organization of the countryside are his crops and livestock. He owned 2 cows, 1 calf, and 1 heifer as well as a variety of swine, but he did not own a draft animal or cart. Sesar was solely a tenant farmer. He rented fields and barn space from several landlords in his district. He grew flax on the "small lot" at Samuel Lindsey's farm, where he lived. He stored his flax in John Hall's barn and his wheat in John Mason's. (Lindsey owned a large farm of 185 acres; Hall was a smallholder with just 30 acres who lived in an 18-by-20-foot, two-story wood house, and, like Cato Dickinson, also rented his "services" to others in the community.) Sesar, like Cato Dickinson, tilled lots on rent or shares from neighboring landholders.[14]

The situation of women in the rural countryside followed the divide between all rateables recorded with or without land. A Chester County, Pennsylvania, widow, Elizabeth Downing, received a bequest from her husband that included "generous amounts of agricultural goods" and "provided the means for her to arrange her material life according to her own judgement but also afforded some defense against economic mischance"—but Downing's bequest was truly exceptional. Rural women taxed for real property in the late eighteenth century appear to have been pursuing one of four economic strategies. The majority of women property holders contracted tenants to work their land but might also have actively managed the farm or simply collected rents. In Tredyffrin Township, Chester County, the 11 women listed with property in the 1799 tax ledger were twice as likely to employ tenants as their male counterparts. Of the 11 women listed on the 1798 dwelling tax schedules, 2 had a male renter designated as the primary occupant within their houses. Thus, women who relied on tenants and laborers to conduct the manual business of the farm had not removed themselves from the business of agriculture. In Mannington Township, Salem County, 3 of the 7 women assessed for land in excess of 50 acres followed the practice of writing leases that rendered their tenants liable for paying taxes on the farm. In these instances the women's income was derived through rents and shares in the harvest. Some women property holders, like Rebecca Allen, however, retained a much stronger role in the stewardship of the land.[15] Allen maintained her 220-acre farm, where she lived in her two-story brick house. The value of her land and buildings placed her in the wealthiest 6 percent of her community. At her death in 1809 she owned no agricultural equipment but possessed $5,350.72 in "Bonds and Notes with Interest thereon." Allen, like the male model farmer, had assumed a managerial role in the organization of the countryside.

Success for women of property was far from certain. Bequests and court decisions protecting widows' rights were often circumvented by scheming neighbors, inattentive executors, and quarrelsome heirs. The 100-acre estate Benjamin Christopher left to his wife, Elizabeth, and their eight children, on the verge of southern Delaware's great cypress forests, was robbed of its value through the depredations of John Jacobs—neighbor, administrator, guardian, and second husband. More tenacious was Elizabeth Jaquett. Elizabeth and her son Peter argued over her legal rights to the family's farm on the banks of the Christina River near Wilmington. The court found in Elizabeth's favor after she had already relocated herself to the town of New Castle and awarded her her portion of the property including a third of the house, garden, smokehouse, well, fields, and meadows. Elizabeth then advertised her share of Long Hook (including her portion of her son's house) for rent in December 1795:

One third part of the PLANTATION now occupied Major Peter Jaquett situated in New-Castle hundred, within one mile of Wilmington, and four miles of New-Castle, containing as follows: a third part of the brick-house, kitchen, barn, barn-yard, stables, smoke-house, garden, nine apple-trees in the orchard, with the use of the well of water, 12 acres and 50 perches wood-land, 13 acres and 20 perches of plough-land, 16 acres and 140 acres of marsh. The above described premises are my thirds, as laid off and confirmed by the [Delaware] Supreme court.

Like Allen across the Delaware River, Jaquett succeeded to a degree as a woman of property.[16]

A very different strategy for women in the possession of agricultural estates was to actually work the farm as an active participant. When her husband died intestate in 1795, Hannah Wells and her children of Mill Creek Hundred carried on the business of farming until her death in 1801. Hannah Wells, like her husband, Harrison, pursued the material world of Rush's model farmer. She and her children lived in the family's stone house, processed and stored crops in the large stone barn, planted diversified crops, and managed livestock.

The fourth economic strategy involved women who possessed or rented smallholds of less than 30 acres. The circumstances of these women smallholders closely paralleled the occupations and means of comparable male rateables. They were not likely farming much beyond a subsistence level. They cultivated a small market garden, keeping a cow for milk, and possibly penned and fattened an extra hog for sale. We know very little about the lives of these women, such as Ann Brown of Tredyffrin Township, who owned 14 acres and resided in a one-story, 14-by-24-foot log house, or Hannah Sims of Mannington Township, who held 20 acres, kept two horses and two cattle, and occupied an 18-by-20-foot, one-and-a-half-story frame house. Sims may have bolstered her income by renting her horses or leasing pasture ground or garden plots to her neighbors. She may have obtained additional cash through home manufactures such as weaving, spinning, or churning butter.[17] Women smallholders and tenants lived much closer to the economic edge than did their propertied neighbors. Their strategies for survival went well beyond farming, but the rural landscape and the society it supported could not have functioned without their presence and abilities.

Although Rush's perfect world of the model farmer made no mention of tenants, the rural countryside was organized in large measure around their presence and contributions. Tenancy was governed and regulated through law and contract specifying action and responsibility. As historian Lucy Simler has demonstrated, rural tenancy existed as a strategy for individuals with upward economic mobility and failed expectations. Tenant-landlord contracts defined the size of the farm on rent, length of the lease, amount of payment, and provisions regarding fences, housing, and gardens. The terms and expectations found in an 1824 lease for Hunterdon County, New Jersey, stipulated the one-year occupancy of a 103-acre farm in exchange for one-half of all the grain raised. Further, William Davis, the tenant, was "to keep all fences in Repair & make what new ones is necessary." Henry Baker, the landowner, was

to find postes & Rails. William Davis to pay all Taxes & to Consume all the hay and straw upon the place & not to sell any off to Cut no firewood without permission. William Davis to have too acres of Land for flaxks & Potatoes for his own use. The said Davis to sow the winter grain with Clover & herd grass seedes to be sown in the month of March. . . . Henry Baker Reserves for his own use the Parlour & Chamber above it with that part of the Caellar that is partitioned of and has a lock to it . . . the quantity of Land to be Tilled are fourteen Acres of corn and sow the present stalk field with oates and winter grain.[18]

It was to the tenant's advantage to invest labor and capital in the cultivation of crops but not to improve land, buildings, and fences beyond the barest passable minimum, so a final clause in the Davis-Baker contract obligated Davis to "leave the place in as good repair as it now is reasonable weare tear and Casualties which may happen by fire or otherwise only excepted," a defensive acknowledgment of the expected fate of rented property.

Landlords habitually railed against what they perceived as unruly and destructive renters. "Weare tear and Casualties" were typically the source of landlord and renter disputes. The 1815 correspondence between Peter Jaquett and Eleuthère Irénée du Pont focused on du Pont's sublessee's actions on Jaquett's farm, where Jaquett was still in residence.[19] "In the course of the last Summer and Fall," wrote Jaquett, "I frequently urged you to come over and visit the Farm and examine for

yourself, if John Weer [du Pont's sublessee] was about to comply with
the lease, this you often promised but always neglected." A furious Jaquett then listed grievances, lease violations, and related costs that included failing to mow and clean the marsh, neglecting to plant potatoes
and other specified crops, allowing fences and bridges to fall into disre-
pair, theft of hay, and broken windows in the brick tenant house.

Frustrated and vulnerable, tenants often had little recourse. Many
retaliated by abusing the landlord's property or fleeing their contractual
obligations. Henry Irwin, a Bucks County tenant, broke his 1805 lease
with John Bradshaw by moving without notice. In an unusual letter to
his former landlord, he wrote:

Friend, I suppose you will conclude I wish to wrong you out of your Rent by the
way I moved. I never new till the evening before I came away that I should move
so soon. I depended on my mother-in-law's waggon and Adam Brinker to move
and I found if I did not move that day I could not move when I should. I confess
I was dispossessed in money very much, but I never intended to defraud you out
of a Cent. I have given you an order on Titus and your Son in law in which they
have both agreed to except. I shall be out in about 10 Days when I expect to receive a sum of Money & will positively call on you and pay you all of. I am with
respect your friend.[20]

The world of the model farmer set forth in the *Columbian
Magazine* similarly omitted mention of rural trades and industries. Agricultural society and landscape, though, incorporated a variety of occupations. In the Middle Atlantic landscape of the late eighteenth century,
alternative occupations were generally in agricultural support industries.
Dominant among these were grist and flour mills that ground for both
neighborhood consumption and export. Mills also functioned as local
brokerages where farmers could store and sell their grain. Most of all,
mills served as nodes of community interaction where people exchanged
information as well as goods and services.

The typical mill seat was composed of a jumble of buildings ranging from the mills themselves through workers' and mechanics' houses,
coopers' shops, barns, and other outbuildings. Representative of one of
these hamletlike enclaves was the Dickerson family's Rock Hole Mill in
southern Sussex County, Delaware. The centerpiece was the 45-by-36-
foot-frame merchant mill built in 1793. Powered by tandem waterwheels, the mill ground flour and meal on three pairs of stones and

processed the final product through "superfine" flour bolters, sifters, and barrel packers.[21] There was also a double sawmill powered by twin waterwheels. An old-fashioned, clapboard-roofed, 14-by-15-foot tubmill powered by a slow-turning, horizontally placed waterwheel and fitted with "country" stones and coarse textured bolters completed the complement of industrial structures. Nearby stood a domestic complex composed of three houses sharing a common garden. Storage and work buildings consisted of a plank-walled granary, two stables, and blacksmith's shop; additional housing included a cooper's tenement and a farmer's tenant house. The scene was completed with disorderly piles of felled timber destined for the sawmill and stacks of milled lumber, farm wagons and wains, fences and gates, and livestock and domestic fowl. The Dickerson mill complex, and countless others like it, was a primary point for commercial interaction in the rural community.

Throughout the Delaware Valley, mills were typically owned by the wealthiest individuals in the neighborhood. George Woodward of London Britain in southern Chester County was the second highest rateable in 1799 township lists. The two mill proprietors in West Bradford and the three in West Caln fell in the richest 12 percent of their respective communities. Grain mill owners, as a group, came closest to possessing the constellation of architectural improvements associated with Rush's image of the model farmer. James Trimble of West Bradford, for example, owned a "good house" of stone and frame construction as well as a "large stone barn." The coincidence between the rural miller's seat and the model farmer's estate is unsurprising in light of the values set forth in Rush's essay. Rush extolled the virtues of the intensive use of the land and a diversified agricultural economy with an emphasis on market crops and goods. The spirit of agrarian republicanism explicit in the model farmer found its counterpoint in the industrial capitalism of the rural flour miller. The same material symbols applied for both.[22]

Flour mills, tanneries, and early textile and paper manufactures in the Delaware Valley offer evidence of the industrialization of the countryside and the changing economic and social order of the rural world in the early nineteenth century. The development of mills and manufactures in this period, however, was constrained by the lay of the land and custom. Natural power sources, such as flowing water, were limited by topography. The development of waterpower required an ongoing investment in shaping and maintaining the landscape and tended to cluster rural manufactures along creek valleys or around impounded ponds. Roads linked these industrial enclaves to the immediate rural hinterland. Consequently, prior to the invention and application of other power sources such as steam, the majority of industrial sites were rural. Industry went beyond processing foodstuffs and included weaving, tailoring, shoemaking, wheelwrighting, and blacksmithing. The 1799 tax list for West Bradford Township, Chester County, identifies 54 individuals by trade. Of those enumerated, 10 worked as shoemakers, 9 as weavers, and 16 in wood and metal work (coopers, joiners, augermakers, blacksmiths, and wheelwrights). Weavers and shoemakers were part of a longstanding tradition of home manufactures that continued well into the nineteenth century even as factory production took over a large part of the market. Artisans in the wood and metal trades typically ran small shops and traversed the countryside to work at specific job sites. Artisans, however, were not divorced from the land. Samuel Wilson of Sadsbury Township, Chester County, worked as a stonemason and built numerous houses, barns, and root cellars. He also owned one farm and tenanted another. Farmers' inventories similarly show that they typically owned complete sets of tools associated with trades like shoemaking. The pursuit of some home manufactures such as weaving was often associated with the productive labor of women. In the model farmer's house Rush noted seasonal demands on women's time, "His sons work by his side all the year and his wife and daughters forsake the dairy and the spinning wheel, to share with him in the toils of the harvest."[23]

Artisans were similarly situated in neighboring townships. In West Caln, 19 percent of the rateable population were recognized artisans, and in London Britain 33 percent of the total were identified by occupations. Significantly, in all three townships these artisans were smallholders, renters, or lodgers. Wood and metal workers were commonly labeled "freemen" on the tax lists. One explanation for this pattern that relates occupational identity with property holding is the notion of "cottage industry," where the home was the center of commercial production. In instances where there was an insufficient agricultural base for a household economy, the dominant means of support provided occupational designation.

A sense of physical movement is central to understanding the organization of the landscape. For the estate of the model farmer to function successfully, the fields, livestock, outbuildings, and house all had to stand in public view. Roads and special events ranging from horse races to auctions bound the countryside as a coherent, contested, interactive, and expressive landscape. When Peter Jaquett, one of Delaware's last surviving revolutionary war officers, died and his body was paraded from his farm outside Wilmington into the city for interment, the *Delaware Gazette* reported, "A larger concourse of citizens, than has often been witnessed in this city, paid the last tribute to the departed hero." Jaquett's last journey from farm to town echoed one he had made countless times during his life. Alexander Lee's neighbors traveled through the countryside to his estate auction in 1822. Their individual paths led them past the mansions of rich landowners and the tenements of landless laborers. Each step of their journey brought them into contact with a material world of architecture and landscape that defined their place in it. In Lee's farmyard black and white, rich and poor, and male and female jostled one another, examining items for sale, signaling their bids over the heads of the crowd, and swapping information and gossip throughout the proceedings.[24]

Even casual movement was symbolically contained and directed. The whole of the countryside was composed of the lesser wholes of individual farms and smallholders' lots; dividing the landscape were miles of fencing. The often contentious nature of the early national rural scene is underscored by the history of fencing. In postrevolutionary Delaware the legislature was besieged with petitions about land and property. The most vocal of these dealt with fencing and an enduring custom of common rights to the land. The conflict apparent in the legislative petitions focused on the practice of allowing free-ranging swine to feed on privately held but unfenced lands. Fencing in the colonial period was the responsibility of the landowner or tenant and was designed to protect crops from the depredations of foraging swine. New laws enacted after the Revolution placed the economic burden of fencing on the animals' owners; they were required to pen (and thereby purchase feed for) their livestock.

Movement through an enclosed countryside typically evoked two levels of response: affirmation and segmentation. Dell Upton, in his work on eighteenth-century Virginia plantation society, defined the planter's landscape as articulated and processional. For the white planter, the countryside "consisted of a network of spaces . . . that was

linked by roads and that functioned as the setting for community interactions." That landscape was a self-affirming construction of a minority
population that possessed land. It also sheltered the movement and activities of slaves, free blacks, and poor whites whose presence both sustained and threatened the greater order. The ability to control and
manipulate public and private landscapes united the model farmer and
the southern planter. Central to their success was the privatization of the
countryside. Its most affecting symbol was the material culture the
model farmer chose to advertise and advance in his own cause. Consequently, protest often took as its seemingly spontaneous targets houses,
barns, fences, livestock, and other material elements of the landscape. In
the stormy political climate of postrevolutionary southern Delaware, for
example, private companies rode at night overturning sawmills, stealing
shingles, and burning buildings. Similar conflicts in central Massachusetts have been characterized as the collision of economic and political
interests between one-story and two-story householders. The abusive
treatment of draft animals constituted a similar form of protest. Accusa-
tions of beating and crippling the landholder's horses were not infrequently leveled at laborers and poor tenants. Thus, Thomas Jackson (a
black tenant) was pursued through the New Castle County courts for
beating the horse of John Aiken (a white farmer) until he broke its nose
and split its skull.[25]

Historic landscapes are defined by the processes—social, economic, cultural, and symbolic—that lend them form and meaning and
invariably are acted out in the local community. The processes advanced
by Benjamin Rush's evocation of the model farmer capture our attention
in the present. While the personification of the third settler advanced in
the *Columbian Magazine* may have been particular to the countryside
of the Delaware Valley, the spirit behind the metaphor was national in
scale. The material world of the model farmer—articulated through
durable stone buildings, orderly fields, and diversified crops—was a
composite of philosophical expectations and practical ambitions. The
material expression of those ambitions had been first stated in the mid
eighteenth century as recorded in the houses of the old colonial elite.
Our access to describing and interpreting those processes depends on
the observation of measurable phenomena: the improvements of land;
the effects of scientific farming and technical innovation; the manipu-

TABLE 3. Changes in Building Materials, Mill Creek Hundred, New Castle County, Delaware

	1798		1804	
	Houses (%)	Barns (%)	Houses (%)	Barns (%)
Stone	19	4	26	8
Log	58	61	54	54
Frame	8	30	6	31
Brick	10	0	11	0
Other/unknown	5	5	3	7
Total	100	100	100	100
	(n=177)	(n=119)	(n=186)	(n=130)
	1816		1828	
	Houses (%)	Barns (%)	Houses (%)	Barns (%)
Stone	38	25	45	30
Log	29	11	31	25
Frame/wood	13	17	13	42
Brick	9	0	10	0
Other/unknown	11	47	1	3
Total	100	100	100	100
	(n=244)	(n=149)	(n=273)	(n=171)

lation of capital (through land, debt, labor, and tenancy); the intensification of rural settlement and agriculture; and the improvement of rural architecture.

In the Delaware piedmont there is also perceptible change over time. By the time of the 1816 tax assessment both the general and the landholding populations had increased 45 percent from their 1798 levels. As Mill Creek Hundred became more densely populated, the total number of farms rose significantly as did the amount of improved acreage per farm, lots of less than 25 acres, and rural industrial and artisan activities. As rural settlement intensified, the local character of agricultural and dwelling architecture also changed. A late eighteenth-century countryside visually dominated by log houses and small barns was increasingly characterized in the 1820s by new stone houses and large multifunctional barns (table 3).[26] But as the number of rural estates corresponding to the model farmer's material condition rose more

Figure 5.   Truman farm, Sadsbury Twp., Chester Co., Pa.,
ca. 1980. (Photo, Charles Thayer.)

rapidly toward the end of the federal period, they still remained the property of a local economic elite (fig. 5).

The Delaware Valley countryside cannot be offered as the paradigm for the organization of the countryside in federal America, but social, economic, architectural, and landscape patterns observed there
spark questions and provide counterpoints applicable elsewhere. The
material world of the model farmer has equivalents in the Chesapeake
region, the Carolina low country, central Massachusetts, and the newly
settled lands of Ohio, Kentucky, and Tennessee. In all these landscapes
are houses and farm buildings of brick, stone, or wood whose plans, finishes, and the very fact of their construction embody the owners' images
of durability, economic attainment, and social authority. The symbolic
compass of the model farmer's countryside extended to farm buildings,
field patterns, crops, fences, and the institutions that made and maintained an emerging middle-class agrarian society. Yet the landscape of
the model farmer was organized around custom. While its owners espoused republican virtue, the organization of their land was intrinsically
hierarchical; while its owners touted self-reliance, their system was necessarily exploitative; while its owners strove to create symbols of agrarian
tranquility, their most persuasive metaphors evoked conflict and conquest. The organization of the countryside as it was advanced in the fig-

ure of the model farmer at the close of the eighteenth century and as it survives in the present is an expurgated text that celebrates the triumph of agrarian progress and social order. The victory of those who realized the material world of the model farmer endures in the iconography of ordinary objects.

---

[1] Benjamin Rush, "An Account of the Progress of Population, Agriculture, Manners, and Government in Pennsylvania, in a Letter from a Citizen of Pennsylvania, to His Friend in England," *Columbian Magazine; or, Monthly Miscellany* 1, no. 3 (November 1786): 117–22. Benjamin Rush concluded, "From a review of the three species of settlers, it appears, that there are certain regular stages which mark the progress from the savage to civilized life. The first settler is nearly related to an Indian in his manners. In the second, the Indian manners are more diluted: It is in the third species of settlers only, that we behold civilization completed. It is to the third species of settlers only, that it is proper to apply the term of *farmers*." As he advanced his analogy the author offered several cautions: his remarks were limited by his own observations; he was uncertain about the applicability of his model to other regions of the United States–particularly the slaveholding South; and he was aware that even in Pennsylvania the changes associated with a succession of migrating settlers might be accomplished by succeeding generations of a single family or by a single individual in the course of his life (Rush, "Account," pp. 120–21). On the material culture of early American gentility, see Kevin M. Sweeney, "Mansion People: Kinship, Class, and Architecture in Western Massachusetts in the Mid Eighteenth Century," *Winterthur Portfolio* 19, no. 4 (Winter 1984): 231–56.

[2] "Prospects of Agriculture in the United States," *Farmers' Cabinet* 1, no. 8 (November 1, 1836): 120; Samuel Henry Black, "An Essay, on the Intrinsic Value of Arable Land; with Some General Remarks on the Science of Agriculture," *American Farmer* 2 (1820): 9.

[3] Rush, "Account," p. 119. The German populations of Pennsylvania established the use of wood-burning stoves in the eighteenth century. Rush admired the stoves and other aspects of Pennsylvania German material life; "An Account of the Manners of the German Inhabitants of Pennsylvania," in Benjamin Rush, *Essays: Literary, Moral, and Philosophical*, ed. Michael Meranze (Schenectady, N.Y.: Union College Press, 1988), pp. 132–45.

[4] Rush, "Account," p. 119.

[5] The organization of the late eighteenth-century cultural landscape in the Middle Atlantic region varied significantly from place to place. The rural prospects around the cypress swamps of southern Delaware, the Pennsylvania German communities of the Lancaster plain, the old Anglo-American settlements of southwestern New Jersey, and the Welsh neighborhoods of Pennsylvania's Great Valley had all been at least a century in the making by 1786. No common standard of development existed between each locale, yet a shared pattern in the order of the countryside is evident.

[6] On Chester Co., see James T. Lemon, *The Best Poor Man's Country: A Geographical Study of Early Southeastern Pennsylvania* (New York: W. W. Norton, 1972); Mary M. Schweitzer, *Custom and Contract: Household, Government, and the*

Economy in Colonial Pennsylvania (New York: Columbia University Press, 1987). For tax lists, see West Bradford Twp. Rateables, 1799, Chester County Historical Society, West Chester, Pa. The average size of farmsteads in West Bradford Twp. was determined by dropping the 18 landholdings of 25 acres or less (244 acres total) from the 11,266 acres listed for the entire township and dividing the 11,122-acre total by the 88 remaining cases. This calculation method is employed throughout this essay to determine mean acreages.

 [7] On West Bradford Twp. houses, see Henry Glassie, "Eighteenth-Century Cultural Process in Delaware Valley Folk Building," in *Winterthur Portfolio* 7, ed. Ian M. G. Quimby (Charlottesville: University Press of Virginia, 1972), pp. 29–57; Arlene Horvath, "The Vernacular Expression in Quaker Chester County, Pennsylvania: The Taylor-Parke House and Its Maker," in *Perspectives in Vernacular Architecture II*, ed. Camille Wells (Columbia: University of Missouri Press, 1986), pp. 150–60. Central Chester Co. houses are discussed in H. John Michel, Jr., " 'In a Manner and Fashion Suitable to Their Degree': A Preliminary Investigation of the Material Culture of Early Rural Pennsylvania," *Working Papers from the Regional Economic History Center* 5, no. 1 (1981). On social status, see Juan Pablo Bonta, *Architecture and Its Interpretation: A Study of Expressive Systems in Architecture* (New York: Rizzoli, 1979), pp. 131–58.

 [8] Assessments, 1797–1830, Mill Creek Hundred, New Castle Co., Delaware, Delaware State Archives (hereafter DSA), Dover. There is some disagreement over the actual amount of acreage that constitutes the threshold for a viable farm. The figure of 25 acres chosen here may, in fact, create the impression that there were more farmers than actually existed; see Lucy Simler, "Tenancy in Colonial Pennsylvania: The Case of Chester County," *William and Mary Quarterly*, 3d ser., 43, no. 4 (October 1986): 542–69.

 [9] For information on the architectural descriptions contained in the court dockets, see Bernard L. Herman, "Delaware's Orphan Court Valuations and the Reconstitution of Historic Landscapes, 1785–1830," in *Early American Probate Inventories*, Proceedings of Dublin Seminar for New England Folklife, ed. Peter Benes (Boston: Boston University, 1989), pp. 121–39. William Wilson, Valuation, H-1-51, 1793, and L-1-191, 1802, New Castle Co. Orphan's Court, DSA.

 [10] Harrison Wells, Valuation, L-1-162, 1801, New Castle Co. Orphan's Court, DSA; Harrison Wells, 1795, Hannah Wells, 1795, New Castle Co. Wills and Inventories, DSA; Ephraim Yarnell, Valuation, H-1-179, 1795, New Castle Co. Orphan's Court, DSA; Ephraim Yarnell, 1793, New Castle Co. Wills and Inventories, DSA; John Dixon, Valuation, G-1-385, 1791, New Castle Co. Orphan's Court, DSA.

 [11] In Salem Co., iron-bearing sandstone was used occasionally for foundations and in a few instances for walling but generally was not a preferred building material. The preference for brick is documented in Michael J. Chiarappa, "The Social Context of Eighteenth-Century West New Jersey Brick Artisanry," in *Perspectives in Vernacular Architecture IV*, ed. Thomas Carter and Bernard L. Herman (Columbia: University of Missouri Press, 1991), pp. 31–42. On the architecture of the county, see Alan Gowans, "The Mansions of Alloways Creek," in *Common Places: Readings in American Vernacular Architecture*, ed. Dell Upton and John Vlach (Athens: University of Georgia Press, 1986), pp. 367–93.

 [12] Liability for taxes was a contractual obligation commonly incorporated into agricultural leases. Lee's nonownership of the land he was taxed for in 1816 is confirmed by his total absence from New Castle Co. deed books and indexes and by his presence in tax lists for 1804 and 1822, where he is listed, but without land (Tax As-

sessments, 1797–1830, St. George's Hundred, New Castle Co., Delaware, DSA). Alexander Lee, Inventory and Estate Sales, New Castle Co.; Probate Inventories, 1822, DSA.

[13] Cato Dickinson Inventory, 1807, Kent Co., Delaware, DSA. The Dickinson material cited here is contained in the John Dickinson Plantation research files, Delaware Bureau of Museums, and is cited courtesy of James Stewart and the bureau.

[14] Jupiter Sesar Inventory, 1808, Salem Co., Probate Records, Salem Co. Courthouse, Salem, N.J.; Rateables, 1795–1800, Mannington Twp., Salem Co., New Jersey State Archives, Trenton. The late eighteenth-century lists for Mannington include both local assessments based on land and livestock and the 1798 Federal Direct Tax List Census "A" list describing housing valued at more than $100.

[15] Elizabeth Downing is discussed in Lisa Wilson Waciega, "A 'Man of Business': The Widow of Means in Southeastern Pennsylvania, 1750–1850," *William and Mary Quarterly*, 3d ser., 44, no. 1 (January 1987): 49; Rebecca Allen Inventory, 1809, Salem Co., Probate Records, Salem Co. Courthouse; 1798 Federal Direct Tax Census, Mannington Twp., Salem Co., New Jersey State Archives, Trenton.

[16] On Elizabeth Christopher, see Bernard L. Herman, *The Stolen House* (Charlottesville: University Press of Virginia, 1992); advertisement, *Delaware Gazette*, December 1795. While Elizabeth Jaquett was able to foil her son's attempts to appropriate her property rights, she was not so fortunate in her other business dealings.

[17] For documentation on the women, see Tax Assessments, 1797–1820, Tredyffrin Twp., Chester Co., Chester Co. Historical Society; 1798 Federal Direct Tax Census, Tredyffrin Twp., Chester Co., National Archives, Washington, D.C.; Rateables, 1795–1800, Mannington Twp., Salem Co., New Jersey State Archives, Trenton. Joan M. Jensen, *Loosening the Bonds: Mid-Atlantic Farm Women, 1750–1850* (New Haven: Yale University Press, 1986), pp. 79–141.

[18] Simler, "Tenancy in Colonial Pennsylvania." On the Hunterdon Co. lease, see information on the indenture between Henry Baker and William Davis, folder 6, Henry Chapman Papers, Bucks Co. Historical Society, Doylestown, Pa.

[19] Peter Jaquett to E. I. du Pont, March 1815, Eleuthère Irénée du Pont Correspondence, box 6, Hagley Library, Greenville, Del.

[20] Henry Irwin to John Bradshaw, ca. 1805, ms. 220, folder 19, Bucks Co. Historical Society, Doylestown, Pa.

[21] On Rock Hole Mill, see Elisha Dickerson, Return of Valuation, H-369-70, Sussex Co., Orphan's Court, DSA. The machinery described within that mill reflects the innovations of Oliver Evans and Thomas Ellicott, both of whom resided in the Middle Atlantic, where they carried out their experiments and installed and tested many of the mechanical devices; see Eugene S. Ferguson, *Oliver Evans, Inventive Genius of the American Industrial Revolution* (Greenville, Del.: Hagley Museum, 1980).

[22] Tax Assessments, 1797–1820, London Britain Twp., West Bradford Twp., and West Caln Twp., Chester Co. Historical Society. Proprietors of other types of rural industries generally failed to achieve the economic position enjoyed by grain millers. The property holdings of tanners, fullers, and sawmill operators ranged considerably lower in the economic ranks of sampled Chester Co. twps.

[23] Rush, "Account," p. 119. On home manufactures, see Michel, "In a Manner and Fashion."

[24] On the organization of the landscape, see Carl Lounsbury, "The Structure of Justice: The Courthouses of Colonial Virginia," in *Perspectives in Vernacular Architecture III*, ed. Thomas Carter and Bernard L. Herman (Columbia: University of

Missouri Press, 1989), pp. 214–26. Peter Jaquett, obituary, *Delaware Gazette and American Watchman*, September 19, 1834. Most historical research on processions and crowds in the eighteenth and early nineteenth centuries has focused on urban phenomena; see Susan G. Davis, *Parades and Power: Street Theatre in Nineteenth-Century Philadelphia* (Philadelphia: Temple University Press, 1986).

[25] Dell Upton, "White and Black Landscapes in Eighteenth-Century Virginia," in *Material Life in America, 1600–1860*, ed. Robert Blair St. George (Boston: Northeastern University Press, 1988), pp. 357–69. On the minority population, see Camille Wells, "The Eighteenth-Century Landscape of Virginia's Northern Neck," *Northern Neck of Virginia Historical Magazine* 37 (December 1987): 4217–55. A fine analysis of inverted symbolic relationships systematically encoded in expressive culture is contained in Peter Stallybrass and Allon White, *The Poetics and Politics of Transgression* (Ithaca: Cornell University Press, 1986); Robert Darnton, *The Great Cat Massacre and Other Episodes in French Cultural History* (New York: Vintage, 1984), pp. 75–104. The argument for symbolic closure in American architecture and landscape has been most forcefully advanced by Henry Glassie, *Folk Housing in Middle Virginia: The Structural Analysis of Historic Artifacts* (Knoxville: University of Tennessee Press, 1975). The circumstances of the Delaware events are advanced in John Kern, "The Election Riots of 1787 in Sussex Co., Delaware," *Delaware History* 22, no. 4 (Fall/Winter 1987): 241–63. Michael Steinitz, "Rethinking Geographical Approaches to the Common House: The Evidence from Eighteenth-Century Massachusetts," in Carter and Herman, *Perspectives in Vernacular Architecture III*, p. 24. John Aiken v. Thomas Jackson (free negro), Interrogatories, Miscellaneous Road Papers, 1798, New Castle, Levy Court, DSA.

[26] The architectural transformation of the Chester Co., Pennsylvania, countryside has been particularly well documented by Gabrielle Milan Lanier, *Samuel Wilson's Working World: Builders and Building in Chester County, Pennsylvania* (Master's thesis, University of Delaware, 1989), pp. 25–41.

Another City
The Urban Cultural Landscape in the Early Republic
Dell Upton

As cashier of the Bank of Germantown and later as secretary of the
Germantown and Norristown Railroad, John Fanning Watson
(1779–1860) helped transform antebellum Philadelphia from a significant port to an even greater manufacturing center.[1] Yet Watson was also
an antiquarian who was deeply interested in Philadelphia's history. Despite his own role in changing the city, he came to believe that the years
around 1800, the period of his own young adulthood and the twilight of
Philadelphia's preeminence as a seaport, were the city's zenith and that
its brilliance had dimmed noticeably ever since.

Watson's *Annals of Philadelphia and Pennsylvania in the Olden
Time* was an elegy for the city of his youth. In a "final appendix of the
year 1856," added to the last edition before his death, Watson offered a
long meditation on the changes he had witnessed during his lifetime.
"Our People are fast changing," he declared. Where once they had been
a "domestic, quiet people, content to rest in their fireside comforts, and

Research for this essay was made possible by fellowships from the Library Com-
pany of Philadelphia, The Historical Society of Pennsylvania, the Center for Ad-
vanced Study in the Visual Arts (National Gallery of Art), and the University of
California, Berkeley, as well as a National Endowment for the Humanities Travel to
Collections grant. I am grateful for all of them. I also thank Karen Kevorkian, Paul
Groth, the late Spiro Kostof, Deryck Holdsworth, Catherine Hutchins, and members
of the Berkeley Americanists for their comments on earlier drafts of this paper, and
Timothy Stokes for research assistance.

indoor society,—they are being all drawn abroad to seek for spectacles and public wonders!" They had become "excitable" as well as "anti-social." To Watson, the proof was the city's landscape. Telegraphing his distress in staccato phrases echoing the growing urban frenzy, he denounced "the *rivalship* of grandeur in houses, the general clatter from crowds of people and confusion now along the streets—no room now to turn or look about—once it was peaceful—pleasant and safe to walk the streets,—now tall houses, are crowded with numerous working tenants—formerly, they were in smaller houses and in bye places.—Tis terrible now to sicken and die at crowded streets, where the rattle of omnibuses is unceasing." Watson the railroad executive was dismayed by railroad and steamship travel where "the people must go by hundreds [and] where they can only stare at, and scan each other without speaking" and by hotels "where all must keep aloof, and look askance at each other." "To my eye," he wrote, "the whole aspect is changing.—It is indeed, already, another City—A *city building on the top of the former!* All the houses now, above *three* stories—present *an elevation* so manifest, as to *displease the* eye;—and particularly, where several, go up so exalted, as to break the former line of equality, and beauty. Even such edifices, lately constructed, as the Bank of North America, Philadelphia and Western Bank, are struck down by the still later, *towering* business houses and hotels, &c., near them. . . . All is now self-exalted and going upon stilts."[2]

Watson's eloquent tirade poured forth conflicting feelings. At the same time that he mourned the eradication of the "line of equality," he also lamented the passing of clear architectural representations of social hierarchy. Where great houses formerly "intimated families of superior grade," now they were signs of nothing more than a temporary cash surplus.[3] He gloried in Philadelphia's commerce, but lamented commercialism. Watson's ambivalence mirrored the conflicted and confusing nature of the changes wrought by commerce and commercialism in the cultural landscape of the largest early republican cities.

Watson's fragmented elegy is characteristic of responses to the transformation of the early republican city. Consequently, historians must seek theme and significance in the urban cultural landscape rather than in the philosophies of individuals. By the cultural landscape I mean a complex artifact that includes the physical fabric of the city and the

artifactual universe of its residents together with the imaginative visions
that urbanites use in constructing, explaining, and evaluating them. To
put it another way, the material city is the product of political, cultural,
social, and economic processes, but it is also a mediating object on
which imaginative structures can be projected and through which they
can be invested with tangible existence. A cultural landscape is not the
product of a collective mind but of many minds working within established, although discontinuous, arenas of power. Physically, cultural
landscapes include buildings but also the spaces between them; the
formal and the official aspects of urban form, but also the informal and
the unofficial; design and intention, but also alteration and use; the built
environment, but also the furnishings and even the clothing adopted by
the urban citizenry or assigned to their neighbors. Mentally, cultural
landscapes are imagined through heterogeneous, imperfect myths that
ascribe significance to the material world.[4] Urban myths constitute a
motley repertoire of metaphors rather than a coherent system. They are
occasionally described but rarely analyzed by contemporaries. Usually
the historian must infer their existence from patterns of space, patterns
of objects, patterns of action, and the rhetorical devices used to characterize space, artifact, and action.

A myth and its artifactual mediators constitute a sublandscape, an
element of the larger urban cultural landscape. Three principal sublandscapes can be identified in cities of the early republic. Despite their
disparate, often contradictory, qualities, they were grounded in a common experience of life in an expanding commercial society. Thus they
offered alternative structures of significance, and early nineteenth-
century urbanites oscillated among them as occasions prompted.

The first I call the systematic landscape. During the decades between George Washington's and Andrew Jackson's elections, some
members of the urban commercial elite articulated a new conception of
the American city. They strove to understand urban society and the urban landscape as a system, and in doing so to reform and reorganize both
into a single, centralized, rational order. By the 1810s and 1820s a quarter century of analysis and experiment had produced a characteristic spatial order that embodied the new social and environmental ideas in
schemes for commercial regulation, public utilities, and urban planning. Most important, the new spatial order reshaped familiar building

types, transforming the jail into the penitentiary, the counting room into the office building, the inn into the hotel, the commercial street into the arcade, and the burying ground into the cemetery.

The second, the competitive landscape, was the product of an individualized understanding of the commercial world. Less often articulated or explicated in the early nineteenth century than the systematic myth, the competitive myth nevertheless had an equally important role in shaping the city. Where the systematic myth promoted a unitary, large-scale urban order, the competitive myth encouraged multiple, small-scale urban orders. Individually the small-scale orders might resemble what the systematic myth proposed for the whole city. Collectively, however, the small orders were discontinuous and decentralized. As a result, the enlarged size and new forms of commercial establishments, domestic and commercial land-use practices, and the density of development infused a new energy and complexity into the urban landscape that sometimes seemed to carry the city beyond rational control.

The systematic and the competitive landscapes shared certain important qualities. For example, both incorporated many common landscape elements of earlier cities, but in extending, intensifying, and reinterpreting these features, early republican city builders created a new kind of city that was notably different from earlier ones. More important, what Watson called "anti-social" tendencies permeated both the systematic and competitive landscapes, because both promoted individual action in commercial and commercialized settings. Public life and public space were subsumed to a collective private; that is, the concept of the public was redefined as the sum of many private goods and actions. The systematic myth assumed that a public order would emerge from this collective private. The competitive myth did not address the issue.

The systematic and the competitive myths were similar, as well, in their commodifying implications. The cross-racial, cross-class frenzy of consumption engendered by both sublandscapes violated traditional moral and social beliefs in ascetic restraint and in innate social and racial hierarchies. These contradictory impulses toward unrestrained consumption and toward rigidly bounded behavior produced the third sublandscape, the shadow landscape. Rhetorically, the multiple urban orders of the competitive landscape were defined as *disorder*, then equated with *moral* disorder, and finally translated into *immoral* order. The shadow landscape thus emerged from a synthesis of the systematic and competitive attitudes toward landscape with traditional social and religious values. It was as single-ordered as the systematic landscape but morally its opposite. In the systematic landscape, explicit theory lead to practice, and in the competitive landscape implicit theory lead to practice, but in the shadow landscape theory interpreted the practices of others.

Late eighteenth-century beliefs about knowledge, human nature, and economics, broadly familiar to educated people, underlay the systematic myth of the relationship between the landscape and its makers. They presumed the existence of inherent relationships among categories of natural phenomena that held out the possibility of knowing and ordering the world systematically. The many learned societies, libraries, schools, and public and private museums that were created in the early republic are familiar testimonies to this intellectual confidence. Charles Willson Peale's Philadelphia museum, its natural specimens arranged according to Carolus Linnaeus's classification, is perhaps the most famous example. Comparable inner essences allowed all living beings to be placed in a single system of relations.[5]

The scientist's belief in a system in the natural world based on comparable essences was paralleled by a similar, if less clearly articulated, belief in system in the moral world. The comparability of inner being, regardless of socioeconomic status, was the foundation of evangelicalism, which placed its faith in personal moral responsibility, and of republicanism, which vested political sovereignty in the people as a whole rather than in extrinsic social estates within the body politic. The similarity of moral and natural essence provided a second ordering principle at Peale's museum, installed in the second-floor Long Room of the Pennsylvania State House (now Independence Hall) in 1802. Above the cases containing the natural history exhibits hung a collection of seventy portraits of physically exceptional people and great Americans. These located humans in the natural order but also depicted a parallel moral order. The visitor might take advantage of "Hawkins's ingenious Physiognomic trace," a device to aid in drawing silhouette portraits, to place herself in the natural and moral orders.[6]

A third stimulus for understanding the world as a system antedated Enlightenment science and Enlightenment and evangelical virtue. In the seventeenth century a theoretical revolution shifted high-level Anglo-American economic theory away from morality and toward a naturalistic image of inner system and regulation that was comparable to that embodied in Peale's representation of the natural world. This new economic understanding was disseminated to the reading public by popularizers like Roger North, whose *The Gentleman Accomptant* celebrated double-entry bookkeeping as an art comparable in beauty and elegance to oratory or dancing. North contrasted the systematic economic understanding of great merchants with the shortsighted and impressionistic thinking of small tradesmen and farmers. To the merchant, double-entry bookkeeping offered a concrete image, complete and true, of the abstract system of relations underlying commercial transactions. North likened well-kept accounts to "the Branches and Leaves of a Tree, in a perpetual Series, all hanging to each other, no less but rather more essentially than [branches] do; for of those, many may be prun'd off, and the Tree left integral and sound; but here not one Accompt, or Line of it can be spared."[7]

The systematic view of economic life also implied belief in an inner essence in the material world. This essence, *value*, translated material goods and immaterial services into comparable commodities. A growing fondness for numerical comparisons in every aspect of daily life is an index of the diffusion of the commodified worldview in America.[8]

The systematic urban myth was founded on these metaphors of unity and essence, which linked the physical, moral, and economic realms in a single discourse. Exposition of the systematic landscape slipped easily from one realm to another. For some writers the connection transcended metaphor; they envisioned concrete relationships among the three realms that could be described precisely. Schemes for rationalizing weights, measures, and monetary systems, for example, were common in the late eighteenth century. They were intended to promote commerce by making the relationship between the physical and economic worlds uniform and transparent. This would equalize all players in the market by eliminating the advantages possessed by those with access to arcane knowledge of systems of exchange and equivalence among local systems. Although the more polished of these schemes seem commonsensical, all depended to some extent on conceptual elisions among the three realms that are most easily recognized in cruder monetary and weights-and-measures schemes. For example, John Dorsey's plan for decimalizing the weights, measures, and monetary system of the United States attempted to reduce the entire material and economic worlds to simple equivalences. Beginning from a mundane empirical observation—that a cubic foot of water at 60° F weighs 1,000 ounces avoirdupois—Dorsey, the city of Philadelphia's keeper of weights and measures, proposed to "establish an uniform System—and by it to reconcile the Unit of Weight, the Unit of Lineal Measure—the Unit of measure of Capacity & the Money Unit of the UStates." Seduced by the idea of comparability, Dorsey wished to legislate a universal, fixed relationship among mass, dimension, and monetary value.[9]

Few observers were as literal-minded as Dorsey. Nevertheless, the assumptions evident in his letter are important for understanding the reciprocal relationship of language and artifact in urban myth. The categories of language form a lens through which we view the material world. Yet the material world is not a mere idea, but an independent entity whose peculiarities and inconsistencies must be confronted. By casting the parallel, discontinuous physical, moral, and commercial worlds into a single discursive system, the metaphors of system and essence became what historian Jean Starobinski has called *emblems*, transcendent images that allow one to bridge the chasms between the physical and mental realms, thus investing metaphor with concreteness and specificity.[10] These emblems encouraged early nineteenth-century urbanites to imagine a systematic landscape that fused the physical, moral, intellectual, and economic aspects of urban life or, more accurately perhaps, it encouraged them to act as if such a landscape already existed.

In the process, traditional urban forms were elevated from habits of practical convenience to matters of principle, and attempts were made to apply them as consistently as possible. The urban grid plan is an example. A centuries-old strategy for real estate platting, grids organized the cities of Philadelphia, Williamsburg, and Savannah as well as innumerable small towns in colonial North America. Yet both gridded colonial cities and those, like Boston and New York, that lacked formal plans, grew in a roughly T-shaped pattern organized around the waterfront and a public/market axis at right angles to it, with concessions made to local topography. For example, Philadelphia's colonial development followed the traditional T pattern and stretched north and south of the official plat rather than filling out the grid from east to west as Penn intended (fig. 1). In the process, the public spaces were built over, and the large blocks were subdivided irregularly. A secondary network of streets and alleys created microcosmic domestic and public realms within the

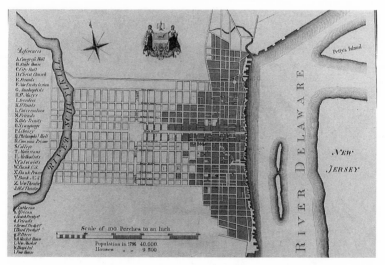

Figure 1.   Thomas Stephens, *Stephens Plan of the City of Philadelphia*, 1796 (facsimile; 1876). (Historical Society of Pennsylvania.)

blocks or squares. These inner-block domestic environments ranged from Benjamin Franklin's quasi-suburban house and garden to the more common, intensively developed residential and industrial courts such as that depicted on the plat of the Carpenter's Company's property drawn by Benjamin Loxley in 1778. The Carpenter's Company replaced the houses on Loxley's plat with two larger houses on Chestnut Street and built its hall behind them.[11] The construction of public buildings behind street-line development was common in the early national period as well.

For postrevolutionary Americans, the grid was not merely a convenient tool of real estate development as it had been to builders like Loxley and his colleagues; it was also believed to generate urban commercial prosperity. The commissioners who created New York City's 1811 plan argued that a grid rendered the city's "situation in Regard of Health and Pleasure as well as . . . the Convenience of Commerce peculiarly felicitous." Vast grids were platted on paper, even as the survey of land crawled along block by block to keep pace with private development. Both New Yorkers and Philadelphians published plans showing the contrast between the existing city and its grid (see figs. 1, 2). The

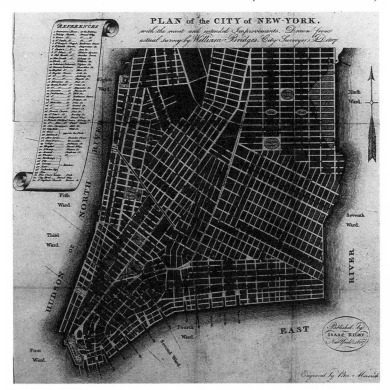

Figure 2.   William Bridges, *Plan of the City of New-York*, 1807. Engraving, Peter Maverick. (Library of Congress.)

newly chartered city of Philadelphia incorporated in its seal "a plough and a Ship representing Agriculture and Commerce, the two great means of Enriching a City," along with "an unfolded Scroll, displaying the Ground plot of the City, between the Rivers Delaware and Schuylkill."[12] These images implied that the promise of future prosperity would be fulfilled.

By the second quarter of the nineteenth century, the grid had acquired great power as an emblem of a vigorous and rational commercial life, as Charles Dickens's famous remarks on Philadelphia suggest. He found the city "distractingly regular" and "would have given the world for a crooked street." "The collar of my coat appeared to stiffen, and the brim of my hat to expand, beneath [the city's] quakery influence. My hair shrunk into a sleek short crop, my hands folded themselves upon my breast of their own calm accord, and thoughts of taking lodgings in Mark Lane over against the Market Place, and of making a large fortune in speculations in corn, came over me involuntarily."[13]

The grid's promise lay in its potential for defining uniform space and promoting perfect internal communication. City governments and members of the mercantile elite worked strenuously to manage the urban landscape in a way that would realize the grid's systematic qualities.

The colonial plans of the major cities had acknowledged the peculiarities of topography. For example, the precise siting of Boston's traditional T plan of wharf and major street, and of its common, were guided by the locations of the town cove, the Trimountain, and the narrow neck connecting the city to the mainland. New Amsterdam/New York also grew along its harbor. A 1625 plan for a regular town within fortifications was superseded by development facing the East River, with three major streets running back from the river front. Attempts to create an evenly settled, canal-laced Netherlandish city never proceeded beyond repeated admonitions to build up the open lots in the city and the construction of one canal, named after Amsterdam's *Prinzengracht*, in 1657. It was filled and converted to a street by the English conquerors.[14]

Builders of cities with regular plans also deferred to topography. Philadelphia's site was originally an uneven plateau, cut by ravines, on a bluff above the Delaware River, chosen not only for its advantages but to avoid encroaching on existing landholdings. Thomas Holmes's 1682 survey relocated the central square and adjusted the sizes of streets and the intervals between them to take the ravines and high points into account. Even as intellectual a plan as Pierre Charles L'Enfant's for Washington in 1791 took advantage of Jenkins Hill as a site for the Capitol. Tiber Creek, a stream that ran along what is now the Mall, was formalized as a canal, and the plan was modified in other ways to accommodate the interests of existing landowners.[15]

Yet as land use intensified, colonial city governments began to alter topography to fit the grid. For example, in the early years of settlement Philadelphia built an arch to carry Front Street over Mulberry (now Arch) Street where it dropped off toward the Delaware River. Just before the Revolution the city covered meandering Dock Creek to create Dock Street, the only winding thoroughfare in the antebellum city limits (see fig. 1).[16]

Early nineteenth-century efforts to accommodate topography to real estate included both small-scale adjustments and projects whose exponential increase in scale of ambition and expenditure created qualitative differences between colonial- and federal-era cities. Boston's leveling of the Trimountain and its many fillings of Back Bay to create level, gridded space are only the most dramatic instances of the topographical alterations every city undertook. In addition, elaborate public works projects of other sorts aimed to realize the grid's implicit spatial interchangability by overcoming natural disadvantages. Philadelphia's waterworks, constructed in 1800 under the supervision of Benjamin Henry Latrobe, are a case in point. They were designed to compensate for differences in the availability and quality of water in the city's neighborhoods and to wash the city's streets and cool its air. Water was conveyed through a brick tunnel from a basin on the Schuylkill River to a pump house built on Center Square, where Penn had intended the city's main public buildings to stand. From there it was distributed through wooden pipes to individual subscribers and public hydrants. Since development was only then reaching the grid's midpoint, the utility of the location was more symbolic than real. Like the plan itself, the waterworks promised that Philadelphia *would* develop in an orderly east-west fashion.[17]

A similar vision inspired a less practical project for lighting Philadelphia using a centrally located three-hundred-foot brick tower with a perpetual coal fire on top. By this means all streets, alleys, yards, and the insides of houses within a three-quarter-mile radius would receive "a light nearly equal to that produced by a full moon." As a result, "there would be an even regular light throughout the city and districts . . . sufficient for almost any purpose for which light is required." Householders would be protected from falls in the dark and would save money on candles and oil. The light would serve as a beacon for travelers and, best of all, there would be "no dark places, in which a person walking would fall over curb stones, or into gutters—and there would be no dark corners, or hiding places, in which thieves or midnight robbers might secrete themselves, to evade the watchman."[18]

Philadelphia's watchmen were themselves governed by the fiction of uniform space. Each watchman was assigned several blocks of a north-south or east-west street to patrol. However densely or irregularly his territory was developed, he was expected to complete his round hourly, turning aside only to walk into each alley that opened off his street. He was to cross paths with other watchmen at fixed intervals. The term "beat" applied to these watchmen's rounds bears an appropriately regular connotation.[19]

The light tower and the watchman's beat also implied a vision of perfect accessibility. Equality of space required that every space be equally available to everyone, physically and psychologically. Early nineteenth-century city dwellers admitted that the narrow, curving streets of cities like New York and Boston were pleasing to tourists' eyes but thought them unsuited to "convenience of living." Job R. Tyson complained to Philadelphia's Roberts Vaux of Boston's "narrow and winding" streets. Although they were clean and presented "an agreeable variety . . . I experienced much embarrassment in attempting to find my way from one part of the city to another, from the numerous intersections and variations of names which the same street undergoes at particular points."[20]

Philadelphia's street system was equally embarrassing, owing to the method of numbering. Although odd numbers had been allocated to the north and east sides of streets and even numbers to the west and south sides early in the colonial era, neither street name nor number was usually posted in the late eighteenth century. Moreover, individual street numbers were assigned as construction proceeded, thus there was no way of telling in which block a given address would be found. Pictorial business directories show that half-numbers were common and residences on business streets often went unnumbered. Efforts to rationalize street numbering began in 1830. The concept of even space and even access irrespective of development underlay the first proposal for numbering, which, like the waterworks and the lighting scheme, focused on Center (by then called Penn) Square and ran north, south, east, and west from there. The city council was to "establish permanent numbers to the corner of each street, letting the same numbers be found to correspond at all the principal streets, running north and south; so that one part of the city would be a complete index for the other." This is the scheme used by most cities currently. However, the city fathers revealed their equalizing assumptions in fixing the intervals between street numbers on each block arbitrarily, allowing six to seven numbers for every hundred feet, regardless of actual density of development.[21]

Street improvements were also based on a presumption of spatial neutrality and equality and were intended to make all addresses equally accessible. New bridges increased points of access to the street systems of early national Boston and Philadelphia. In Philadelphia, New York, and Boston, traffic was expedited still further by leveling streets and reducing the differences in elevation among the major streets. Yet New Yorkers continually complained that the condition of the streets impeded easy transaction of business. An undated cartoon, part of a series entitled "New-York As It Is," depicted a city street filled with holes, garbage, and pigs (owned by the city and used as garbage scavengers). A man has been knocked down by an omnibus, and respectably dressed pedestrians are mired in mud.[22]

Metaphors of equal space and equal access informed two unsuccessful projects in 1820s Philadelphia. Merchant Paul Beck, Jr., upset by the city's irregular waterfront, held out the apparently forgotten Penn plan as a reproach to the city, as did many Philadelphia reformers of the early nineteenth century. In a redevelopment proposal of 1820, Beck contrasted Penn's desire that the waterfronts remain public commercial property, available to all Philadelphians, with the extensive and irregular private wharves and stores that had taken over the Delaware River shore. The irregular waterfront impeded general public use, harbored "dram shops and other immoral nuisances," and encouraged disease, which, Beck claimed, "always commences in the neighborhood of the wharves." Citing the model of Boston's newly rebuilt wharves, Beck wanted the city government to buy the entire waterfront and start over. The land beyond Front and New Water streets could be replatted into a series of equal lots with identical storehouses and rented out (fig. 3). This would restore Penn's plan, eradicate disease and license, "make Philadelphia the handsomest of cities," and offer an example of rational planning for others.[23]

Beck's plan "failed [for want] of like spirits to carry out the idea," but the irascible Stephen Girard, who had opposed Beck's effort, bequeathed $500,000 in 1831 to give Philadelphia a second chance by building a new waterfront street, Delaware Avenue, between Water Street and the river and constructing regular public wharves along it, together with steps at stated intervals to facilitate access to the waterfront (fig. 4).[24]

Wholesale merchants and city governments in other cities were no more successful than Beck and Girard in reforming waterfront space.

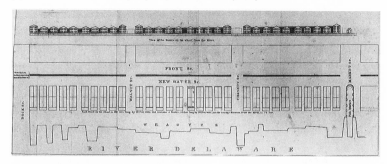

Figure 3.   William Strickland, elevation and plan, waterfront, Philadelphia. From [Paul Beck, Jr.], A *Proposal for Altering the Eastern Front of the City of Philadelphia* (Philadelphia: William Fry, 1820), frontis. (Library Company of Philadelphia.)

Figure 4.   Front Street steps, Philadelphia, built 1830s or later. (Photo, Dell Upton.)

Retail merchants and real estate developers compiled a better, although still spotty, record in rationalizing downtown shopping space. As with Beck's scheme, their allegiance to the ideas of equal space and equal access is most evident in their grandest projects, notably in the construction of shopping arcades to American cities in the 1820s. The first was in Philadelphia, built in the 600 block of Chestnut Street by Peter A. Browne, Edward Shippen Burd, architect John Haviland, and other investors in 1824–26 (figs. 5, 6). With its two levels of commercial space and its third floor designed as a new home for Peale's museum, the Philadelphia Arcade brought together under one roof the commercial and intellectual aspects of the systematic model of early republican urbanism. The modularly planned, identical shops, grouped on the commercial floors into three blocks separated by two avenues, were intended to reduce the differences in land value between frontage on a major street and space inside the block. Yet the arcade failed. The proprietors attributed the failure to a conspiracy among merchants located in the established business district on Second and Third streets, while Browne added that the inclusion of lottery agencies had offended genteel shoppers. Contemporary historian Daniel Bowen thought that the arcade went under because the entire city, in its "great uniformity," already possessed the attributes of an arcade. "Philadelphia has almost all the conveniences of an extensive Arcade, so beautiful are the arrangement of its streets, for shade, and side-walks, &c."[25]

The systematic urban myth was dynamic. The grid was conceived as a nonspecific system that could accommodate any number of specific meanings. Each person's purposeful movements through the streets connected otherwise independent spaces in a network of personal values. In other words, the street was the negative between the positives of private values; it traced the boundaries and described the location of parcels with no fixed relationships to one another other than their shared inner comparability. The fundamental order grew from within, shaped by the value of the parts rather than being imposed from without. For this reason the cost of every proposed urban amenity to the state and its economic benefit to the citizen occupying the city's parcels was closely calculated. The proponents of Philadelphia's light towers, for example, estimated that the scheme would cost the city $73,000 per year less than gas-fueled street lamps and that it would save private citizens an additional $100,000 per year in oil and candles.[26]

When the principle of comparable inner essences was applied to human life, it generated a view of citizenship that was as commodified and individualized as that of urban development. Individual worth was assessed by setting off each person's cost to the state against productivity

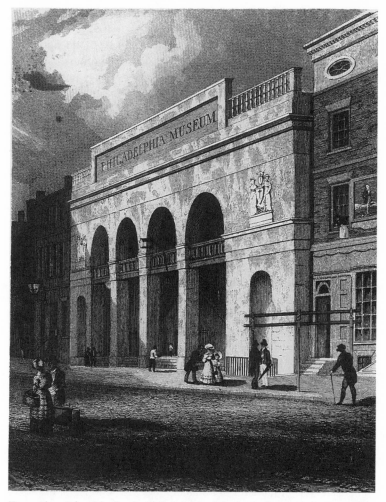

Figure 5. John Haviland, Philadelphia Arcade, built 1824–26. Engraving, Fenner, Seans and Co., 1826. (Library Company of Philadelphia.)

or potential productivity. Annual reports of the governors of public schools, prisons, almshouses, houses of refuge, and asylums of every sort included analyses of clients processed and costs per client. In addition, the managers expected all institutions except public schools to supply

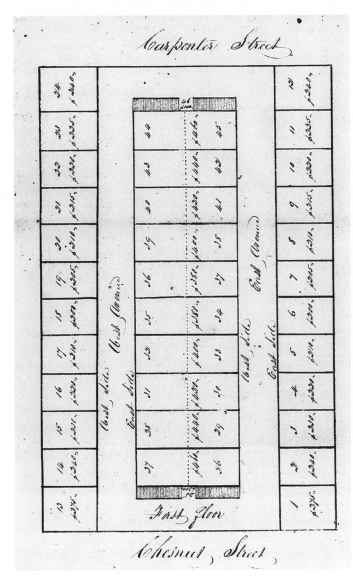

Figure 6.   John Haviland, first-floor plan, Philadelphia Arcade, ca. 1825.
(Burd Papers, Historical Society of Pennsylvania.)

much—eventually, they hoped, all—of their operating capital from the proceeds of inmate labor. Although some critics realized that cost analysis and social reform were incompatible, most opponents of repressive penal and welfare proposals felt constrained to frame their counterarguments in terms of cost.[27]

Cost analysis of care and punishment was only the most obvious form of social commercialization. The commodification of human behavior and morality was more subtle but even more pervasive. Educational and therapeutic institutions struggled to shape the inner person to a common standard. Metaphors of system and essence led once more to conceptual elision, as social managers envisioned differential civic merit in landscape terms. Through visible marks and spatial organization, a sort of human map would plot people in relation to one another so that, as with street numbers, one part of society "would be a complete index for the other." These considerations underlay the obsession with visual classification of social aspiration and failure. Paupers were to be removed from their homes and collected in almshouses for cost effectiveness and to serve as a deterrent to other poor people. If "there is no visible change in [the pauper's] condition [what] would prevent others asking relief?" Convicts were given distinctive, outlandish uniforms (fig. 7). Juvenile delinquents in the Boston and New York houses of refuge were to be divided according to their conduct into classes signified by uniforms and badges, respectively, each of which implied a degree of privilege or deprivation.[28]

The goal was to create a society in which there was no need for such cues. All members would act as one from inner impulse rather than from outer compulsion. Like the street grid, laws and regulations described the limits of conduct rather than its substance. Higher standards than the legal ones were expected in the republican city. "Therapeutic" institutions, with their carefully contrived material environments, were one way of instilling them. In this spirit the managers of the Philadelphia House of Refuge, a juvenile reformatory that emulated the nearby Eastern State Penitentiary in its architecture and discipline, wrote that children who had done no wrong but who merely seemed insufficiently sheltered from criminal temptation were "entitled to a place within these walls. . . . The imputation of a crime is not a necessary passport to admission."[29]

Figure 7.   *Prisoners at the State Prison at Auburn*. From John Warner Barber, *Historical Collections of the State of New York . . .* (New York: S. Tuttle, 1842), p. 78. (Library of Congress.)

The notion of commoditized citizenship and the techniques used to manufacture it were similar in nearly every penal and social welfare institution. Indeed, prisons, houses of refuge, almshouses, schools, and the many varieties of asylum were sometimes described as branches of a single system. Within their walls, bells controlled inmate action, and elaborately choreographed physical drills were the fundamental disciplinary tools. Paupers went to and from work and meals in step. Prisoners moved in lockstep, an intentionally humiliating, close-order march with their bodies nearly touching, forcing each convict to move when and as his neighbors did, while speech and eye contact were strictly forbidden (see fig. 7). By these means, wordless, synchronized movement arduously pantomimed an ideal, inner-directed society.[30]

Metaphors of system and essence also shaped efforts to direct individual moral and intellectual development. Projects such as the Lancasterian system of education were the human equivalent of John Dorsey's scheme for rationalizing weights and measures. The difference was that where Dorsey's ideas remained unpublished and untried Joseph Lancaster's guided the public school systems of most early national-period cities. Lancasterian instruction was introduced, often under Lancaster's personal supervision, into the public school systems of New York (1805), Georgetown (1811), Washington, D.C. (1812), Albany (1815), Philadelphia (1817), Baltimore (ca. 1821), and Boston (1824) and employed in orphanages, houses of refuge, and almshouses as well. Civic leaders in small towns and growing cities as far south as Fayetteville, North Carolina, and as far west as Cincinnati sought information or assistance in establishing their own Lancasterian schools.[31]

Joseph Lancaster (1778–1839) was an English teacher who adapted his system from one devised in India by Andrew Bell. For Lancaster, knowledge was a simple, hierarchically structured system that could be broken down into its constituent parts for student consumption. Reading students, for example, first learned to form the characters of the alphabet correctly, then moved on to one-letter words, followed by two-letter words, three-letter words, and so on. The teacher was not to expose the student to the next level of knowledge until she or he had mastered those below it.[32]

The Lancasterian system treated facts as so many pennies, to be deposited in student piggy banks until nickels, dimes, and dollars of knowledge were amassed. It assessed individual performance according to the balance accumulated. Students were evaluated and ranked within their peer groups daily. Good performances were rewarded with tickets of merit that could be used to purchase small prizes. Lancasterians gloried in constant reshuffling of the student hierarchy and stressed the importance of making it visible. The best student in each group wore a medal until he or she was dethroned by another student during the same or a subsequent lesson.[33]

This microcosmic social turmoil was integrated into an orderly macrocosm of knowledge by a prescribed pattern of movement. Recitations took place at stations along the walls of the classroom, the students standing in rank order, and Lancasterian manuals illustrated traffic patterns by which study groups should move to and from their desks (figs. 8, 9). "It is better that they stand behind their seats until the signal is given to sit all together." When seated, students were to write their lessons on slates, or in trays of sand in front of them (fig. 10). They were to write on cue, stop on cue, and erase on cue. They were to recite on cue and be silent on cue, "even if a word is half pronounced." For Lancasterians, the preferred architectural envelope for this choreographed

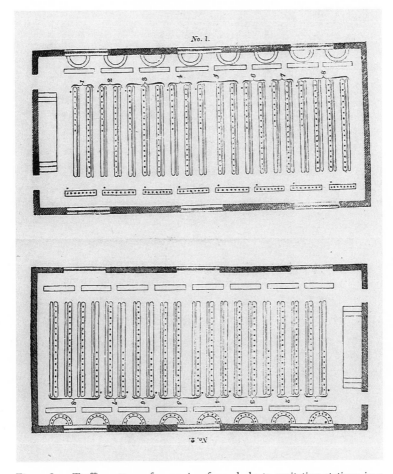

Figure 8.   Traffic patterns for moving from desks to recitation stations in a Lancasterian school. From Joseph Lancaster, *The British System of Education: Being a Complete Epitome of the Improvements and Inventions Practised in the Royal Free Schools* (London: By the author, 1810). (Library Company of Philadelphia.)

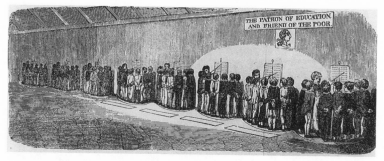

Figure 9.   Students at recitation stations. From Joseph Lancaster, *The British System of Education: Being a Complete Epitome of the Improvements and Inventions Practised in the Royal Free Schools* (London: By the author, 1810). (Library Company of Philadelphia.)

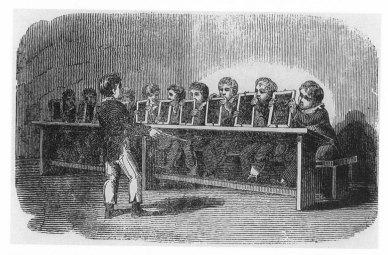

Figure 10.   Students displaying lessons on slates. From Joseph Lancaster, *The British System of Education: Being a Complete Epitome of the Improvements and Inventions Practised in the Royal Free Schools* (London: By the author, 1810), frontis. (Library Company of Philadelphia.)

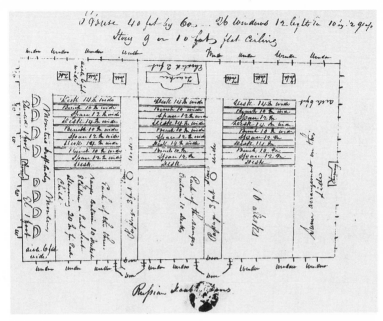

Figure 11.   J. M. Patton, proposed design for Lancasterian school in Milton, Pa. (Patton to Roberts Vaux, April 1, 1828, Roberts Vaux Papers, Historical Society of Pennsylvania.)

movement was a rectangular building with one room to a floor, each containing a raised teacher's platform at one end, rows of benches and desks the width of the room, and fixed stations for recitation groups along the wall (figs. 11, 12). Boys and girls, blacks and whites, were all to have separate classrooms.[34]

To its supporters, the great advantage of the Lancasterian method was the "monitorial" or "mutual" system of teaching. Each subgroup of eight to ten pupils was instructed by a student from the next level above. The teacher supervised the group, monitored the highest grades, and heard the monitors' recitations. By this means every pupil was actively occupied at all times.

Cost was the clincher. A single teacher could supervise 500 to 700 pupils in a single large classroom. Slates replaced expensive copy books,

Figure 12.   Mifflin School, Philadelphia, designed in 1825. (Photo, Dell Upton.)

and sand trays could in turn be substituted for slates (see fig. 10). Individual books might be dispensed with in favor of communal books printed in large type and attached to the wall. Since each pupil could only look at one page at a time of a regular book, leaving the other pages unavailable to anyone else, the wall-mounted book offered economy of scale. Lancasterian economies of scale and efficiency in the use of teachers' and pupils' time appealed to philanthropists and public officials in the early nineteenth century. The governor of New York compared Lancaster's system to the great labor-saving machines of the burgeoning manufactories, while New York City's Public School Society tried without success to have monitors legally bound to its service as apprentices until the age of twenty-one.[35]

Thus, notions of system and essence stimulated Lancasterians to conceive of human knowledge, orderly instruction, individual accomplishment, and spatial order as interlocking realms in which the material world could act as a tool for shaping the moral and intellectual faculties decisively and efficiently. From the first it was intended for poor children and for public schools. Better-off children were instructed in private schools by traditional methods. Lancasterianism taught habits of system and discipline intended to fit the lower classes for productive roles in the new commercial economy, at an attractive cost per unit.[36]

The Lancasterian fusion of the intellectual world of rational ordering, the human world of personal motivation, and the economic world of comparative evaluation dramatically illustrates the congruity of early nineteenth-century social and spatial thinking. Yet Lancasterianism also serves as a reminder that the early national period was an era of experiment. The precise material order that would unite social and spatial precepts was uncertain. Lancasterians tried to devise one, yet despite the extensive paraphernalia of slates, badges, tickets of merit, and communal books, their spatial framework for education—a single large room and a traffic pattern—was necessarily unspecialized.

Yet the germ of a more precise spatial order was present in the fascination with separation and classification that Lancasterians shared with other Anglo-American social reformers of the late eighteenth and early nineteenth centuries. Separation and classification of people, acts, and things in space was widely promoted as the key to rationalizing and reforming life. By the second decade of the nineteenth century social reformers had devised a fusion of social and spatial ideals based on these watchwords. Social separation and classification were achieved spatially by the use of repetitive, multicelled, often vaulted buildings. In this new form, each person or activity was given its own space, but all were alike. As with Lancasterianism, the goal was economy of scale, but this spatial model served even more important aims. Separation and classification allowed for comparison, analysis, and understanding of activities and populations. In addition, most observers of the era accepted social theories based on models of medical pathology. Separation and classification therefore had the complementary advantage of preventing social infection and contagion by obstructing undesirable associations.

Multicelled buildings were not a new idea. Neither was the standard arrangement of the cells along a neutral circulating system (usually a corridor) that made each independently accessible. Both had occasionally been used in the colonial era. (The familiar Georgian-plan house, with its rooms opening off a central passage, is an example.)[37] What was new was the specific articulation of people and spaces. Although the solution seems obvious after nearly 200 years of use, it took several decades, from the Revolution until the mid 1810s, for the two to

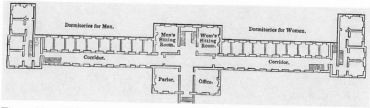

Figure 13.　William Strickland, ground-floor plan, Asylum for the Relief of Persons Deprived of Their Use of Reason, Philadelphia, 1814 and 1830s. From *Thirty-Eighth Annual Report of the Asylum . . .* (Philadelphia, 1853), p. 28. (Library Company of Philadelphia.)

be brought into alignment. The first example is the Asylum for the Relief of Persons Deprived of Their Use of Reason (also called Friends' Asylum), built outside Philadelphia in 1814 (fig. 13).

On the exterior the Friends' Asylum adopted the traditional five-part massing of a pavilion with wings and hyphens, an eighteenth-century, Anglo-American visual formula favored for all sorts of institutions. Where earlier hospitals such as Philadelphia's Pennsylvania Hospital—built in stages between 1751 and 1805—used a plan corresponding to their massing, incorporating one or a few large rooms in each wing, the Friends' Asylum divided the wings into single-loaded corridors with individual cells while retaining the customary Georgian-plan central block for administration and staff lodging.[38]

In individualizing treatment by assigning each patient to a single cell, the Friends' Asylum provided a solution to a planning problem with which Americans had wrestled for a quarter of a century. Yet the one-to-one matching of user and space was not commonsensical; it appeared after much halting experimentation, as the history of prisons during the era illustrates.

A new prison, Walnut Street Jail, was built in Philadelphia in 1773. From the front it appeared as a pavilion flanked by wings, an arrangement obviously similar to that used at the Pennsylvania Hospital (fig. 14). In plan it was a U-shape structure with ells projecting back from each end of the main block. Eight large groin-vaulted rooms opened off a single-loaded, barrel-vaulted corridor in the main block, with five rooms off a corridor in each of the ells. In 1787, when penal reformers convinced the Pennsylvania legislature to adopt imprisonment as a means

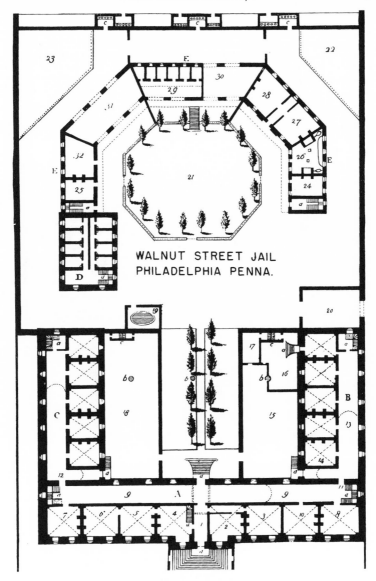

Figure 14.   Plan, Walnut Street Jail, Philadelphia, 1773–74. From Negley
Teeters, *The Cradle of the Penitentiary* (Philadelphia: Pennsylvania Prison
Society, 1955), facing p. 85.

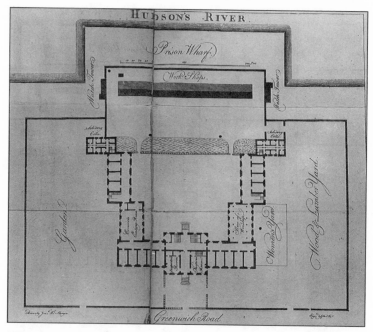

Figure 15.   Joseph Mangin, plan, New-York Prison, 1797. From [Thomas Eddy], *An Account of the State Prison or Penitentiary House in the City of New York* (New York, 1801), frontis. (New-York Historical Society.)

of reform, rather than merely safekeeping or punishment as it was traditionally used, Walnut Street was chosen as the model penitentiary. Where prisoners had traditionally been housed in large rooms in buildings often constructed for other purposes, Walnut Street Jail inmates were classified by gender and seriousness of offence (felony, misdemeanor, vagrancy, arrested but not yet tried) and held in a purpose-built structure. The ideas of social separation and classification and of the vaulted, celled building were both employed at Walnut Street Jail, but ten to twenty convicts occupied each cell as in the older prisons. Thus, while social contagion was ameliorated by classification, it was not eliminated, since treatment was not individualized. Reform prisons with similar plans and regimes were erected in most states over the next quarter century, for example at New York City (1797) (fig. 15) and Charlestown, Massachusetts (1804–5).[39]

Figure 16. John Haviland, cell, Eastern State Penitentiary, Philadelphia, 1823–35. (Photo, Dell Upton.)

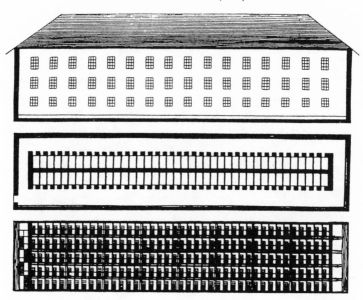

Figure 17.   Elevation, plan, cross-section, north wing, New York State Penitentiary, Auburn. From W. David Lewis, *From Newgate to Dannemora: The Rise of the Penitentiary in New York, 1796–1848* (Ithaca: Cornell University Press, 1965).

It was not until the second decade of the nineteenth century that the next step—individual confinement of each prisoner in a separate cell—was taken (fig. 16). By matching prisoners to cells, classification and separation could be refined, allowing treatment to focus on the single convict. The facilities and reformative techniques—contemplative isolation and occupation denied or tedious work imposed—were common, but their severity could be individually regulated according to the seriousness of each inmate's crime and the degree of his reform. Penitentiaries with many small, vaulted cells opening off single- or double-loaded corridors were built at Auburn, New York (1816–18), Pittsburgh (1818–26), and Philadelphia (1823–35) (figs. 17, 18).[40] Other states and large cities followed suit in the 1830s. In each, the penological theory, or prison discipline as the builders called it, was somewhat different, but the social-spatial assumptions underlying the building were shared.

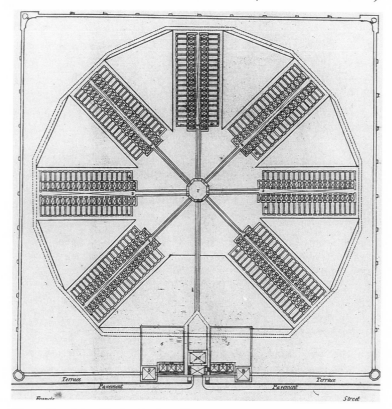

Figure 18. John Haviland, plan, Eastern State Penitentiary, Philadelphia. From *Views of Philadelphia and Its Environs from Original Drawings Taken in 1827–30* (Philadelphia: G. C. Childs, 1830), p. 39. (Library Company of Philadelphia.)

The active complement of the cell was the treadmill, an English device employed by some American authorities, most notably those supervising New York City's almshouse and the penitentiary (fig. 19). Like the Lancasterian school, the treadmill was a cheap way to ensure efficient use of the prisoners' time. All worked the same amount of time at the same task; there was no possibility of slacking. Like the prison cell, it had the advantage of individualizing standardized treatment: individual labor was automatically apportioned to the convict's body size.[41]

Figure 19.   Treadmill, New York City Penitentiary. From
S. Allen, *Reports on the Stepping . . . Mill* (New York, 1824),
frontis. (Library of Congress.) While Allen presented this as
a view of the New York treadmill, it is a widely disseminated
illustration originally published as a view of the treadmill at
Brixton prison, England.

The celled building and the treadmill were attractive because both
regulated conduct by impersonal, physical means rather than by resent-
ment-generating human force. Separate cells and carefully contrived devices for preventing transmission of visual and aural signals prevented
convicts from associating with one another. The treadmill forced prisoners to work continuously to keep up. It had a clockwork mechanism
that sounded a bell at intervals to mark changes of shifts; it also sounded
an alarm if the convicts colluded in operating the mill too slowly.

These measures established a "connection between morals and architecture" that the Boston Prison Discipline Society thought could be
useful in many other settings. They urged that the cellular principle be
extended from prisons and almshouses, where it was already used, to "all
establishments, where large numbers of youth of both sexes are assembled and exposed to youthful lusts," including boarding schools and colleges and even the houses of "large families."[42]

The repetitive, often vaulted, celled building was an ideal architecture for commoditized citizenship. It encompassed the transitive

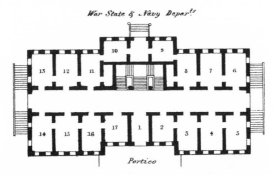

Figure 20. Plan, executive offices, Washington, D.C., ca. 1800, rebuilt ca. 1819. From Robert Mills, *Guide to the National Executive Offices* (Washington, D.C., 1841), facing p. 14.

essence of people, money, space, and action that Dorsey and Lancaster envisioned. It was rapidly translated back to everyday life, where it was used to individualize work and consumption, matching workers to spaces and consumers to commodities. The spatial history of the office building, for example, paralleled that of the prison. The typical office in the mid eighteenth century had consisted of a common counting room for the clerks and an elaborately decorated boardroom for the directors or managers, who took an active role in the business and met as often as weekly. In the late eighteenth century, larger office buildings were constructed for government agencies, the first large-scale bureaucratic organizations. The first purpose-built government offices in the United States, the four executive office buildings that flanked the White House in the first decades of the nineteenth century, used rooms of various sizes organized along corridors to multiply old-style clerks' rooms (fig. 20). These were large, unvaulted chambers connected by internal doors to allow them to be combined in suites; there was no indication of a clear one-to-one distribution of functions or personnel. New-model offices appeared as early as 1826 with the construction of Jones Court in New York City, where offices opened off an interior court on the principle of the shopping arcade. The form was perfected at Robert Mills's United States Treasury Building, 1836–42 (fig. 21). Mills modeled the general layout of

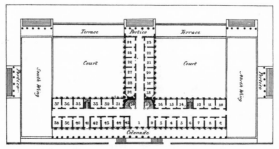

Figure 21.   Robert Mills, plan, United States Treasury
Building, 1836. From Robert Mills, *Guide to the National
Executive Offices* (Washington, D.C., 1841).

the building on its predecessor, one of the executive offices, but scaled
the groin-vaulted rooms for occupation by two clerks each.[43]

Repetitive-celled buildings were ubiquitous in the American urban landscape by the 1820s. They were most commonly seen in long,
identical rows of houses. William Sansom's block-long row on George
(now Sansom) Street in Philadelphia was hailed a few years after its construction in 1799 as "the first that has been built in America with strict
attention to uniformity." The claim was untrue. There were many
shorter, but still uniform rows built before the Revolution, even in
Philadelphia. Yet it is significant that Sansom's row was perceived as a
first, for it suggests that the public had developed a new appreciation for
such modular landscapes.[44]

Familiar building types like the tavern-hotel were more thoroughly
transformed. In the old tavern one partook en masse of common facilities. By the 1820s a guest in the best hotels rented a separate, specific
space and paid for services that were individually priced and itemized.
Each guest's personal consumption remained essentially the same as
every other guest's: the behavior was individualized, as John Watson
noted in his final appendix, but the experience was common and coor-
dinated by an elaborate system of bells.[45]

In addition to transforming old building types, the celled formula
created new ones, such as the shopping arcades of the 1820s and even the
commercial cemeteries that first appeared in the same decade. Traditional burial grounds were public property, usually owned by churches.
Like the old-fashioned tavern guest, the deceased had the right to use the

common facility. Interment was a temporary privilege, granting non-exclusive use of a grave until the corpse decomposed, as an English court noted. The commercial cemetery offered a new concept, one akin to renting a private room in a hotel: perpetual personal ownership of a specific plot. The Philadelphia, or Ronaldson's, Cemetery of 1827 was the first commercial cemetery there. A miniature city, it was laid out on a rectilinear grid, and its plots were sold to private purchasers who often took them as land speculations. At Ronaldson's and at the picturesque cemeteries that were founded in the 1830s, promoters stressed that because the purchaser owned a specific tract of land rather than the simple right to be in the cemetery, the remains would be free from disturbance.[46]

By the time of Andrew Jackson's election, spatial and social principles of separation (into individual spaces), classification (by crime, disease, age, gender, family, wealth), and equal access (through corridors, pathways, streets) had been fused into a systematic urban myth. The system was imagined as transparent, neutral, and nonhierarchical. As a consequence there was little place in the systematic landscape for a public realm. The public morality was the personally moral and industrious behavior of individuals. The public prosperity was the sum of many private prosperities. The public welfare was promoted by facilitating easy movement of citizens going about their personal business. The streets held no intrinsic public value other than as publicly supported tools for the pursuit of the collective private. Public space, in other words, was defined by what it lacked—impediments to private good—rather than by what it possessed—symbols of common values or facilities that promoted the general welfare. Thus, while the systematic landscape could be realized in limited, controlled situations like public institutions and relatively small private enterprises, it never achieved the domination of urban space that it required. Atomistic itself, the systematic landscape had little defense against the unsystematic atomism of the competitive landscape.

My label "competitive" encompasses two distinct urban spatial orders. One was the traditional aristocratic pattern of land use, the assignment of space based on social merit rather than economic value. It was evident in the continuing predilection of some of the postcolonial elite for using large amounts of center-city space unproductively as sites for large free-

Figure 22.   Benjamin Henry Latrobe, Bank of Philadelphia, 1804. Lithograph, 1809. (Library Company of Philadelphia.)

standing houses surrounded by gardens. However, these disappeared relatively early in the nineteenth century, with the exception of the largest public and quasi-public institutions such as government buildings and banks. In Philadelphia the Bank of Pennsylvania (1799) and Bank of Philadelphia (1805), both private institutions, and the First Bank (1797) and Second Bank (1818) of the United States were all sited in gardens in the heart of Philadelphia's business district (fig. 22). As late as the mid 1830s Ammi B. Young's preliminary plans sited the new customs house in a large landscaped park on Boston's busy waterfront.[47]

These institutions, highly visible but relatively few in number, undermined the vision of equal space equally accessible but were rarely criticized both because they were familiar and because they were controlled by the urban elite. Rather, it was the dense, apparently chaotic, land use of the burgeoning commercial cities that seemed new and noteworthy. Overintensive land use in the single-minded pursuit of individual gain appeared from the systematic viewpoint to result from the

Figure 23.   Shop fronts, South Front Street, Philadelphia, 1846. Lithograph, Thomas S. Wagner and James M'Guigan. (Library Company of Philadelphia.)

kind of shortsightedness or failure to see the big picture that Roger North attributed to the farmers and shop-traders of early eighteenth-century England.

The grid was fundamentally two-dimensional. The competitive landscape was multidimensional. Space was not a transparent or neutral medium of commerce but a limited commodity to be battled for, claimed, and exploited to the fullest. Watson believed that this attitude was introduced to New York and Philadelphia from England in the 1790s. Among the "flaunting signs of competition" that characterized the new order were stores the full depth of the building (rather than being confined to the front of a house), "bulk" (projecting bay) windows, and lighting and late-night hours in retail stores (fig. 23). He wondered that these tradesmen and women did not realize these measures were futile. Everyone worked harder, but no one made any headway.[48]

The bulging commercial buildings of the 1790s inflated conspicuously in the first decades of the nineteenth century. Commercial spaces were extended back and to the upper floors (fig. 24). More important, commercial spaces gradually took over the streets. Merchandise was piled on the sidewalks, and parcels were stacked at curbside to await the

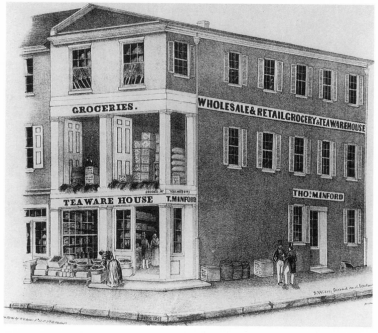

Figure 24.   Multifloor shop, Second and Walnut streets, Philadelphia, 1847. Lithograph, W. H. Rease. (Library Company of Philadelphia.)

freight wagon. Shopkeepers erected wooden frames at the curb to support the outer edge of a canvas awning that covered and claimed the entire sidewalk. The capture of the sidewalk was complemented in the late 1820s by the introduction of stores whose first floors were supported by granite piers and enclosed with glazed doors and french windows (see fig. 23).[49] The entire front of the building could be opened up and the sidewalk drawn into the shop. Lithographs of the 1830s and 1840s show that these new stores were arranged in aisles leading back into the interiors from the openings, on the same principle as the interior streets of a shopping arcade.

Visually as well as spatially, merchants commandeered public space. Signs were cantilevered over sidewalks or painted on the never-removed end panels of awnings. They were placed on buildings where they could be seen from the greatest distance. They were painted or at-

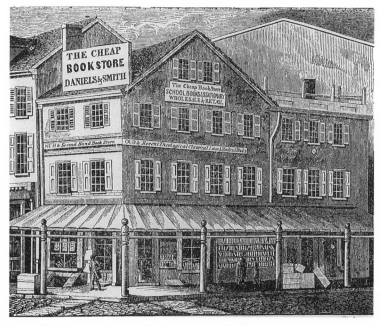

Figure 25. Awning-protected shop front, Philadelphia, 1846. Woodcut. (Library Company of Philadelphia.)

tached to the facade, sometimes even covering the windows (see fig. 23). They stood on the eaves (fig. 25).

In short, the use of individual spaces intensified to the point where the cell-defining bounds of the systematic grid were obliterated visually and spatially by merchants. At the same time, wheelbarrowmen, vendors from carts, and hucksters operated in the streets from no specific address, to the dismay of settled shopkeepers and in violation of city ordinances.[50]

In contrast to the imagined equality and transparency of systematic space, competitive space was unequal and opaque. Unwanted scraps of space above and below ground level could provide a site for a marginal business, such as the African-American-run oyster cellars that were created in the nineteenth century (fig. 26). Because they were out of public view, the same sorts of spaces were ideal for marginal, even illicit uses. Like grog houses and tippling shops, oyster cellars were places for the consumption of hard liquor. Many had a separate inner room parti-

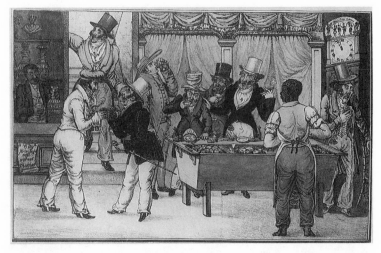

Figure 26. *James Akin, Philadelphia Taste Displayed; or, Bon-Ton be-low Stairs*, ca. 1830. Lithograph, Kennedy and Lucas. (Historical Society of Pennsylvania.)

tioned into small cubicles for patrons who desired greater privacy. Male enclaves—unmarked, semirespectable coffee houses, and brothels— were often found above street level.[51]

In the colonial era the waterfronts, for all their traditional faults as incubators of disease and immorality, had also been the residences as well as workplaces of great merchants, and thus a scene of working-class and elite intermixture. By 1830 the merchants in most American cities had retreated inland. Philadelphia's Stephen Girard (1750–1831) was reported to have been the last great merchant to live next to his counting house, and a watercolor of his then-curious Water Street establishment was made to commemorate the passing of an era (fig. 27).[52] Henceforth, the docks were off-limits to the respectable.

Like the systematic landscape, the competitive landscape had a social as well as commercial dimension. Outside the business district social territoriality was the rule. The firehouses of numerous volunteer companies, in many cities no more than fronts for gangs of rowdy young men, were the capitals of competing ethnic and class domains, the foci of assaults and defenses during riots. In commercial public gardens coffee and

Figure 27. Stephen Girard house, Water Street, Philadelphia. Watercolor, ca. 1831. (Library Company of Philadelphia.)

tea drinking, botanical displays, and entertainments of several sorts, such as fireworks and balloon ascensions, competed with alcoholic indulgence and more rough-hewn entertainments and were increasingly taken over by one or another political faction. Philadelphia's Lebanon Garden, for example, was the scene of Jacksonian bear roasts. To celebrate Andrew Jackson's first inauguration, his followers purchased a buffalo for $70, tied it to a tree in the garden, and watched as "a Mr. Peal, who had frequently shot buffaloes on the prairies" pumped several bullets into it, with little effect. The buffalo was finally dispatched with an axe.[53]

The systematic and competitive, social and commercial landscapes intersected in the streets, a scene of conflict between the genteel and the

Figure 28.   *Life in Philadelphia: A Crier Extraordinary*, ca. 1830. Lithograph, C. Hunt. (Library Company of Philadelphia.)

rough-hewn. The flaunting signs of competition that characterized the commercial landscape were matched socially. It was impossible to walk down the streets without being aware of people whose sights, sounds, and smells were at best unwelcome and sometimes even threatening to the genteel. The sight of drunks, beggars, and free blacks were all offensive to the respectable, as were the cries and shouts of hawkers and vendors (fig. 28). Smoking and chewing of tobacco became a symbol of the ag-

Figure 29. E. W. Clay, *The Smokers*, 1837. Lithograph, H. R. Robinson, New York. (Library Company of Philadelphia.)

gressive presence of the rough-hewn (fig. 29). An anonymous English traveler noted "the great number of persons to be met with in every street, smoking segars. In passing along you are assailed by those fragrant perfumers, for this being a free country, they puff and spit, to the right and left, to the great annoyance of those who may happen to have no taste for delicacies of this description." Worse, young toughs were likely to harass people of all classes, while even ostensibly respectable young men felt free to make remarks and even to accost single young women.[54]

There were several societies operating on the competitive street, and it was not always easy to recognize them all, much less separate or classify them. In the competitive landscape the complement of the orderly visual separation and classification imposed through the badges and uniforms of institutional inmates was the often-outlandish dress of fashionable whites and blacks on the streets (figs. 30, 31).[55]

A second strategy of the genteel and the aspiring was to seek spatial segregation. In some cases they avoided areas popular with ordinary people. Francis Grund noted ironically that the Battery and others of the most beautiful parts of New York were the domain of "the people," who "follow their inclinations, and occupy what they like, while our exclusives are obliged to content themselves with what is abandoned by the

Figure 30. *Life in New York: St. John's Park, September 28, 1829. Inconvenience of Tight Lacing.* Lithograph, Anthony Imbert. (Library Company of Philadelphia.)

crowd," while the elite withdrew to private St. John's Square. In other cases the upper classes did not concede public space so passively but sought to seize it from the crowd. In Philadelphia the eastern public squares (Franklin to the north, and Washington to the south), were used as lumber yards, potters' fields, and dumps until the early nineteenth century. Washington Square was also the scene of Sunday drumming and dancing for Philadelphia's African Americans. Both were landscaped in the 1810s, and Washington Square was claimed by genteel promenaders while the southwestern (now Rittenhouse) square, surrounded by a working-class neighborhood, was left unimproved (see fig. 31). Significantly, smoking was prohibited in Washington Square.[56]

Figure 31.   E. W. Clay, *Promenade in Washington Square*, Philadelphia, 1829–30.   Watercolored etching.   (Library Company of Philadelphia.)

The systematic urban landscape created transparent urban space; the competitive landscape obscured space. Spatial conflict in commerce, offenses to social sensibilities, and occasional incidents of genuine danger in the streets were troubling to many urbanites. Through the lenses of traditional morality and modern systematic order, the third, or shadow, myth provided an interpretation of urban cacophony that resolved urban confusion into a clearly perceived threatening landscape in the eyes of those middle-class and elite observers who wrote about the city's problems.

The competitive material world seemed to promote the loosening of traditional standards of personal discipline. Just as Watson saw commercial competition as a futile and arrogant struggle for place, so he condemned the splendid dress and personal arrogance of free blacks who, he thought, had become unmanageable "since they got those separate churches, and received their entire exemption from slavery." Although black finery was galling, it was only the most conspicuous instance of a general lack of discipline that was responsible for the confusion on the streets. From this point of view, the genteel were often as guilty as the rough-hewn. It is significant that Watson connected perceived arrogance with the failure of churches, for the myth of the shadow landscape interpreted immodesty and indecorous behavior as sin.[57] From the moral point of view the urban landscape presented a prospect of sinful disorder.

Yet notions of separation and classification promoted a more specific analysis of urban space. In addition to the inherent evils of drinking, fornication, rowdiness, and insolence that characterized the competitive landscape and its undisciplined denizens, the landscape itself was at fault, for it encouraged promiscuous mixing of classes, races, and sexes. This complaint was as conspicuous in denunciations of informal public gathering places as the sins themselves. The grog houses, oyster cellars, tippling shops, hose and engine houses, and other places of informal gathering and public entertainment encouraged mingling. The streets were the worst of all. There, children were exposed to corruption even more easily, and casually, than in immoral premises. To people who accepted a contagious model of social disorder (even though they disagreed whether medical disease spread that way) the danger was clear: unseparated, unclassified spaces threatened to spread social disorder throughout society.[58]

What is more, corruption failed to confine itself to the disreputable parts of the city. Even the new elite neighborhoods were not safe for gentility. In New York, for example, just as merchants moved away from the waterfront, so did prostitutes after 1820. Prostitutes moved into every neighborhood of the city, often sorting themselves by class of their clients, forming a kind of dimly glimpsed parallel society to the respectable city.[59]

The notion of a parallel society is the key to understanding the third landscape. The cacophony of the streets was finally transformed from innocent disorder, to immoral disorder, to immoral *order*—a shadow landscape that linked alley dwelling, tavern, oyster cellar, brothel, theater, dock, and street in a system that was largely invisible to, but threatened, respectable society. These places were not simply the fringes and backsides of the commercial city, but an aggressive, morally and medically subversive landscape that was the reverse of the therapeutic landscape of prison and almshouse and the respectable commercial landscape of hotel and cemetery. The opposition between the two was explicitly drawn in the early republican era, as in the 1829 decision of the state of New York to support the New York City house of refuge by a tax on groceries, taverns, ordinaries, grog shops, public gardens, theaters, and circuses.[60]

Early republican city dwellers believed the landscape affected their lives directly and decisively. The material landscape was envisioned as a determinative framework for social, economic, and hygienic order. They looked to the landscape to shape their society, provide their livelihoods, give meaning to their social rituals, and depict their successes and failures. Behind these truisms, however, lay uncertainty, inconsistency, and conflict.

While the material landscape is a text that can be read for symptoms of social health or pathology, spatial and social conflict within the city has concrete roots in the competing interests of social classes and ethnic groups. Yet these rarely worked out in simple, easily interpreted ways. As culturally imagined representations of a city, urban myths served as filters through which group and individual interests were diffused. Because they were loosely based on common experiences, yet capable of variable applications, they appealed to people of a variety of social classes. Their metaphorical qualities made it possible even for individuals to slip from one myth to another as the occasion demanded. As a result, space and human action in the city are fragmented and complex.

Middling merchants and tradespeople, for example, found both competitive and systematic myths appealing. These people were the builders of the signs, awnings, and other obstructions to orderly movement through the city that comprised a significant element of the competitive landscape. In other contexts, however, they found the disciplinary aspects of the systematic model attractive as well. The clear but nonhierarchical territorial demarcation of the gridded city promised a strict maintenance of boundaries among things and people and consequently offered clear, objectively based, social position. The grid was also a spatial device for bringing together bodies and things and comparing inner essences by fusing being and owning into commercialized personhood. Cutler George Frederick Boyer understood the connection between person and property. As depicted by nineteenth-century business historian Abraham Ritter, Boyer "was . . . tenacious of his right, title and interest in his domicil, which, during his ownership, he used to his liking, and went whithersoever he would; but, in process of time, he sold his house to William Folwell, and fell sick and bed-ridden with consumption. His cough was troublesome, and expectoration frequent; but being no longer the owner, he refused the benefit of the soil, and [in] spite of his wife's entreaties to 'spit out,' he would crawl to the window to discharge the encumbrance."[61]

Merchants and tradespeople were often victims of the chaotic life of the streets. Thus they were drawn to a model that sought to bring social life and spatial order into a single focus and eliminate the ambiguities of the competitive city and the shadow landscape. In this respect the discipline of the systematic city was something to be applied not only to oneself but even more to others. The ethos of the systematic landscape was deeply repressive, as its proponents freely admitted. Writing in 1817 of the poor children—the "pure liberty boys"—who pilfered small items from taxpayers' shops rather than attend the public schools provided for them, Philadelphia schoolmaster John Ely thought that they "should be removed from the streets, as the wheel-barrow-men were," by a "spirited and vigilant police . . . to prevent them from contaminating the morals of other boys." He feared it would never be done, however, from a weak-minded concern for "the natural rights of the citizens."[62]

The systematic model took no account of the possibility of conflicts among legitimate private interests, but instead assumed equality of opportunity and consequently expected a general acceptance of the justice of hierarchies of wealth and social standing.[63] In this respect it was attractive not only to the middling but also to the elite. Its implications for power beyond the personal scale attracted wealthy and politically powerful citizens who were able to see the urban picture whole and were confident of their ability to affect it.

Yet the transparent ideal of the systematic landscape was undermined by customary models of land use based on personal standing rather than on economic power. Job R. Tyson noted the Boston habit of siting houses so that they would be "hid behind trees or corners, or concealed by hills & other buildings of moderate dimensions & little attractiveness." In other respects, traditional elite culture served to alleviate some of the savagery of the republican social ideal. Some wealthy people clung to older models of benevolence based on fatalistic but more humane, less accusative views of economic equality than the dominant early nineteenth-century ones. Other wealthy people attacked the systematic model analytically. Philadelphia Roman Catholic Mathew Carey, for example, spent much of his time and money after his retirement publishing pamphlets that undermined the fundamental premises of the systematic model of society and of the shadow landscape, calling for a more open-handed treatment of the poor.[64]

By default, the competitive landscape was the landscape of the poor. True, the systematic model addressed the problem directly and in depth, through the creation of asylums and therapeutic institutions, while the competitive model, with its cutthroat competition for space and resources, took no explicit notice of the poor and the marginal. In contrast to the repressive and often mean-spirited vision of social reform put forward in the systematic myth, however, the competitive accommodation of small producers at least left cracks in which the wheelbarrow men, hucksters, oyster sellers, and others of the most marginal people could survive, however badly. It was much more difficult to get by within the framework of public support and intermittent employment approved by elite authority, as Carey demonstrated.

Between 1790 and 1830 three principal ways of imagining the city held sway in the United States. Using these transitive patterns of metaphor and practice, urban dwellers had created all the significant urban patterns and building types of antebellum America by 1830. By the third quarter of the nineteenth century a largely despairing conception of the city had replaced them. Yet while the American city changed radically after the 1850s, and with it explicit models of urban process, the early nineteenth-century cultural landscape continues to shape our responses to urban space and urban social life in the late twentieth century.

---

[1] *The Biographical Encyclopedia of Pennsylvania of the Nineteenth Century* (Philadelphia: Galaxy Publishing Co., 1874), pp. 462–63; John F. Watson, *Annals of Philadelphia and Pennsylvania in the Olden Time*, 3 vols. (3d ed., rev. and enl. by Willis P. Hazard, 1875; reprint, Philadelphia: Edwin S. Stuart, 1905), 3:13–14; Deborah Dependahl Waters, "Philadelphia's Boswell: John Fanning Watson," *Pennsylvania Magazine of History and Biography* 98, no. 1 (January 1974): 3–52.

[2] John F. Watson, *Annals of Philadelphia and Pennsylvania, in the Olden Time; Being a Collection of Memoirs, Anecdotes, and Incidents of the City and Its Inhabitants*, 2 vols. (2d ed.; Philadelphia: J. B. Lippincott, 1868), 2:588–91. Subsequent quotations from Watson are derived from this edition except as noted. Since Watson

inserted and deleted material in each version, and his successor Willis Hazard added an entirely new third volume, it is sometimes necessary to cite the 1st and 3rd editions.

[3] Watson, *Annals*, 2:591.

[4] I use *myth* to mean a metaphoric model of action and judgment rather than in the colloquial sense of a religious tale or a fanciful or untrue belief.

[5] "A Guide to the Peale Museum," *Port Folio* 4, no. 19 (November 7, 1807): 293–95.

[6] Daniel J. Boorstin, *The Lost World of Thomas Jefferson* (Boston: Beacon Press, 1948), pp. 111–16; Rhys Isaac, *The Transformation of Virginia, 1740–1790* (Chapel Hill: University of North Carolina Press, 1982), pp. 263–64, 309–11; Gordon S. Wood, *The Creation of the American Republic, 1776–1787* (Chapel Hill: University of North Carolina Press, 1968); "Guide to the Peale Museum," p. 295.

[7] Roger North, *The Gentleman Accomptant; or, An Essay to Unfold the Mystery of Accompts* (2d ed.; London: E. Curll, 1715), pp. 17–18, 2, 57–58, 62, 201; Joyce Oldham Appleby, *Economic Thought and Ideology in Seventeenth-Century England* (Princeton: Princeton University Press, 1978).

[8] Patricia Cline Cohen, *A Calculating People: The Spread of Numeracy in Early America* (Chicago: University of Chicago Press, 1982).

[9] John Dorsey to William Jones, president of the Second Bank of the United States [ca. 1818], William Jones Papers, Uselma Clark Smith Collection, Historical Society of Pennsylvania (HSP). Thomas Jefferson, "Notes on Coinage" (1784), and "Reports on Weights and Measures" (1790), *The Papers of Thomas Jefferson*, ed. Julian P. Boyd, 24 vols. to date (Princeton: Princeton University Press, 1953–), 7:150–203, 16:602–75; Charles Varlo, *Schemes Offered for the Perusal and Consideration of the Legislature, Freeholders, and Public in General . . .* (London: J. Chapman, 1775), p. 141.

[10] The inescapability of language is a familiar story to twentieth-century scholars. For an early statement, see Benjamin Lee Whorf's essays of the 1920s and 1930s, collected in *Language, Thought, and Reality: Selected Writings of Benjamin Lee Whorf*, ed. John B. Carroll (Cambridge: MIT Press, 1956); for a more recent exploration, see Jonathan Culler, *On Deconstruction: Theory and Criticism After Structuralism* (Ithaca: Cornell University Press, 1982), esp. pp. 89–110. Jean Starobinski, *1789: The Emblems of Reason*, trans. Barbara Bray (Cambridge: MIT Press, 1988).

[11] Hannah Benner Roach, "The Planting of Philadelphia: A Seventeenth-Century Real Estate Development," *Pennsylvania Magazine of History and Biography* 92, no. 1 (January 1968): 3–47, 92; no. 2 (April 1968): 143–94; Anthony N. B. Garvan, "Proprietary Philadelphia as Artifact," in *The Historian and the City*, ed. Oscar Handlin and John Burchard (Cambridge: MIT Press, 1963), pp. 177–201; Gary B. Nash, "City Planning and Political Tension in the Seventeenth Century: The Case of Philadelphia," *Proceedings of the American Philosophical Society* 112 (1968): 54–73; John W. Reps, *Town Planning in Frontier America* (1969; reprint, Columbia: University of Missouri Press, 1980); Clement Biddle, *The Philadelphia Directory* (Philadelphia: James and Johnson, 1791), p. v; Paul Groth, "Streetgrids as Frameworks for Urban Variety," *Harvard Architectural Review* 2, no. 2 (Spring 1981): 68–75; Richard S. Dunn and Mary Maples Dunn, eds., *The Papers of William Penn*, vol. 2, *1680–1684* (Philadelphia: University of Pennsylvania Press, 1982), pp. 118–21; Walter Muir Whitehill, *Boston: A Topographical History* (2d ed.; Cambridge: Harvard University Press, 1968), pp. 1–46; John Kouwenhoven, *The Columbia Historical Portrait of New York: An Essay in Graphic History* (New York: Harper and Row, 1953); Claude-Anne Lopez, *Benjamin Franklin's "Good House"* (Washington, D.C.: U.S.

Department of the Interior, 1981); Benjamin Loxley memo book, 1768, Benjamin Loxley Papers, Uselma Clark Smith Collection.

¹²City commissioners as quoted in M. Christine Boyer, *Manhattan Manners: Architecture and Style, 1850–1900* (New York: Rizzoli, 1985), p. 9. Philadelphia City Council minutes, April 24, 1789, p. 92, City Archives, Philadelphia. The New York commissioners went on to note that "from the same causes the price of Land is so uncommonly great [that] it seemed proper to admit the principles of Economy to greater influence than might under circumstances of a different kind have consisted with the dictates of Prudence and the sense of Duty" (Boyer, *Manhattan Manners*, p. 9). In a similar vein, Clement Biddle noted that Penn had intended Front Street in Philadelphia for public access and enjoyment, but that "the inhabitants were soon convinced that the ground . . . was too valuable to be kept unimproved, in any degree, merely for the sake of a prospect" (Biddle, *Philadelphia Directory*, p. v). The most perceptive analysis of the New York grid's commercial implications can be found in Hendrik Hartog, *Public Property and Private Power: The Corporation of the City of New York in American Law, 1730–1870* (Chapel Hill: University of North Carolina Press, 1983), pp. 158–75. Contrasts between New York City and Philadelphia are discussed in Boyer, *Manhattan Manners*, p. 9; Edward K. Spann, "The Greatest Grid: The New York Plan of 1811," in *Two Centuries of American Planning*, ed. Daniel Schaffer (Baltimore: Johns Hopkins University Press, 1988), pp. 11–39; Martin P. Snyder, *City of Independence: Views of Philadelphia before 1800* (New York: Praeger Publishers, 1975), pp. 198–205.

¹³Charles Dickens, *American Notes and Pictures from Italy* (Oxford: Oxford University Press, 1957), p. 98.

¹⁴Whitehill, *Boston*, pp. 1–46; Reps, *Town Planning*, pp. 126–30; Berthold Fernow, ed., *The Records of New Amsterdam from 1653 to 1674 Anno Domini*, 7 vols. (New York: Knickerbocker Press, 1897), 1:33, 36–37.

¹⁵Roach, "Planting of Philadelphia," pp. 22–24, 33–37; National Capital Planning Commission, *Worthy of the Nation: The History of Planning for the National Capital* (Washington, D.C.: Smithsonian Institution, 1977), pp. 15–36; Kenneth Bowling, *Creating the Federal City, 1774–1800: Potomac Fever* (Washington, D.C.: American Institute of Architects Press, 1988), pp. 91–98.

¹⁶Watson, *Annals*, 1:364–66; Thomas Condie and Richard Folwell, *History of the Pestilence, Commonly Called Yellow Fever, Which Almost Desolated Philadelphia, in the Months of August, September, and October, 1798* (Philadelphia: R. Folwell, 1799), pp. 6–7.

¹⁷Whitehill, *Boston*, pp. 73–94; Darwin H. Stapleton, ed., *The Engineering Drawings of Benjamin Henry Latrobe* (New Haven: Yale University Press, 1980), pp. 28–36, 196; Jane Mork Gibson, "The Fairmount Waterworks," *Philadelphia Museum of Art Bulletin* 84, nos. 360–61 (Summer 1988): 2–11.

¹⁸D. B. Lee and W. Beach, "Lighting the City by Towers," *Hazard's Register of Pennsylvania* 13, no. 4 (January 25, 1834): 55–56.

¹⁹Broadside, "Regulations for the Government of the Nightly Watch of the City of Philadelphia," Philadelphia, May 13, 1823; *Philadelphia in 1824* (Philadelphia: H. C. Carey and I. Lea, 1824), pp. 169–70.

²⁰On convenience of living, see Watson, *Annals* (1st ed.), app., p. 73. Tyson to Vaux, July 24, 1829, Roberts Vaux Papers, HSP.

²¹"Proceedings of Councils," *Hazard's Register of Pennsylvania* 5, no. 25 (June 19, 1830): 390. Biddle, *Philadelphia Directory*, p. xii; J. P. Brissot de Warville, *New Travels in the United States of America, Performed in 1788* (Dublin: W. Corbet, 1792),

p. 315. Uniform street numbering, along with rationalization of street names, was not enacted until 1858 (Howard Gillette, Jr., "The Emergence of the Modern Metropolis: Philadelphia in the Age of Its Consolidation," in *The Divided Metropolis: Social and Spatial Dimensions of Philadelphia, 1800–1975*, ed. William W. Cutler II and Howard Gillette, Jr. [Westport, Conn.: Greenwood Press, 1980], p. 11).

[22] Bridges are discussed in Whitehill, *Boston*, pp. 74–78; "A Statistical Account of the Schuylkill Permanent Bridge," *Port Folio*, n.s., 5, no. 11 (March 12, 1808): 168–71; no. 12 (March 19, 1808): 182–87; no. 13 (March 26, 1808): 200–204; no. 14 (April 2, 1808): 222–24. On traffic, see Watson, *Annals*, 1:232–35; Elizabeth Blackmar, *Manhattan for Rent, 1785–1850* (Ithaca: Cornell University Press, 1989), p. 99. "New-York As It Is. Respectfully Dedicated to the Corporation of the City of New York by Serrell and Perkins," ca. 1850, Print Room, Library Company of Philadelphia (LCP). Watson attributed the grading of Philadelphia to "bad taste and avidity for converting every piece of ground to the greatest possible revenue" (Watson, *Annals*, 1:233). For similar efforts in late antebellum Philadelphia, see Gillette, "Emergence of the Modern Metropolis," p. 12.

[23] [Paul Beck, Jr.], *A Proposal for Altering the Eastern Front of the City of Philadelphia, with a View to Prevent the Recurrence of Malignant Disorders, on a Plan Conformable to the Original Design of William Penn* (Philadelphia: William Fry, 1820), pp. 3–6, 10–11; Henry Simpson, *The Lives of Eminent Philadelphians, Now Deceased* (Philadelphia: William Brotherhead, 1859), pp. 37–48.

[24] Abraham Ritter, *Philadelphia and Her Merchants, as Constituted Fifty [to] Seventy Years Ago* (Philadelphia: By the author, 1860), p. 66; *The Will of the Late Stephen Girard, Esq., Procured from the Office for the Probate of Wills, with a Short Biography of His Life* (Philadelphia: Lydia R. Bailey, 1839), pp. 30–34; Simpson, *Lives*, pp. 43–44.

[25] Daniel Bowen, *A History of Philadelphia* (Philadelphia: By the author, 1839), p. 157; Johann Friedrich Geist, *Arcades: The History of a Building Type* (Cambridge: MIT Press, 1983), pp. 4, 12–13, 536–38; *An Act to Incorporate the Stockholders of the Philadelphia Arcade* (Philadelphia, 1829), pp. 5–6; Peter A. Browne to Edmund Shippen Burd, September 4, 1827, and Browne to Managers of the Arcade, ca. 1827, Edmund Shippen Burd Papers, HSP. The surviving Philadelphia Arcade documents, including sketch plans, are in the Burd Papers. The Providence, R.I., arcade, begun in 1828 and still operating, was also envisioned as a complete downtown organized on rational principles and was intended to compete with an existing business district; Robert L. Alexander, "The Arcade in Providence," *Journal of the Society of Architectural Historians* 12, no. 3 (October 1953): 13–16. Geist, *Arcades*, pp. 64–68, traces the origins of the arcade to Paris in the late eighteenth century.

[26] Lee and Beach, "Lighting the City by Towers," p. 56.

[27] Michael B. Katz, *In the Shadow of the Poorhouse: A Social History of Welfare in America* (New York: Basic Books, 1986), pp. 22–23, 32; Franklin Bache, "Penitentiary System," *Hazard's Register of Pennsylvania* 3, no. 13 (March 28, 1829): 197–99; [Stephen Allen], *Reports on the Stepping or Discipline Mill, at the New-York Penitentiary* (New York: Van Pelt and Spear, 1823), p. 28; Mathew Carey, *Essays on the Public Charities of Philadelphia, Intended to Vindicate the Benevolent Societies of This City from the Charge of Encouraging Idleness . . .* (4th ed.; Philadelphia: J. Clarke, 1829). For examples of cost analysis of public assistance, see Howard [Mathew Carey], *Pauperism—No. II: To the Citizens of Philadelphia, Paying Poor Taxes* (Philadelphia, 1827), pp. 1–2; *Philadelphia in 1824* (Philadelphia: H. C. Carey and I. Lea, 1824), p. 63; [Thomas Eddy], *An Account of the State Prison or Peniten-*

tiary House, in the City of New-York (New York: Isaac Collins and Son, 1801), pp. 35–36, 40–45. Eddy calculated that efficient kitchen equipment had reduced the daily cost of cooking fuel from 22 mills per inmate to 1 285/315 mills (p. 47). For examples of accounting of income from public institutions, see *A View of the New-York State Prison in the City of New-York* (New York: T. and J. Swords, 1815), pp. 53–54; "Statement of Some of the Advantages That May Be Derived from Removing the Philadelphia Alms House and House of Employment to the Country," ca. 1810, LCP Collection, HSP.

28 "To the Honourable Senate and House of Representatives of the Commonwealth of Pennsylvania . . . , the Memorial of the Guardians for the Relief and Employment of the Poor in the City of Philadelphia" (Philadelphia, ca. 1836), n.p.; *Fourth Annual Report of the Board of Managers of the Prison Discipline Society, Boston, 1829* (Boston: T. R. Marvin, 1829), pp. 13–14; *Seventh Annual Report of the Managers of the Society for the Reformation of Juvenile Delinquents in the City and State of New-York* (New York: Mahlon Day, 1832), p. 15.

29 James Mease, *The Picture of Philadelphia*, continued by Thomas Porter, 2 vols. (Philadelphia: Robert Desilver, 1831), 2:41.

30 *Rules for the Government of the Board of Guardians, Its Officers, Business and Affairs; and for Regulating and Controlling the Alms-House, Hospital, and House of Employment* (Philadelphia: William Brown, 1835), p. 24; *Tenth Annual Report of the Managers of the Society for the Reformation of Juvenile Delinquents in the City and State of New-York* (New York: Mahlon Day, 1835), pp. 6–7; William Russell, *Manual of Mutual Instruction; Consisting of Mr. Fowle's Directions for Introducing in Common Schools the Improved System Adopted in the Monitorial School, Boston* (Boston: Wait, Greene, 1826), pp. 16–17; Dickens, *American Notes*, p. 31. Convicts counted the lockstep among the most degrading elements of prison discipline, and its replacement in the Ohio penitentiary in the 1850s by military drill was a significant reform (R. S. M'Ewen, *The Mysteries, Miseries, and Rascalities of the Ohio Penitentiary* [Columbus, Ohio: John Geary, Son, 1856], pp. 60–61). See Michel Foucault, *Discipline and Punish: The Birth of the Prison*, trans. Alan Sheridan (New York: Vintage Books, 1979), pp. 147–53, for a discussion of the relationship between bodily movement and moral formation and of the origins of synchronized movement in military discipline. As with many of Foucault's most provocative observations, the truth of this one was openly acknowledged in nineteenth-century documents; for example, see the comparison of schools to regiments in the 1826 report of the Albany Lancasterian school as quoted in Russell, *Manual of Mutual Instruction*, p. 105.

31 John Franklin Reigart, *The Lancasterian System of Instruction in the Schools of New York City* ([1916]; reprint, New York: AMS Press, 1972), pp. 1–2; John Claggett Porter, "Joseph Lancaster and the Lancasterian Schools in the District of Columbia," *Records of the Columbia Historical Society of Washington, D.C.* 25 (1923): 5–7; Russell, *Manual of Mutual Instruction*, p. 105; *First Annual Report of the Controllers of the Public Schools of the First School District of Pennsylvania; With Their Accounts* (Philadelphia: Board of Control, 1819), p. 5; Joseph Lancaster to Vaux, March 5, 1821, Vaux Papers; *First Biennial Report of the Trustees and Instructor of the Monitorial School* (Boston: Thomas B. Wait and Son), p. 5. For schools outside the large cities, see Ithiel Town to Roger S. Baldwin, March 15, 1823 (Fayetteville, N.C.), folder 175, box 14, ser. 1, group 55, general correspondence, Baldwin Family Papers, Yale University Manuscripts and Archives; Coudy Raquet to Roberts Vaux, March 30, June 15, 1821 (Cincinnati), Vaux Papers. "Lancasterian" was the preferred form of the adjective in the nineteenth century.

114   *Everyday Life in the Early Republic*

³² Joseph Lancaster, *The British System of Education: Being a Complete Epitome of the Improvements and Inventions Practised in the Royal Free Schools* (London: By the author, 1810).

³³ Lancaster, *British System of Education,* pp. 29–30; *First Biennial Report of the Trustees,* pp. 18–19.

³⁴ Lancaster, *British System of Education,* p. 2–3, 7; Russell, *Manual of Mutual Instruction,* pp. 3–7, 17–18; Benjamin Shaw to Controllers of the Public Schools, Philadelphia, April 16, 1818, Vaux Papers. Lancaster published his own *Hints and Directions for Building School-Rooms,* which I have not seen.

³⁵ Reigart, *Lancasterian System,* pp. 8, 91.

³⁶ One estimate was $3 per pupil per annum; Shaw to Controllers of the Public Schools, April 16, 1818, Vaux Papers.

³⁷ There is extensive literature on the Georgian-plan house. For a succinct definition, see Henry Glassie, "Eighteenth-Century Cultural Process in Delaware Valley Folk Building," in *Common Places: Readings in American Vernacular Architecture,* ed. Dell Upton and John Michael Vlach (Athens: University of Georgia Press, 1986), p. 400.

³⁸ *Account of the Rise and Progress of the Asylum, Proposed to Be Established, Near Philadelphia, for the Relief of Persons Deprived of Their Use of Reason . . .* (Philadelphia: Kimber and Conrad, 1814); John D. Thompson and Grace Goldin, *The Hospital: A Social and Architectural History* (New Haven: Yale University Press, 1975), pp. 97–99; *Account of the Present State of the Asylum for the Relief of Persons Deprived of the Use of Their Reason* (Philadelphia: W. Brown, 1816), p. 3. Compare the plan of The Retreat (York, England) in Thompson and Goldin, *The Hospital,* pp. 72–73, with the Friends' Asylum model.

³⁹ Michael Ignatieff, *A Just Measure of Pain: The Penitentiary in the Industrial Revolution, 1750–1850* (New York: Penguin Books, 1989), pp. 15–43; Robert J. Turnbull, *A Visit to the Philadelphia Prison* (Philadelphia: Budd and Bartram, 1796); Negley K. Teeters, *The Cradle of the Penitentiary: The Walnut Street Jail at Philadelphia, 1773–1835* (Philadelphia: Pennsylvania Prison Society, 1955); Eddy, *Account of the State Prison,* pp. 12–13; *State Prisons and the Prison System Vindicated, with Observations on Managing and Conducting These Institutions . . .* (Charlestown, Mass.: S. Etheridge, 1821); Harold Kirker, *The Architecture of Charles Bulfinch* (Cambridge: Harvard University Press, 1969), pp. 214–15.

⁴⁰ Prison reformers were never certain that these prisons were appropriate for women, who were often locked up in old-style communal cells even in prisons, such as Auburn, where male prisoners were housed in individual cells. Although individual confinement was proposed by English reformer Jonas Hanway as early as 1776, it was used only for punishment of recalcitrant convicts until the American prisons adopted it in the second decade of the nineteenth century. The American example stimulated its adoption in Europe (U. R. Q. Henriques, "The Rise and Decline of the Separate System of Prison Discipline," *Past and Present* 54 [1972]: 65, 72–73). For the intellectual history of individual confinement and its architectural container, see Foucault, *Discipline and Punish,* esp. pp. 143–49, 195–228.

⁴¹ Allen, *Reports;* James Hardie, *The History of the Tread-Mill, Containing an Account of Its Origin, Construction, Operation, Effects . . .* (New York: Samuel Marks, 1824), p. 17; "Description of the Tread Mill, Recommended by the Society for the Improvement of Prison Discipline," *Port Folio,* 4th ser., 14, no. 5 (November 1822): 428–32. Some treadmills, like that at New York, were used as power sources for prison industries, but many prison governors believed that the

futility of arduous, useless labor was a more powerful deterrent to crime, and their treadmills were harnessed to nothing; Allen, *Reports*, p. 15; Henriques, "Rise and Decline," pp. 67–68.

[42] Boston Prison Discipline Society, *Fourth Annual Report of the Board of Managers* (Boston: T. R. Marvin, 1829), p. 55.

[43] Robert Mills, *Guide to the National Executive Offices and the Capitol of the United States* (Washington, D.C.: P. Force, 1841); Mills to [Louis McLane?], Secretary of the Treasury, April 6, 1833, no. 1809, Robert Mills Papers, National Museum of American History, Smithsonian Institution; "Jones Court," fol. drawing, June 8, 1826, box 1, group 299, Ithiel Town Papers, Yale University Manuscripts and Archives; Robert Mills to House Committee on Public Buildings, February 21, 1838, no. 0226, Mills Papers, National Museum of American History, Smithsonian Institution. (I am grateful to Pamela Scott for allowing me to examine the Mills Papers while they were being edited.)

[44] "A Brief Sketch of the Origin and Present State of Philadelphia," *Port Folio*, n.s., 5, no. 13 (April 6, 1805): 98.

[45] Doris Elizabeth King, "The First-Class Hotel in the Age of the Common Man," *Journal of Southern History* 23, no. 2 (May 1957): 173–88 (I am grateful to Barbara Carson for this reference); Jefferson Williamson, *The American Hotel: An Anecdotal History* (New York: Alfred A. Knopf, 1930), pp. 10–11, 22; William H. Eliot, *A Description of Tremont House, with Architectural Illustrations* (Boston: Gray and Bowen, 1830), pp. 9–10; Dickens, *American Notes*, p. 60.

[46] Rights of the deceased are discussed in "Iron Coffins," *Port Folio*, 4th ser., 11, no. 1 (March 1821): 119–24. Philadelphia Cemetery, *Copy of Deed of Trust, April 2, 1827* (Philadelphia, 1827), pp. 1–10. The proprietors of Laurel Hill Cemetery discouraged the use of family vaults, grave enclosures, and ostentatious grave markers, arguing that "the boundaries are defined, and the grounds perfectly dry" (*Regulations of the Laurel Hill Cemetery, on the River Schuylkill, near Philadelphia* [Philadelphia: A. Waldie, 1837], p. 7).

[47] Ammi B. Young, Boston customs house site plan, ca. 1835, Prints and Drawings Collection, AIA Foundation, Washington, D.C. The existing customs house was built to a different Young design in 1837–47.

[48] Watson, *Annals* (1st ed.), app. p. 73; Watson, *Annals*, 1:221–22, 242.

[49] Asa Greene, *A Glance at New York* (New York: By the author, 1837), pp. 7–8.

[50] Hucksters were poor women who bought no-longer-fresh food at the market and resold it.

[51] Watson, *Annals*, 1:240; Francis J. Grund, *Aristocracy in America, from the Sketch-Book of a German Nobleman*, 2 vols. (London: Richard Bentley, 1839), 1:278–90.

[52] Joan H. Geismar, "Patterns of Development in the Late Eighteenth- and Nineteenth-Century American Seaport: A Suggested Model for Recognizing Increasing Commercialism and Urbanization," and Diana diZerega Wall, "The Separation of Home and Workplace in Early Nineteenth-Century New York City," *American Archeology* 5, no. 3 (1985): 175–84, 186–87; Watson, *Annals*, 1:225. On Girard, see Simpson, *Lives*, p. 415.

[53] Watson, *Annals* (3d ed.), 3:402–3; Bruce Laurie, *Working People of Philadelphia, 1800–1850* (Philadelphia: Temple University Press, 1980), pp. 58–61, 153–55; Samuel L. Mitchell, *The Picture of New-York* (New York: I. Riley, 1807), pp. 156–57; John Davis, *Travels of Four Years and a Half in the United States of America during 1798, 1799, 1800, 1801, and 1802*, ed. A. J. Morrison (New York: Henry Holt, 1909), p.

351. Jacksonian bear roasts are documented in an unsigned note, *Hazard's Register of Pennsylvania* 13, no. 26 (June 28, 1834): 416.

54 "Letters from an Englishman in the United States to His Friend in Great Britain," *Port Folio*, 4th ser., 12, no. 2 (December 1821): 305; Grund, *Aristocracy in America*, 1:29, 30; James Flint, *Letters from America* (Edinburgh: W. and C. Tait, 1822), p. 34; "Proceedings of Councils," *Hazard's Register of Pennsylvania* 5, no. 25 (June 19, 1830): 390–93; Brissot de Warville, *New Travels*, pp. 155–56; Davis, *Travels*, p. 355; Timothy J. Gilfoyle, "Strumpets and Misogynists: Brothel 'Riots' and the Transformation of Prostitution in Antebellum New York City," *New York History* 68, no. 1 (January 1987): 57–59.

55 For foppish fashions, see the prints in the numerous English and American variations of the series *Life in Philadelphia*, racist lampoons of black social aspirations that also included a few images of fashionable whites, and similar series such as *Life in New-York* (many copies of all versions of both series on deposit in Print Room, LCP), also "The American Lounger—by Samuel Saunter, Esq.," *Port Folio*, 4th ser., 7, no. 4 (April 1819): 325; Greene, *Glance at New York*, pp. 80–81.

56 On shared space, see Grund, *Aristocracy in America*, 1:19. "It is very vulgar . . . to be seen walking in the same grounds with mechanics, house-servants, and laboring people" ([William M. Bobo], *Glimpses of New-York City* [Charleston: J. J. McCarter, 1852], pp. 181–82). Smoking is discussed in Petition to the Common Council from Some Citizens, ca. 1790, folder 2, box 42, Philadelphia General Petitions, 1692–1799, Society Miscellaneous Collection, HSP; *Philadelphia in 1830–1* (Philadelphia: E. L. Carey and A. Hart, 1830), pp. 145–47; "Proceedings of Councils," *Hazard's Register of Pennsylvania* 5, no. 8 (February 20, 1830): 334–35; Watson, *Annals* (1st ed.), p. 483; Greene, *Glance at New York*, pp. 216–17, 219–20; Bobo, *Glimpses*, p. 182. Smoking was permitted in New York's more democratic Battery, although reclining was forbidden; Bobo, *Glimpses*, pp. 181–82. For the significance of promenading, see Daniel M. Bluestone, "From Promenade to Park: The Gregarious Origins of Brooklyn's Park Movement," *American Quarterly* 39, no. 4 (Winter 1987): 531–38.

57 Watson, *Annals*, 2:261. For a different analysis of African American behavior, see Gary B. Nash, *Forging Freedom: The Formation of Philadelphia's Black Community, 1720–1840* (Cambridge: Harvard University Press, 1988). On black churches and white hostility, see Emma Jones Lapsansky, " 'Since They Got Those Separate Churches': Afro-Americans and Racism in Jacksonian Philadelphia," *American Quarterly* 32, no. 1 (Spring 1980): 58, 61–63; Nash, *Forging Freedom*, pp. 100–133.

58 William D. Kelley, *Address Delivered at the Colored Department of the House of Refuge . . . on December 31st, 1849* (Philadelphia: T. K. and P. G. Collins, 1850), p. 13; Marcia Carlisle, "Disorderly City, Disorderly Women: Prostitution in Ante-Bellum Philadelphia," *Pennsylvania Magazine of History and Biography* 110, no. 4 (October 1986): 549, 557, 568; G. M. Dallas, "Correspondence—House of Refuge," *Hazard's Register of Pennsylvania* 3, no. 16 (April 18, 1829): 250; Christine Stansell, *City of Women: Sex and Class in New York, 1789–1860* (Urbana: University of Illinois Press, 1986), pp. 203–9; Erwin H. Ackerknecht, "Anticontagionism between 1821 and 1867," *Bulletin of the History of Medicine* 22 (1948): 562–93; George Rosen, "Political Order and Human Health in Jeffersonian Thought," *Bulletin of the History of Medicine* 26 (1952): 32–44; Charles Rosenberg, *The Cholera Years: The United States in 1832, 1849, and 1866* (Chicago: University of Chicago Press, 1987), pp. 75–79; and François Delaporte, *Disease and Civilization: The Cholera in Paris, 1832*, trans. Arthur Goldhammer (Cambridge: MIT Press), pp. 163–70; Dell Upton, "The City As

Material Culture," in *The Art and Mystery of Historical Archaeology: Essays in Honor of James Deetz*, ed. Anne Elizabeth Yentsch and Mary C. Beaudry (Boca Raton, Fla.: CRC Press, 1992), pp. 51–74.

[59] Timothy J. Gilfoyle, "The Urban Geography of Commercial Sex: Prostitution in New York City, 1790–1860," *Journal of Urban History* 14, no. 4 (August 1987): 371–93; compare to Carlisle, "Disorderly City," pp. 550, 554–56.

[60] Street life is discussed in "The Petition and Memorial of the Subscribers, Licensed Inn and Tavern-Keepers," January 12, 1804, McAllister Collection, LCP Collection, HSP; "Ardent Spirits," *Hazard's Register of Pennsylvania* 3, no. 6 (February 7, 1829): 96; Carlisle, "Disorderly City," p. 564; *Documents Relative to the House of Refuge, Instituted by the Society for the Reformation of Juvenile Delinquents in the City of New-York, in 1824* (New York: Mahlon Day, 1832), pp. 4, 17, 221, 307–8; *First Annual Report of the Managers of the Society for the Reformation of Juvenile Delinquents in the City of New-York* (New York: Mahlon Day, 1825), p. 36. Groceries sold hard liquor by the drink.

[61] Ritter, *Philadelphia and Her Merchants*, p. 149. J. B. Jackson says that the essence of his Landscape Two (similar to my systematic landscape) is "its belief in the sanctity of place. It is place, permanent position both in the social and topographical sense, that gives us our identity. The function of space according to this belief is to make us visible, allow us to put down roots and become members of society" (J. B. Jackson, *Discovering the Vernacular Landscape* [New Haven: Yale University Press, 1984], p. 152).

[62] Ely to Vaux, June 4, 1817, Vaux Papers.

[63] A good, brief account of early republican attitudes toward opportunity and achievement is Paul Gilje, *The Road to Mobocracy: Popular Disorder in New York City, 1763–1834* (Chapel Hill: University of North Carolina Press, 1987), p. 205.

[64] Tyson to Vaux, July 24, 1829, Vaux Papers. Stansell, *City of Women*, pp. 30–34; Katz, *In the Shadow of the Poorhouse*, pp. 4–10; [Mathew Carey], *A Plea for the Poor: An Enquiry How Far the Charges Against Them of Improvidence, Idleness, and Dissipation, Are Founded in Truth. By a Citizen of Philadelphia* (3d ed.; Philadelphia, 1836); Carey, *Essays on the Public Charities of Philadelphia*; James N. Green, *Mathew Carey, Publisher and Patriot* (Philadelphia: Library Company of Philadelphia, 1985), pp. 29–31.

Reading the Landscape of
Federal America
David S. Shields

Poetry has a curious value as a means of insight into the domestication of the landscape in early America. During the federal era poetry assumed the task of reflecting on the "progress of refinement" in the material and cultural circumstances of American citizens. It attended especially to the circumstances of persons who often escaped notice in other forms of writing—the poor, the enslaved, the dislocated. This attentiveness was a legacy of a project devised by certain English poets of the 1710s and 1720s to present the unremarked conditions of the lives of the commonality, an ambition roughly analogous to the mystique of the unrecorded life that now animates many historians. The doctrines of philanthropy, besides instigating such projects for the amelioration of society as the workhouse system, inspired Whiggish poets to bear witness to the conditions of the "meaner sort of people." Lockean anthropology directed poets to evaluate the human condition in terms of a material and social environment. Landscape ceased to be the ornamental backdrop for human affairs; it became the material context of human action, demanding interpretation if the life of the subject were to be known. In the 1730s English arbiters of taste began placing a premium on the poetic testimonies of common men: Stephen Duck, the "thresher poet," composed "Poverty," inaugurating a tradition that would culminate in Robert Burns's masterly evocations of Scottish life and land.[1]

During the 1730s British American poets began to treat landscape in terms of a cultural geography. Richard Lewis, in "Food for Criticks"

(1731), documented the depredations of Philadelphia's hunters on the wildlife of the Schuylkill valley. Thomas Makin's "On the Instant Cold Weather," (1732–33) measured the effects of climate on the different classes of Pennsylvanians. The anonymous author of "The Rape of Fewel" charted the destruction wrought in winter months on wood:

By frugal Palatine, or poor Hibernian,
Or British Convict; or a native born Whom Rum and Strumpets
    have to Darkness doom'd.
. . . .
Bald antiquated Oaks, and Bark-shed Gums,
Mansions untenable, dismantled Barns,
Storm-shaken Fences, thin broad Rails oblique,
Distorted Posts, Gates clad with dismal Moss.
And rotten rooted Stumps; all bear the Marks
    of needy Thieves Perdition.

This literature did not suffer from an upper-class myopia. Yet these writings do not possess the innocence of those sorts of texts that are most frequently the resort of historians of the landscape—tax assessments, accounts, inventories, insurance records, court records, laws, and so forth. Works of art do not aspire to the status of documents; even works inspired by an aesthetic of reportage cannot be reduced to the status of a factual record. They are, instead, interpretations. As such they should be viewed as occasions of meaning akin to the articles collected in this volume.[2]

Neoclassicism, the dominant literary mode of the European empires during the eighteenth century, offered two paradigms for representing landscape: the Horatian picture of a domesticated countryside fixed in timeless arrest, and the Virgilian representation of the landscape as the arena of a war between man and nature—an ongoing war of creative destruction. In Europe there was a marked predilection toward the Horatian view; several popular genres—the prospect poem, the great house poem, the country walk poem—portrayed the Old World's landscape as a locus of achieved civility. It was finished, static, and ordered. In America the Virgilian georgic predominated. It portrayed American landscape as temporal, dynamic, vital, wearing several aspects in an unsteady progress from wilderness to cultivation. Man's interactions with the landscape were processual. An obvious circumstance explains in part why New World poets differed from Old in their embrace of the Virgilian paradigm. In British America there was no fixed ancestral countryside. Throughout the eighteenth century property boundaries were extraordinarily fluid; many estates were created from scratch; inherited land underwent compulsive improvement. In Britain the vast majority of estates had long been cultivated by the eighteenth century; even with the enclosure movement in the north, the creation of new agricultural lands was exceptional. The "paternal acres" of Horatian formula aptly characterized the condition of property in Britain. As fundamental as this disparity of circumstance between Old World and New was the different demographics of land ownership. In Britain the countryside remained in the hands of a small segment of the population throughout the eighteenth century. In British America an expanding population of freeholders from a broad range of economic backgrounds swarmed over the countryside, forming it in the image of their wills. How violent this process could be is suggested in "On National Prospects and Improvements" by Philip Freneau, the most prolific and celebrated of federal poets. "Dame Nature" speaks:

To man I gave the power, the art, the skill
To mould creation's surface, at his will,
Oceans to tame, rude forests to reduce,
Enjoy my toils and turn them to his use.
Here, rivers flow, while cataracts intervene,
There, mountains rise, to discompose the scene,
But all, subjected, yields to man's control;
His is the task to reign where oceans roll,
To level mountains, or exalt the plain,
To act, contrive, like nature's self again.[3]

This endorsement of man's capacity to recreate nature in his own image renovates the classical doctrine that cultivation is the human "improvement" of the wild.

Of all classical works Virgil's *Georgics* examines most comprehensively how man's will improved the landscape by molding it into an image of his "reasonable" desires. These desires were to own property, to mark the bounds of human dominion, to build shelter, to tame the wild profusion of the land and redirect its vitality to useful ends, to prosper from one's produce, and to improve one's domicile and expand one's holdings. The order of these matters is important because it reveals the close attention to the practical conditions of de novo cultivation. Virgil had studied these matters as the Roman Empire developed its "new lands." Americans of the 1750s to 1830s, reapproximating the situation of the imperial Romans in their territorial expansions, embraced the georgic as a vehicle for reflecting artfully on the task of improvement.[4]

DESIRING AND OWNING PROPERTY

The wish to own property was general in federal America, and the countryside was viewed in light of this wish. Literature invariably portrayed the transformation of the countryside from common landscape to private freehold. On the margins of settlement where tracts of land had not been atomized into plots, the wishful eye could indulge ambitions in a general way, judging areas in light of an abstract standard of utility. The desirous eye sought signs that promised increased value. George Ogilvie, in his georgic on the creation of a rice plantation, *Carolina; or, The Planter* (written in 1776 and published in 1791), supplies a catalogue of the signs of fertile rice land. In the wild swamplands of the low country a would-be planter seeks a place

Where some vast river rolls a gentle tide,
Rich vallies wide expand on either side;
There the tall Cypress rears his moss-crown'd head,
There Tupilos their cumbrous branches spread,
Th'Iberian Oak aloft expands his boughs;
Beneath the wax producing Myrtle grows;
. . . .
And where the sandy heights embrace the vale,
The Great Magnolia wide perfumes the gale.
Where such the native growth, shall doubts remain,
That Phoebus warms a more prolific plain?
No! from the surface scarce more distant rise
Those trees, whose branches seem to prop the skies,
Than deep, beneath the black superior ground,
Rich loamy earth, and marly clay are found;
A fruitful compost, formed in lapse of time,
Of putrid shells, and plants, and settling slime.[5]

The profusion of foliage and the presence of these particular species of plant signal the presence of "a fruitful compost." Ogilvie's depiction is controlled by a theory of vitalism. The passive verbs characteristic of prose description have been systematically supplanted with active verbs in this vision. These trees are spreading, expanding, producing, waving, thriving, trembling, perfuming, and propping the skies. The universal animation of the foliage signifies that the trees draw vitality from a common source, the richly composted soil. The compost's vitality can be redirected by a planter to his cultivars. In the phenomenology of landscape, "native growth" is a substitute sign for the vitality of future crops. Native growth has symbolic significance more than intrinsic worth. Only the river and the soil have immutable and absolute value in the imagination of the would-be property owner.

The question of who could act upon their desire and obtain land assumed critical weight during the federal era. After the confederation was consolidated into a national government in 1789, property ownership became a troublesome issue. Thirteen years of anxiety over the authority by which land titles were issued ended. A host of enterprisers exploited the new security by projecting—making speculative purchases of tracts of western land in the hopes of founding settlements. The land craze generated projects in western Georgia, western Pennsylvania, Ohio, and Kentucky. Concurrently the parceling out of western lands became politicized. Promoting a land-based economy, the Jeffersonian faction encouraged the western development. Opposing Jeffersonian agrarianism, the Federalists encouraged urban growth, the development of manufactures, and international trade. The most striking portraits of the speculative mania of the era came from the Federalist wits who ridiculed land fever. Lemuel Hopkins of Hartford in 1796 complained how

Much people—both the high and low
The squire, the deacon and the beau
With judges, generals, legislators,
(All melted down to Speculators)
Flow'd in amain, from every quarter,
Like Windham frogs from dry'd-up water.
. . . .
Conven'd they sever'd into *squads*
And talk'd of townships, miles, and rods,
. . . .
And deem'd by din't of purse or brain,
The largest *wastes* of woods to gain.

Hopkins was particularly concerned about speculations in the Ohio territory, but the satire had a more general application. Speculators attempted to secure tracts at low cost, then subdivide them, selling lots to immigrants and greenhorns at inflated prices. A town, rather than a landscape of freeholds, was the goal, but the superfluity of speculators forced them to settle with anyone sporting ready cash.[6] The effect of land speculation was not that envisioned by Jeffersonian agrarians. Competition among projectors quickly imposed a cash economy in the West, putting cash-poor would-be settlers at a disadvantage in the market for land and hindering development.

The usual resort of the land-hungry poor was squatting. Early American literature possesses many extraordinary portraits of illegal tenants on the frontier, beginning with plantation owner William Byrd's bemused observations of derelict Carolinians. The landscape of his squatters was virtually uncultivated: "We observed very few corn-fields in our Walks, and those very small, which seem'd the Stranger, to us, because we could see no other Tokens of Husbandry or Improvement." Hogs and cattle ran free-range in the swamps. Land was not cleared. For those who attempted to create fields on the margin of the forest there was peril from theft by those too indolent to work fields themselves, from vagabonds passing through, and from wild creatures. Jonathan Boucher's "Absence, a Pastoral: Drawn from the Life, from the Manners, Customs, and Phraseology of Planters" (written around 1780; published in 1833) portrays crop plundering in frontier Maryland:

Our man-boy, Jack, did, in his new-ground patch,
A runaway a' grabbling 'moodies [yams] catch:
The rogues escap'd, but all the 'moodies I
For Mollsey, in my 'tatoe-hole, put by.
Ah, woe is me! these dainties are no more'
Some bugs or grubs did every one devour.[7]

The influx of speculators in the territories during the 1790s—all of whom desired clear title and secure jurisdiction over "waste lands"— cleared the squatters from the forest. Indeed, the compulsion to secure control as well as title to tracts resulted in a legal fantasy among the projectors that Native Americans were a species of squatter. This fantasy came into its own after the Louisiana Purchase:

And when our children leave our fost'ring arms
And roam the western wilderness for farms. . . .
Is better far than on the self same place
To meet with squatters of a different race,
With whom, perhaps, possess'd of better right,
We cannot get along unless we fight.

An "overflowing stream of population" pushed the Native American:

His wigwam swept away, his patch of corn,
Before the fury of the torrent borne;
Drove him from wood to wood, from place to place
And now for hunting leaves him little space.[8]

Once the speculator had secured title and wrested control of his plot, he dispatched surveyors to mark the bounds of the holdings. While topography might dictate the limits of one's sway, more often the countryside was partitioned according to the harsh geometries of the quadrant and chain.

MARKING BOUNDS

Viewed retrospectively, a freehold estate radiates from the household— this is the way estates are represented in the Horatian literature. Viewed during the process of creation, the Virgilian image, an estate develops from the perimeter to the center: the limit of the scope of property is drawn, then fields, pens, and buildings are created within the circumscribed zone. The marking of the bounds is a civil exercise advertising the extent to which one's legally recognized sway operates. The landscape of federal America was in great measure a countryside of fences and blazed trees.

First, of your destin'd field the *outlines* mark,
Not groping devious thro' the woodland dark;
But let the compass to the pole-star true,
Direct your progress, and assist your view.[9]

Just as the deedbook in the courthouse testified publicly to one's holdings, fences and blazes announced the publicly attested extent of property—publicly attested because the surveyor, a civil official, presided over the marking of the bounds.

The mystique of private property obscures the extent to which social institutions presided over the partitioning of the countryside. Because rival claims and bounds were adjudicated by public agents to prevent violence between property owners, resentment was frequently transferred from neighbors to civic agents. The extent of the civic presence in matters of property is attested by the tendency to make the local surveyor into a scapegoat figure. Consider "On John Wood's Surveying," a satire from one of federal Virginia's more capable poets, William Munford:

The boundaries that lie betwixt
Old neighbours, & of old time fixt,
He alters at his sov'reign pleasure
Without regard to mete or measure
And ev'rything's turned upside down
By this Surveyor of the Town.
Whole squares which people held by Plat
The Body moved "quite out of That,"
And by his mischeif-making pother
Sets them to jostling one another.
He will not leave one stone at rest,
But keeps them moving East or West:
And blames forsooth, for all this rumpus,
The Variation of the Compass,
Pray, might not this conceited sot,
Whither the Needle erred or not,
Run a straight line from stone to stone,
And thus give ev'ry man his own.[10]

The peace of the countryside depended on the visibility and regularity of the bounds of private property.

SHELTER

After marking the bounds of property, the freeholder erected a building to shelter him and his dependents and engaged in the initial tasks of clearing and cultivation. Whether constructed on a huge tract or by the emigrant on his few acres, the building was provisional, a refuge that would be destroyed, rebuilt, or consigned to subsidiary status as soon as feasible. Often this rude shelter was built by settlers fully conscious of the disparity between the structure and the image of a house cherished in their wishes. George Ogilvie is quite eloquent about the discommodiousness of Myrtle Grove, his plantation house on Santee River:

> Myrtle Grove a terrestrial Paradize? let me see what Paradizial objects would present themselves to your mere Corporial view (not that of your fertile fancy). A few Rough boards naild together so nicely as to admit the wind and light through every seam—placed on the top of a sandy hillock about five feet above the level of the water forms what we call a House of 26 by 14 feet which divided into two rooms contain last night—My overseer his Wife two Children John Smith two Gentlemen who came to see me, and your most humble Servant—in all Seven Whites besides two or three Negroes—how do you like my accommodation within doors?

Ogilvie did not doubt that "Myrtle Grove will in a few years be both pretty and pleasant, at least at the time of year when the Muskitoes are quiet." It was well capitalized and well supplied with slave labor. It produced rice, a staple crop that did not suffer the volatile price swings of the staple luxuries—tobacco, indigo, silk, and rum. Ogilvie could well afford to think ahead to the improved condition of his household.[11]

The tension between the rude and the improved household was a dynamic not tied to class or region. Even in the poorest frontier freeholds the cycle of improvement was at work, as may be seen in a 1795 poem written by a stonemason (Samuel Ward? Nathaniel Chandler?) about his visit to a primitive household in the bounty lands of northern Vermont. It affords a rare glimpse of the circumstances of life on the margins of New England:

> It was on a little eminence this little cottage stood
> Compris'd of logs piled up enclosed in a wood
> I met the rural Cottager and then as I shall say
> We interchanged Compliments and past the time of day
>
> And when our conversation had ended on the spot
> He kindly invited me to walk into his Cot
> But when I was within I solemly declare
> A Maide sat in the corner which caused me to Stare
>
> And half a dozen Children all dirt from feet to head
> And on the bed the wife who had lately got to bed

Four Chaires a Chest a Table two beds a sive and Chest
Was all the parlors furniture I solemly protest

This house not being divided one room it did contain
It having but one window was very dark within
Now [Rachal] served supper it being late at night
We had to feel for victuals becaus[e] there was no light

Now supper being ended the evening I did spend
In reading of a shipwreck unto my jovel friends
Our supper it consisted of potatoes bread and pork
Myself the only one who had a knife and fork

Our drink they call'd it tea though Mistaken I believe
I forsed down the first cup which maid my bosom heave
And now a great conjecture came with in my head
I knew not which to sleep with the Mistress or the Maid

But soon from this suspense they did me extricate
I slept with son and husband as I to you relate
Early in the morning as soon as I arose
They e[a]rnestly surveyed me while I put on my cloth[es][12]

While this verse has its fascinations as a depiction of the living conditions of a borderer family, what most commends consideration is the emulation of polite manners. The value of tea and literacy is attested
humorously. And when we consider that the writer was present at this
household to construct a stone chimney, mitigating the darkness he had
remarked, we see that this is a family that has material aspirations as well
as a respect for the protocol of hospitality.

The improvement of the homestead was a project motivated by a
freeholder's desire. The improvement of the land was a matter of neces-
sity. Only by diligent cultivation could householders subsist or hope to
prosper. Consequently, clearing and improving fields took priority over
upgrading the house.

CLEARING AND CULTIVATING

In no other aspect of the domestication of the landscape did the varying
conditions of nature exercise such determinative force. In the swamp

thickets of South Carolina, for instance, the labor requisite to hack roots from the adhesive soil and trench fields for drainage made all but the wealthiest slaveholders incapable of creating rice plantations. The piedmont forests from Maine to Georgia offered a more hospitable landscape for the middling freeholder. Enoch Lincoln, governor of Maine, in 1816 published a poem entitled "The Village," detailing the process of clearing the New England frontier. First a lumberman felled the marketable trees on frontier tracts, sledging off logs in midwinter. Spring brought the farmer who cleared trunks, branches, and unmarketable timber:

His cumber'd land the sturdy yeoman clears.
Fell'd by his strokes, the forest prostrate lies;
Its vital sap the glowing summer dries,
And last the bonfires burn, the boughs consume,
And spreading flames the hemisphere illume.

Sometimes an unwanted consequence of clearing the forests was the premature improvement of the dwelling:

See yon simple hut, of structure rude,
Of unplaned boards contrived and logs unhew'd:
The threat'ning fires pursue their blasting way,
And the low fabric falls their certain prey.[13]

While other writers supply more detailed accounts of stumping, clearing stones, plowing, and manuring soil, Lincoln's account aptly conveys the violence of the transformation wrought on the land. The forests are leveled, the vegetation burned, the ground broken.

The farmer's triumph in the Virgilian war with nature was marked by the act of cultivation whereby the soil's vitality was restored and redirected by human will to new growth. The planter derived his identity from his actions with the soil. The scenes most familiar to literary and graphic depictions of rural life were those of sowing, planting, and harvesting. The classical literature on planting was particularly detailed about the method of planting. Eighteenth-century Anglo-American writings lent a scientific cast to the particularity:

Summer Fallows best your Crops ensure,
And far exceed all Species of Manure.
By this the nitrous Particles of Air
When loose the Surface, and the Passage fair,
With Ease descend, and to the Soil adhere.

Following classical precedent, the American writers of georgics provided a practical method for planting, based on the latest experimental results.

Let Two Feet void 'twixt every Trench remain.
Tho' some, imprudently, their Room confine,
Allowing half that Space to every Line.
Give Room, one Stem as much as three full yards
And richer far the Weed.[14]

As this excerpt from a poem on indigo attests, success in cultivation was measured not only by the abundance of produce but also by its quality. To reap a profit the farmer had to produce goods attractive in the market stalls. Besides fighting a war with nature, the farmer battled in the marketplace with his neighbors.

THE IDEAL OF ESTATE

The reward for the farmer's struggles characteristically took one of two forms: the creation of a rural estate (the individual ideal) or the founding of a village (the social ideal). The former exerted greater power over the literary imagination. The most popular poem of the eighteenth century, according to Dr. Samuel Johnson, was John Pomfret's "The Choice" (1699), describing the ideal life in its material and social circumstances. Because Pomfret supplied an ideal portrait, he employed the timeless and static Horatian representation of achieved civility. The poem was imitated ad nauseum by scores of New World litterateurs, appearing with particular frequency in the decade following the revolutionary war. According to Pomfret,

Near some fair town I'd have a private seat,
Built uniform, not little nor too great;
Better if on a rising ground it stood,
Fields on this side, on that a neighbouring wood.
It should, within, no other things contain
But what are useful, necessary, plain.
Methinks 'tis nauseous, and I'd ne'er endure
The needless pomp of gaudy furniture.
A little garden, grateful to the eye,
And a cool rivulet run murmuring by,
On whose delicious banks a stately row

Of shady limes or sycamores should grow;
At th' end of which a silent study placed
Should with the noblest authors there be graced.[15]

The appositeness of these lines to Monticello, or at least to Jefferson's characterization of his estate as an instantiation of republican simplicity, is striking. They could serve, too, as the description of that other Virginian estate that assumed iconic value during the last decades of the century, Mount Vernon. It is not, however, my purpose to end this excursus by suggesting that the domestication of the landscape was in effect a progress from the teeming wild to achieved civility. The image of the perfectly cultivated piedmont farm outside of Charlottesville—like the period room in a museum display—presents a world in arrest, an aestheticized landscape of sufficiency and repose.

Poetry affords another representation, more familiar in its dynamism and disarray. In contraposition to the Monticello of Horatian ideality, poetry directs attention to another Virginia plantation of the same era, a Virgilian site of perpetual change and labor. At William Munford's Richland, time has not been frozen. The task of improvement has not been completed, indeed it appears incapable of completion. The struggles of the planter remain unremitting. The difficulty of a farmer's working his will to satisfaction in the material world in human society is demonstrated with comic point.

The Disasters of Richland
The Author's Place of Residence. Written in 1795.

FAST by where roaring Roanoke
His stream doth roll o'er many a rock,
A building stands upon a hill,
Which these disasters follow still;—
Most luckless wights of all the nation,
Who make this house their habitation!
Imprimis, thro' th' unshingled top,
The waters, so uncourtly drop,
Descending on the ladies' heads,
And wet their gowns, the floor, and beds.
With these the whistling winds combine,
And in a charming concert join,
With noise of children to distract;
You'd think your very scull was crack'd.

To drive these bustling guests away,
Good Mr. Kennon to il[l]s all day.
To stop the window-lights with board,
Where clothes and pillows oft are stor'd. —
From room to room to make your way,
Is dang'rous on a rainy day.
The porches all are sadly falling,
And needlessly for help are calling.
While two a nat'ral death have died,
And spread their ruins far and wide,
Another, like a tree uptorn,
Whose roots high in the air are borne,
Suspended stands, with poles for prop,
No part remaining but the top;
The last, dejected, and alone
Seems it's companions' fates to moan;
Benches and banisters are gone;
The rotten sills and quaking floor
Threat him who carelessly walks o'er;
But while these evils I unfold,
A multitude remains untold,
For Satan, sure a scheme pursuing,
Brings all things on this land to ruin,
The Cats, Rats, Horses, Sheep and Hogs,
Cows, Goats and Pigeons, Dear and Dogs;
Negroes and Overseer to plague
Unite their forces in a league.
The Cats and Rats devour the meat,
Horses and Hogs the corn and wheat,
The Cows and Sheep feed on the cotton,
The Horses tread it down to rotten;
The ruthless goats tobacco spoil,
And disappoint the lab'rer's toil;
High as they reach, they brouze and tear
The youthful trees, which flourish'd fair,
And least the ruin should diminish,
The deer takes care their work to finish.
Thus, while destruction 'round us thickens,
The dogs destroy eggs, ducks and chickens,
And Mrs. Kennon doth determine
To raise no more to feed such vermin. —

The pigeons peck the new-sown pease,
The negroes plunder all the trees,
And eat green fruit to sick'n and gripe 'em,
While not a morsel's left to ripen.
The Overseer, with strife and jarrings,
Keeps all the family a warring,
And all his fuss cannot avail
Nor put in place a single nail.
Thus all the Land's a prey to foes,
At least as numerous as those,
Who Babylon in pieces trampled,
Or is perhaps quite unexampled.—
Thick weeds throughout the garden grow,
Which like a tow'ring forest shew;
With these the crop is overspread,
And scarce a plant dares lift it's head;
The fences all so wond'rous low,
That ev'ry creature in may go,
And feast him to his heart's content,
That nothing may be idly spent:
And when at last, the crop so thin
With mickle pains is gather'd in,
The wheat in roofless barns they pour,
For birds and weavil to devour,
To sun and rain expos'd 'tis laid,
Till quite destroyed, and nought is made—
The corn, because they love not eating,
They naked leave, where rains are beating,
In pens, the fence of which they leave
Down to the ground, least cows shou'd grieve.—
Tobacco, 'cause it costs so little,
The negroes think not worth a tittle?
Cut down it lies, and goes to pot,
With unregarded dust to rot.—
The people who attend the mill,
Are quarr'ling with the miller still,
Dispute accounts, and make a pother,
Which almost serves to kill my mother,
Who with her cares and debts perplex'd,
So oft is cross'd, so often vex'd,
So often melancholy sits,

'Tis wonderful she keeps her wits.—
The picture now exactly fits,
And when to Richland house you go,
Reader, the likeness you will know.[16]

Munford's descriptive excursion around Richland traces the phenomenological structure of a finished estate, moving from the central household to the periphery of the property, from the house interior to the far fences. Instead of revealing the scope and reasonability of the planter's will, the poet's transit shows the extent of the forces frustrating the planter's project. The suprahuman potency of nature is revealed in the disasters at Richland. All man-made items—shelter, barns, fences—decay before the onslaught of the elements. The ancient battle between the wild and the cultivated is further complicated by depredations performed by livestock on produce. Even in the human sphere the planter's will is confounded. Conflicts pitting the self-interest of slaves against the authority of the master and the desires of the foreman against the will of the master imbue the planter's travail with a social dimension. Munford's mock georgic explores the negative potential of the Virgilian understanding of farming as a process. If work was not its own reward on the farm, but a never-ending encounter with natural, economic, and social disasters, one can, perhaps, understand the reasons for the extraordinary exodus from the countryside in the nineteenth century. Even when work provided the farmer with moral satisfactions, they might not be sufficient to counter the elements, the incompetence (studied or not) of the labor force, the appetite of livestock, and the demands of the bill collector. Even Monticello itself, when read with Munford's lens, loses its timeless aura and monumental cast, appearing instead as an extravagant symbol of the restless activity of planting and building. The hilltop estate near Charlottesville conveys the primary truth inscribed in the countryside of federal America when we understand it as a working farm rather than a sublime artifact.

---

[1] The phrase "the progress of refinement" is taken from the title of Thomas Odiorne's important poem, *The Progress of Refinement* (Boston: Young and Etheridge, 1792). I. B. Kirkman Gray, *A History of English Philanthropy . . .* (1905; reprint, New York: Augustus M. Kelley, 1967), pp. 46–63. Robert Southey, *The Lives*

of the Uneducated Poets, ed. J. S. Childers (Oxford, Eng.: Oxford University Press, 1925). Landmarks in the development of a literature of common life include Matthew Prior, *Down-Hall* (1723), John Gay, *Rural Sports* (1713), James Thomson, *Winter* (1726), John Dyer, *Grongar Hill* (1726), Walter Harte, *Essays on Husbandry* (collected 1764), and John Philips, *Cyder: A Poem in Two Books* (1709).

[2] "The Rape of Fewel: A Cold-Weather Poem," *Pennsylvania Gazette*, October 26, 1732, published in Franklin's newspaper nearly a decade to the day after he first entered Philadelphia, having warmed himself by a fire of fence rails. [Richard Lewis], "Food for Criticks," *Pennsylvania Gazette*, July 17, 1732; J. A. Leo Lemay surmises an earlier version of the poem may have appeared in 1731 in a lost issue of the *Maryland Gazette*. [Thomas Makin], "On the Instant Cold Weather," *American Weekly Mercury*, February 6, 1732/33. The employment of paintings, particularly genre paintings, as documents of material culture, offers an apt analogy. While the design of a painting is determined by aesthetic (or ideal) concerns, the details represented in the painting often denote what is ready to hand. In poetry, too, the evidentiary worth of a discourse is greatest on the level of detail rather than of argument. When interpreting poems one must judge the extent to which an argument would warrant the distortion of things and states of affairs.

[3] Philip Freneau, "On National Prospects and Improvements (July 27, 1822)," *The Newspaper Verse of Philip Freneau: An Edition and Bibliographical Survey*, ed. Judith R. Hiltner (Troy, N.Y.: Whitson, 1986), pp. 683–85. The articulation of a Virgilian pragmatics of agriculture was not restricted to belles lettres. Manuals such as R. Bradley's *A Survey of the Ancient Husbandry and Gardening, Collected from Cato, Varro, Columella, Virgil, and Others, the Most Eminent Writers among the Greeks and Romans* (London, 1725) digested the practices of ancient agriculture for use in the British empire.

[4] For an evaluation of the program of the *Georgics* see Michael C. J. Putnam, *Virgil's Poem of the Earth: Studies in the Georgics* (Princeton: Princeton University Press, 1979). The importance of the *Georgics* has been misjudged by historians. Leo Marx, *The Machine in the Garden* (Oxford, Eng.: Oxford University Press, 1964) and Lewis Simpson, *The Dispossessed Garden* (Athens: University of Georgia Press, 1975) promote the theme of early American pastoralism. Neither of the writers treats the tradition of eighteenth-century georgics as expressed in Charles Woodmason, "Indico," in "A Colonial Poem on Indigo Culture," ed. Hennig Cohen, *Agricultural History* 30 (1956): 42–43; [James Sterling], "Verses Occasioned by the Success of the British Arms in the Year 1759," *Maryland Gazette*, January 3, 1760; James Grainger, *The Sugar-Cane*; and George Ogilvie, *Carolina; or, The Planter* (1776).

[5] George Ogilvie, "Carolina; or, The Planter. Written in 1776," ed. David S. Shields, *Southern Literary Journal* (special issue, 1986): 11–12. The plantation was located on Crow Island, contiguous to the Deas family lands in Santee Delta.

[6] [Lemuel Hopkins], "Guillotina; or, The Annual Song of the Tenth Muse," in *The Echo, with Other Poems*, 1807, ed. Richard Alsop (1807; reprint, Upper Saddle River, N.J.: Literature House/Gregg Press, 1970), pp. 221–22. John Reps, *Town Planning in Frontier America* (Princeton: Princeton University Press, 1969), introd.; William Wyckoff, *The Developer's Frontier* (New Haven: Yale University Press, 1988).

[7] William K. Boyd, ed., *William Byrd's Histories of the Dividing Line betwixt Virginia and North Carolina* (New York: Dover Publications, 1967), p. 54; Jonathan Boucher, "Absence, a Pastoral: Drawn from the Life, from the Manners, Customs, and Phraseology of Planters (or, to Speak More Pastorally, of the Rural Swains) Inhabiting the Banks of the Potomac in Maryland," in *Southern Writing, 1585–1920*, ed.

Richard B. Davis, C. Hugh Holman, and Louis D. Rubin, Jr. (New York: Odyssey Press, 1970), p. 229.

[8] Richard Alsop, "Echo No. XX: March 4, 1805," in Alsop, *Echo*, pp. 169–70.

[9] Ogilvie, "Carolina," pp. 87–90.

[10] William Munford, "On John Wood's Surveying," [ca. 1816], poems and miscellaneous writings, Munford-Ellis papers, Perkins Library, Duke University, Durham, N.C. Poem published by permission of the Perkins Library.

[11] "George Ogilvie to Margaret Ogilvie. November 22, 1774," *Southern Literary Journal* (special issue, 1986): 122. Ogilvie, a loyalist, was forced to leave South Carolina in 1778 because he refused to take the oath of allegiance to the revolutionary government. The family papers are held by the University of Aberdeen and contain a wealth of material about plantation life from 1760 to 1820 in South Carolina.

[12] [Nathaniel Chandler?], untitled poem on a visit to a cottager at "Eden," Ward-Chandler manuscripts, American Antiquarian Society, Worcester, Mass. The site of the cottage was in the bounty lands granted to Col. Seth Warner and officers of his revolutionary army regiment in the plain southeast of Belvidere Mountain, Lamoille Co., Vt.

[13] Enoch Lincoln, "The Village," in *Specimens of American Poetry, with Critical and Biographical Notices*, ed. Samuel Kettle, 3 vols. (1829; reprint, New York: Benjamin Blom, 1967), 2:304–5. For analogues, see James K. Paulding, *The Backwoodsman* (New York, 1818); and P. Bayley, *Canada, a Descriptive Poem, Written at Quebec, 1805* (Quebec: John Neilson, [1806]). This motif was sentimentalized in the 1830s and 1840s by the popular Thomas Cogswell Upham.

[14] As cited in Woodmason, "Indico," pp. 42–43.

[15] John Pomfret, *The Choice* (London, 1699), p. 1.

[16] William Munford, "The Disasters of Richland," in *Poems and Compositions in Prose on Several Occasions* (Richmond: Samuel Pleasants, 1798). Richland was located in Mecklenburg Co., Va.

City Living, Federal Style
Damie Stillman

The well-known image of Benjamin Henry Latrobe's perspective drawing of his proposed Bank of Pennsylvania of 1798 or 1799 (fig. 1) is generally used to illustrate the advanced form of neoclassicism he brought
to America in 1796—with its geometric shapes, plain-wall aesthetic, and
archaeological Greek Ionic order derived from the Erechtheum in
Athens. The beautifully rendered drawing does present a striking edifice,
achieved in part by contrasting the bank with the buildings flanking it.
These two buildings can, however, serve just as readily as the backdrop
for a consideration of domestic architecture in the young republic. For
it is against a cityscape filled with colonial buildings that newly built
urban housing in the federal period can best be understood.

The building on the extreme right of Latrobe's bank, the older of
the two, is characteristic of numerous Philadelphia houses built in the
first half of the eighteenth century, with their stolid proportions, string
courses, and characteristic pent roofs and door hoods. The more up-to-
date edifice to the left of the bank is City Tavern of 1773. Representing
well not only the commercial buildings but the very similarly designed
houses erected on the eve of the Revolution, it features a slightly projecting pedimented central section and a fairly elaborate pedimented
doorway. A decade or so after completion of the tavern, Philadelphia
and other urban centers began to see the first intimations of a still newer
style and newer approaches to machines for urban living, to paraphrase
Le Corbusier.[1]

To comprehend the nature of those first federal-period town houses
as well as those that succeeded them during the first two decades or so

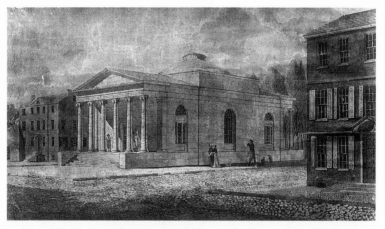

Figure 1.   Benjamin Henry Latrobe, Bank of Pennsylvania, Philadelphia, drawing of 1798–99. (Maryland Historical Society, Baltimore.)

of the nineteenth century, we need to examine the forms they took, the innovations and conservative retentions they displayed, how they functioned, and the reasons they are the way they are. Also significant are the English patterns of urban housing during the late eighteenth and early nineteenth centuries. Despite certain New World interpretations, we would do well to bear in mind James Fenimore Cooper's comment of 1824: "You will also see by what I have written, that the Americans have not yet adopted a style of architecture of their own. Their houses are still essentially English, though neither the winters nor the summers of their climate would seem to recommend them." Although Americans might contract with someone "to Build . . . a dwelling House . . . in a good and Workman like manner," as Jared Lane did with John Couch on November 14, 1790, in Sharon, Connecticut, the houses, and especially city ones, certainly reflected the prevailing English trends.[2]

Like their British counterparts, although not necessarily in the same proportions, American urban houses of the federal period fall into five basic types: the freestanding house, common in smaller towns but also appearing in cities, particularly among wealthier individuals; the narrow, typically three-bay house that was generally intended to fill spaces in the existing urban fabric; the double or semi-detached house; the row of three or four houses, usually each three bays wide; and the

Figure 2. Charles Bulfinch, elevation, Joseph Coolidge, Sr., house, Boston, 1791–92. (I. N. Phelps Stokes Collection, Miriam and Ira D. Wallach Division of Art, Prints, and Photographs, New York Public Library, Astor, Lenox, and Tilden Foundations.)

grander architectural compositions, commonly called terraces in England but more often denominated rows in this country, by which a substantial number of three-bay houses are grouped together in a more comprehensive scheme. The first two types were not new, for they were frequently found in colonial towns; the other three were more nearly innovations of the postrevolutionary era. All reflect certain ties to the past as well as new tendencies, although the last type is especially indicative of the transformations that characterized the urban image in the young republic.

The larger freestanding variety ranged from late colonial modifications of the format represented by Philadelphia's City Tavern—similar but generally more elongated in proportion—to such neoclassical adaptations as the house Charles Bulfinch designed for his sister's father-in-law, Joseph Coolidge, Sr., on Cambridge Street in Boston, of 1791–92 (fig. 2). Inspired by his one-and-one-half-year trip to Europe in 1785–87, the still-amateur gentleman-architect took a flat and slightly elongated Adamesque composition (similar to Robert Adam's Society of Arts in his Adelphi project in London, circa 1771–74 [fig. 3]), simplified it, and affixed it to a traditional four-square New England seacoast house with hipped roof and captain's walk. The center-hall, four-corner-room plan is both straightforward and conventional, although the so-called imperial staircase, with one straight flight splitting into a dou-

Figure 3.   Robert Adam, elevation, Society of Arts, Adelphi, London, 1771–74. Engraving. From Robert Adam and James Adam, *The Works in Architecture* vol. 1, no. 4 (London, 1774), pl. 4. (Winterthur Library.)

ble return, like the central facade treatment, probably reflects works Bulfinch saw in England.[3]

Grander and more elaborate is the celebrated house erected for William Bingham in 1785–86 on Third Street in Philadelphia, one of the earliest fully neoclassical houses to go up in America. Although demolished after a fire in 1847, it can be visualized through William Birch's engraving of 1800, a plan and elevation sketched by Bulfinch on his visit there in 1789, written descriptions, and the catalogue of the sale held there in 1805 following Bingham's death the previous year (figs. 4, 5). Designed by John Plaw, an English architect of such small elegant villas as the oval Belle Isle of 1774 on an island in Lake Windermere, and the au-

Figure 4.   John Plaw, William Bingham house, Philadelphia, 1785–86. Engraving, William Birch, ca. 1800. From William Birch, *The City of Philadelphia* (Philadelphia: By the author, 1800), pl. 22. (Winterthur Library.)

thor of a number of smaller-scale architectural books, including *Rural Architecture*, of 1785, this structure was commissioned in London by Bingham, an extremely wealthy Philadelphian who had gone there with his family shortly after the Treaty of Paris ended the revolutionary war. On December 29, 1783, Bingham wrote his father-in-law, Thomas Willing, that he had "sketched out the plan" of a new house in Philadelphia and "employed an architect to execute it properly." The identification of Plaw as that architect is confirmed by his exhibiting in 1790 at the Incorporated Society of Artists, of which he was then president, a "design for a house in Third Street, Philadelphia," which can only be the Bingham house.[4]

Occupying a large lot surrounded by a high wall, the "Mansion House," as it was known at the time, had a front facade distinguished by a delicate and elaborate fan- and side-lit door surmounted by a balconied Palladian motif with a beautifully traceried semicircular window above.

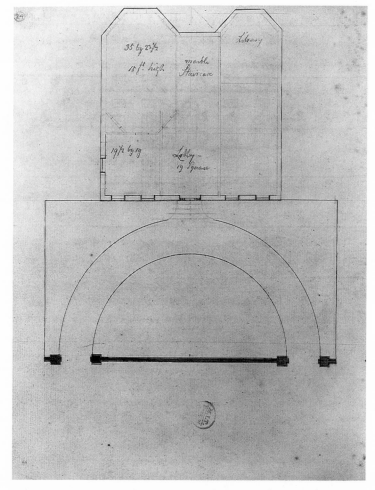

Figure 5. John Plaw, plan, William Bingham house, Philadelphia, 1785–86. Drawing, Charles Bulfinch, 1789. (Library of Congress.)

Also present on the entrance facade were swag panels and delicate pat-erae. The garden facade featured two polygonal ends—a treatment found in a number of English neoclassical designs—reflected on the in-terior in a library with one half-octagonal end and a larger rectangular room with two half-octagonal projections. In between the two was a white marble staircase that complemented a lobby whose floor was laid in a marble mosaic. Probably even more impressive were the rooms on the floor above, for, in the proper English fashion for town residences, "the best rooms," as Bingham informed his father-in-law, "will be on the first Story," or what in present-day America is the second floor. Judging by the auction catalogue of the contents of the house in 1805, just after Bingham's death, imported English architectural features included "composition stone ornaments, from the manufactory of Coade, London, consisting of Fascia Medallions Entablatures Mouldings, and Key stones." These items, presumably extras left over from the construction, were listed on the uppermost floor.[5]

Many visitors were impressed. An Englishman named Henry Wansey reported in 1794: "I found a magnificent house and gardens in the best English style, with elegant and even superb furniture." Bulfinch, a budding young amateur architect from Boston who had himself been to both England and France, described it as "in a stile which would be esteemed splendid even in the most luxurious parts of Europe. Elegance of construction; white marble staircase, valuable paintings, the richest furniture and the utmost magnificence of decoration make it a palace, in my opinion far *too* rich for *any* man in this country." This did not prevent Bulfinch from using his exterior drawing of the house as the basis for his Harrison Gray Otis house in Boston seven years later. Joseph Manigault, a wealthy South Carolinian who visited Philadelphia in 1790, wrote to his architect-brother Gabriel that "Mr. Bingham's House is more handsomely finished than I supposed [he had originally written 'than any I have seen in America,' but scratched it out in favor of 'I supposed']; though I had heard you speak much of it. Many people think it too much ornamented, but it does not strike me in that light; I think it proves him to be a man of Taste."[6]

Freestanding houses with projecting bows, not only polygonal, as at Bingham's, but also semicircular, began to appear all along the seaboard about 1790, the year the young John McComb, Jr., created at least four such designs for Government House in New York, the proposed home for the new president. None seems to have been executed, and the president, indeed the federal government, left that city before the building was more than begun. Two years later the designs for two other presidential houses—on Ninth Street in Philadelphia and the present White House in Washington, D.C.—that featured curved exedrae on their garden facades, were carried out, although no president ever lived in the Philadelphia structure. Other early examples of this motif include a house designed by English architect Joseph Bonomi in 1797 for John B. Church at 59 Broadway in New York. Like the President's House in Philadelphia, it had a segmental projection along its garden front.[7]

Within the next few years it was no longer necessary to own a lavish freestanding house—designed by an English or American architect and situated on a large parklike expanse of property—in order to have a projecting exedra. A case in point is the Moses Myers house in Norfolk (fig. 6). The east portion (visible at the far left of figure 6) was erected circa 1796 as a three-bay, side-hall plan. Soon thereafter a front porch was added on the east and a polygonal rear exedra on the west, aggrandizing the house and making it more elegant and reflective of the new neoclassical ethos.[8] In the process the entrance was changed from the end bay of a narrow, three-bay, side-hall plan to the center of the gable end, providing a wide entrance hall with stairway at one end, just as was standard practice at the back of a side-bay entrance hall.

This transformation of a traditional urban house plan could also be seen in newly built houses, especially as settlers and ideas were carried westward. John W. Hunt, a merchant and later a hemp manufacturer, banker, and financial speculator who had come from New Jersey, built a house with this sort of arrangement in Lexington, Kentucky, around 1812 (fig. 7). The principal entrance to his freestanding house is through the elaborate fan- and side-lit door in the center of the gable end, which opened into a broad cross hall with the stairway in a room at the right end. The builder also included an additional doorway, subsequently reconstructed from existing evidence, at the other end of the hall bay, opening into an office, an opening that corresponded to the traditional side-bay entrance into a three-bay town house facade. Lexington was not at this time a rural outpost devoid of urban attractions. Although founded in April 1779, by the first years of the nineteenth century it boasted a population of 2,500 and in 1807 had a coffeehouse with newsroom attached, receiving forty-three newspapers from throughout the country. A number of subscribers themselves built elegant houses in the new style. A Frenchman visiting at that time pronounced the houses "as well built as any in the United States. The streets," he added, "are paved and ornamented with footways."[9]

Figure 6.   Moses Myers house (view from northeast), Norfolk, Va., ca. 1796, before 1818. (Property of the City of Norfolk, operated by the Chrysler Museum, Norfolk, Va.)

Figure 7. Hopemount, the Hunt-Morgan house (view from southeast), Lexington, Ky., ca. 1812. (Bluegrass Trust, Lexington, Ky.)

The kind of organization seen in the side facade of Hunt's house or in the original Myers house was typical of an urban house type that proliferated in American cities of the era, as it had earlier in London. One example is the now-demolished John B. Coles house at 1 State Street in New York, of 1797–99 (fig. 8). Designed by John McComb, Jr., who became the leading architect of federal New York, it is characterized by such late colonial features as the flat arch with keystone above all of the windows.[10] More indicative of the newer neoclassical taste are the proportions, the oval and rectangular panels above the second-floor windows, and the delicate ornamentation atop the door and on the porch railing.

As a corner house it had a gable end facing Whitehall, but, unlike the Hunt-Morgan house in Lexington, the Coles house had no entrance on that side. In plan the Coles house (fig. 9) combined the traditional side-bay hall and straight-return stairway with a neoclassical semicircular alcove at one end of the dining room, a motif extremely common in the work of Adam and his English contemporaries. In addition to his

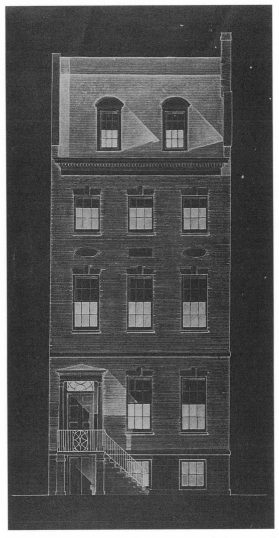

Figure 8. John McComb, Jr., measured drawing of front elevation, John B. Coles house, New York, 1797–99. (Index of American Design, on permanent loan to Avery Architectural and Fine Arts Library, Columbia University, New York City.)

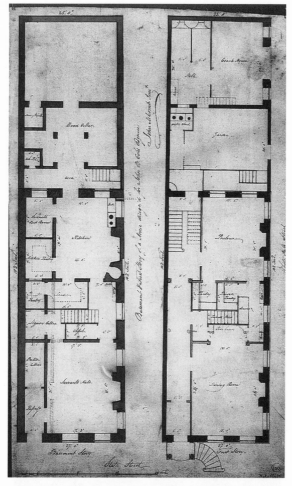

Figure 9.   John McComb, Jr., plan, John B. Coles house,
New York, 1797–99. (New-York Historical Society.)

elegant provision for a place for the sideboard, McComb also paid attention to practical matters, including pantries, back stairs leading up
from the basement kitchen, and three water closets in a space off the garden behind the parlor. Coles, "a flour merchant with large ventures over-
seas," was a member of the Common Council for the first ward, "where

Figure 10.   Charles Bulfinch, elevation, town house, 1800–
1805. (Rotch Library of Architecture and Planning, MIT
Libraries.)

all the wealth, aristocracy and dignity lived," and in 1806 was one of the
two Federalists nominated for Congress.[11]

    A Bulfinch design for a Boston town house of a few years later
(fig. 10) provides a variation on this formula.[12] The ground-floor windows

Figure 11.   Nathaniel Russell house (view from southeast), Charleston, S.C., 1809–11. (Library of Congress: Photo, Frances Benjamin Johnston.)

evince the conservative flat-arch-and-keystone treatment; the second floor, which would have contained the most impressive rooms, exhibits not only swags but delicate fanlights. The house has both a less-common central entrance and a flat balustrated roofline.

Combining features of the McComb and Bulfinch designs is a third example, the Nathaniel Russell house in Charleston, South Carolina, built in 1809–11 (fig. 11). It contains a doorway in the central bay and a flat-roof balustrade but is accompanied by more traditional window crestings. The extreme attenuation of the second floor and the delicate doorway are the most avant-garde features of the facade, but the plan (fig. 12) reveals the neoclassical delight in spatial play that is exemplified by both the oval staircase and the oval saloon projecting into the garden as a polygonal bay. The iron balcony outside that exedra has delicate decoration that parallels the ironwork on McComb's Coles house. The owner, Nathaniel Russell, had moved to South Carolina from Rhode Island in the 1760s as a young man in his twenties, later

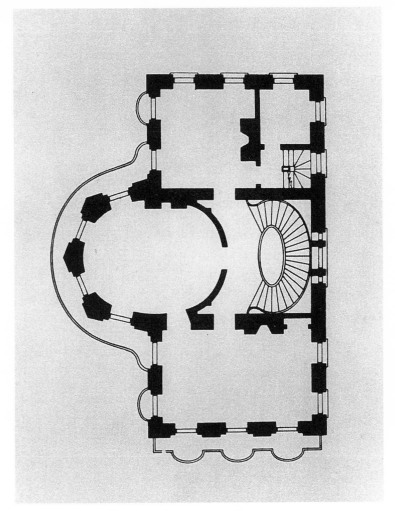

Figure 12.   Plan, Nathaniel Russell house, Charleston, S.C., 1809–11. (Historic Charleston Foundation.)

becoming so wealthy that he was dubbed "King of the Yankees."[13]

Both flat and bowed surfaces, conservative and newer window treatments, and swags and delicate iron balconies could be found in

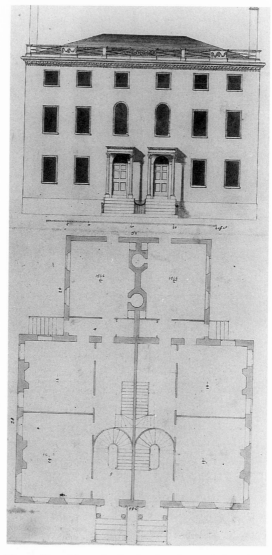

Figure 13.   Alexander Parris, elevation and plan, double house, probably for Thomas Hovey and Jonathan Stevens, Portland, Maine, 1803. (Parris sketchbook, Boston Athenaeum.)

Figure 14.   Asher Benjamin, James Colburn houses, Boston, 1808. (Society for the Preservation of New England Antiquities, Boston.)

double or semi-detached houses, such as the two New England examples shown in figures 13 and 14. The former is twenty-three-year-old Alexander Parris's 1803 design, probably for 92–98 Free Street in Portland, Maine, which presents two three-bay houses joined together in a mirror image. Except for the two porches and the windows above them, the structure looks like a typical four-square New England house with a flat balustrade punctuated by neoclassical panels. (This last feature probably derived from Bulfinch's contemporary work in Boston.) Inside, the only innovative spatial features are the twin semicircular staircases. The clients for this scheme may have been commission merchants Thomas Hovey and Jonathan Stevens.[14]

Both spatially and decoratively more neoclassical are the James Smith Colburn houses built in 1808 at 54–55 Beacon Street in Boston by the thirty-five-year-old Asher Benjamin, whose principal fame rests with the architectural books he authored. The client was a twenty-eight-year-old who boasted then that he was "worth over half a million dollars."[15] The new taste is most obvious in the bowed fronts, indicating oval-ended rooms within, but it is also evident in the extreme attenuation of both the second-floor windows and Corinthian pilasters, as well as in the fan- and side-lit doors, the delicate porch stretching all across the front, and the similar refinement of the iron balconies.

Colburn described the building of this double house in his diary: "About the year 1807 I purchased a lot of Jonathan Mason, Esq., in Beacon Street, enough for two houses, and had two beautiful houses built thereon. One I intended for myself and the other for my sister. They were planned by myself and the work executed by A. Benjamin, Architect. They were two superb houses with two bowfronts, circular dining rooms, and drawing rooms over, with folding doors." In 1808 Colburn and his brother-in-law William Gill sold the eastern house, still under construction, to Nathan Appleton for $13,500, with the purchase price including "iron railings to the piazza & an Iron railing in the front of the lower story, —paper hangings suitable for said house as imported for the said Colburn & Gill & Glass-plates for the mirror windows in the dining room." Further, the contract stipulated "that the materials so furnished by the said Colburn & Gill shall be of equal quality with those furnished for the adjoining house building for them by the said Benjamin."[16]

Other bowfronted double houses soon followed, with two examples on the opposite, or south, side of Boston Common being the Everett-Denny and Gray-Welles houses on Summer Street, both built about 1812. Straightfronted double houses could be found in various places. Among those in New York is one by McComb with fan- and side-lit doorways in rusticated bays at two edges of the structure and a rusticated arch leading to a passage between the houses.[17]

Bulfinch may be the direct source for the projecting bows at the Colburn and subsequent houses, as for example, in his Jonathan Mason house on Beacon Hill of 1799–1802 (which also includes flanking attenuated pilasters), but comparable British examples can also be identified, as at 39–43 Castle Street in Edinburgh, 1792–93 (fig. 15).[18] Although built of stone rather than brick, with a broad pediment providing a central emphasis, this Scottish triple house, with its bows, giant pilasters, and differentiated lower level, clearly relates to Benjamin's double house in Boston.

Without the bows and pilasters, the Edinburgh house can be seen as a distant model for a triple house in Charleston, Vander Horst Row at 78 East Bay, built circa 1810 (fig. 16). Constructed as an investment by the wealthy merchant and former South Carolina governor Arnoldus Vander Horst, this building combined the colonial Palladian great-house formula of a projecting and pedimented central pavilion with the neoclassical oval and rectangular panels above the second-floor windows and delicate fanlight in the pediment.

In his will of May 14, 1810, Vander Horst directed that "the Three tenements fronting on East Bay Street, engraved on the Marble Pannels in the front, Vander-Horst's North Row 1810, be neatly but plainly finished in the inside, the Chimnies in the two Rooms on the Second floor in each tenement to have Plain Marble front pieces and slabs, all the other chimnies to have front pieces of Stone as a Security against fire." Demonstrating his concern for practical matters as well, he went on to decree that "the three Cisterns [are] to be finished and tin gutters to be fixed to the eaves of the buildings, sufficient to carry rain water into them, with a pump to each."[19]

Conservative in certain aesthetic respects, this triple house nevertheless demonstrates the possibility of unifying a series of town houses into a larger and more palatial composition, as John Wood the Elder had demonstrated three-quarters of a century earlier at Queen Square in Bath, 1729–36.[20] The anonymous designer of the Castle Street houses in Edinburgh had transformed Wood's idea into a neoclassical version.

Another composition of this type is the 1794–95 Wheat Row at 1315–21 Fourth Street SW, Washington, D.C. Conservative in design, it was a product of the fevered speculation that struck builders in the national capital as it prepared for the arrival of Congress and the administration. In this case James Greenleaf from Massachusetts formed a

Figure 15.   39–43 Castle St., Edinburgh, 1792–93. (Royal
Commission on the Ancient and Historical Monuments of
Scotland, Edinburgh.)

Figure 16.   Vander Horst Row, Charleston, S.C., ca. 1810. (Gibbes
Museum of Art/Carolina Art Association, Charleston, S.C.)

Figure 17.   Charles Bulfinch, elevation, Park Row, Boston, 1803–5.
(Massachusetts Historical Society.)

syndicate with Philadelphians Robert Morris and James Nicholson to create a quadruple house with pedimented central section.[21]

Three or four—or more—houses could also be designed as a row or terrace without any unifying elements, a technique common in Britain throughout the eighteenth century. Introduced across the Atlantic during the federal period, this is exemplified by Bulfinch's Park Row at 1–4 Park Street, Boston (fig. 17). Four houses, each four bays and thirty-nine feet wide, feature fan-lit doorways, arched entries leading to the rear (the latter necessitated by the absence of alleyways behind), and flat-arched-and-keystoned windows under blind arches in the lowest floor. Elongated windows, delicate iron balconies, and flat balustrades with decorative panels complete the neoclassical touches. Comparable English examples range from Robert Mylne's Albion Place in London, 1772–ca. 1792, to the Crescent, Town Walls, Shrewsbury, Shropshire, circa 1800. Bulfinch's plan (fig. 18) includes ample semi-elliptical stairways in the new taste. When completed, these four houses were assessed at an impressive $10,000 each, and twelve years later they were still described as "in an improved style of architecture after the modern English models."[22]

Manifestations of this type of row can also be found in other cities and in the hands of different architects and developers, as in the Seven

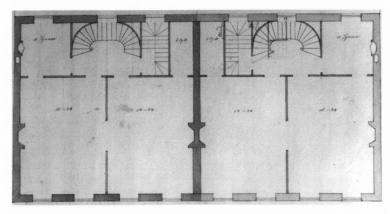

Figure 18.   Charles Bulfinch, second-floor plan, Park Row, Boston, 1803–5. (Massachusetts Historical Society.)

Buildings, erected on Pennsylvania Avenue in Washington near the President's House between 1794 and 1796 by William Lovering, ultimately financed, like Wheat Row, by the Greenleaf Syndicate of Greenleaf, Morris, and Nicholson.[23]

Long rows, known as terraces, are undoubtedly the most characteristic form of neoclassical urban housing in England. The term *terrace* seems first to have been applied to the houses themselves, rather than the promenade on which they stood, in Robert Adam's Royal Terrace at the Adelphi in London of 1768–75 (fig. 19).[24] Although it was composed of a series of individual town houses, these were unified by ornamented pilasters at the center and ends. Unlike John Wood the Elder's Queen Square in Bath or its progeny in the United States, such as the Vander Horst or Wheat rows, the Royal Terrace had no central pediment. In keeping with a neoclassical tendency toward unaccented centers, its horizontal emphasis was balanced by the pilasters and pedimented ends of the flanking units. Within the Adelphi, but further back from the river, a central exclamation *was* provided on John Street—in this case by the pedimented house for the Society of Arts (see fig. 3).

That Americans were familiar with the Adelphi and connected it with Adam's style and fame was indicated as early as 1773 in Philadelphia, when William Williams, "[a] native of this city, . . . having lately returned from London, where he has for some time studied ARCHI-

Figure 19. Robert Adam, Royal Terrace, Adelphi, London, 1768–75. Engraving, B. Pastorini. From Robert Adam and James Adam, *The Works in Architecture* (London, 1778–1822), 3: pl. 1. (Winterthur Library.)

TECTURE in its various branches," advertised in the *Pennsylvania Packet* that he "proposes carrying on the business of House Carpentry in the most useful and ornamental manner, as is now executed in the city of London, and most parts of England . . . in a new, bold, light and elegant taste, which has been lately introduced by the great architect of the Adelphi Buildings at Durham Yard; and which is now universally practised all over Britain."[25]

Despite the appearance of this advertisement before the Revolution, it was twenty years later that America saw anything approaching such a terrace. The first was Charles Bulfinch's Tontine Crescent in Boston in 1793–94 (fig. 20). Erected on Franklin Place in the former garden of Joseph Barrell's estate in the South End, this development was named for and intended to be financed by a scheme under which the last survivor of a group of shareholders became heir to the entire property, a form of gambling that was quite popular in the eighteenth century.[26]

In Bulfinch's original conception two curved terraces were to occupy a shallow ellipse. As a description in the *Massachusetts Magazine* asserts: "The figure of a crescent has been adopted, as, independent of the beauty of the curve, it afforded an opportunity of introducing a green or grass plat surrounded by trees, which will contribute to the ornament of the buildings, and be useful in promoting a change and circulation of air." Financial difficulties and the narrowness of the site forced him

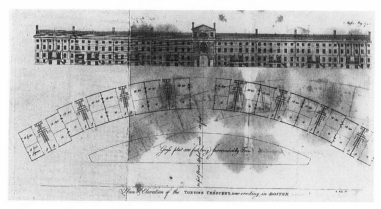

Figure 20. Charles Bulfinch, elevation and plan, Tontine Crescent, Boston, 1793–94. Engraving, S. Hill. From *Massachusetts Magazine* 6 (February 6, 1794): frontis. (American Antiquarian Society.)

to complement the crescent on the south, seen in the engraving that accompanied the description, with a flat row on the north that was constructed as four double houses.[27]

The encomium of the project further stated that "the entire range will be four hundred and eighty feet long, and consist of sixteen dwelling houses, and one ornamental pile in the centre devoted to public uses. These houses are built in a substantial manner of brick, with party walls of the same materials between them, and are finished in the most approved stile of modern elegance; the rooms are spacious and lofty, and attention is paid to procuring all possible conveniences for domestic use."[28]

As at the Adelphi, Tontine Crescent was articulated by giant orders at its center and ends. Bulfinch further emphasized the center with a pediment and Palladian motif within relieving arch (both employed at Adam's Society of Arts in the Adelphi complex [see fig. 3], although not at the Royal Terrace). Equally neoclassical are the urns in niches and laurel-draped medallions that Bulfinch sketched in between the half-columns and pilasters on his drawing for the central section and the ornamental panels in the entry bays of the various houses. As on John Street in the Adelphi, the central unit was to be occupied by cultural institutions, Bulfinch having given the main space there to the

Boston Library Society and the room above it to the Massachusetts Historical Society.[29]

In plan Tontine Crescent shows a relatively common row-house arrangement, with straight-return stairs at the end of the side hall, but with service stairs behind them. The principal interest in the plan is, however, the curved shape, derived from the Royal Crescent in Bath, of 1766–74, and its progeny, including, for example, John Eveleigh's Camden Crescent at Bath, begun in 1788. Elegantly designed and highly praised, Tontine Crescent was nevertheless a financial disaster, although Bulfinch made certain "that not one of my creditors was materially injured." In February 1795 he sold two of the houses, 12 and 13, still in an unfinished state but with a guarantee to complete them "at my own expense in like manner as the other houses in said Crescent," for £1,680, which was equivalent to $5,600, or only a little over half the valuation of his Park Row houses of a decade later. A quarter century after its completion Tontine Crescent was still an elegant address, judging by Henry Sargent's view of the dining room at No. 10, with its beautifully ornamented archway from the parlor, tall windows, and fashionably attired guests.[30]

Despite the beauty of this conception and its popularity in Britain, no other crescents were erected in federal America. There were, however, other attempts at grand but straight terraces of this type. Bulfinch, himself, created a series of nineteen houses, all joined by a continuous one-story attenuated Doric porch topped by an ironwork balcony, on the south side of Boston Common in 1810–12. Even earlier, about 1806, Parris conceived for Portland a block of nine houses (fig. 21) stretching 245 feet, as opposed to the Tontine Crescent's sixteen houses and 480-foot length. Its central columned unit was ornamented with an enormous swag-and-wreath panel topped by an eagle. The segmental-arched lower floor is similar to various Bulfinch designs, such as Park Row (see figs. 17, 18), as are the oval stairhalls. The two arched windows in the center, on the other hand, are reminiscent of Parris's own double-house design for Portland a few years earlier (see fig. 13). A slightly more modest but more aesthetically successful scheme for a terrace of eight houses by Parris, this time actually dated 1806 (fig. 22), also features oval stairways, but the more reticent facade is unified only by the reversing repetition of the three-bay pattern and the swag panel in the center of the flat balustrade.[31]

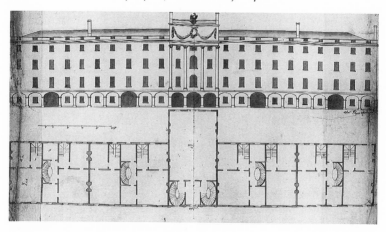

Figure 21.   Alexander Parris, elevation and plan, row houses, Portland, Maine, ca. 1806. (Parris sketchbook, Boston Athenaeum.)

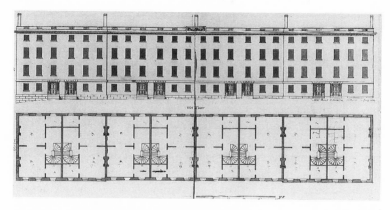

Figure 22.   Alexander Parris, elevation and plan, row houses, Portland, Maine, 1806. (Parris sketchbook, Boston Athenaeum.)

In Philadelphia, probably in the latter 1790s, William Priest reported that "several *uniform* and elegant rows of houses have *lately* been built." These may have included the two long rows back-to-back between Seventh and Eighth streets on Sansom and Walnut, which were up by the first years of the nineteenth century. Developed by

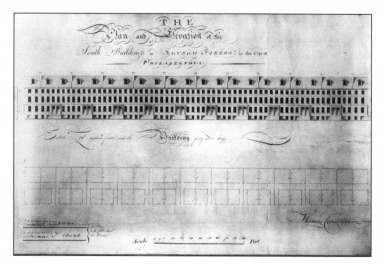

Figure 23.   Thomas Carstairs, elevation and plan, Sansom Row, Philadelphia, 1799. (Library Company of Philadelphia.)

William Sansom on property sold by Robert Morris to pay his debts, the row on Sansom was designed by Thomas Carstairs, who had emigrated from London just after the Revolution. That on Walnut is often attributed to Benjamin Henry Latrobe, who arrived a little over a decade later. Very little of each survives, but Carstairs's Sansom Row can be gauged by his design (fig. 23). Like the Parris drawing of a few years later (see fig. 22), it features a series of three-bay houses arranged in mirrored pairs, though with arched fan-lit doorways and dormer windows instead of a balustrated roof line. In his plan Carstairs inserted straight-return stairs in a cross hall between the two principal rooms, rather than Parris's oval stairs behind the entry. The houses on the north side of Walnut seem to have been similar to those of Carstairs and quite different from Latrobe's typical manner, which raises questions about the Latrobe attribution. The sources for these terraces were the long rows of similar houses that lined the streets of London and other British cities of the late eighteenth century, as on the west side of Merrion Square, Dublin, although the doorways in the Irish version are more elaborate. Closer to the Dublin example because of their elaborate fanlights, although still characterized by the late colonial flat-arch-with-keystone windows, were the Philadel-

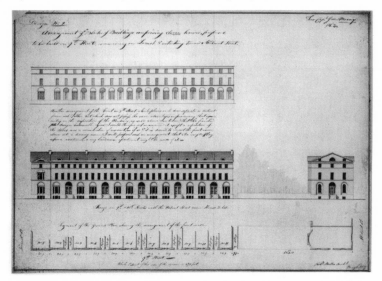

Figure 24.   Robert Mills, elevations and plan, Franklin Row, Philadelphia, 1809. (Private collection.)

phia houses that graced the south side of Walnut, known as York Row, built in 1807 by the carpenter Joseph Randall. The few that survive from this familiar terrace arrangement have very delicate Adamesque tracery around the door.[32]

Plainer, more austere, and more indicative of the later neoclassical manner of the 1790s in England and of Latrobe's usual work in America was Franklin Row in Philadelphia on the west side of Ninth Street, between Locust and Walnut. Designed in 1809 by Latrobe's former student, Robert Mills, for Capt. John Meany, this was at one point conceived as a complete square of buildings, although the designs shown in the drawing in figure 24 call for only eleven houses on one street. Two alternatives are indicated, but both employ triplet windows under a blank relieving arch. As executed the following year, the lower scheme was more nearly followed. The most notable change entailed a repetition of the overarched triplet window on the second floor. Of the ten houses actually built, only one has survived, and it has been both altered and moved.[33]

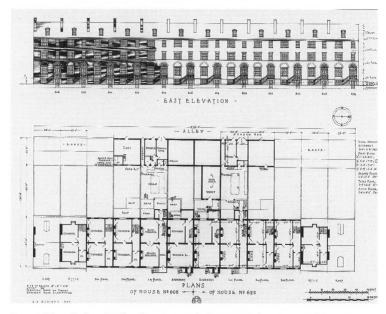

Figure 25.   Robert Mills, elevation and plan, Waterloo Row, Baltimore, 1816. Measured drawing, G. P. Schott. (Library of Congress.)

An insurance survey of 1840 for one of the buildings, 8 Franklin Row, reveals the houses had marble sills, a fanlight over the door, a twenty-light "Venetian" (or triplet) window front and back topped by a twelve-light one, white and black marble mantels in each first-floor room, "neat wood" ones on the floor above, and mahogany and curled maple double folding doors in the parlor.[34] The plan accompanying that survey indicates a transverse arch across the hall, with the straight-return stairs behind that arch.

A slightly later version of the Franklin Row scheme was used by Mills in 1816–18 or 1819 for a "range of houses for Water company" on Calvert Street between Center and Monument in Baltimore (fig. 25). Shortly thereafter named Waterloo Row, these twelve two-bay houses, all of which are now demolished, featured an arcaded main floor with alternating triplet windows under blind tympana and narrower doorways with delicate fanlights. On the upper two floors the triplets were repeated, but without the relieving arches. Six white marble steps parallel to the facade led to each doorway, which opened onto a narrow hall, crossed by an arch, as in Franklin Row, and flanked on one side by double parlors with folding doors between them.[35]

On their completion some of the houses were insured for $8,000 and the others for $7,000, representing only two-thirds of the actual value. A number of the owners were craftsmen, taking them for investments, with the other houses being insured by Baltimore Water Company. Despite their refined design and elegant interiors, including black marble chimney pieces with Doric colonnette stiles, the houses did not sell well. At least five of the twelve had their policies canceled, forfeited, or not taken up, with the company reinsuring these in 1822 for $5,300 or $5,100 each. This may have been due to the depression of 1819 or to their distance from the main center of the city and its business district, especially at the original high valuations. Yet, even fourteen years after completion, when the policies were up for their second seven-year renewal, six were still owned by Baltimore Water Company and one by stonemason-investor William Stewart, who had not lived there even in 1822–23.[36]

The original valuations are impressive, especially if compared with most of the other houses insured by the Equitable Society, the vast majority being valued at considerably less. On the other hand, there were a few houses with higher valuations, such as one very near the center of the city insured for $10,000 or the City Bank of Baltimore, which was insured for $15,000.[37]

Shortly after the erection of Mills's elegant Waterloo Row, Baltimore saw another row of slightly larger but less grandly conceived houses. Developed by Lewis Pascault and denominated Pascault Row, these houses on West Lexington Street were three bays and twenty-eight feet wide as opposed to Waterloo Row's two-bay and twenty-three-foot width. Although lacking Mills's tripartite openings, they did feature oval panels within square plaques between the second and third floors. When insured in 1822, they were valued at $4,000.[38] Unlike their grander competitors, they have survived and have recently been restored.

These types of composed rows or terraces, echoing first the Adamesque neoclassicism of the 1770s in England and then the austerity and plain-wall aesthetic of the 1790s there and, in Latrobe's hands, here, always remained the exception. Through them parts of certain American cities, in the East as well as further west, as in Louisville, de-

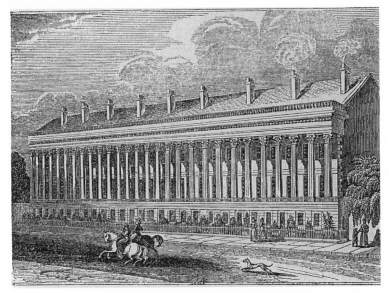

Figure 26.   La Grange Terrace, New York, 1830–33. Woodcut. From *Mirror* 30, no. 864 (November 1837): 329.

veloped an urban fabric akin, at least in part, to that proliferating in London, Bath, Dublin, Edinburgh, and other British centers. After the federal period ended, more elaborate terraces ornamented with grand colonnades appeared here, just as they had in Regency England. One example, La Grange Terrace, built on Lafayette Street in New York in 1830–33, even achieved the distinction of high praise in a British publication, the *Mirror* (November 18, 1837): "Of a truth, this superb specimen of transatlantic embellishment almost eclipses the terraces of our Regent's Park, overloaded as they are with ornament and fantastic design. Its material is far more costly than artificial stone; for it is of white marble, the material of Rome in the Augustan age; so that in art, the Americans may be said to have begun where the Romans left off."[39]

Seen in the illustration that accompanied that tribute (fig. 26), La Grange Terrace appears very grand, a fact that can be partially surmised from its present less elegant and truncated state. Its authorship is in dispute, with Robert Higham, James Dakin, A. J. Davis, and a Mr. Geer all being suggested as its designer.[40] The writer's allusion to the terraces of

Regent's Park can certainly be understood when the New York row is compared, for example, with John Nash's Cumberland Terrace of 1826. By the 1830s the United States could boast urban housing equivalent to, or even better than, London's. The comparison also demonstrates, however, the truth of Cooper's reflection, for in the United States, city living, federal and Greek-revival style, was still very much city living, English style, even if there were some independent developments—such as the gable-end entrance with cross hall—and even though the grander unified terraces were both less prolific and aroused some resistance.

----

[1] Le Corbusier's famous phrase that "we must look upon the house as a machine for living in" appears in Le Corbusier, *Vers une architecture* [Towards a new architecture], trans. Frederick Etchells (1927; reprint, New York: Praeger Publishers, 1960), p. 222.

[2] James Fenimore Cooper, *Notions of the Americans Picked Up by a Travelling Bachelor*, 2 vols. (3d ed.; Philadelphia: Carey, Lea, and Blanchard, 1838), 1:150. Contractual indenture, November 14, 1790, Jared Lane Miscellaneous Papers, New York Public Library, New York City.

[3] For more on the Coolidge house, see Harold Kirker, *The Architecture of Charles Bulfinch* (Cambridge: Harvard University Press, 1969), pp. 41–43. On Bulfinch's European trip, see his autobiographical memoir, quoted in Susan Ellen Bulfinch, *The Life and Letters of Charles Bulfinch, Architect* . . . (Boston: Houghton, Mifflin, 1896), p. 42; and Kirker, *Architecture*, pp. 6–7. Apparently developed in Spain in the sixteenth century, though based on earlier Italian ideas, the imperial type of staircase appeared not infrequently during the baroque era and flourished in late eighteenth-century England; see Damie Stillman, *English Neo-Classical Architecture*, 2 vols. (London: A. Zwemmer, 1988), esp. 1:289; Nikolaus Pevsner, *An Outline of European Architecture* (8th ed.; Harmondsworth, Eng.: Penguin Books, 1974), pp. 81–83; and Sandra Blutman, "Geometrical Staircases," *Journal of the Society of Architectural Historians* 26, no. 1 (March 1967): 37. Although Bulfinch undoubtedly saw numerous examples in Europe, he may have been encouraged by seeing one in Philadelphia at the Bingham house in 1789.

[4] William Bingham to Thomas Willing, December 29, 1783, Correspondence, 1780–89, Bingham Papers, Historical Society of Pennsylvania, Philadelphia (hereafter cited as HSP). For Bingham and his trip to Europe, see Robert C. Alberts, *The Golden Voyage: The Life and Times of William Bingham, 1752–1804* (Boston: Houghton Mifflin Co., 1969), pp. 120–56. For the Bingham house, see William Birch, *The City of Philadelphia* (Philadelphia: By the author, 1800), pl. 22; Bulfinch, drawings executed on a trip to Philadelphia and New York, 1789, Prints and Photographs Division, Library of Congress; and "Catalogue of the principal articles of furniture and plate," an advertisement of the William Bingham sale by A. Pettit and Co., *United States Gazette* (Philadelphia), November 16, 1805, reprinted in Alberts, *Golden Voyage*, app. 4, pp. 467–73. For Plaw's 1790 exhibited design and more on

Plaw, see Howard Colvin, *A Biographical Dictionary of British Architects, 1600–1840* (London: John Murray, 1978), pp. 642–43. On Belle Isle, see Stillman, *English Neo-Classical Architecture*, 1:152, pl. 90.

[5] For a description of the grander rooms on the floor above, see Bingham to Thomas Willing, January 18–February 19, 1784, Correspondence, 1780–89, Bingham Papers, HSP. The contemporary reference to the Mansion House appears in Alberts, *Golden Voyage*, p. 162. On the auction, see the Pettit catalogue, reprinted in Alberts, *Golden Voyage*, app. 4, p. 471. In 1785 Willing advised Bingham to bring back a variety of materials for the house that were either better, less expensive, or more readily available in London, including sash glass, sash boards, cogs for pulleys, locks, hinges, bolts, padlocks, brass nails, sheet lead, and "Colours all Ready ground in Oil" (Willing to Bingham, March 12, 1785, Correspondence, 1780–89, Bingham Papers, HSP).

[6] Henry Wansey, *Journal of an Excursion to the United States in the Summer of 1794* (1796), ed. David John Jeremy (Philadelphia: American Philosophical Society, 1970), p. 105; Charles Bulfinch to his parents, April 2, 1789, quoted in Bulfinch, *Life and Letters*, pp. 75–76; Joseph Manigault to Gabriel Manigault, September 17, 1790, Manigault Family Papers, South Caroliniana Library, University of South Carolina, Columbia. (The author is grateful to Frankie Webb, Charleston Museum, for suggesting this reference.) The design of the facade for Bulfinch's first house for Otis, on Cambridge St., circa 1796, preserved at Massachusetts Historical Society, is extremely close to the one in the drawing in Library of Congress that he made of the Bingham house in 1789. The principal differences are in the door, which lacks the Gibbs surround with its vermiculated blocks; the panels above the second-floor windows, which substitute swags topped by paterae for other, less conventional neoclassical decorative motifs; and the tops of the windows, which, on the first and second floors, employ flat lintels rather than pronounced keystones. In the executed Otis house the second-floor panels were eliminated, thus lessening somewhat the resemblance. For photographs of both drawings and the extant Otis house, see Kirker, *Architecture*, figs. 50–52.

[7] McComb's Government House designs are in the McComb Collection, nos. 54–58a, New-York Historical Society, New York City. The last numbered of these has a semicircular exedra in the center of the garden facade. The others feature either a half-octagonal projection in that location or two such forms on the ends of the entrance front, or both; see Damie Stillman, "Artistry and Skill in the Architecture of John McComb, Jr." (Master's thesis, University of Delaware, 1956), p. 21, figs. 4–8. In the Philadelphia house of 1792–97 the garden projection was segmental, reflecting the horizontal oval room within. A plan of the first floor dating around 1800–1802 (when the building, having been acquired by the University of Pennsylvania, was adapted for educational purposes) shows the oval room labeled "Provost's room" (University of Pennsylvania Archives, MS 2012). The university's committee on the new building reported to the trustees in the spring of 1802 that they had "fitted up the west Bow Room on the second story for the Medical School" (quoted by George W. Corner, *Two Centuries of Medicine* [Philadelphia: J. B. Lippincott Co., 1965], p. 49). The President's House in Washington, D.C., designed by James Hoban for the 1792 competition, exhibits the dramatic projecting exedra on its garden facade. Bonomi's drawings, labeled "design of a house now building in the City of New York in America by John Barker Church Esqr.," are preserved in a private collection in Oxfordshire; for the plan, see Stillman, *English Neo-Classical Architecture*, 1: pl. 117.

[8] The present porch on the north side is a modern reconstruction. (The author is deeply indebted to T. Patrick Brennan for opening the house and to Bernard Her-

man for providing information on insurance policies from which these dates are derived.) Mutual Assurance Society policies, nos. 226 (1797), 2638 (1818), Virginia State Library, Richmond. Dates from insurance surveys.

⁹ François-Marie Perrin du Lac, *Travels through the Two Louisianas* (London, 1807), p. 41, as quoted in Rexford Newcomb, *Architecture in Old Kentucky* (Urbana: University of Illinois Press, 1953), p. 18. On Hunt and his house, see Newcomb, *Kentucky*, pp. 50–51. (Patrick Snadon provided information about the reconstruction of the side door.) For the newsroom and its newspaper subscribers, see Noble E. Cunningham, Jr., "Political Dimensions of Everyday Life in the Early Republic," elsewhere in this volume. On the early nineteenth-century population of Lexington, see Perrin du Lac, *Travels*, p. 41, as quoted by Newcomb, *Kentucky*, p. 18. Lexington's impressive collection of federal houses, a number of which are located around the same square (now called Gratz Park) as Hopemount, the name given to the Hunt (now Hunt-Morgan) house, can be surveyed in Newcomb's volume or in Clay Lancaster, *Ante-Bellum Houses of the Bluegrass* (Lexington: University of Kentucky Press, 1961). Here, as elsewhere, architecture confirms Daniel Boorstin's concept of "frontier boosterism." For an excellent example of this on the northern frontier, see William Newell Hosley, Jr., "Architecture and Society of the Urban Frontier: Windsor, Vermont, 1798–1820" (Master's thesis, University of Delaware, 1981). For Boorstin's concept, see Daniel J. Boorstin, *The Americans: The National Experience* (New York: Random House, 1965), esp. pp. 113–68.

¹⁰ Drawings for the Coles house (McComb drawings, nos. 100, 101, 102a, New-York Historical Society) can be compared with measured drawings completed for the Index of American Design (on loan to Avery Architectural Library, Columbia University) before demolition of the structure. Although Coles bought the property in 1797, his name first appeared at that address in the 1800 *City Directory*, as noted by I. N. Phelps Stokes, *The Iconography of Manhattan Island . . .* , 6 vols. (New York: Dodd, 1915–28), 1:424. For more on the house, see Stillman, "Artistry and Skill," pp. 39–41. On McComb, see Stillman, "Artistry and Skill," or *Macmillan Encyclopedia of Architects*, s.v. "McComb, John, Jr."

¹¹ Dixon Ryan Fox, *The Decline of Aristocracy in the Politics of New York* (New York: Columbia University Press, 1919), p. 18; Walter Barrett [J. A. Scoville], *The Old Merchants of New York*, 5 vols. (New York: J. W. Lovell, ca. 1889), 2:42.

¹² Kirker, *Architecture*, p. 223, suggests that this may be the house for Daniel Raynerd, Bulfinch's favorite plasterer; Jack Quinan ("Daniel Raynerd, Stucco Worker," *Old-Time New England* 65, nos. 3–4 [Winter–Spring 1975]: 9–10) thinks the Raynerd house may be by Asher Benjamin, although not, of course, this drawing. (The author is indebted to Janice Timinski for a reminder of this controversy.)

¹³ Junior League of Charleston, *Across the Cobblestones* (Charleston, S.C.: By the league, 1965), reissued by the Historic Charleston Foundation as *Historic Charleston Guidebook* (9th pr.; 1975), p. 68. Exedrae projecting from the side of a town house, especially one presenting a three-bay front to the street, are naturally less common within a tight urban fabric. Bulfinch employed one in this fashion at his third house for Harrison Gray Otis, 45 Beacon St., Boston, in 1806–8. The house next to the Otis house was built later using a concave curve on its side to accommodate the projection from the Otis structure. Both still exist.

¹⁴ Earle Shettleworth, "Notes Pertaining to the Parris Portfolio at the Boston Athenaeum," April 10, 1965, Boston Athenaeum; Edward Francis Zimmer, "The Architectural Career of Alexander Parris (1780–1852)" (Ph.D. diss., Boston University, 1984), p. 49. The example cited for Bulfinch is Park Row, 1803–5. Despite the sug-

gestion in Kirker, *Architecture*, p. 181, that the balustrade was not executed, Zimmer, "Parris," p. 52, points out that it is shown with those panels on a painted chimney-board at the Bostonian Society, Boston.

[15] James Smith Colburn, *The Personal Memoirs of James Smith Colburn* (Boston: Massachusetts Society of the Colonial Dames of America, 1949), p. 67.

[16] Colburn, *Personal Memoirs*, p. 66; the wording of Colburn's memoirs has caused some scholars (e.g., Abbott Lowell Cummings) to suggest that perhaps Colburn designed the houses and Benjamin just built them. It seems more likely, given the general practice of the time and mention of Benjamin here and in the contract, that Colburn offered suggestions that Benjamin then both worked up and executed. For a discussion of the various possibilities, see Zimmer, "Parris," p. 316 n.29. In 1982 Cummings listed the house as the work of Benjamin; *Macmillan Encyclopedia of Architecture*, s.v. "Benjamin, Asher." Contract between Nathan Appleton and James S. Colburn and William Gill, April 16, 1808, Appleton Family Manuscripts, Massachusetts Historical Society, Boston.

[17] The Everett-Denny house is very close in design to those by Benjamin. Jack Quinan, "Asher Benjamin and American Architecture," *Journal of the Society of Architectural Historians* 38, no. 3 (October 1979): 253, attributes the house to Benjamin, although he dates it ca. 1808. Zimmer, "Parris," p. 170 n.170, suggests that the date is ca. 1814 because the outline of the house appears on John G. Hales's 1814 map of Boston. Photographs of it are available at the Society for the Preservation of New England Antiquities, Boston. That institution, as well as the Bostonian Society, has photographs of the Gray-Welles house, which was built as a speculative development by Israel Thorndike, who was assessed for an unfinished double house in 1812, according to Kirker, *Architecture*, p. 377, who sees no reason to connect it with Bulfinch. The McComb double house is preserved in the McComb Collection, New-York Historical Society, and another double-house design in that collection features column-framed arched doorways in the two central bays; both are illustrated in Agnes Addison Gilchrist, "John McComb, Sr., and Jr., 1784–99," *Journal of the Society of Architectural Historians* 31, no. 1 (March 1972): 20.

[18] Although destroyed in the 1830s, Bulfinch's Mason house can be seen in a lithograph by William S. Pendleton, reproduced in Kirker, *Architecture*, fig. 76, with documentation on pp. 156–57. Bulfinch had used a projecting exedra on various country houses, beginning with Pleasant Hill, Charlestown, for Joseph Barrell, 1791–93, and including Col. James Swan's house in Dorchester, circa 1796–the latter featuring the projection on the entrance front, more analogous to its use on the Mason town house a few years later. Quinan, "Asher Benjamin," p. 251, cites the Bulfinch precedent for the Colburn houses.

[19] May 14, 1810, Charleston Co., S.C., Wills, 32:924, recorded at the Museum of Early Southern Decorative Arts, Winston-Salem, N.C. (The author is grateful to Frank Horton for making these extensive and valuable files available.)

[20] John Summerson, *Architecture in Britain, 1530–1830* (1953; 6th ed., Harmondsworth, Eng.: Penguin Books, 1977), pp. 386–88.

[21] Restored in 1966, Wheat Row can be seen in Historic American Buildings Survey measured drawings, DC-10; see also, U.S. National Capital Planning Commission, *Worthy of the Nation: The History of Planning for the National Capital* (Washington, D.C.: Smithsonian Institution Press, 1977), p. 41; Diane Maddex, *Historic Buildings of Washington, D.C.* (Pittsburgh: Ober Park Associates, 1973), p. 28. (The author is indebted to Susan Brizzolara for the reminder of this example.)

[22] Shuabel Bell, "An Account of the Town of Boston Written in 1817," *Bostonian Society Publications* 3 (1919): 23, quoted by Kirker, *Architecture*, p. 182, who also gives the valuation, from Boston Assessors Taking Books, 1805, ward 9, City Hall, Boston. Plans and elevations for the row are preserved at Massachusetts Historical Society. (The author is indebted to the late Ross Urquhart for allowing examination and photography of these drawings.) See also Kirker, *Architecture*, pp. 181–83. For the Mylne terrace, which was part of his urban planning scheme at the south end of Southwark Bridge, but no longer exists, see Stillman, *English Neo-Classical Architecture*, 1: pl. 176. The Shrewsbury example, which is smaller and curved, is extant.

[23] The building was on the northwest corner of Pennsylvania Avenue and Nineteenth St. NW; see James M. Goode, *Capital Losses: A Cultural History of Washington's Destroyed Buildings* (Washington, D.C.: Smithsonian Institution Press, 1979), p. 140.

[24] Stillman, *English Neo-Classical Architecture*, 2:560 n.49, points out that Adam's print specifically refers to the "Royal Terras" and that the *Oxford English Dictionary* gives 1769 as the date for this particular definition.

[25] Williams advertisement, *Pennsylvania Packet*, January 4, 1773. For examples "all over Britain," see Stillman, *English Neo-Classical Architecture*, chap. 7.

[26] Named for Lorenzo Tonti, a Neapolitan banker who introduced the scheme into France around 1653, tontines were popular in eighteenth-century England as well as in America, as in the Tontine Coffee House in New York, 1792–94.

[27] "Description of the Plate," *Massachusetts* 6 (February 1794): 67. On the financial situation, see Charles A. Place, *Charles Bulfinch, Architect and Citizen* (Boston: Houghton Mifflin Co., 1925), pp. 63–64, 68–75. On the four houses at 17–24 Franklin Pl., see Kirker, *Architecture*, pp. 89–91.

[28] "Description," p. 67.

[29] Bulfinch's drawing is in the Department of Prints and Photographs, Library of Congress, and is illustrated in Kirker, *Architecture*, fig. 34. The presentation of the upper room is noted in "Description," p. 67. Kirker, *Architecture*, p. 80, notes the assignment of the lower room.

[30] Bulfinch, *Life and Letters*, p. 99; Kirker, *Architecture*, p. 79. The contract for 12 and 13 Tontine Crescent—in Suffolk County, Massachusetts, Deeds, book 179, p. 257a—was brought to the author's attention by Sylvia Lahvis. For the valuation of the Park Row houses, see p. 321. Sargent's painting (Museum of Fine Arts, Boston), is reproduced in Kirker, *Architecture*, fig. 36.

[31] If the Tontine Crescent had no immediate progeny, it did in the 1980s on Main St., Charlestown, Mass. Of red brick with groups of white pilasters at the outer ends of its two curving blocks, this crescent features at its center not an elaborate pedimented pavilion but an intervening street. It reveals its late twentieth-century date by bay windows on that street and the two flanking ones and by the rear facade treatments typical of the 1980s. Facing Boston Common on Common (later Tremont) St., between Mason and West sts., Bulfinch's terrace of nineteen houses was a speculation by David Greenough and James Freeman; see Kirker, *Architecture*, pp. 258–61. Parris's terrace designs are preserved in the Parris sketchbook, MS L.333, pp. 22–23, 18–19, Boston Athenaeum. Neither Shettleworth, "Notes," nor Zimmer, "Parris," pp. 85–88, sheds any more light on these two projects; Shettleworth says not built in Portland and Zimmer concurs. The latter notes how someone might have contemplated or even commissioned such a project in 1806, given the thriving business situation then, but reasons that the Embargo of 1807 and its results would have dissuaded anyone from continuing.

[32] William Priest, *Travels in the United States of America; Commencing in the Year 1793, and Ending in 1797* (London: J. Johnson, 1802), p. 31. The exact date of this reference is uncertain, for, although it is tempting to connect this with Sansom and Walnut rows, this comment was added to his letter of March 3, 1794, during the editing of his letters for publication, which probably took place in 1797. This likelihood seems to be confirmed by a similar addition on pp. 31–32 stating that "the seat of government of the United States, will, in the year 1800, be removed to the federal city, now building in the district of Columbia." The reference to the rows could, however, have been added anytime prior to the 1802 publication. Carstairs's advertisement that he had "lately arrived in this city from London" is cited in Alfred Cox Prime, ed., *The Arts and Crafts in Philadelphia, Maryland, and South Carolina, 1786–1800* (Topsfield, Mass.: Walpole Society, 1933), p. 293. Latrobe arrived in Norfolk in March 1796 and first visited Philadelphia in March 1798 (see Talbot Hamlin, *Benjamin Henry Latrobe* [New York: Oxford University Press, 1955], pp. 64, 121). For Sansom's rows on Sansom and Walnut sts., see Kenneth Ames, "Robert Mills and the Philadelphia Row House," *Journal of the Society of Architectural Historians* 37, no. 2 (May 1968): 142–43. Latrobe's traditional involvement with Sansom's houses on Walnut rests on Latrobe to Richard Dale and William Wilmer, February 10, 1814: "In 1800, when Sansom's row in Walnut Street was built, I had the best means of ascertaining the actual cost" (as quoted in Hamlin, *Latrobe*, p. 152). The style of these houses causes one to wonder about the degree of Latrobe's involvement in the actual design. For an earlier examination of the possible reasons for the difference between the Walnut St. houses and Latrobe's usual style, see Ames, "Robert Mills," p. 143. For York Row, see Ames, "Robert Mills," p. 143; Edward Teitelman and Richard W. Longstreth, *Architecture in Philadelphia: A Guide* (Cambridge: MIT Press, 1974), p. 62.

[33] Originally on the west side of Ninth between Locust and Walnut, the sole surviving house is now on the southwest corner of Eighth and Locust. For more on the project, see Ames, "Robert Mills," pp. 140–41.

[34] Franklin Fire Insurance Surveys, no. 3049, May 7, 1840, HSP. (This source was brought to the author's attention by Jeffrey A. Cohen.) In that particular house the wall and doors between the two parlors had been removed in the 1830s.

[35] Robert Mills, Daily Journal, August 7, 1816, Robert Mills Papers, Library of Congress. Begun in 1817, the houses were completed either by autumn 1818 or spring 1819, when they were insured by the Baltimore Equitable Society. See Robert I. Alexander, "Baltimore Row Houses of the Early Nineteenth Century," *American Studies* 16, no. 2 (Fall 1975): 70–71; William Voss Elder III, *Maryland Period Rooms* (Baltimore: Baltimore Museum of Art, 1987), pp. 28–29. The houses were renamed by January 1, 1822; "Record of Policies Issued," E:228–30, Baltimore Equitable Society. For details of the houses, see the measured drawings by G. P. Schott, Historic American Buildings Survey; Alexander, "Baltimore Row Houses," pp. 70–71; Elder, *Maryland Period Rooms*, pp. 28–29.

[36] On the initial insurance and the first renewals, see "Record of Policies Issued," E:35–37, 152, 228–30 (January 1, 1822), Baltimore Equitable Society: 8 houses were valued at $8,000, with $7,600 for the main or front portion; 4 at $7,000, with $6,600 for the front part. (The author is deeply grateful to Stephen Bernhardt, president and treasurer of Baltimore Equitable Society, for allowing examination of these records and for discussing the ratio of insurance to valuation.) For the first owners as artisan-investors, see Alexander, "Baltimore Row Houses," pp. 70–71. On subsequent insurance renewal, see "Record of Policies Issued," F:645–46, 796 (June 1, 1833); and G:49–50 (January 1, 1836). For Stewart's address, see *The Baltimore Directory for*

1822–23 (Baltimore: Hatchett, 1822). (For knowledge of the 7-year duration of the policies, the author is indebted to Stephen Bernhardt.)

[37] "Record of Policies Issued," E:59 (November 1, 1819), Baltimore Equitable Society. The house, belonging to Jacob I. Cohen, was on Baltimore St., near Calvert; the bank, also near the center, was at the corner of Gay and Second.

[38] "Record of Policies Issued," E:249 (April 11, 1822), E:291–92 (October 15, 1822), Baltimore Equitable Society. See also Alexander, "Baltimore Row Houses," pp. 21–22, fig. 5; and Natalie W. Shivers, *These Old Placid Rows: The Aesthetic and Development of the Baltimore Rowhouse* (Baltimore: Maclay, 1981), p. 26. Although Shivers dates this development 1816, and Thomas Griffith, *Annals of Baltimore* (Baltimore, 1824–29), pp. 250–51, says 1819, the latter date can mark the beginning at most; even that is unlikely, given the economic conditions that year. Completion in 1822 seems indicated by the issuance of insurance policies at that time.

[39] *Mirror* 30, no. 864 (November 18, 1837): 329–30. On Louisville, see Samuel Thomas, *Views of Louisville since 1760* (Louisville: Courier-Journal Publishing Co., 1971). (This was brought to the author's attention by Richard Jett of Kentucky Heritage Council.)

[40] Geer is cited as the architect in *New York Views*, as quoted in the *Mirror* 30, no. 864 (November 18, 1837): 330. Talbot Hamlin, *Greek Revival Architecture in America* (New York: Oxford University Press, 1944), p. 130, attributes it to Davis and even cites a drawing in the Davis collection at Avery Architectural Library, Columbia University, labeled "approaching what Lafayette Terrace ought to be"; but *Macmillan Encyclopedia of Architects*, s.v. "Town and Davis," lists only "1833, La Grange Terrace (interiors)" under the works of the firm, and it is not mentioned at "Davis, Alexander Jackson." In "Works and Projects," in Amelia Peck, ed., *Alexander Jackson Davis, American Architect, 1803–1892* (New York: Rizzoli, 1992), p. 107, Jane B. Davies lists it as the work of Dakin and Davis, with Davis credited only with "Details" and Geer cited as the client. As Dakin was a partner in the firm in 1832–33, that seems to explain why some have credited him with it, but it does not appear under his name in *Macmillan Encyclopedia*. Higham was suggested by Regina Kellerman, "La Grange Terrace: The Question of Authorship" (Paper delivered at the annual meeting of the Society of Architectural Historians, New York, 1966). Although half of the houses in La Grange Terrace have been demolished, the rest of the row still stands — albeit in deteriorated condition — just below Astor Pl. on the west side of Lafayette St., across from the former Astor Library, which now houses the Public Theatre.

From "Country Mediocrity" to "Rural Improvement"

Transforming the Slovenly Countryside in Central Massachusetts, 1775–1840

Jack Larkin

This essay examines an episode of cultural change. It will consider how, in the late eighteenth and early nineteenth centuries, as part of a great social and economic transformation, the rural people of central Massachusetts reshaped the material world they had inherited. It looks at the slovenly countryside, the vision of rural improvement, and the pattern of historical change in which one version of the domestic environment replaced the other.

Speaking in 1819, the gentlemanly agricultural reformer Josiah Quincy described what he said had long been the common usage of ordinary farm families in Massachusetts. Often, their doors were "barricadoed by a mingled mass of chip and dirt" around the entrance. Chickens roosted on the windowsills, geese guarded the entryways, and pigs rooted around the doorsteps or lay under the abandoned relics of sleds and carts. Worst of all, each yard was "an inlaid pavement of bones and broken bottles, the relics of departed earthen ware, or the fragments of abandoned domestic utensils."[1]

The basis for Quincy's critique can be verified in the archaeological record; research on rural Massachusetts sites suggests that broadcast trash disposal was the common practice of ordinary folk in the countryside. To the archaeologist such seemingly chaotic scenes exhibit an important and complex ordering. Casually strewn waste can be analyzed to reconstruct patterns of movement and work and to understand the changing shape of activity around the house.[2]

More to the point of this essay is Quincy's perception, and that of earlier observers, both English and American, of disorder. If dirt is "matter out of place," then there were two different definitions of dirt at issue in the early nineteenth-century New England countryside: the "slovenly" and the "improved" versions of the domestic landscape.[3] One had no articulate spokesmen; it can be recovered through the material record and the words of its critics. The other had many vocal proponents. They articulated a different vision of the domestic landscape—a vision that would, for instance, see the chips and dirt cleared away, the livestock segregated from the house, and the sherds and bones picked up.

Before 1800 central Massachusetts—Worcester County, the eastern parts of Hampshire, Hampden, and Franklin counties, and the westernmost parts of Middlesex County—was a landscape of dispersed agricultural settlement with farms and farmhouses, as the Reverend Peter Whitney wrote in 1793, "scattered all over the place without much order." Each town had a centrally located meetinghouse and common, but with the exception of Worcester, the shire town, there were only a few tiny villages. Most of that landscape was still in woodlands; in 1781 over three-fourths of it was "unimproved" in the language of the tax assessors. Travelers passed through substantial forested stretches to find patches of land opened for tillage and pasture. Clear views and lines of sight between farmsteads were rare.[4]

Across that landscape farm families shared the patterns and practices of southern New England's mixed agriculture. They grew rye and corn for breadstuffs, cut hay and pastured cattle and sheep, produced salt beef and pork, butter and cheese, and wool and flax to be spun and woven in households. Undergirding this rural economy were the diverse agricultural and domestic arts of men and women and the technologies of rural life—small-scale, low-powered, slow, and heavy, as pioneering rural ethnographer Francis Underwood described them from the perspective of the late nineteenth century. Transportation proceeded by oxdrawn carts and sleds on exceedingly difficult roads. The tools of agriculture were epitomized by heavy wooden plows and shovels whose working parts were shod with iron. Predominantly part-time artisans

Figure 1.   Illustration. Woodcut. From Samuel Goodrich, *A Pictorial Geography of the World* (Boston, 1840), p. 145. (Old Sturbridge Village.)

worked in small scattered shops, and water-powered grist and saw mills of a few horsepower each dotted the region's streams.[5]

The majority of families lived in a domestic material world organized extensively and casually, one whose boundaries and practices have only recently been explored. Archaeological evidence converges with contemporary descriptions to testify to the roughness of its texture. Housewives tossed broken vessels and trash out the most convenient door or window and threw bones and food scraps into the yard to be picked over by the domestic animals. Few houses boasted grassy lawns or enclosed front yards; their unfenced spaces were trampled and bare or sprouted straggly uncut weeds (fig. 1). Two early nineteenth-century domestic sites excavated by Old Sturbridge Village, the Emerson Bixby and Cheney Lewis houses in the Four Corners neighborhood of Barre, Massachusetts, exemplify this practice; for substantial periods of time after they were built, the soil immediately around the houses consisted of coarse gravel fill and little vegetation.[6]

Families did not share shelter with their livestock, but the outdoor realms of humans and animals were not sharply differentiated. Privies were not only prominently visible but located with obvious functionality. The evidence of a heavily used pathway suggests that the Bixby family probably used a corner of the barn until midcentury. At the Stratton farm and tavern site in Northfield, Massachusetts, the "necessary house" was aligned parallel to the house facing the road and backed right up onto the pig lot. Robert B. Thomas, writer and publisher of *The Farmer's Almanack*, attested that this pattern of placement was widespread; he fulminated against the many farmers who built their outhouses "within the territory of a hog yard, that the swine may root and ruminated and devour the nastiness thereof."[7] Woodpiles were massive, irregular heaps sometimes found near the front or side door of the house. Although abundant stretches of woodland remained, farmhouses were devoid of shade, a cultural consequence of long warfare with the forest.

The houses standing on these slovenly lots were small. The Federal Direct Tax List of 1798—that remarkable and never-since-repeated inventory of the nation's housing stock—disclosed that two-thirds of the houses in Worcester County, Massachusetts, were of a single story. One Worcester County house in four was valued at under $100; many of these, with three to six windows and dimensions of 20-by-24 feet or 20-by-18 feet, were dwellings described by the assessors as "indifferent," "poor and old," "small and mean," "an old poor house," or even "one building 20-by-18 feet called a house." Evidence also strongly suggests that in 1800 the majority of dwellings were unpainted and "dusky with weatherstain." Most farmers allowed clapboards to weather to the uncertain color they usually called "brown."[8]

Similar patterns of organization can be observed indoors as well. One of the best "thick descriptions" we have of late eighteenth-century domestic arrangements in rural New England is Edward Parry's account in his intimate and revealing journal of his sojourn with the Parker household of Sturbridge, Massachusetts, in 1775. Parry, a Royal Navy agent interned in Sturbridge by the suspicious revolutionary government, found a material world that he described as sparse, crowded, unkempt, dirty, and malodorous. His sense of appropriate boundaries and uses of space, as well as his senses, seemed constantly under assault. Parker's house, of a form and size common in the countryside, "was a very miserable one" to Parry's mind. Eleven people shared the dwelling's four ground-floor rooms and "a garrett without any divisions." Heavy work went on in the kitchen. Parker, his wife, and their five small children slept in another room in which the entire household ate meals. A couple of "dirty servant girls," two white laborers, and Parker's "negro man" bedded down in the garret. By the standards of his hosts, Parry was signally honored with "a room solely for my purpose," a small space 7-by-10 feet. The "best room," which Parry observed was used only on "extraordinary occasions," boasted the house's greatest finish; it had a tall case clock, a small corner cupboard, and a floor painted with squares of "Spanish brown and Oker."⁹

Everywhere in the dwelling the needs of agricultural and household processing and storage intruded on space for sleeping or socializing. Parry's private chamber was decorated with all the family's stockings, "sundry Peticoats, Gowns, female shoes," and "the industry of the Family being all the Skains of Yarn, & linnen for the next weaving." Members of the household who slept in the garret had to arrange themselves around the loom and spinning wheels. Most of the time the best room was a repository for what the household was producing, full of "Milk pans, baked apples, and rough dry cloaths." Parry's relief at having his own bed was severely compromised by Parker's insistence that he follow country custom and allow men visiting the house overnight "to partake of my bed and among the rest a journeyman Shoemaker who made shoes for the family."¹⁰

The house was pervaded by the smells of apples, cheese, slightly souring milk, and strongest of all, the "constant perfume" of a "dye Pot filled with chamber lye"—the highly concentrated leavings of the household's chamber pots. There was also the dirt. The Parkers' tablecloth was never clean, the knives and forks were "black and dirty—never Scoured, seldom whetted, and sometimes Washed," and the pewter tankards for drinking cider were encrusted with "the Liquor &c that dryd upon it from time to time."¹¹

It seems fairly clear that the Parker household's way of life was widely shared in the central Massachusetts countryside during the last decades of the eighteenth century and beginning of the nineteenth. Timothy Parker was not a poor farmer but one of Sturbridge's wealthier citizens, a man whose land and possessions ranked him 8 out of 230 taxpayers in the town's tax list of 1781; the Parkers' tall case clock would have markedly distinguished them from the majority of their neighbors. After Parry had visited widely throughout the community— he thought himself nearly "universally acquainted" in the town after a few months—he testified that such was the common standard, the "country mediocrity."[12]

The 1798 tax list shows many artisans and farmers living in roughly built dwellings of two or three rooms, ones that would have made Parker's seem spacious and comfortable. Visiting one such meager habitation in the area a few years after the 1798 assessment, teamster Asa Sheldon noted that "it had two rooms on the base, and was one story in height." There were "two small glass windows in front and a board one in the rear that could be taken down at pleasure." The hearth was "rough stone," and in the center of one room there was a pine post used to support the garret floor; over the years it had been whittled down "almost to a splinter" for fireplace kindling.[13]

In these small and crowded houses families were still very large. Households in central Massachusetts averaged over six people in 1790; women who married in the 1780s could expect to have seven or eight children. There was little sensory separation among individuals. Families in the smallest houses necessarily slept within sight and hearing of each other; the use of a chamber pot, or even parents' sexual intercourse, could not have been concealed. The notion of one's own bed was foreign to most people, and the concept of one's own room even stranger.[14]

A look at a sample of probate inventories that provide us with detailed, if partial, anatomies of central Massachusetts domestic interiors tells us that by the standards of Edward Parry, and later generations, the interiors of houses were bare, sparsely furnished, often dark, and sometimes cold. Families walked at night in darkness between the flickering fire and the "feeble circle of light," as Harriet Beecher Stowe was to describe it, made by "the dim gleam of a solitary tallow candle." Households used candles sparingly. In a group of central Massachusetts inventories taken between 1790 and 1810, over half of the households owned only one or two candlesticks; more than four was rare. A very wealthy family could awe others with a prodigal lighting display of nine or a dozen candles. The visual world created by these small islands of illumination was shadowy at best, making reading and close work difficult at night.[15]

The floors and windows that inventory listers saw were bare and unadorned, for the most part. In 1800 "carpets were then only known in a few families," as the rural New England memoirist Samuel Goodrich recalled. Window coverings were equally rare. In central Massachusetts the majority of houses had no floor coverings and not a single pair of curtains.[16]

Most walls were bare of formal images as well; fewer than one household in ten had a painting, print, or engraving. Only looking glasses shared the walls with occasional broadsides and homemade art, and most houses had no more than one or two. Their rarity made them important objects, prominently placed in the parlor or sitting room.

The furnishings and spatial arrangements of these dwellings permitted slovenliness at a more intimate level. The furnishings and patterns of room use made more than the most superficial washing a rare event. In the farm households of his native Enfield, Massachusetts, wrote Francis Underwood, there was no bathing; each household member would go "down to the 'sink' in the lean-to next the kitchen . . . to wash his face and hands." Even in 1815 in the comfortable household of prominent minister Lyman Beecher in rural Litchfield, Connecticut, all family members washed in the kitchen, using a stone sink and "a couple of basins." With such an exercise being carried out in full view of others, most country folk did not do much more than "washing the face and hands" once or twice a day, usually in cold water.[17]

Within the sea of rural slovenliness there were some families connected to New England's urban commercial and professional elite who lived differently. Parry found one beacon of civilization in Sturbridge, the household of the Harvard-educated minister Joshua Paine. The Paines lived in a domestic world that Parry found reasonably recognizable. There he discovered a comparative abundance of books and furniture and greater facilities for privacy and comfort, "far above the country mediocrity." The house, a central chimney lean-to dwelling of two stories and six rooms, was a paragon of civility, "thoroughly built according to the taste of the times." Its grounds were "ornamented and rendered useful" by Sturbridge's first decorative plantings of fruit trees and flowering bushes. Parry found everything "tranquil and regular, neat and clean."[18]

The material world that Parry thought almost intolerable at the time of the Revolution, and which Quincy was still describing four decades later, did not emerge out of total isolation from markets and their attendant streams of goods, or illiteracy and complete separation from the fashions and cultural promptings of Boston and the Atlantic world. Studies of probate inventories suggest that it embodied a standard of living that had been slowly expanding over many decades.

In the late eighteenth century a patient roadside recorder would have registered slow-moving but important flows of goods in and out of every central Massachusetts community and virtually every household. There were streams of goods — butter, cheese, livestock, some hay and grain — going east to Boston and surrounding towns. Central Massachusetts farmers were sufficiently attuned to the distant markets for these commodities that the prices for goods traded in their account books had already begun to reflect those determined in the Boston markets. There was also a contrary flow, "assortments for the country trade," returning in a westerly direction by the same conveyances. These goods were not enormous in quantity but were vitally important to the consumption standards rural households had adopted: sugar and tea, tobacco, rum, spices, teapots, teacups, sugar bowls, individual sets of cutlery and crockery, window glass, and a few accoutrements of fashionable dress.[19]

Weighed against the domestic environments of an even earlier America, the houses of central Massachusetts would have in some ways been fairly impressive. Between 1790 and 1810 most had enough chairs for family members to sit down to meals or to offer seats to visitors; three-fourths of the inventories from this period list at least half a dozen chairs, and the average was nine. All twelve members of Timothy Parker's household, for example, could sit around the table. Although they usually ate salted meat boiled with vegetables "brought to the table in a single pot," they dined with individual plates, drinking vessels, and utensils. Such goods, once the trappings of luxury in colonial America, had gradually become widespread in their consumption or ownership.

This provincial countryside was a place where material standards were not only rising but considerably in advance of those in many parts of rural Europe. To the eyes, noses, and minds of more cultivated observers it was disorganized, loose, and painfully coarse, lacking regularity and indifferent to neatness, order, and finish. Such was "the Country life, to which I was unaccustomed," Parry wrote.[20]

Parry was a reasonably cultivated Englishman who found his New England jailer-hosts' political views as irregular and disheveled as their domestic environments. Yet there also seems to have been an awakening sense among members of New England's political and cultural elite — men whose houses, domestic arrangements, and habits of sanitation were akin to those of Parry and Joshua Paine — that rural

slovenliness was now shameful. Even as the elite might praise farmers
for their sturdy independence and instinctive political wisdom or deni-
grate their ignorance, depending on electoral results, the "select" shared
with Parry a distaste for country mediocrity.

Among the select was clergyman and president of Yale University
Timothy Dwight, one of the most articulate observers of New England's
landscape at the end of the eighteenth century. Dwight turned a sharply
categorical moral analysis on rural slovenliness. To his eye the domestic
landscape was an outward and visible sign of moral character, civil society, and the possibilities of greater prosperity. Dwight preferred to think
of New England's rural landscape as typified by the street villages,
painted houses, and neat dooryards of the prosperous families of the agri-
culturally wealthy lower Connecticut Valley; he was uneasy with much
of what he encountered elsewhere in the region. Small brown dwellings
with barren homelots, scattered refuse, and prominent privies were what
he came to see as "uncouth, mean, ragged, dirty houses" and the objec-
tive correlative of "coarse, groveling manners." Families living in such
shabby malodorous dwellings were too likely to ignore the regularities
"from which the chief enjoyments of society spring." Another index of
the lack of regularity, a clue to the presence of coarse, groveling manners, might have been a demographic one. The incidence of premarital
pregnancy was at its peak in late eighteenth-century central Massachusetts, and in some towns as many as one couple in three in the countryside was anticipating wedlock.[21]

In the minds of the elite, traditional patterns for the use of domestic space became profoundly distasteful. Such patterns were not just old-
fashioned or rustic but filthy and chaotic; they signified not a casual
unconcern for ornament but a lack of control. The naked evidence of
human appropriation and use of space, the far-flung detritus of habitation, was increasingly unacceptable.

Parry simply endured, described, and departed. Dwight hoped for
moral and material improvement. He described a process of emulation
and cultural diffusion. Ordinary folk would be attracted by the self-evident material superiority of cleanliness, symmetry, neatness, and privacy. "The very fact that men see good houses built around them," he
wrote, "will more than almost anything else awaken in them a sense of
superiority in those by whom such houses are inhabited. The same sense
is derived in the same manner from handsomer dress, furniture and

equipage. . . . This I apprehend is the manner in which coarse society is first started toward improvement."[22]

The vision of improvement set out by Dwight was potently expressed in New England's literature of agricultural reform. From the end of the eighteenth century, in addresses delivered before state and county agricultural societies and in Robert B. Thomas's widely read *Farmer's Almanack* and agricultural periodicals like the *New England Farmer*, an array of reformers insistently urged farmers to select better stock and crop varieties, use more manure, build tighter fences and larger barns, keep better accounts, and manage their time, labor, and capital more efficiently. Along with this advice went a thoroughgoing critique of slovenly country ways and exhortations to take on the improved style. The literature ridiculed traditional trash disposal, condemned the siting of farmers' privies as showing "a want of taste, propriety, and decency," argued for an end to "barnlike" houses for farm families, and agitated for dooryards, paint, and neatness and finish everywhere. Slatternly housewives were condemned for dribbling snuff into their butter or letting geese befoul their yards. Lydia Maria Child's *American Frugal Housewife*, dedicated "to those who are not ashamed of economy," was published in 1832 and already in its twelfth edition by 1833. Readers were admonished to value "neatness, tastefulness" as well as "good sense" and to see "the true economy of housekeeping" as the "art of gathering up all the fragments." Along with recipes, Child filled her book with formulas and descriptions for cleaning and scouring.[23]

Country folk heeded this abundantly available advice, or at least acted as if they had. From 1800 to 1840 there was great change. The rural economy of New England, and central Massachusetts in particular, was transformed. In the process its material world was to a large extent made new.

By 1840 the landscape had been strikingly reshaped. Year by year the region's usable agricultural land was extended by clearing and by improvement for cultivation as tillage, hayfields, and pasture. Between 1781 and 1831 the percentage of improved land had more than doubled, from 24 percent to 54 percent. In the most improved towns, pasture land was being pushed up hillsides to steeper and steeper slopes. Travelers and landscape painters described a domesticated agricultural landscape of open sight lines. Almost everywhere farm families could see the lights in their neighbors' windows.[24]

As cleared acreage expanded, total farm output and agricultural productivity rose. The patterns of production on farms and in farm households changed. Central Massachusetts remained a semipastoral region of mixed farming, but its array of crops and its balance between tillage, mowing, and meadow, and oxen, cattle, sheep, and swine, was shifting markedly in the direction of market specialization. Cloth and breadstuffs, once enormously important forms of household production, were leaving the orbit of farm and household as flax cultivation virtually disappeared and the production of wool and rye steadily diminished, replaced by factory-made cottons and woolens and wheat flour from the west. With the steady diminution of wooded land, the area's timber supply had "been reduced more than half" by 1845, and "the price more than doubled."[25]

The pattern of rural settlement was likewise transformed. Commercial/artisanal villages arose around the common and meetinghouse that marked the center of virtually every town; a network of central places of varying size and complexity extended across the countryside. Manufacturing villages grew up on almost every exploitable water-power site, first producing yarn and thread, then cotton and woolen cloth. These were outposts of commerce and small-scale production, settlements of merchants and full-time artisans growing as centers of trade and service for the farming populations, or clusters of transient families drawn from the most marginal rural folk to tend the water-powered, mechanized production of cloth and furniture. The landscape was sprinkled with thousands of "ten footers," small shops in which many of Worcester County's young men worked to make heavy shoes. From a handful in the early 1820s, their numbers had grown to nearly 2,000 in 1832 and over 4,000 by 1837. The county also became a center for agricultural implement and edge-tool production as some country blacksmiths became manufacturers. Thousands of women in farmers' and artisans' households participated in a growing web of outwork: braiding straw, weaving palm-leaf hats, and sewing the upper parts of shoes that men "bottomed."[26]

Goods had trickled into and out of the countryside in the late eighteenth century; in the 1830s they flowed in torrents, moving in heavily loaded horse-drawn wagons over better roads. Butter, cheese, livestock, hay, and oats moved in much larger quantities and on far more complex paths of exchange into the conurbations of eastern Massachusetts and into the new villages — what writer Samuel Goodrich called "home markets in every valley."

Shoes, machine-produced cloth, chairs, plows, axes, scythes, palm-leaf hats, braided straw, and even printed books moved from villages and scattered shops into centralized urban channels of distribution, then out to wider markets, and sometimes back into the countryside that produced them. The stores of country merchants had greatly expanded in size, and their shelves were weighed down with a plenitude of consumer goods: English and American textiles in profusion, plates, bowls, cups and saucers, looking glasses, and toothbrushes.[27]

More restrained, prudential, and calculated ways of childbearing and courtship took shape for the people of the region. Since Timothy Parker's day the birthrate had fallen steadily. The people of central Massachusetts were not only marrying later each decade but had begun to practice conscious family limitation. Patterns of courtship and sexuality shifted as well; the incidence of premarital pregnancy fell steadily, in some communities dipping below 5 percent by 1840.[28]

What also emerged out of the transformation of the rural economy and society was a reshaped domestic environment. Although the great nationwide housing assessment of 1798 was never repeated, it is clear from less complete censuses, settlement maps, and an extensive survey of surviving structures that over the next four decades the people of central Massachusetts built many new dwellings and rebuilt and added on to many existing ones. Two-story houses became more common; a rare dwelling-house map for the town of Shirley, Massachusetts, reveals that their proportion in that community increased from just over one-third in 1798 to well over one-half by 1832. As the size of households decreased, houses became larger, and crowding decreased. With increasing size came the articulation and separation of room functions and the beginnings of the possibility of privacy.[29]

Many rural families made efforts to impose a new order on their domestic surroundings, a deep but largely unspoken shift in the way they saw and treated the spaces immediately around them. Archaeological, architectural, and documentary study of the Bixby site provides the most fully worked-out example of this process, but it was clearly a widespread phenomenon. The detritus-strewn landscapes that Josiah Quincy described became less common. Rural households made boundaries outdoors and defined and separated the functions of spaces around their houses with greater precision. They gradually took up the practice of dumping their refuse in well-defined pits or over boundary walls instead of scattering it broadcast.

Between 1800 and 1840, as pioneer-ethnographer Francis Underwood recounted, households in the central Massachusetts community of Enfield took on "a more general air of neatness in houses, dooryards, and gardens," planted "more ornamental trees," cleaned up their "old straggling heaps of wood," and had them "cut and piled undercover"; an increasing number of farmers were seeing to it that their houses "were painted and in good repair." The houses of the countryside became white rather than brown as rural people used increasingly affordable white lead pigment to create the white-hued villages and country neighborhoods that came to typify the neat and finished landscape of rural New England.[30]

As early as 1807 men in central Massachusetts country villages were undertaking the improvement of the landscape, planting trees in front of their houses, along nearby roads, and on town commons. By the 1830s and 1840s some communities had street improvement and rural improvement societies to plant shade trees along the roads and to encourage their placement around homes. Pliny Freeman's house in Sturbridge had been built in 1812 and for almost three decades had gone without paint or fence. Eventually Freeman decided to participate in the reformation of his domestic landscape. "I was glad to hear," wrote a friend in 1840, "that you had your house painted and a dooryard."[31]

Within doors as well "all this is changed," wrote Newton Hubbard of the central Massachusetts town of Brimfield, reminiscing about the transformation of the rural domestic interior from the vantage point of the mid nineteenth century. Curtains "protect the windows and ornament the house, carpets cover the floors, and stoves are through the house."[32]

The new rural economy made a new material world available, in a quiet domestic revolution. As textiles, carpeting, wallpaper, chairs, and looking glasses became less expensive, families filled the rooms of their houses and embellished bare walls, windows, and floors. As domestic consumers they created a material world of greater abundance and comfort.[33]

We can trace this development in the probate inventories of Worcester and Hampden counties. Every decade the mean number of chairs rose, from just below eleven in 1790–99 to nearly twenty-one in 1830–39. The number of candlesticks and looking glasses doubled, and the proportions of households with oil lamps, clocks, and carpets grew markedly. Cookstoves, sofas, and other cushioned furniture appeared in significant numbers after 1820.

By the mid 1820s central Massachusetts manufacturers were marketing factory-made fancy chairs by the thousands and underselling the local cabinetmakers who made chairs for ordinary folk. By 1840 there were dozens of artisan-turned-entrepreneurs, inventive New England mechanics who adapted water-powered lathes and saws to the production of standardized parts.

With mass-produced chairs selling for 30¢ to 75¢ each, families bought in increasing numbers. Old habits of domestic display thus became democratized; many families of fairly modest wealth could fill a parlor and sitting room with matched sets, as only more prosperous families could have done earlier. This increase also extended the social capacity of the household. Families could entertain larger groups and offer them uniform and genteel seating. Households with eighteen or twenty-four chairs rather than six or ten could entertain not only the minister but the Masonic Lodge, not only the neighbors but a full meeting of the Ladies' Charitable Society.

Nighttime seeing became easier as more households were able to move beyond Stowe's "feeble circle of light." Farm families who continued to make their own candles saw better because they were using more; families owned nearly twice the number by the 1830s. Inventories show oil lamps in village homes after 1810, fueled by the rapidly expanding American whale fisheries. Lamps burned brighter and more evenly than candles. By the 1830s the majority of nonfarming families with a pair or two of lamps were buying lamp oil at stores, continually pressing New England's whaling fleet to supply them with the means for light.

After 1820 central Massachusetts village families began to install cookstoves to replace kitchen fireplaces and accepted the most significant change in the technology, and experience, of domestic heat since the fireplace itself had come into common use in the Middle Ages. By the late 1830s even modest artisans' households were adopting stoves to economize on expensive wood. Farm families, who cut wood from their own lots, were slower to abandon their hearths and brick up their fireplaces but by 1850 had begun to do so.

Cookstoves and then ornamental parlor stoves displaced the traditional functions of the hearth and changed the way an increasing number of families used their houses. Stoves stood near the center of the kitchen, parlor, or sitting room, radiating heat evenly and invisibly, enlarging the room's usable space during the winter.

Carpets became far more common in central Massachusetts parlors. The application of the power loom to their manufacture had brought them within reach, the inventories suggest, of one household out of four or five by 1830. Cushioned furniture appeared for the first time. Along with the sofa, the parlor carpet, adding a soft texture to a previously hard, bare floor, became a crucial symbol of genteel comfort. Window curtains appeared in substantial numbers as well, giving families some visual privacy from passersby on increasingly busy roads; curtains were also part of the house's facade, speaking to those same passersby about the householder's standard of living.

The pianoforte, which had become urban America's most culturally decisive piece of parlor furniture, appeared in the countryside as well. A few central Massachusetts families—less than one in a hundred—were able, as one observer described it, "to beautify the room by so superb an ornament." Its introduction had a powerful effect. "It is impossible to exaggerate the sensation that was produced in the village," remembered one central Massachusetts man, "when that instrument was first heard." Pianofortes, he made clear, were coming to symbolize an expanded range of material and social aspirations even for humble families who would never achieve this ultimate "badge of gentility" for themselves.[34]

Central New England houses became less barren of pictures. Rural New England was crisscrossed by the routes of an expanding number of country limners, itinerant painters who offered their skills in portraiture at varying prices. These artists were primarily engaged in supplying middling and prosperous householders with likenesses of themselves and other family members, while booksellers ran an increasing trade in engravings of heroes and statesmen like John Quincy Adams, Andrew Jackson, or Napoleon Bonaparte. At least one Massachusetts house in four or five had a painting or engraving on its walls by the 1830s, although before the advent of cheap lithographs in the 1840s professionally produced art was still for a minority.[35]

Looking glasses ceased being singular objects; households had two, three, or more. More families were decorating walls with amateur art: family registers, printed or hand-drawn records of marriages, births, and deaths, or schoolgirl-produced "mourning pictures" that memorialized departed family members.

The likeliest place to look for pictorial expression in American households after 1820 was on the dining table or in the cupboard. Another new technology, the transfer printing of images on relatively inexpensive mass-produced English pottery, brought depictions of English, European, and Chinese scenery into thousands of homes that had seen nothing before except small woodcuts and engravings in books. Archaeological investigation has revealed ordinary central Massachusetts households in the 1830s eating off plates bearing select views of "Eashing Park" and "Wilderness of Kent," England; "Batalha, Portugal"; and Verona, Italy.[36]

The presence of a clock in a central Massachusetts household became less a symbol of affluence than of time consciousness. Tall case clocks and clocks with finely finished brass movements remained expensive and relatively rare, but the development of mass-produced clocks with inexpensive wooden works, beginning with Eli Terry's shelf clock in 1806, brought time pieces within reach of a wide range of families. By the 1830s central Massachusetts estate appraisers found clocks in the households of virtually all storekeepers and professional men, two-thirds of the craftsmen, and one-half of the farmers.

Along with greater abundance came the possibility of greater regularity, neatness, and finish in more intimate matters as well. Larger houses and smaller households made for more privacy, and the chamber set of basin, ewer, washstand, and towel began to appear in the furnishings of the household. New spatial arrangements and utensils, and mind-sets, made complete bathing possible.[37]

In these multifarious ways rural slovenliness gave way to improvement. Change was not sudden or uniform, but it was impressive. By the 1830s the remaining pockets of the older rural world—farms with yards "littered with old shoes, dead cats, and broken jugs" and interiors of unpainted houses where "every thing [was] in chaos"—were seen differently in the literature of improvement and criticism. They were the dwelling places not of traditionalists but of the drunken and vicious.[38]

Can we reconstruct any part of this subtle and complex process of cultural transmission that led to rural improvement? One set of clues may lie in the relationship between village and countryside. Villages were engines of economic change and small-scale outposts of urban society in the countryside. Center villages became the first outposts of improvement, nodal points from which new standards were disseminated.[39]

A minister's wife described one encounter around 1820 when she traveled with her husband to pay pastoral calls, leaving her white-painted village to go to the town's farthest outlying neighborhood, the locality of Westwoods, some three miles distant. When at last they arrived in the district she found herself deep in country mediocrity. With a sure eye the minister's wife categorized the exteriors and interiors of the district's homes. The houses were small and brown with low and cracked ceilings and sparsely furnished rooms. Afraid to put down her cloak and bonnet lest they be soiled, she catalogued the deficiencies of their furniture and noted that some houses still had beds in their parlors. Taking tea at a "rickety" table, she observed with fastidious distaste that her hostess poured from a "black earthen" pot and served the ceremonial beverage in "common, coarse" blue-edge cups for "the homeliest tea-drinking in which she had ever participated."[40]

These encounters were jarring for her hosts as well. Such interactions were surely part of the process by which country people took their cues about standards of material life. A genteel visitor's poorly concealed disdain would remind country families both of their aspirations and the difficulty of achieving them. Farm families went into the villages to trade, worship, vote, and sometimes visit. They saw new furnishings and standards of domesticity and order that became powerful guides to aspiration, just as villages took as their own models the fashionable ways of Worcester, Northampton, and Hartford, or those yet greater central places, Boston, Providence, and New York.[41]

To catch an ordinary country family in the act of moving from country mediocrity to rural improvement, we can look at blacksmith and farmer Emerson Bixby of Barre, Massachusetts, his wife, Laura, and their daughters. Their house, domestic landscape, family life, and rural economy have been exhaustively studied as the Bixby dwelling, built in 1807, has become Old Sturbridge Village's newest exhibit. As it stood in its country neighborhood, in its original architectural configuration with three rooms, unfinished garret, and unpainted clapboards, the Bixby house was an exemplar of country mediocrity. A visitor from the village would have seen a brown house—set in a yard littered with broken dishes and household refuse—with no proper entryway, dark interior colors, painted imitations of baseboards and moldings, and a parental bed prominently displayed in the best room.[42]

In the 1830s the Bixby family began to create a new pattern for their domestic life. They put white paint on the brown clapboards. They began to dump trash in pits. They attached an ell, with shed and dairy room, to the house and changed the traffic pattern so that visitors entered through the ell door and then gained entry to the kitchen. In the early 1840s they continued their domestic revolution, further expanding and redefining their living space and seeking greater separation and privacy. They built two new bedchambers and created a parlor by removing the bed, with its reminders of sleep, undress, and sexuality, from the best room. They painted over their old decorative scheme with a light, fashionable color, but without amplifying the extent and symmetry of the woodwork.[43]

Some changes were in direct imitation of genteel ways. Others were adaptations. The house, for example, never became completely symmetrical. The visitor entryway was an unfinished ell. A factory-woven parlor carpet never appeared, nor did a cookstove, although a fireframe did around midcentury. Although never able to afford an elegant empire-style sofa, they seem to have cut down a bedstead to play that role and upholstered and padded some of their own chairs. Taken as a whole, the Bixbys' achievement was substantial.

The timing of these changes coincided with the coming of age of the Bixby daughters, three young women who added substantially to the family's resources for improvement with their earnings in outwork — braiding straw, making palm-leaf hats, and sewing shoe uppers — and who were a most receptive audience for village fashions. The outwork of wives and daughters in the Massachusetts countryside, maintained a Massachusetts congressman in 1823, was ensuring that "the comforts of the farmer were increased . . . his decaying house was repaired, taste came in with her embellishments."[44]

With painfully accumulated savings and the income provided by a combination of blacksmithing, small-scale dairy farming, and outwork, the family had narrowed the gap of respectability between the Four Corners and the center village. The precise constellation of changes at the Bixby house was unique, but thousands of central Massachusetts families achieved changes in the early and middle decades of the nineteenth century.

The improvers, who looked at all the arrangements of their society in highly moralizing ways, saw the shifts as the simple triumph of decency and right-mindedness and another example of Whig historiography, the celebration of the victorious march of progress. Slovenliness, after all, has had few spokesmen or defenders. Our understanding of the triumph of a new view of "matter out of place," however, needs to go beyond celebration.

Along the paths that have been here sketched out, people of the central New England countryside adopted improving ways. If asked, they surely would have said that they were making these changes to please themselves. In adopting new standards and transforming their living spaces, they were also acknowledging the nature of cultural and economic power in their communities and society. The changes rode in on a tide of economic transformation, which provided ordinary people with new resources and opportunities, and pressed them to adopt new ways of seeing and ordering their own, close-at-hand material world.

Even the severest of critics of the Whig history of domestic life would probably agree that for most New England families material life became indisputably better, cleaner, more comfortable, and probably healthier. The landscape took on a different order, one more orderly in our eyes. There was also a greater abundance of furnishings.

It is a final twist of this story, however, that some instigators of rural improvement began to feel that the process had gotten out of hand. In the literature on agricultural improvement and country life of the 1830s and 1840s, the gentlemen farmers, editors, and ministers who concerned themselves publicly with these issues—the intellectual descendants of Timothy Dwight and Josiah Quincy—were viewing the material achievement of the countryside in a profoundly ambivalent way. That there had been great changes in neatness and finish and substantially increased space and comfort could not be denied. Yet there was considerable unease about what this signified.

Since the late eighteenth century, country folk had replaced many small and mean dwellings with larger ones, but by 1832 the *New England Farmer* was publishing articles maintaining that they had gone too far, that farmers and rural mechanics were building "houses too large for comfort, convenience or beauty." There was now too much emulation throughout the countryside, too much concern with acquiring objects of luxury and convenience. Edward Parry and Timothy Dwight had devoutly wished for emulation of more refined and tasteful ways; in 1830 eminent lawyer and progressive farmer Theodore Sedgwick complained that "our villages, which should glory in pure manners, ape the very silliest fashions of the cities." Country folk were going beyond achieving decency and order. They were striving too much "to be alike, and to appear one as well as another," trying to disguise real differences in wealth and status.[45]

Rural households came under indictment for overconsumption and wasteful expenditure indoors as well. Young country families spent too much on furnishing their houses. Daughters and wives were draining away their fathers' substance in their insistence on expensive furniture and dress. The spinning wheel and loom, female implements that were fast disappearing from central Massachusetts households, became symbols not only of household self-sufficiency but of lost domestic virtue. The wholesome tools of textile production were contrasted with the pianoforte, the artifact of feminine refinement and domestic extravagance *par excellence*, although precious few rural households had one.[46]

What these critics—upper-class men unsettled by a perplexing and powerful transformation—wanted may have been a new version of country mediocrity. It would be cleaner and neater than the old one, to be sure. Unpleasant odors and slovenly front yards would stay banished, and beds would remain decently removed from parlors. Country houses, however, although neat and well finished inside and out, would be appropriately humble in size. There would be no vulgar attempts at ostentation, no ordinary families trying "to appear one as well as another." Within the simply furnished rooms of these dwellings would be wives and daughters plying the spindle and shuttle to make the family's clothes and other textiles, not dreaming of dresses, fancy chairs, cookstoves, and carpets. This discomfort with rural improvement was part of a larger unease. The material orderliness of the new countryside was accompanied by a far more intimate connection with the ways of the city and the marketplace. The old world the critics missed was not one of premarital pregnancies, rum-soaked barn raisings, and foul smells but that of comparatively stable agricultural communities with their household economy, focus on the local community, and habits of deference to established leadership. These too had waned along with rural slovenliness. Elite commentators on rural life, the humbler folk who lived it, and scholars today would probably disagree as to whether the price for improvement had been too high.

----

[1] Josiah Quincy, "An Address Delivered before the Massachusetts Agricultural Society, at the Brighton Cattle Show, October 12, 1819," *Massachusetts Agricultural Journal* 6, no. 1 (January 1820): 5.

[2] James J. F. Deetz, "Ceramics from Plymouth, 1621–1835: The Archaeological Evidence," in *Ceramics in America*, ed. Ian M. G. Quimby (Charlottesville: University Press of Virginia, 1973), pp. 15–40; James J. F. Deetz, *In Small Things Forgotten: The Archaeology of Early American Life* (Garden City, N.J.: Anchor Press/Doubleday, 1977), pp. 125–27; John E. Worrell, "Scars Upon the Earth: Evidence of Dramatic Social Change at the Stratton Tavern," in *Proceedings of the Conference on Northeastern Archaeology*, ed. James A. Moore (Amherst: University of Massachusetts Press, 1980), pp. 133–45; Stephen A. Mrozowski, "Prospect and Perspective on an Archaeology of the Household," *Man in the Northeast* 27, no. 1 (1983): 27–38; Mary C. Beaudry, "Archaeology and the Historical Household," *Man in the Northeast* 28, no. 1 (1984): 27–38; Geoffrey Moran, Edward Zimmer, and Anne Yentsch, "Trash Disposal Patterns," in *Archaeological Investigations at the Narbonne House, Salem Maritime National Historic Site, Massachusetts*, Cultural Resources Management Studies, no. 6 (Boston: Massachusetts Historical Commission, 1982), pp. 163–86.

[3] Dell Upton has distinguished between two emerging forms of urban landscape, the "neat" and the "messy," in early nineteenth-century America in his "Another City: The Urban Cultural Landscape in the Early Republic," elsewhere in this volume.

[4] Peter Whitney, *History of the County of Worcester . . .* (Worcester, Mass.: Isaiah Thomas, 1793), p. 160; Joseph S. Wood, "Elaboration of a Settlement System: The New England Village in the Federal Period," *Journal of Historical Geography* 10, no. 4 (October 1984): 331–56; Hugh Raup, "The View from John Sanderson's Farm," *Forest History* 10, no. 1 (April 1966): 2–11; Jack Larkin, *The Reshaping of Everyday Life, 1790–1840* (New York: Harper and Row, 1988), pp. 6–9; Richard L. Bushman, "Opening The American Countryside," in *The Transformation of Early American History: Society, Authority, and Ideology*, ed. James A. Henretta, Michael Kammen, and Stanley N. Katz (New York: Alfred A. Knopf, 1991), pp. 239–56.

[5] Andrew Baker and Holly Izard Paterson, "Farmers' Adaptations to Markets in Early Nineteenth-Century Massachusetts," *The Farm*, Proceedings of Dublin Seminar for New England Folklife, vol. 11, ed. Peter Benes (Boston: Boston University, 1988), pp. 95–108; Francis H. Underwood, *Quabbin: The Story of a Small Town with Outlooks on Puritan Life* (1893; reprint, Boston: Northeastern University Press, 1986), pp. 18–26, 96–106, 266–73; Percy Wells Bidwell, "Rural Economy in New England at the Beginning of the Nineteenth Century," *Transactions of the Connecticut Academy of Arts and Sciences* 20 (1918): 241–81; Percy Wells Bidwell, "The Agricultural Revolution in New England," *American Historical Review* 26, no. 4 (December 1921): 683–702; Roger Parks, "Roads in New England, 1790–1840," (Ph.D. diss., Michigan State University, 1964).

[6] Worrell, "Scars Upon the Earth"; David Simmons, Myron O. Stachiw, and John Worrell, "The Total Site Matrix: Periodization of the Architectural and Archaeological Evidence of Emerson Bixby's Homelot, Barre, Massachusetts," in

Practices of Archaeological Stratigraphy, ed. Edward Harris and Marley Brown III (San Diego: Academic Press, 1993), pp. 181–98; John Worrell, "People Lived in Those Houses, and They Recorded Their Personalities in the Dirt" (Paper presented at the conference on New England archaeology, 1983); John Worrell, "Getting from Here to Barre Four Corners; or, Plotting Trajectories through Space and Time" (paper presented at the annual meeting of the Northeastern Anthropological Association, 1988); John Worrell, "Landscape as Artifact: Archaeological Evidences of Artificial Site Formation" (paper presented at the conference on New England archaeology, 1991); David Simmons, "Computers and a Blacksmith: Sorting Out the World of Emerson Bixby" (paper presented at the Microcomputer Applications in Archaeology Symposium, Princeton University, 1986); David Simmons, "Dirt, Documents, and Databases" (paper presented at the annual meeting of the Council for Northeast Historical Archaeology, 1986); David Simmons, "The Emerson Bixby Project: Family, Work, and Community of an Early Nineteenth-Century Blacksmith" (paper presented at the annual meeting of the Society for Historical Archaeology, 1987). The above cited unpublished papers are on file at the Research Department, Old Sturbridge Village (OSV).

[7] Robert B. Thomas, *The Farmer's Almanack for 1826* (Boston: Hill and Andrews, 1825), p. 5.

[8] Michael Steinitz, "Landmark and Shelter: Housing in the Central Massachusetts Uplands in the Eighteenth Century" (Ph.D. diss., Clark University, 1988); Lee Soltow, "Egalitarian America and Its Inegalitarian Housing in the Federal Period," *Social Science History* 9, no. 2 (Spring 1985): 199–213; Schedules for Worcester County, Federal Direct Tax of 1798, microfilm, Research Library, OSV; Larkin, *Reshaping,* pp. 127–32; Underwood, *Quabbin,* pp. 19–20; Samuel G. Goodrich, *Recollections of a Lifetime; or, Men and Things I Have Seen . . . ,* 2 vols. (New York: Miller, Orton, and Mulligan, 1857), 1:70; Myron O. Stachiw, "The Color of Change: The Bixby House and the Social and Economic Transformation of the Household, 1807–1850," in *Paint in America,* ed. Sara Chase and Patricia Weslowski (Boston: Society for New England Antiquities, forthcoming); Jack Larkin, "Center Villages in Rural New England: A Preliminary Report" (1978, Research Dept., OSV); extensive documentation of the painting and appearance of buildings in rural New England is in Historical Landscape File, Research Dept., OSV.

[9] James H. Maguire, "A Critical Edition of Edward Parry's Journal, March 28, 1775, to August 23, 1777" (Ph.D. diss., Indiana University, 1970), pp. 52–53. For similar conditions elsewhere, see *A Journal by Thos. Hughes for His Amusement . . . (1778–1789)* (Cambridge, Eng.: Cambridge University Press, 1947), pp. 24–26; Richard L. Bushman, "High-Style and Vernacular Cultures," in *Colonial British North America: Essays in the New History of the Early Modern Era,* ed. Jack P. Greene and J. R. Pole (Baltimore: Johns Hopkins University Press, 1984), pp. 345–83.

[10] Maguire, "Edward Parry's Journal," pp. 53–54.

[11] Maguire, "Edward Parry's Journal," pp. 53–57.

[12] Maguire, "Edward Parry's Journal," pp. 59, 61–62; Town of Sturbridge Tax List for 1781, Research Library, OSV.

[13] Asa Sheldon, *The Life of Asa Sheldon: Wilmington Farmer* (Woburn, Mass.: E. H. Moody, 1862), p. 23; a rare view of a small New England house is "At Preston, Ct.," in Benjamin H. Coe, *A New Drawing Book of American Scenery* (New York: Saxton and Miles, 1845), p. 8.

[14] Nancy Osterud and John Fulton, "Family Limitation and Age at Marriage: Fertility Decline in Sturbridge, Massachusetts, 1730–1850," *Population Studies* 30,

no. 3 (1977): 481–94; Helena Temkin-Greener and Alan Swedlund, "Fertility Transition in the Connecticut Valley, 1740–1850," *Population Studies* 31, no. 2 (1978): 221–35; David H. Flaherty, *Privacy in Colonial New England* (Charlottesville: University Press of Virginia, 1972), pp. 33–84.

[15] The discussion of central Massachusetts domestic environments in the paragraphs that follow and later in this essay is based on probate inventory studies undertaken at Old Sturbridge Village: probate inventories for the towns of Brimfield, Palmer, Chester, Sturbridge, Shrewsbury, and Barre, Mass., 1790–1850, and a probate inventory sample of Worcester Co. farmers, mechanics, and merchants, 1790–1850. Originals are in Worcester and Hampden Co. courthouses, Worcester and Springfield, Mass. Transcripts and analyses are in Research Dept., OSV. See also Abbott Lowell Cummings, *Rural Household Inventories . . . 1675–1775* (Boston: Society for the Preservation of New England Antiquities, 1964), pp. v–xxi; Edgar DeN. Mayhew and Minor Meyers, Jr., *A Documentary History of American Interiors: From the Colonial Era to 1915* (New York: Charles Scribner's Sons, 1980), pp. 49–125. Harriet Beecher Stowe, *The Pearl of Orr's Island* (1862; reprint, New York: H. L. Burt, 1900), p. 4; Harriet Beecher Stowe, *Poganuc People: Their Loves and Lives* (New York: Fords, Howard, and Hurlbut, 1878), p. 91; Reminiscences of Susan Blunt, Manchester Historic Association, Manchester, N.H., transcript, Research Dept., OSV.

[16] Goodrich, *Recollections*, 1:74; Lydia Howard Sigourney, *A Sketch of Connecticut: Forty Years Since* (Hartford, Conn.: Oliver D. Cook and Sons, 1824), p. 141; Edward Everett Hale, *A New England Boyhood* (New York: Cassell Publishing, 1893), pp. 7–8.

[17] Underwood, *Quabbin*, pp. 18–19; Catherine C. Webb, "Diary 1815–1816," in Emily Noyes Vanderpoel, comp., *Chronicles of a Pioneer School from 1792 to 1833 . . .* , ed. Elizabeth C. Barney Buel (Cambridge: Harvard University Press, 1903), pp. 148–50; Richard L. Bushman and Claudia L. Bushman, "The Early History of Cleanliness in America," *Journal of American History* 74, no. 4 (March 1988): 1213–38; Caroline Fuller Sloat, "No Soap! The Story of Dishwashing in the Bixby Household," (1988, Research Dept., OSV); Larkin, *Reshaping*, pp. 157–66.

[18] Maguire, "Edward Parry's Journal," p. 59; George Davis, *A Historical Sketch of Sturbridge and Southbridge* (West Brookfield, Mass.: O. S. Cooke, 1856), pp. 36–37.

[19] Bettye Hobbs Pruitt, "Self-Sufficiency and the Agricultural Economy of Eighteenth-Century Massachusetts," *William and Mary Quarterly*, 3d ser., 41, no. 3 (July 1984): 333–64; Winifred B. Rothenberg, "The Market and Massachusetts Farmers, 1750–1855," *Journal of Economic History* 41, no. 2 (June 1984): 283–314; Carole Shammas, "The Domestic Environment in Early Modern England and America," *Journal of Social History* 14, no. 1 (Fall 1980): 3–24; Carole Shammas, "Consumer Behavior in Colonial America," *Social Science History* 6, no. 1 (Winter 1982): 67–86; Gloria L. Main and Jackson T. Main, "Economic Growth and the Standard of Living in Southern New England, 1640–1774," *Journal of Economic History* 48, no. 1 (March 1988): 27–46; Lois Green Carr and Lorena S. Walsh, "Inventories and the Analysis of Wealth and Consumption Patterns in St. Mary's County, Maryland, 1658–1777," *Historical Methods* 13, no. 3 (Spring 1980): 81–105.

[20] Maguire, "Edward Parry's Journal," pp. 49–50.

[21] Timothy Dwight, *Travels in New-England and New-York*, ed. Barbara Miller Solomon, 4 vols. (Cambridge: Harvard University Press, Belknap Press, 1969), 2:346–47. See also Dwight, *Travels*, 1:244–46; 2:160–61, 230–33, 239–40, 321–29; Tim-

othy Dwight, *Greenfield Hill: A Poem in Seven Parts* (New York: Childs and Swain, 1794), pp. 42–46 (lines 393–520).

[22] Dwight, *Travels*, 2:346–48.

[23] Lydia Maria Childs, *The American Frugal Housewife* . . . (12th ed.; Boston: Carter and Hendee, 1833), p. 17. Quincy, "An Address Delivered," pp. 1–8, combines strictly agricultural advice with admonitions about order and cleanliness; Robert B. Thomas's *Farmer's Almanack* (Boston) was clearly a vehicle of rural reform from its inception in 1787; those for 1800, 1808, and 1818 have statements on housing, landscape, and sanitation; also see Thomas Fessenden, *New England Farmer* (Boston) for 1823 and 1824. Tamara Plakins Thornton, "Between Generations: Boston Agricultural Reform and the Aging of New England, 1815–1830," *New England Quarterly* 59, no. 2 (June 1986): 189–211, provides an important interpretation of the reformers in the context of New England agricultural and social change, and Tamara Plakins Thornton, *Cultivating Gentlemen: The Meaning of Country Life among the Boston Elite, 1785–1860* (New Haven: Yale University Press, 1990), is an illuminating discussion of the elite's internal world of agricultural change.

[24] The state tax valuations for Worcester Co. towns, 1781–1850, show decade-by-decade increases in the acreage of cleared or "improved" land: state valuation lists, Worcester Co., 1781, 1791, 1801, 1841, 1850, 1860, Massachusetts State Archives; state valuation lists, Worcester Co., 1811–21, American Antiquarian Society, Worcester, Mass. Transcripts and computer files are at Research Dept., OSV. See also Raup, "The View from John Sanderson's Farm"; Michael Bell, "Did New England Go Downhill?" *Geographical Review* 79, no. 4 (October 1989): 450–66; William Cronon, *Changes in the Land: Indians, Colonists, and the Ecology of New England* (New York: Hill and Wang, 1983), pp. 108–70.

[25] Findings on change in landscape, economy, population, and settlement patterns are based on the central Massachusetts towns database, Research Dept., OSV, including town-by-town data for Worcester Co. from the state valuation returns, 1781–1860; population schedules, federal censuses, 1790–1860; schedules of manufactures, federal censuses, 1820, 1840, 1850; agriculture schedules, federal censuses, 1840–50; published federal and state schedules of manufactures, 1832–65; settlement pattern data from the Massachusetts town map series of 1794 and 1831 and the Worcester Co. map of 1857.

[26] Wood, "Elaboration of a Settlement System"; Joseph S. Wood, "The Origins of the New England Village" (Ph.D. diss., Pennsylvania State University, 1978); for manufacturing village development, see Jonathan Prude, *The Coming of Industrial Order: Town and Factory Life in Rural Massachusetts* (Cambridge, Eng.: Cambridge University Press, 1983); Gary Kulik, Roger Parks, and Theodore Z. Penn, eds., *The New England Mill Village, 1790–1860* (Cambridge: MIT Press, 1982); for change in the New England rural economy, see Jack Larkin, "The Merriams of Brookfield: Printing in the Economy and Culture of Rural Massachusetts in the Early Nineteenth Century," *Proceedings of the American Antiquarian Society* 96, pt. 1 (April 1986), pp. 39–73; Andrew H. Baker and Holly Varden Izard, "New England Farmers and the Marketplace, 1780–1865: A Case Study," *Agricultural History* 65, no. 3 (Summer 1991): 27–45; Robert A. Gross, "Agriculture and Society in Thoreau's Concord," *Journal of American History* 69, no. 1 (June 1982): 42–61. On outwork, see Caroline Fuller Sloat, "A Great Help to Many Families: Straw Braiding in Massachusetts before 1825," in *House and Home*, Proceedings of Dublin Seminar for New England Folklife, vol. 13, ed. Peter Benes (Boston: Boston University, 1991), pp. 89–100; Myron O. Stachiw, "Work at Home and for

Hire: Outwork in the Early Nineteenth Century" (1988, Research Dept., OSV); Thomas L. Dublin, "Women's Work and the Family Economy: Textiles and Palm-Leaf Hatmaking in New England, 1830–1850," *Toqueville Review* (1983): 297–316; Thomas Dublin, "Women and Outwork in a Nineteenth-Century New England Town: Fitzwilliam, New Hampshire, 1830–1850," in *The Countryside in the Age of Capitalist Transformation: Essays in the Social History of Rural America*, ed. Steven Hahn and Jonathan Prude (Chapel Hill: University of North Carolina Press, 1985), pp. 71–102.

[27] Caroline Fuller Sloat, "The Center of Local Commerce: The Asa Knight Store of Dummerston, Vermont, 1827–1851," *Vermont History* 53, no. 4 (Fall 1985): 205–20.

[28] Osterud and Fulton, "Family Limitation"; Smith and Hindus, "Premarital Pregnancy in America."

[29] Claire Dempsey and Michael Steinitz, "Settlement and Social Development," and Charlotte Worsham, "Architectural Development," in Claire Dempsey et al., *Historic and Archaeological Resources of Central Massachusetts* (Boston: Massachusetts Historical Commission, 1985), pp. 51–198, 199–270; map of Shirley, Mass., 1832, Massachusetts State Archives.

[30] Underwood, *Quabbin*, pp. 266–67; Larkin, *Reshaping*, pp. 127–32; Stachiw, "The Color of Change"; Historical Landscape File, OSV.

[31] Mary Pease to Pliny Freeman, February 6, 1840, Freeman Family Papers, Research Library, OSV; *History of Bolton, 1738–1938* (Bolton, Mass.: By the town, 1938), p. 70; George F. Daniels, *History of the Town of Oxford* (Oxford, Mass.: By the town, 1892), p. 258; Beaman Papers [West Boylston, Mass.] 1806–7, Worcester Historical Society, Worcester, Mass.; record book, Shrewsbury [Massachusetts] Street Improvement Society, 1840–42, Research Library, OSV.

[32] Newton Hubbard, *The Hubbard Homestead* (Brimfield, Mass., 1895), n.p.

[33] Mayhew and Meyers, *Documentary History*, pp. 49–125.

[34] Underwood, *Quabbin*, pp. 199–206; Larkin, *Reshaping*, pp. 143, 248–51.

[35] David Jaffe, "One of the Primitive Sort: Portrait Painters of the Rural North, 1760–1860," in Hahn and Prude, *Countryside*, pp. 103–38.

[36] Simmons, "Emerson Bixby Project."

[37] See Catharine E. Beecher, *A Treatise on Domestic Economy . . .* (Boston: Marsh, Capen, Lyon, and Webb, 1841), pp. 360–61.

[38] *New England Farmer* 16 (July 1, 1837): 3.

[39] Richard D. Brown, "The Emergence of Urban Society in Rural Massachusetts, 1760–1820," *Journal of American History* 61, no. 4 (June 1974): 29–51; Larkin, "Center Villages"; Jack Larkin, "The Various and Conflicting Interests of the Town: The Neighborhoods of the New England Countryside" (1988, Research Dept., OSV).

[40] Martha Stone Hubbell, *The Shady Side; or, Life in a Country Parsonage* (Boston: J. P. Jewett, 1853), pp. 77–81.

[41] Underwood, *Quabbin*, pp. 194–206, 266–73, provides an account of emulation and cultural diffusion in the central Massachusetts countryside. See also Brown, "Emergence of Urban Society"; Bushman, "High-Style and Vernacular Cultures"; Bushman, "Opening of the Countryside"; Bushman and Bushman, "Early History of Cleanliness"; Larkin, *Reshaping*, pp. 121–48.

[42] Myron O. Stachiw and Nora Pat Small, "Tradition and Transformation: Rural Society and Architectural Change in Nineteenth-Century Central Massachusetts," in *Perspectives in Vernacular Architecture, III*, ed. Thomas Carter and Bernard L. Herman (Columbia: University of Missouri Press, 1989), pp. 135–48.

[43] Abbott Lowell Cummings, "Notes on Furnishing a Small New England Farmhouse," *Old-Time New England* 48, no. 3 (Winter 1958): 65–84, documents a similar process of transformation by the Walkely family of Southington in Hartford Co., Conn.

[44] "On the Manufacture of Straw and Grass Bonnets. No. VII. . . . Remarks of Mr. Baylies of Massachusetts," *New England Farmer* 2, no. 44 (June 11, 1823): 348; Sloat, "A Great Help to Many Families"; Stachiw, "Work at Home and for Hire"; Dublin, "Women and Outwork."

[45] *New England Farmer* 10, no. 37 (March 28, 1832): 292–93; 13, no. 25 (December 31, 1834): 197–98; Theodore Sedgwick, *Address Delivered before the Berkshire Agricultural Society, October 7, 1830* (Pittsfield, Mass.: Phineas Allen and Son, 1830), pp. 3–4.

[46] *New England Farmer* 6, no. 32 (February 29, 1828): 256; 7, no. 13 (October 16, 1829): 101; 17, no. 51 (June 26, 1839): 406; 19, no. 19 (November 11, 1840): 197; 21, no. 2 (July 13, 1842): 13; no. 9 (August 31, 1842): 72.

Marketing and Competitive Innovation
Brands, Marks, and Labels Found on Federal-Period Furniture
Barbara McLean Ward

It has long been recognized that after the Revolution American artisans began to develop a different attitude about marketing the wares they produced. Historian Gary Nash observes that on the eve of the Revolution artisans were vacillating between two forms of economic thought. One, the traditional outlook, emphasized the mutuality of relationships among all members of society, fostered strong bonds among craftsmen at different ranks within each trade, and stressed the community of responsibility within each trade. Challenging this corporate view of the community was a rising laissez-faire ethos that "celebrated entrepreneurial, competitive, and accumulative activity."[1] This entrepreneurial attitude gained ground during the years following the Revolution.

Historians of American decorative arts and United States history generally have recognized a fundamental change in the nature and volume of craft production toward the end of the eighteenth century, but a definition of the underlying change in the attitudes of which these developments are the symptoms has remained elusive. In this article I seek to illuminate some of the basic shifts in thinking that fostered a new breed of entrepreneurial artisan in the federal period through a close examination of the marks, brands, and labels they used on furniture.

Labeled furniture is valued today principally for the information it provides about makers. We may justifiably ask, however, what an individual cabinetmaker's purpose was in marking, branding, or labeling his furniture.

The tradition of marking wares to signify *quality* probably began in France in the thirteenth century. Standards were set for the goldsmiths of Paris in 1260, and in 1275 it was ordered that each city in France have its own distinctive mark. In England, in 1300, during the reign of Edward I, a law was passed introducing the sterling standard; it required that all objects made in silver be of the same alloy as coin: 925 parts per thousand silver and 75 parts per thousand copper. Marks signifying compliance with this standard have varied considerably throughout the history of the practice, but for the most part four have been used: one indicating that the object has been assayed, or tested for purity; one indicating the town where it was assayed; one indicating the maker of the object; and one indicating the year in which the object was made. The charter of the Goldsmiths' Company of London was granted in 1327, and guild members became the official superintendents of their craft. Standard alloys for English pewter were established by statute in 1348; in 1503/4 Parliament passed a law requiring all makers to identify their pewter wares with a distinctive mark registered with the guild. Brass, on the other hand, escaped regulation and is rarely marked. In France beginning in 1743 *ébénistes* (cabinetmakers) were required to stamp their furniture with an initial identifying the wares as the work of officially sanctioned craftsmen. In colonial America sealers of leather and sealers of weights and measures helped to regulate the trades in many towns; however, bread was the only commodity for which town governments are known to have enacted a required marking system. Marks indicated the quality of the flour used so customers could determine the fair price of the bread. American silversmiths and pewterers were not required by law to mark their wares to indicate quality, but most used maker's marks voluntarily. The silversmith's mark was a personal guarantee that the wares were up to the sterling standard. At first both pewterers and silversmiths marked goods with their initials. Gradually pewterers began to use full-name and quality marks that imitated those used on London-made pewter. Silversmiths also gradually adopted full-name marks. During the federal period many silversmiths began to use additional marks that identified the city where they worked.[2]

Figure 1.   Maker's name, on drawer backboard. John Pimm, high chest, Boston, 1720–35. (Winterthur.)

Many of the earliest marked or signed pieces of American furniture bear the initials of their owners rather than those of their makers. Ownership was more important than authorship during the seventeenth and early eighteenth centuries. When we occasionally do find the name of a maker inscribed on an object, it appears that the brand or inscription was a form of communication between shops of specialist artisans. Thus, the well-known Boston caned chairs stamped with the letter *I* were probably marked by the caner so that he could identify the chairs he had caned and receive payment for the proper amount of piecework. Japanned furniture, which required the work of many craftsmen, is often marked several times on the case with the name of the cabinetmaker for whom the object was being decorated. The high chest by John Pimm in the Winterthur collection is known to be Pimm's work because the backboard of each drawer bears his name (fig. 1).[3] Lumber merchants also occasionally inscribed boards with the names of the cabinetmakers for whom the boards were being reserved.

Only a relatively small number of objects made before 1750 are signed, labeled, or branded. When done, it was more for the satisfaction of the maker than for the customer, since most signatures are concealed in places where owners never would see them—the inside backs of chests and high chests and the bottoms and backs of drawers. Many

Figure 2.   Signature on drawer side. Job Coit and Job Coit, Jr., desk-and-book-case, Boston, 1738. (Winterthur.)

objects that bear proud inscriptions declaring the maker's name, and sometimes his place of residence and date of manufacture, appear to be an artisan's first substantial piece of workmanship or pieces that were in some way outstanding when compared to his other works. By signing an object in this way, the maker preserved the fact of authorship for posterity and maintained a degree of psychological ownership of an object's design and workmanship even after it was sold (fig. 2). The Job Coit and Job Coit, Jr., desk-and-bookcase, the earliest dated example of the block-front form made in Boston, may represent the successful solution of an especially difficult design problem, a solution that was a major innovation in the stylistic history of New England furniture.[4] As such, it certainly was worthy of the makers' signatures, which it bears on two of the small drawers of the desk section.

Another example of a cabinetmaker declaring his role in the development of a design is the bombé desk and bookcase dated 1753 and signed by Benjamin Frothingham and D. Sprague of Charlestown, Massachusetts. This is the earliest dated example of the bombé form by an American cabinetmaker, and, by signing his work, Frothingham succeeded in forever attaching his name to the development of this distinctive case shape. Sprague was either Frothingham's journeyman or colleague. Frothingham is an intriguing artisan; he was one of the first members of his craft in the Boston area to recognize the potential of using his own products as a means of advertising his business. Many labeled Frothingham pieces survive, securely establishing his reputation as a design innovator.[5]

After the Revolution, changes in the American economy—opening up of trade barriers between states, institution of tariffs, repayment of war debts, establishment of a national currency, and disruption of prewar trade patterns—encouraged entrepreneurs to invest in many kinds of domestic manufacture. Artisans used the interest earned on money lent to the revolutionary cause and the contacts they had made during military service to establish manufacturing concerns, many of which served markets at a considerable distance from their base of operations. Perhaps the most famous of these artisan-turned-manufacturers is Paul Revere, the silversmith and patriot who began producing sheet copper after the war. Others such as clockmaker Eli Terry and pewterers Thomas Danforth and Thomas Boardman merely committed themselves to widespread distribution of the same goods they had made in smaller quantities before the war.[6]

In the furnituremaking trades, chairmakers in particular had long known of the potential market for their wares in other localities. Even in the early eighteenth century, Boston chairmakers disrupted the markets of their Philadelphia colleagues by shipping cheap ready-made chairs to that city. But, in general, the favored status granted to English imports made it difficult for American furnituremakers to sell their wares in southern ports. The Revolution changed this; while inexpensive English imports began to reenter American ports in significant numbers, they were generally subject to tariffs. With the advent of the federal monetary system in 1792, domestic trade items were able to compete more successfully with foreign imports; the craftsmen-entrepreneurs of cities such as Salem and Boston quickly responded to these new conditions.[7]

Furniture historians are aware that much more branded, labeled, and signed furniture survives from the federal period than from any previous period in our country's history. What I am arguing is that this increase is not due solely to the greater number of surviving objects, although survival is certainly a factor. Rather, it is due to a fundamental change in the attitude of cabinetmakers toward the objects they produced. Faced with renewed competition from imported goods and provided with the prospect of increased markets for their products, they began to recognize the value of identifying themselves with the designs of their furniture and their furniture designs with their businesses. This awareness of an "ownership" of skill embodied in a product even after its manufacture and sale would eventually culminate in the patenting of furniture designs and construction techniques in the first half of the nineteenth century.[8]

That cabinetmakers labeled their furniture *at all* suggests another major shift in the artisan's attitude toward production. When an artisan decided to seek out a printer to make labels or a metalworker to create a brand or cut a stencil, he did so because he was beginning to think about producing his wares in quantity. He also knew that even if he were present at the shop, the sheer volume of furniture that the shop was now producing—attested to by such documents as the inventory of the estate of Jacob Sanderson of Salem, which lists 240 bureau fronts—might make it impossible for him to sign every piece.[9] The texts of extant labels, like the signatures, provide clues to the changing attitude of craftsmen toward their work during the late eighteenth century.

In recent years British scholars have focused attention on the revolution in marketing and consumer behavior that occurred in the final years of the eighteenth century. Josiah Wedgwood used marketing techniques that are well known today, including celebrity (or, in his case, aristocratic) endorsements and the timely issuing of wares celebrating popular public events. George Packwood, a maker of razor strops, catapulted his small enterprise into a large-scale export business through hyperbolic newspaper advertising. American artisans in the more traditional trades were not enamored of these techniques, and research has shown that many who advertised actually produced very little and advertised primarily because they had been unable to obtain public notice any other way. Advertisements placed by these same artisans also announced their departures from town, as many are known to have engaged in their crafts for very short periods of time.[10]

What, then, was the accepted manner of advertising one's wares in the late eighteenth century, and how did practices differ from one city or production center to another? In answering these questions it is helpful to divide the identifying inscriptions, brands, and labels found on federal-period furniture into several groups. Initials branded or painted on pieces of furniture were used primarily as vehicles of communication between producers and retailers and appear primarily on objects made on speculation meant for sale in distant domestic or foreign ports. The cabinetmakers of Newburyport, Salem, and Boston were leaders in this wholesale trade. The manuscript record left by the enterprising brothers Jacob and Elijah Sanderson of Salem provides ample evidence of the extent of their business dealings in this speculative realm. In January 1802 Elijah Sanderson sent nine cases of mahogany furniture "on his own account and Reisk" on board the brigantine *John* bound for the East Indies. The cases contained two secretary-and-bookcases, a "sash-cornered" sideboard, a bureau, two lady's secretaries (with the "heads" packed in the sideboard), and one field bedstead and sacking. Each object was numbered and marked with the branded or painted initials *ES* (fig. 3). This marking system was standard among shippers and consignors, and similar directions appear in the records of a number of Salem merchants. Sanderson directed Captain Gotteshall to sell the furniture "to the beste advantage you Can on your Voyage out Either at the Cape of Good Hope or Isle of France or Else where in the East Indies as you may find best for my Intrest." Thus, the secretary-and-bookcase bearing the label of Nehemiah Adams of Salem that Henry Francis du Pont found in Capetown, South Africa, was hardly an anomaly (figs. 4, 5).[11]

Customs records indicate that Newburyport cabinetmakers engaged in a similar trade. Household furniture appears as part of the cargo consigned on ships bound for the French, British, and Dutch West Indies; the East Indies; "French and European ports on the Atlantic"; "other African ports"; Louisiana and the "British American colonies [Canada]." In late 1810 more than $2,856 worth of furniture was shipped from Newburyport to Africa aboard the bark *Ossipee*; this was the town's largest consignment of furniture as venture cargo up to that date.[12]

Although exotic ports may have offered the highest potential profits to the consignors, during the years of the embargo (1807–9) the

Figure 3.   Initials on back rail. Card table, attributed to Elijah Sanderson, Salem, Mass., ca. 1802. (Museum of Early Southern Decorative Arts, Winston-Salem, N.C.)

Sandersons and their Salem colleagues searched for new domestic markets. In addition to letters written regarding the prospects in Virginia and Carolina ports, the Sanderson manuscripts contain at least two receipts for furniture sold at auction in Baltimore. Shipping furniture, however, was not always as lucrative as its makers hoped it would be. In 1803, for example, the captain of a ship carrying furniture on consignment for the Sandersons reported from Richmond, Virginia, that he could not sell their portion of the cargo there because a ship from New York had recently arrived loaded with furniture that was auctioned at very low prices.[13] This intense competition with artisans from other cities meant that furnituremakers wishing to sell their products beyond the traditional local markets had to anticipate consumer taste and produce wares attractive to customers whom they would never know.

In contrast to the brands and painted initials that are evidence of involvement in impersonal marketing schemes, printed labels often contain messages representing attempts by the cabinetmaker or chairmaker to appeal directly to local customers. Such labels built upon the word-of-mouth advertising that had traditionally brought furnituremakers the bulk of their business. They also assured that satisfied customers could quickly bring to mind the name of the firm that had

Figure 4. Nehemiah Adams, secretary-and-bookcase, Salem, Mass., 1795–98. Mahogany, satinwood; H. 89$\frac{1}{4}$″, W. 67 $\frac{3}{4}$, D. 17$\frac{13}{16}$″. (Winterthur.)

produced a given table, chair, or settee, at a time when warerooms were increasing in size and small manufactories proliferated. Individuals might actually seek out the shop of a particular maker if they were impressed with the furniture he made—furniture they had the opportu-

Figure 5.   Label on back of upper section of the secretary-and-bookcase in figure 4.

nity to see either in the homes of friends or on display in the warerooms of general merchants.

Labels containing information of value to potential customers vary in significant ways. All give the name of the maker or firm and the business location (fig. 6). This kind of minimal information was of value only to a customer or retailer living in another town who would be likely to send an order rather than come to the shop. On the other hand, the label that Joseph Short of Newburyport affixed to a card table of about 1806 (fig. 7) provides detailed information on the exact location of the shop, greatly assisting a customer wanting to make a personal visit. After having the labels printed, Short apparently found the description to be inadequate and went so far as to provide additional handwritten directions. Thus, the label in figure 7 has now been altered to read:

Warranted, Cabinet work of all kinds, Made and sold by, Joseph Short, At his Shop Merrimack-Street, between market-Square and Brown's Wharf, Next below Mr John Boardman's Newburyport.

Figure 6.   Label on underside of top. Joseph Rawson, Sr., card table, Providence, ca. 1800. (Winterthur.)

John Boardman was apparently a successful businessman, thus Short's decision to use Boardman's shop as a convenient landmark for customer's wishing to find Short's place of business. What is important is that Short recognized the need to give potential customers more detailed information about the location of his shop and that to do so he took advantage of another shopkeeper's higher visibility within the community.

Short's label also makes a special appeal to customers desiring custom work by declaring that "ALL orders for Work will be gratefully received and punctually executed." Some makers chose to provide information on their labels about the range of forms they produced, indicating wholesale trade, retail trade, custom work, or the availability of a large assortment of ready-made wares. The label of George Shipley of New York, found on a Rhode Island card table he imported for his cabinet wareroom, emphasizes his role as a retailer with a large assortment of ready-made items on hand.[14]

Less often, labels indicate something of the nature of a cabinetmaker's competition and, more particularly, the reason why the maker's goods were superior to those provided by others. Michael Allison of New

Figure 7.   Label. Joseph Short, card table, Newburyport, Mass., 1806. (Yale University Art Gallery, gift of Benjamin A. Hewitt, in honor of Patricia E. Kane.)

York, for instance, used a simple name and address stamp early in his career but by 1817 employed labels that included a handsome engraving of a large brick building with a sign identifying it as "Allison's Cabinet Warehouse." By 1823 he was using a new label declaring that:

M. ALLISON, CABINET-MAKER, No. 46 & 48 Vesey-Street, Greatful to his friends and the public for past favours, relying on the superior quality of his work for fashion and durability, takes this method to inform them that he has constantly on hand, and constantly making CABINET FURNITURE, SOFAS, MAHOGANY and ROSEWOOD CHAIRS, Of all descriptions, faithfully made of the best materials, which he sells as cheap as any regular Cabinet-Maker in this city. Knowing the deception in work made for Auction, he trusts that if people would examine for themselves, and compare the work and the price, that that business so destructive to all good work, a deceptive to the public, would have an end.[15]

Allison was complaining about men like Jacob and Elijah Sanderson, who made furniture for the export trade. The entrepreneurial spirit that motivated the Sandersons was not universally appreciated. Men like Allison still clung to the belief that the artisan owed something to his client and that the members of his craft had certain basic responsibilities to the public.

The simple act of labeling a piece of furniture implied, in the traditional mode of marking wares established within the metalsmithing trades, that the maker was willing to stand behind his work. It is significant that during the federal period cabinetmakers increasingly declared in their labels that their furniture was "warranted." The presence of this word implies that inferior wares were being presented to the public. It also suggests that maker and customer were no longer personally acquainted with one another and that the patron could not withhold payment if he was not satisfied, as was common with "bespoke" (custom-made) goods. Further, it suggests that without printed evidence the customer had little idea of which cabinetmaker had made his desk, chest, or table. The warranty would be of little use to an owner who lived a thousand miles from the maker and who spoke a different language from that of his supplier, but, that a maker was willing to accept responsibility for the quality of an item he manufactured may have provided the buyer with some assurance.

It is more likely that labels containing warranties—especially when they also include specific information on the location of a particular shop as in the label of Mark Pitman of Salem (fig. 8)—were meant to attract local customers. Michael Allison certainly directed the message in his 1823 label to local buyers. He trusted that under close examination the "superior quality of his work for fashion and durability" would be apparent. It may be significant that many of the labels bearing warranties come from the shops of cabinetmakers who worked in large furniture- producing centers. Those in the craft who were heavily involved in export did not, for the most part, profess to warrant their furniture, and, at least in Salem, cabinetmakers who did warrant their furniture were those who geared their production to local tastes and pocketbooks.

In his analysis of federal-period card tables, Benjamin A. Hewitt identified significant differences in the quality of craftsmanship and sturdiness of construction among tables made in different regions. Areas well known as centers of furniture production for export—Newburyport, Salem, and Boston—produced tables of noticeably light construction

Figure 8.   Label on bottom panel. Mark Pitman, enclosed pier table, Salem, Mass., 1800–1810. (Winterthur.)

that often incorporated scrap wood and thin boards. The Sanderson manuscripts reveal that freight was charged according to bulk rather than weight; it is therefore doubtful that cabinetmakers made light-weight furniture in an effort to save shipping costs. Rather, the overall appearance of furniture from these areas suggests that cabinetmakers who produced furniture for export lavished more attention on facade decoration than they did on durability of construction. These objects were designed to look appealing on the auction block rather than to withstand the scrutiny of discriminating buyers visiting a furniture ware-room. Out of touch with their eventual customers and identified as the makers of objects only by their initials, these artisans were less interested in how long a piece of furniture lasted than they were in how quickly it sold. In contrast to the stunning furniture exported from the town, most documented objects with histories of local ownership in the Salem area are both plain in decoration and conservative in design.[16]

Card tables made in New York, on the other hand, are notable for the variety of shapes in which they were made, their subtle use of attractive matched-grain veneers, and their meticulous quality of construction. Although many New York cabinetmakers produced furniture for export, the city's large population also made it the home of the largest furniture warerooms in the United States, and many cabinetmakers had to import furniture themselves to keep their establishments well stocked. Intense local competition probably explains why New York cabinetmakers took the lead in introducing new table shapes and in devising new mechanisms for opening and closing these convertible pieces of furniture.

Evidence suggests that most furniture made in Philadelphia continued to be custom made. Here, too, there was innovation in the shape of tables produced, yet not to the extent found in New York. Very few Philadelphia cabinetmakers routinely labeled their furniture, and there was no appreciable increase in the practice during these years. Most of the furniture is dark and does not display the contrasting veneers found on objects made in exporting areas.[17]

In Baltimore, like Philadelphia, the lack of labeled furniture may indicate that most cabinetmakers concentrated on custom work. Except for chairmaking, the cabinetmaking trade remained relatively small, and it appears that most furniture made in the city was produced for local consumption. John Shaw, cabinetmaker of Annapolis, however, labeled a large proportion of the objects that he made. Why did Shaw, who worked in a town with no more than twenty-five hundred inhabitants, label furniture when his Baltimore counterparts did not? The answer may lie in Shaw's business goals. Labeling was probably the best way for him to advertise his business and thereby gain the patronage of Baltimore residents who regularly did business in the state's new capital.[18]

After the Revolution competition and the prospect of increased markets for their products caused artisans to produce goods that bore distinctive indications of individual design and creativity. For the first time successful design ideas were standardized and replicated for broad distribution. Customers interested in a certain design were expected to seek out its creator and buy from the individual who had developed a particular interpretation of the prevailing style. Exported wares were expected to compete on the shipper's auction block on the basis of appealing design, and makers consciously produced objects that were distinctive. They also organized their shops to produce these wares efficiently in quantity. Products of skill—goods in the wareroom—now became the commodities that artisans owned. Skill itself, as the outstanding cabinetmakers of New York learned, was not enough to give them economic security. It was this shift from selling skills directly to *patrons* in the custom-work tradition to selling ready-made goods on the shoproom floor to *customers* in a new retail mode that marked the metamorphosis of artisan to manufacturer during the federal period.

This new mentality was not universally applauded, however, nor was it adopted by all producing artisans. When the Sandersons faced financial ruin in 1811, diarist and cleric William Bentley confided to his journal that these men had thrust themselves "from mechanic employments into mercantile affairs, and venturing largely upon credit, and breaking embargo laws, and making promises they had plunged themselves into the greatest evils." These were men who "came into [Salem] to get wealth by other means than the slow gains of its inhabitants."[19] Clearly Bentley disapproved; equally clearly from our historical vantage point, the change was irrevocable. The furniture industry would increasingly be dominated by factory production, and consumer-producer relationships would become increasingly impersonal. Large-scale production required a means of advertising; labels fulfilled this function for the first generation of cabinetmaker- entrepreneurs in the United States and marked the advent of a new mode of communication between furnituremakers and their potential customers.

---

[1] Gary B. Nash, "A Historical Perspective on Early American Artisans," in *The American Craftsman and the European Tradition, 1620–1820*, ed. Francis J. Puig and Michael Conforti (Minneapolis: Minneapolis Institute of Arts, 1989), pp. 1–13; see also Barbara McLean Ward, "Hierarchy and Wealth Distribution in the Boston Goldsmithing Trade," *Essex Institute Historical Collections* 126, no. 3 (July 1990): 129–47.

[2] Goldsmiths' Company of London, *Touching Gold and Silver: Five Hundred Years of Hallmarks* (London: By the company, 1978), pp. 7, 14; Howard Herschel Cotterell, *Old Pewter: Its Makers and Marks* (1929; reprint, Rutland, Vt.: Charles E. Tuttle Co., 1963), pp. 5, 6; Rupert Gentle and Rachel Feild, *English Domestic Brass, 1680–1810, and the History of Its Origins* (New York: E. P. Dutton, 1975), p. 3; F. J. B. Watson, *Louis XVI Furniture* (New York: St. Martin's Press, 1973), pp. 63–65; Richard B. Morris, *Government and Labor in Early America* (1946; reprint, Boston: Northeastern University Press, 1981), pp. 161–63; Louise Conway Belden, *Marks of American Silversmiths in the Ineson-Bissell Collection* (Charlottesville: University Press of Virginia, 1980), pp. 9–23; Martha Gandy Fales, *Early American Silver* (rev. ed.; New York: E. P. Dutton, 1973), pp. 245–48.

[3] Benno M. Forman, *American Seating Furniture, 1630–1730* (New York: W. W. Norton, 1987), pp. 258–67. I am indebted to Nancy E. Richards, who, while preparing a catalogue of New England case furniture in the Winterthur collection, provided me with the Pimm information.

[4] One good example of a hidden signature is that of Brewster Dayton of Stratford, Connecticut, on a high chest in the Winterthur collection. It is only decipherable when all the drawers are removed from the upper section; see Edward S. Cooke, Jr., "Craftsman-Client Relations in the Housatonic Valley, 1720–1800," *Antiques* 125, no. 1 (January 1984): 272–80. For a thorough discussion of the design and construction of the Job Coit desk-and-bookcase, see Margaretta Markle Lovell, "Boston Blockfront Furniture," in *Boston Furniture of the Eighteenth Century* (Charlottesville: University Press of Virginia, 1974), pp. 90–94; Nancy Goyne Evans, "The Genealogy of a Bookcase Desk," in *Winterthur Portfolio 9*, ed. Ian M. G. Quimby (Charlottesville: University Press of Virginia, 1974), pp. 213–22.

[5] Clement E. Conger and Alexandra W. Rollins, *Treasures of State: Fine and Decorative Arts in the Diplomatic Reception Rooms of the U.S. Department of State* (New York: Harry N. Abrams, 1991), pp. 94–95.

[6] Patrick M. Leehey, "Reconstructing Paul Revere: An Overview of His Ancestry, Life, and Work," and Edgard Moreno, "Patriotism and Profit: The Copper Mills at Canton," in *Paul Revere—Artisan, Businessman, and Patriot: The Man Behind the Myth* (Boston: Paul Revere Memorial Association, 1988), pp. 15–39, 95–115; Charles F. Montgomery, *American Furniture: The Federal Period . . .* (New York: Viking Press, 1966), pp. 11–18; Barbara McLean Ward, "Metalwares," in *The Great River: Art and Society of the Connecticut Valley, 1635–1820*, ed. William N. Hosley and Gerald W. R. Ward (Hartford: Wadsworth Atheneum, 1985), pp. 273–78, esp. pp. 276–77.

[7] Boston chairmakers are discussed in Brock Jobe, "The Boston Furniture Industry, 1720–1740," in *Boston Furniture of the Eighteenth Century* (Boston: Colonial Society of Massachusetts, 1974), pp. 3–48, esp. pp. 5–6. For a recent discussion of the economic resurgence in the United States during the 1780s and 1790s and the factors involved—including new federal trade regulations, the Bank of the United States and commercial banks, and government securities speculation in fostering commercial and industrial innovation—see Thomas M. Doerflinger, *A Vigorous Spirit of Enterprise: Merchants and Economic Development in Revolutionary Philadelphia* (Chapel Hill: University of North Carolina Press, 1986), pp. 283–344.

[8] For a discussion of the U.S. Patent Office and criteria used for the granting of furniture patents, see Rodris Roth, "Nineteenth-Century American Patent Furniture," in David A. Hanks, *Innovative Furniture in America from 1800 to the Present* (New York: Horizon Press, 1981), pp. 20–46.

[9] Mabel M. Swan, *Samuel McIntire, Carver, and the Sandersons, Early Salem Cabinet Makers* (Salem, Mass.: Essex Institute, 1934) includes an excerpt from Jacob Sanderson's inventory, on pp. 38–39. In this volume Swan reprinted a number of the bills, receipts, and invoices in the Sanderson Family Papers in the James Duncan Phillips Library, Peabody and Essex Museum, Salem, Mass.

[10] Neil McKendrick, John Brewer, and J. H. Plumb, *The Birth of a Consumer Society: The Commercialization of Eighteenth-Century England* (Bloomington: Indiana University Press, 1982), pp. 99–194; Barbara McLean Ward, " 'The Most Genteel of Any in the Mechanic Way': The American Silversmith,"

in *Silver in American Life: Selections from the Mabel Brady Garvan and Other Collections at Yale University*, ed. Barbara McLean Ward and Gerald W. R. Ward (Boston: David R. Godine, 1979), p. 16.

[11] Sanderson Family Papers, Derby Family Papers, Phillips Library, Peabody and Essex Museum; Charles F. Montgomery, *American Furniture: The Federal Period, 1788–1825* (New York: Viking Press, 1966), pp. 225–26.

[12] Newburyport Customs Records, Peabody and Essex Museum.

[13] Sanderson Family Papers, Peabody and Essex Museum.

[14] Benjamin A. Hewitt, Patricia E. Kane, and Gerald W. R. Ward, *The Work of Many Hands: Card Tables in Federal America, 1790–1820* (New Haven: Yale University Art Gallery, 1982), p. 150.

[15] For illustrations of these and other Michael Allison labels and stencils, see John L. Scherer, *New York Furniture at the New York State Museum* (Alexandria, Va.: Highland House, 1983), pp. 32, 38, 43, 56, 72, 73.

[16] Hewitt, Kane, and Ward, *Work of Many Hands*, pp. 39–54, 55–106; Sanderson Family Papers, Peabody and Essex Museum; Gregory R. Weidman, *Furniture in Maryland, 1740–1940: The Collection of the Maryland Historical Society* (Baltimore: By the society, 1984), p. 71; Dean A. Fales, *Essex County Furniture: Documented Treasures from Local Collections, 1660–1860* (Salem, Mass.: Essex Institute, 1965).

[17] Hewitt, Kane, and Ward, *Work of Many Hands*, pp. 55–106. Although Hewitt suggests that additional study may reveal some card tables attributed to Baltimore makers to be those from Philadelphia, a dearth of labeled examples makes this mere speculation.

[18] Weidman, *Furniture in Maryland*, pp. 44, 70–71, 86; see also William Voss Elder III and Lu Bartlett, *John Shaw: Cabinetmaker of Annapolis* (Baltimore: Baltimore Museum of Art, 1983).

[19] *The Diary of William Bentley, D.D. . . . ,* 4 vols. (1905–; reprint, Gloucester, Mass.: Peter Smith, 1962), 4:51–52.

Changing Consumption Patterns

English Ceramics and the American Market from 1770 to 1840

George L. Miller,
Ann Smart Martin, and
Nancy S. Dickinson

Ceramics available to—and selected by—American consumers changed significantly during the early years of the republic. These changes were the result of a series of technological innovations in the Staffordshire potteries that Josiah Wedgwood capitalized on with his brilliant marketing of creamware. This paper examines the impact that changes in Staffordshire had on the American market as it was trans-

This research was made possible by grants from the National Endowment for the Humanities and Garrow and Associates of Atlanta, Ga. The Department of Archaeological Research, Colonial Williamsburg Foundation, provided matching funds that made the NEH grant possible. The authors thank the department's director, Marley Brown, and interns Jean McFarlane and Donna Sawyers. Many institutions generously granted access to their records: Wedgwood Archives, Barlaston, and Keele University; Spode Archives, Stoke-on-Trent, and Keele University; Minton Archives, Stoke-on-Trent; Stoke-on-Trent City Museum and Art Gallery, Horace Barks Reference Library, Hanley; Stafford Record Office, Stafford; Winterthur; New York Historical Society; Historical Society of Pennsylvania; Smithsonian Insti-

formed from an insignificant dumping ground in the eighteenth century to the prime market for the English ceramic industry in the nineteenth century.

THE RISE OF STAFFORDSHIRE AND THE EXPORT MARKET

Development of the English ceramic industry was influenced by the introduction of three types of imported ware: Chinese porcelain, German salt-glazed stoneware, and Dutch delft. All three were adopted for production in England and influenced the evolution of the white wares for which the Staffordshire industry became famous.

Introduction of Chinese porcelain into England during the sixteenth century inspired a quest to discover the secret of its production. It was not until the 1750s that English potters succeeded in producing a soft-paste version of porcelain. In 1768 William Cookworthy was awarded a patent for the production of a true hard-paste porcelain made with English clay and china stone from Cornwall.[1] Development of the English porcelain industry, however, was overshadowed by the success of Josiah Wedgwood's creamware, which undercut the porcelain market.

In Staffordshire the quest for porcelain and white-firing wares was aided by good local clays and clean-firing coal close at hand. Experimentation by potters led to the adoption of innovations such as calcinated flint, Cornish clays, plaster molds, bisque firing, liquid glazes, and

tution; Hagley Museum and Library; National Archives; Massachusetts Historical Society; Kress Library of Business and Economics, Harvard University; Maryland Historical Society; Morris Library, University of Delaware; Swem Library, College of William and Mary; Alderman Library, University of Virginia; Research Library, Colonial Williamsburg Foundation; Virginia State Archives; Virginia Historical Society. Many friends and colleagues aided the authors: Robert Copeland, Helen Dent, Martin Phillips, Gaye Blake Roberts, Patricia Halfpenny, Kathy Niblett, Deborah Skinner, David Barker, David Furniss, Christine Fife, Margaret Morris, John Smith, Arnold Mountford, Terrence Lockett, Una des Fontaines, John des Fontaines, Audrey Dudson, Arlene Palmer Schwind, Susan Myers, Regina Blaszczyk, Lynne Sussman, Barbara Carson, Cary Carson, Elizabeth Collard, Mary Beaudry, Carl Martin, Suzanne Spencer-Wood, Georgeanna Greer, Barbara Teller, Robert Hunter, Jr., Patricia Samford, Lorena Walsh, Harold Gill, Silas Hurry, Henry Miller, Catherine Hutchins, Neville Thompson, Richard McKinstry, Beatrice Taylor, Karen Stuart, Kathryn Arnold, Steven Pendery, and Thomas Dunning. The authors' apologies to those they have neglected to mention.

salt glazing. Out of these developments emerged white salt-glazed stoneware, which was succeeded by creamware and pearlware. These wares nearly replaced a great variety of imported and domestically produced ceramics by the 1780s.

A major factor in the success of creamware was its creative marketing by Josiah Wedgwood. By selling to the likes of Queen Charlotte of England and Catherine the Great of Russia, Wedgwood elevated creamware to a status that enabled it to compete with porcelain. As a fine enameled-painted ware, it could serve the royal and wealthy families of the world, while undecorated, it was cheap enough for the working classes. Development of creamware, use of transfer printing, innovative marketing by Josiah Wedgwood, and the building of a canal improving transport between Staffordshire and Liverpool soon gave the potteries a commanding position in the world market.[2]

By the end of the eighteenth century, the Staffordshire industry had become dependent on the growing export trade. A petition from the potters to Parliament in 1785 estimated that "not less than five-sixths of the earthenware manufactured in Staffordshire is exported." The major market was the Continent. Wedgwood's correspondence from the 1760s to the 1780s shows his sales expanding into Russia, Spain, the Low Countries, France, Italy, Germany, and Turkey.[3] These were all large, important markets frequently mentioned in his letters. In contrast, references to his wares being sent to America in this period are rare. In one example, Wedgwood, in 1767, did request that his partner Thomas Bentley dump some out-of-style wares on the American market. By the early nineteenth century, however, a shift occurred as European markets were closed to English trade by tariffs. The former North American colonies went from being a marginal market to English potters' most important customer. From 1815 to 1860 the United States absorbed between 40 and 50 percent of the ceramics exported from England—more English ceramics than were being sold in the home market.[4]

These changes can be seen in the ceramics recovered from archaeological sites in the United States. Before the 1770s many types of wares were imported from several countries. Examples include German salt-glazed stoneware, Dutch delft, French faience, Chinese porcelain, Spanish majolica, and a variety of English wares such as combed slip, Buckley, white salt-glazed stoneware, agate, red stoneware, delft, and others. By the 1780s creamware and pearlware were displacing these from the market. From the 1790s to the Civil War, English refined earthenwares constituted the vast majority of table-, tea-, and toiletwares used in the United States.

CHANGES IN DECORATION

Among the most visible changes in ceramics was the type of decoration. Before the 1760s the techniques of painting and enameling with mineral colors in England were primarily confined to porcelains and tin-glazed earthenwares. For centuries the decoration of earthen- and stonewares was primarily limited to the use of clay slips and molding, with clay slips confined to a range of earth colors such as yellow, tan, brown, or black. The Staffordshire potters did not have a tradition of enameling or painting. As creamware began to eliminate delft from the market and cut into the demand for porcelain, some enamelers and painters from those industries migrated to Staffordshire for employment.[5]

Nonetheless, the vast majority of creamware was undecorated. One of the striking characteristics of American archaeological assemblages from the 1770s to the 1790s is the high percentage of undecorated creamware they contain. For example, at Michigan's Fort Michilimackinac, abandoned in 1780, only 2.3 percent of the 3,549 creamware sherds excavated were color decorated.[6]

Creamware enjoyed a high level of popularity at home and abroad from its introduction in the 1760s through the 1780s. Wedgwood's correspondence, however, shows that he was under increasing pressure from the early 1770s to produce a whiter ware; he came up with "pearl white" in 1779. Other potters had produced a whiter ware, called China glaze, by 1775.[7] Modern scholars have renamed both of these products pearlware.

Unlike creamware, pearlware was rarely undecorated. It became one of the most common types of ceramics used from the late 1790s through the 1820s. Archaeologist Ivor Noël Hume has described pearlware as a "forgotten milestone of English ceramic history."[8] It was forgotten because it was overshadowed by a revolution in decoration that accompanied the transition from creamware. As a distinctive innovation, creamware was able to compete successfully with porcelain in prestige, and it set the style for many consumers until the 1780s. Pearlware, on the other hand, was an imitation of Chinese porcelain. Because it was a copy of porcelain, it was unable to exceed it in status. Importation of Chinese porcelain into England was the monopoly of the British East India Company. By the late 1780s the honorable company was in conflict with the London chinamen who traditionally purchased their imported wares at auction. As a result, the company stopped importing porcelain in 1791 with the exception of "private lots" brought in by company officers. The final blow to the importation of Chinese porcelain into England came in 1799, when a customs duty higher than 100 percent was placed on these wares as a revenue measure.[9]

Pearlware filled the niche created by declining exports of Chinese porcelain. Consider the evidence from its development. First, in 1775 potters gained the right to use kaolin clays from Cornwall but could not legally produce porcelain, as Richard Champion retained that right when he renewed Cookworthy's patent. Around the time that kaolin came into use in Staffordshire, several potters developed China glaze, a ware with a blue-tinted glaze that was an excellent visual imitation of Chinese porcelain. In addition, potters decorated most of their painted wares from the mid 1770s to the War of 1812 in a Chinese style (fig. 1). The first underglaze transfer-printed wares, introduced around 1784, were also decorated in patterns borrowed from the Chinese and remained popular until the War of 1812. Willow was one of the Chinese-style patterns introduced in the 1780s and is still in production.[10]

Widespread use of color decoration was the major change that accompanied the introduction of pearlware. Whereas the vast majority of creamware was undecorated, pearlware was almost always decorated. Nearly all of the undecorated refined earthenwares from American sites dating between 1790 and 1830 are creamware; almost all the other wares are decorated. The dominant color of those that are decorated is cobalt blue.

Three factors led to the predominance of cobalt blue on pearlware. First, it is a strong color that can stand the high temperatures necessary for underglaze decoration. Second, Roger Kinnaston set up an air furnace in Cobridge, Staffordshire, in 1772 to refine cobalt for use in the potteries, but because of his drinking problem sold copies of the recipe for preparing cobalt "for trifling sums" of £10 or £12 to gratify his "Bacchanalian propensities."[11] Thus the knowledge of how to prepare the

Figure 1.   Plate, Staffordshire, Eng., 1780–90. Shell-edge pearlware, painted in a Chinese style; Diam. 9½″. (G. L. Miller Collection.)

color became fairly common in Staffordshire in the early 1770s. Finally, cobalt was one of the main colors associated with Chinese porcelain, which was what pearlware copied. The use of cobalt was also facilitated by the migration of skilled "blue painters" from the declining delftware factories, seeking employment in the expanding Staffordshire potteries.

Here again there is a contrast with creamware. The small amount of creamware that was decorated was overglaze decorated, whereas the vast majority of pearlware was underglaze decorated. The impact of cobalt is readily apparent when comparing archaeological assemblages dating from 1770 to 1795 to those from 1810 to 1830. Plain white creamware is by far the most common ceramic type in the earlier period, while blue-decorated wares dominate the later sites.

The revolution in decoration was one of the great changes in eighteenth-century ceramic production and consumption. Almost all assemblages have large quantities of decorated wares after 1795. By this time creamware had become the cheapest refined ceramic available. Its production began to be limited to utilitarian vessels such as bowls, mugs, table plates, and chamber pots. For example, one-fourth of the 8,250 vessels sold in 1825 by the Philadelphia china merchant George M. Coates to five country merchants were plain creamware. However, while less than 5 percent of the cups and saucers were creamware, almost 90 percent of the chamber pots were.[12] In short, creamware was increasingly used for utilitarian vessels that were less involved as vehicles of status display.

One last striking visual change took place in the wares of Staffordshire at the end of the 1820s. In the last chapter of *History of the Staffordshire Potteries* author Simon Shaw states that "very recently" some manufacturers had begun printing in red, brown, and green under the glaze and that "owing to the Blue having become so common, the other is now obtaining a decided preference in most genteel circles."[13] Printed wares in red, brown, green, and purple are common in potters' invoices to the United States from 1829 through the 1840s, and excavated assemblages from 1830 to 1850 are distinctive because of the great variety of colors used to decorate the vessels.

STANDARDIZATION OF THE STAFFORDSHIRE WARES

The changes in decoration just described are a pale reflection of the effects of industry standardization, which began in the eighteenth century. By the 1780s the wares of Staffordshire potters had become standardized products, making it possible to substitute items from one factory for those of another. For example, when Wedgwood did not have enough ceramics on hand to fill orders, he substituted products of his fellow potters.[14]

More than a hundred potteries were operating in Staffordshire from the 1770s through the nineteenth century. No one, not even Wedgwood, had control of the market. Innovations were quickly adopted, and the successes of any potter were soon copied by others. Few patents were taken out. One of the best-known cases of potters following the success of others was the imitation of Wedgwood's cream color (creamware), which he renamed Queen's ware. The market he created soon had others adopting his improvements, and in his own words: "When Mr.

Wedgwood discovered the Art of making Queen's Ware . . . he did not ask for a Patent for this important Discovery. A Patent would have limited its public Utility. Instead of one hundred Manufactories of Queen's Ware, there would have been one." In addition to duplicating one another's wares, potters copied one another's patterns. The best example of this is the willow pattern, introduced around 1790 by Josiah Spode and quickly copied by his competition.[15] A wide range of vessels in willow ware were listed in the Staffordshire potters' 1814 price-fixing list, indicating that it had become a generic pattern by that time.

Success itself was a factor in standardization; yet, it also had a negative aspect. Production capacity grew as potters exported more of their wares, but foreign trade also made them more vulnerable to wars, embargoes, and depressions. During these times production capacity exceeded demand, forcing potters into severe price competition for the remaining market. Such conditions led to a series of price-fixing agreements that attempted to keep prices from falling and prevent destructive price competition.

Staffordshire price-fixing lists have been located for fifteen different years between 1770 and 1873 (fig. 2).[16] These lists formalized the standardization of products by naming vessels and enumerating their sizes, types of decoration, and list prices. Better than 90 percent of the tea-, table-, and toiletwares excavated from American sites from 1790 to 1860 are among the types included in the lists.

More than a hundred potters produced generic wares that competed on the basis of price. Only three or four of the better potters were able to establish brand-name recognition and sell their wares above the price-list levels. Their products became recognized by consumers as Wedgwood, Spode, or Minton wares. These are noticeably absent in American assemblages from before the Civil War. One explanation may be their high cost; letters from Minton's partner John Boyle to a Philadelphia importer in January 1837 described Minton wares as too expensive for the United States market. Boyle stated that Minton's "have not nor had this house ever [had] any agent in the States."[17]

Ceramics listed in the potters' price-fixing agreements ranged from creamware, the cheapest type, to printed wares, the most expensive. Printed wares generally cost three times as much as creamware. Small quantities of English bone china and French porcelain were also imported, and they appear to represent the upper range of what was avail-

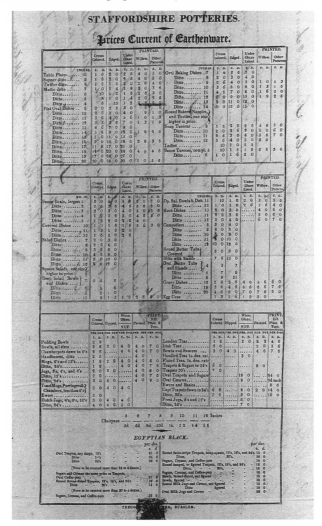

Figure 2.   Staffordshire potteries, broadside, "Prices Current of Earthenware," 1817. (Ferguson, Day, and Successor Company Papers, New-York Historical Society.) This is a revision of the 1814 price list, and on the reverse is a letter from Staffordshire potter J. J. Holden to Day, Downs, and Eastburn of New York, concerning the selling of their products in the American market.

able. Gold-banded French porcelain in the 1830s was almost fifteen times the cost of creamware.[18]

Sets of index values, based on the cost of plain creamware, have been generated from the Staffordshire potters' price-fixing lists and invoices. These index values have been used to analyze numerous excavated assemblages of nineteenth-century ceramics. Almost all of these collections had an average value that ranged from one and one-half to two times the cost of creamware.[19] Thus, all evidence indicates that the American market consumed the cheaper standardized Staffordshire wares.

GROWTH OF THE AMERICAN MARKET FOR ENGLISH CERAMICS

The transition of the United States from an unimportant to a prime market for the Staffordshire pottery industry can also be illustrated by the length of time it took for new wares and patterns to arrive here. Research in account books of ten merchants in the Chesapeake area shows that creamware did not make its appearance in retail stores there until 1768 and did not become common until after 1770. This was at least seven years after Wedgwood began producing the product. The seven-year lag is in stark contrast to the speed with which potters catered to the United States market after the War of 1812. When the revolutionary war hero Marie-Joseph Lafayette visited the United States in 1824, several potters produced patterns with his picture. Lafayette landed in New York on August 16, 1824. A print of this landing was sent to Ralph and James Clews, who promptly had it engraved for printing on tablewares (fig. 3). By December 30, 1824, the Clews brothers were shipping tablewares with the Lafayette pattern to their New York agents, taking fewer than five months to have it ready for the United States market.[20]

A further indication of the changing relationship is the increased amount of correspondence between American merchants and Staffordshire potters. Until the late eighteenth century most ceramics were exported by merchants rather than potters. As some of the more successful potters prospered, they entered into partnerships with merchants and became directly involved in marketing their wares. Wedgwood became a partner of the Liverpool merchant Thomas Bentley, while Spode took on the London merchant William Copeland. Miles Mason, a London

Figure 3.   Ralph Clews and James Clews, *Landing of Gen. La Fayette at Castle Garden, New York, 16 August, 1824,* Staffordshire, Eng., 1824–28. Dark blue transfer-printed platter; L. 15 ½″, W. 12″. (Ellouise Barker Larsen Collection, Division of Ceramics and Glass, National Museum of American History, Smithsonian Institution.)

china merchant, purchased a pottery in Lane Delph in 1799. James Neale, a London merchant, entered into partnership with the Hanley potter Humphrey Palmer in 1778.[21]

Nearly all the documents related to ceramic importation before the revolutionary war are those of general merchants. Direct correspondence with potters did not become common until after 1790, the same time when importers specializing in ceramics also began to appear in the larger cities. A marked increase of potters' correspondence and invoices to the United States occurs following the War of 1812. Part of this may be due to changing customs regulations, which after 1818 required exporters to declare their wares before the United States trade counsel in the country of origin.[22] The Staffordshire potters declared their invoices in Liverpool. It appears that after 1818 they routinely prepared at least three invoices: one to file with the United States counsel, one to accompany the goods, and one to remain with the owner of the wares. Many invoices have survived for the post-1818 period, and they are generally more detailed than those of earlier dates.

The growing importance of the United States market is also indicated by several hundred transfer-printed patterns produced by a number of Staffordshire potters between 1816 and 1840 depicting American heroes, buildings, and ships. Some potters, including William Adams and Enoch Wood, even incorporated the American eagle into their makers' mark. An indication of the strength of the American market for English wares is provided by an 1806 description of the export activities of the Staffordshire potter John Davenport: "Though Mr. D [Davenport] ships immense quantities of Ware to America, very little of his own Manufacture is sent—being too good for the American Market—I am told he keeps a person constantly going amongst The Potteries & purchasing ware for exportation."[23] This suggests that by 1806 Davenport and possibly other potters had already begun to ship wares to the United States on their own account, and that a strong market had developed for the cheaper Staffordshire wares.

Most of the English ceramics imported by American merchants were ordered by correspondence; however, some importers also made buying trips to Staffordshire. When the Baltimore merchant Matthew Smith was setting up his pottery-importing business in 1806, he spent six days in Staffordshire selecting wares from potters in Cobridge, Burslem, Longport, Lane End, Shelton, and Stoke-on-Trent and had difficulty obtaining what he needed. He summed up his frustration as follows: "On Monday, Tuesday & Wednesday we were engaged in ordering what goods I wanted—but from the orders the Potters had on hand, we could get none to undertake to furnish more than 6 or 8 Crates—and were obliged to order a few things at one place and a few things at another, to make something like an assortment. There has been for some time past a great demand for Wares—no Quantity fit for the American Market is on hand—and it is a kind of favor to get Goods for Money."[24]

Throughout most of the nineteenth century, potters had a surplus of wares and were begging for customers, which suggests that Smith began his business during an unusual time. The task of selecting wares became easier after 1815, when potters' agents became more common in the United States. That change, however, would prove to be a mixed blessing since it brought the importers into direct competition with the potters.

THE MARKET FOLLOWING THE WAR OF 1812

Perhaps the most significant change in the way ceramics were supplied to the United States market occurred after the War of 1812. Like most English manufacturers, Staffordshire potters went through difficult times in the early nineteenth century. The Napoleonic Wars, Embargo Act of 1807, and British Orders of Council for 1807 and 1809 all disrupted their trade. During the War of 1812 English merchandise was warehoused in Liverpool, Bermuda, and Halifax in preparation for the reopening of the United States market with the return of peace. Even during hostilities, importers such as Horace Collamore of Boston and Matthew Smith of Baltimore were able to send orders on cartel ships to England for the wares they wanted shipped as soon as the war was over.[25]

As great as postwar demand was, it was not as great as the potters' ability to produce, a situation that led to a surplus of wares. Before 1815 American merchants controlled the types and quantities of wares imported. Following the return of peace the importers ordered what they felt would sell, but much to their irritation found themselves competing with ceramics shipped on consignment by Staffordshire potters.

Large consignments wound up at public auction in Boston, New York, and Philadelphia, where prices sometimes fell below importers' prime costs or to such a low level that the expected margin of profit was reduced. The market for all kinds of English products became glutted, and sales were slow. Jonathan Ogden, a New York importer and commission merchant, wrote to his Liverpool correspondents in June 1816 that he was not able to sell copperas, salt-, iron-, or earthenware. He added that earthenware could not be sold for more than 20 percent of its cost and charges.[26]

These conditions caused importers to protest to the potters. An association of earthenware dealers was established in Boston to take action on the issue. The dealers began by boycotting auctions. When an auction was advertised they would send two members to inform the auctioneer that the dealers would not be attending and would offer to purchase the wares at an advance over the invoice price. If that failed, two members would attend the auction to buy the cheap wares, which were then divided among the dealers.[27] Efforts by the importers to retain control of their market failed partially because the potters' capacity to produce exceeded the market's ability to consume.

Competition for the United States market led English potters to produce a great variety of printed patterns with American views, buildings, and heroes. This campaign seems to have had little success, as these patterns are not commonly found in archaeological assemblages. The limited popularity of these views is suggested in an 1816 letter by the New York merchant Jonathan Ogden, who wrote to his suppliers in Liverpool that "handled cups & saucers will Never never sell in our Market there cannot be a worse article and the same is the case for printed mugs & I never knew General Heads or any National devices in any Article ever to meet a ready sale in any Country."[28] In their zeal to capture the United States market, potters seemed to copy any print with an American subject that fell into their hands. One can only wonder what made the Clews brothers think that people would want to finish their dinner to stare at a platter or plate with a view of a penitentiary in Allegheny, Pennsylvania, or an almshouse in New York (fig. 4).

In addition to borrowing from American prints, potters copied one another's patterns. The Clews brothers wrote to their agent F. Wilby in New York in December 1833 asking him to send a plate of John Ridgway's new pattern if he considered it worth copying. Several letters to Wilby indicated that he collected other potters' patterns that were selling well and shipped them back to Staffordshire to be copied by the Clews brothers.[29] There is a sense of urgency in the Clewses' letters to Wilby, indicating that patterns had to be copied quickly because their popularity was short lived. The Clewses' correspondence to New York indicates that they were bringing out new patterns every year and that, with few exceptions, the same pattern was rarely mentioned for longer than three years.

PRICE COMPETITION AND THE FALL OF CERAMIC PRICES

Competition to supply the market with patterns in the American taste has left an imprint that can be seen in archaeological and museum

Figure 4.   Ralph Clews and James Clews, *Penitentiary in Allegheny, near Pittsburgh*, Staffordshire, Eng., 1832–34. Blue transfer-printed platter; L. 15″, W. 12³/₄″. (Ellouise Barker Larsen Collection, Division of Ceramics and Glass, National Museum of American History, Smithsonian Institution.)

collections. The main battle, however, was waged on the basis of prices and discounts, which have not left the same kind of physical evidence. Information on prices can come only from documents. Fortunately, fifteen different Staffordshire price-fixing lists have survived, providing a base for plotting the rates of discounts given by potters from the 1790s to the 1880s. This information can be used to establish the cost of ceramics to American consumers. These are supplemented with more than two hundred potters' invoices that have discount information, provide a detailed inventory of the wares sold, and give the "list" price for each entry.[30] List prices in the invoices were taken from the various Staffordshire potters' price-fixing lists. At the bottom of the invoices the list prices for wares were summed, and the total was discounted.

Five major types of wares were enumerated in the price-fixing lists, and these account for over 99 percent of the wares in the potters' invoices:

CC   The potters' term for cream color or creamware, which was undecorated and the cheapest type available.

Edged   The potters' term for blue and green shell-edge wares, mostly tablewares such as dishes (platters), plates, twifflers, muffins, sauce boats, and tureens. Edged wares were the cheapest tableware with decoration.

Dipt   A catch-all term applied to wares that were decorated with colored slips. Dipt wares included mocha, common cable, variegated, and other annular types. Dipt wares were mostly mugs, bowls, jugs (pitchers), and chamber pots. They were the cheapest hollowwares available with decoration.

Painted A term most commonly used to refer to underglaze painted vessels, which generally were teaware. (Some of the lists had columns for enameled wares, which were overglaze painted and more expensive.)

Printed The potters' term for transfer-printed wares. Printed wares included tea-, table-, and toiletwares. Generally they were the most expensive wares on the lists.

The list price for CC, edged, dipt, and painted wares remained fairly stable throughout the period under consideration, while that of printed wares dropped slightly after the 1820s. This general stability is shown in figure 5, which plots the combined list prices of forty-eight dozen vessels, one-third of which were CC, edged, and printed wares, against the New York All Commodities Index of Wholesale Prices. Figure 5 suggests that prices for Staffordshire wares were very stable from 1796 to 1859. This stability, however, is an illusion. Figure 6 illustrates the price of the same wares after deducting the potters' discounts and graphically demonstrates an extensive fall in prices. This chart is helpful in understanding the ferocity of competition for the United States market and the speed with which potters were developing new patterns. It also clearly illustrates that for the consumer, ceramics were becoming cheaper from 1810 until 1850.

IMPACT OF LOWER PRICES ON CERAMIC CONSUMPTION

Economists would describe the demand curve for ceramics as elastic: as prices declined, people either consumed more and/or changed the types

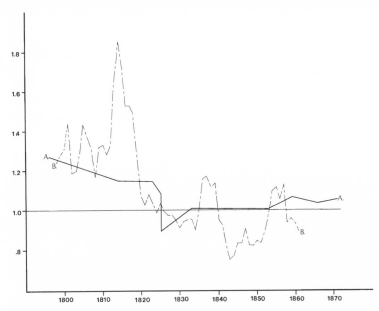

Figure 5.   Net list prices compared to the New York All Commodities Index of Wholesale Prices, both indexed to 1824–42. A= list prices for 48 dozen vessels: 16 dozen creamware, 16 dozen shell-edge, and 16 dozen printed wares for 1796, 1814, 1816, 1817, 1818, 1823, 1825, 1833, 1846, 1853, 1859, 1866, and 1871. From George L. Miller, "A Revised Set of CC Index Values for Classification and Economic Scaling of English Ceramics from 1787 to 1880," *Historical Archaeology* 25, no. 1 (1991): 2. B= New York All Commodities Index of Wholesale Prices. From Arthur Harrison Cole, *Wholesale Commodity Prices in the United States, 1700–1861* (1938; reprint, New York: Johnson Reprint Corp., 1969), pp. 135–36.

of ceramics they purchased. We do not have quantitative studies that can measure changes of per capita consumption for ceramics as prices dropped; however, an analysis of invoices illustrates changes that took place in the types of wares being selected. The primary change from the 1770s to the 1820s was from undecorated creamware to a variety of decorated pearlwares. Most of these changes in comsumption patterns took place following the War of 1812.

    Consider three assemblages of wares sold in 1789, 1806, and 1825 (table 1). The first example is forty-three crates imported by Archibald

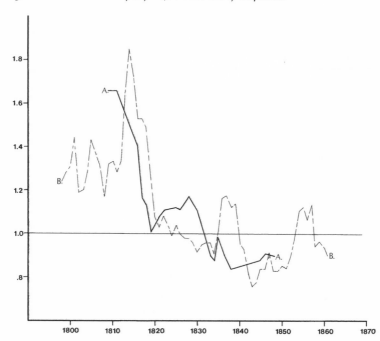

Figure 6.   Wholesale prices of ceramics in Staffordshire compared to the New York All Commodities Index of Wholesale Prices, both indexed to 1824–42. A= wholesale prices for 48 dozen vessels: 16 dozen creamware, 16 dozen shell-edge, and 16 dozen printed wares, 1809–48. From George L. Miller, "A Revised Set of CC Index Values for Classification and Economic Scaling of English Ceramics from 1787 to 1880," *Historical Archaeology* 25, no. 1 (1991): 3. B= New York All Commodities Index of Wholesale Prices. From Arthur Harrison Cole, *Whole-sale Commodity Prices in the United States, 1700–1861* (1938; reprint, New York: Johnson Reprint Corp., 1969), pp. 135–36.

Freeland of Manchester, Virginia, for five country merchants. Those crates contained 32,862 pieces of table- and teaware. An 1806 invoice for fifty crates of ware, containing 26,562 vessels, imported by Hobson and Boulton of New York from the potters John Robinson and Sons, provides the second sample. The third assemblage consisted of 8,250 vessels sold to five country merchants in 1825 by George M. Coates, a Philadelphia earthenware dealer.[31] Almost all of the decorated vessels in the 1789 as-

TABLE 1. Comparison of Plain and Decorated Ware in Three Assemblages

	1789 (%)	1806 (%)	1825 (%)
Plain creamware	71.4	56.1	24.5
Decorated wares	28.6	43.9	75.5

TABLE 2. Comparison of Teaware in Three Assemblages

	1789 (%)	1806 (%)	1825 (%)
Creamware teas	51	42	4.2
Decorated teas	49	58	95.8

TABLE 3. Comparison of Vessel Forms and Sizes Available

	1814		1846	
	Forms	Sizes	Forms	Sizes
CC	39	125	82	147
Edged	18	73	31	108
Printed	24	69	124	259

semblage were teaware. The plates, however, were all undecorated creamware. In the 1806 order shell-edge plates had been added to the creamware, while the 1825 assemblage had creamware, shell-edge, and printed plates. When the cups and saucers for the three assemblages are compared, the contrast is again striking (table 2). The figures demonstrate that as prices declined, consumers upgraded the type of ceramics they purchased to include more decorated wares.

In broad terms, the sequence of replacement for the federal period starts with plain creamware, which begins to be displaced by edged, dipt, and painted wares in the 1780s. These in turn begin to be superseded by printed wares following the War of 1812. By the 1830s printed wares had become the most popular tea- and tableware. As the price of printed wares fell, the variety of vessels and range of sizes increased. Table 3 compares the number of vessel forms and sizes available in different types of wares, as taken from the potters' 1814 and 1846 price-fixing lists. While all three types increased in both the variety of vessels and ranges of sizes available, the most noticeable change was in the availability of printed wares, which increased fivefold from 1814 to 1846. The availability of creamware forms increased twofold.

AVAILABILITY AND CONSTRAINTS ON CONSUMPTION PATTERNS

Tea- and tablewares were separate purchases for most consumers until late in the nineteenth century, when large sets that combined them became common. Initially, the separation of tea drinking from dining was inextricably linked to the introduction of tea from China. Rodris Roth has provided excellent documentation of the tea ceremony in her study of tea drinking in America.[32] There is, however, a side to the story that is missing. Consumers would have had a difficult time matching table- and teawares until the 1830s because of what was available as well as a mind set that separated the two.

The Staffordshire potters' price-fixing lists divide the wares into three basic groupings: table-, tea-, and toiletware. Some lists also have a grouping labeled "mugs and jugs ware," which roughly corresponds to kitchen and tavern wares. Vessels in these broad groupings were made, measured, and generally decorated differently. For example, tableware was press molded or, in the case of some smaller vessels, slip cast. Teaware was wheel thrown, with the exception of some teapots that were press molded or slip cast. Toiletwares were wheel thrown and press molded. Mugs and jugs were for the most part wheel thrown.

The Staffordshire potters also used two different measurement systems to define the sizes of their vessels: one for pressed wares and the other for thrown wares. Tableware and pressed ware were measured in inch sizes. Teaware and other hollowwares were measured by the potters' dozens.

The potters' dozen began as a unit of pay for throwers and other workers. After a vessel was thrown it was placed on a six-foot drying board. A board full of wares of a single size counted as a dozen, although the actual number could range from six one-gallon basins on one board to thirty-six half-pint bowls on another.[33] The size of the former would be "6s," while the latter would be referred to as "36s." Potters' dozens are usually multiples of six; some of the most common sizes were 3s, 6s, 9s,

12s, 18s, 24s, 30s, 36s, 42s, and 48s. Sometimes size numbers were impressed on the bases of hollowwares. These vessels were also priced by the potters' dozen, a practice that further complicates the process of establishing a vessel count and unit price from invoices.

Pressed and thrown vessels were decorated differently because of the technology of their production. By the 1740s plaster-of-paris molds had been introduced into the potteries.[34] This new material led to an increased production of pressed flatwares. The clay was rolled out like pie dough into a flat disk of appropriate thickness and diameter. This was then picked up and draped over a convex mold that formed the inside surface of the plate. The bottom was smoothed by the potter and the excess clay trimmed from the rim. Most plaster-of-paris plate molds from the 1750s to the early nineteenth century had molded decoration that produced raised areas on the inside surface of the vessel. Some of the most common molded patterns include the following:

white salt-glazed stoneware	basket, dot, and diamond; gadroon; and barleycorn patterns
creamware	feather edge; Queen's; royal; and shell-edge patterns
pearlware	shell-edge patterns

These became generic patterns produced by many potters, and each was popular for a period of years between 1750 and 1830 (fig. 7). Plain unmolded plates were uncommon before the 1790s. The molded patterns listed here are almost exclusively used on tableware. Molding on teaware, toiletware, and kitchen wares was limited because of the technology used to produce them. Thus, pressed wares commonly have molding, while thrown wares rarely do. Both round-pressed and thrown wares commonly went through another step of production called turning, which was a factor in the use of molded patterns.

Turning pottery is like turning wood on a lathe. It was a process used to thin the vessel, create foot rings, and give the object a sharper and cleaner profile. Turning was done after the vessel had dried to a leather-hard state. A piece of hollowware, such as a teacup, was slipped onto a conical chuck, and the outside surface was cut away with a metal tool. With a piece of flatware, such as a plate, the vessel was laid face down on a flat bat, and the bottom side was shaped, again with a metal tool. In the process, the plate was thinned, and the foot ring was created.

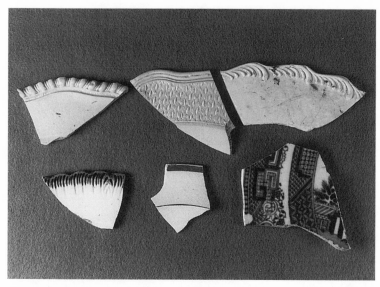

Figure 7.   Common tableware types, Hanley, Staffordshire, Eng., 1750–1840. Top row (*left to right*): gadroon, white salt-glaze stoneware (1750–75); barleycorn, white salt-glaze stoneware (1750–80); feather edge, bisque (1760–90). Bottom row (*left to right*): blue shell edge, pearlware (1780–1840); brown line, creamware (1770–1825); willow pattern, pearlware (1790–1840). The dates are ranges for the types of decoration, and not dates of specific variants illustrated.

Clearly a cup with a molded exterior surface could not be turned. This explains why the great majority of cups found on archaeological sites from the 1750s to the 1830s were thrown, while plates were pressed. It also explains why matching tea- and tableware in that period was almost impossible. This also applies to the other hollowwares that were wheel thrown, such as toiletware, mugs, and jugs.

Tableware of white salt-glazed stoneware with molded surface decoration was at the height of its popularity from the 1750s to the 1770s. Molding was less effective on creamware because the thicker glaze obscured some of the detail. Molding on creamware became confined to the rim, and the emphasis shifted to simple classical vessel forms with smooth unmolded surfaces. Use of molding was further reduced with pearlware, which was almost always color decorated.

Although the surfaces of pearlware were mostly unmolded, except for shell edge, tableware continued to be separated from teaware in types of decoration. Examples of tableware that lacked a teaware counterpart include blue and green shell edge, lined, and willow pattern. (Willow teas do exist; however, they are almost always on whiteware and date from the second half of the nineteenth century.) Brosley, a popular printed oriental landscape pattern, was limited to teaware. The vast majority of pearlware teas were either painted or printed.

In addition to differences between tea- and tableware produced from white-firing clays, there was a continuous production of redware teapots, creamers, and sugars that had no counterpart in tableware or cups and saucers. Along with the tea introduced from China came red stoneware Yi-hsing teapots, which were the source of the English copies. Among the earliest Staffordshire teapots were some made of red stoneware by the Elers brothers in the 1690s.[35] Then came Jackfield teawares, which had a dense, dark red body and a shiny black glaze, and red earthenware teapots with a plain lead or black glaze. Redware teapots have been in continuous production in England from the eighteenth century. (Some connoisseurs claim that they make the best tea.) While one could have a redware teapot, matching cups and saucers or tableware were not available (fig. 8).

Dipt wares are another example of the strong segregation of a decorative type to a limited range of vessel forms. These were generally restricted to hollow forms such as bowls, mugs, jugs, chamber pots, salts, and castors. Dipt wares—slip-decorated refined wares—are common in excavated assemblages dating from the 1780s to the twentieth century (fig. 9).

Consumers today think of ceramics in terms of a "place setting" made up of the table plate, bread plate, and a cup and saucer. This concept is a twentieth-century American marketing device. Until the last quarter of the nineteenth century, table- and teaware were purchased separately. Given the choices available, consumers would have had difficulty assembling matching sets before the 1830s. While it was possible to match a few printed patterns, this was rarely done before the second half of the nineteenth century.

Ceramic purchase patterns from excavated assemblages also provide strong evidence that consumers accepted the separation of tea- and tableware. The most common practice was for consumers to purchase

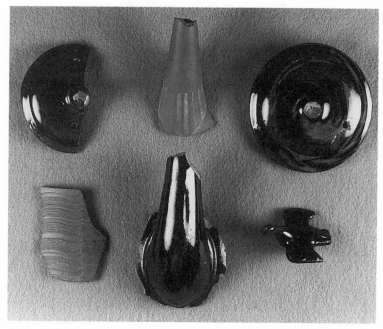

Figure 8.   Common redbodied teaware fragments, Hanley, Staffordshire, Eng.,
1740–1900. Top row (*left to right*): lead-glaze redware teapot lid (1750–1850), red
stoneware teapot spout (1690–1780), agateware teapot lid (1740–75). Bottom row
(*left to right*): engine-turned red stoneware bowl fragment (1763–80), black-glaze
redware teapot spout (1740–1900), bird finial for a Jackfield teapot (1740–80).
The dates are ranges for the types of decoration, and not dates of specific variants
illustrated.

teaware of a higher cost than tableware. William Adams and Sarah Jane
Boling assembled information on expenditure practices from forty-five
archaeological collections dating from the 1790s to the 1850s. The average expenditure on cups and saucers was twice the cost of creamware,
while the average expenditure on plates was only one and two-thirds
times the cost.[36]

Purchase patterns for table- and teaware appear to differ in another
way as well. In the account books of the Philadelphia earthenware dealer
George M. Coates, teas were consistently sold as sets consisting of six
cups and saucers. Tableware, however, was sold by the piece with vary-

Figure 9.   Common dipt ware fragments, Hanley, Burslem, and Cobridge, Staffordshire, Eng., 1775–1880. Top row (*left to right*): blue-spattered pearlware bowl (1775–1800), engine-turned pearlware mug (1790–1830), variegated bisque bowl (1775–1835), cable bisque bowl (1775–1835). Bottom row (*left to right*): variegated pearlware bowl (1775–1835), mocha pearlware mug (1795–1835), variegated pearlware mug (1780–1835), blue-band whiteware mug (1840–1900). The dates are ranges for the types of decoration, and not dates of specific variants illustrated.

ing numbers being purchased at one time. In Coates's account book, only two sets of matched tableware were included among the over 37,000 vessels purchased by five country merchants between 1824 and 1831. Both sets were printed tableware and did not include teas.[37] As the price of printed wares declined, the consumption of matched sets increased. By the 1840s more printed patterns were available in both tea- and tableware. Large matching sets, however, did not become commonly available until the end of the century.

COMPOSITION OF TEA- AND TABLEWARE ASSEMBLAGES

This overview of availability and how it was affected by technology and prices sheds some light on the formation of typical household assemblages of ceramics from the 1770s to the 1850s. One of the most common table assemblages for the last two decades of the eighteenth century consisted of creamware plates, painted pearlware or porcelain teas, and dipt or delft bowls. From the late 1790s blue and green edge plates began to replace creamware as the most popular tableware, holding that position well into the 1820s. Along with them, the householder would most likely have used painted or printed teas and dipt or painted bowls. Beginning in the 1820s printed plates moved into wider use in combination with painted or printed teas. By the 1840s it was common to have both printed tea- and tableware, but usually in different patterns. These combinations would naturally vary for differing economic classes, although by the early nineteenth century edged and painted wares were appearing even in slave and tenant households.[38]

Until now scholars have viewed ceramic replacement sequences in terms of one ware rising in popularity and then falling from grace to be replaced by another. The effects of marketing, prices, technology, and availability on the choices people made have not been taken into consideration. This research is just beginning to shed some light on the process of changing consumption patterns.

In *The Birth of a Consumer Society*, Neil McKendrick, John Brewer, and J. H. Plumb describe a consumer revolution that began in eighteenth-century England.[39] They delineate an expanding world of goods driven by consumer demand and marketing. In this paper we have attempted to describe the impact of that revolution on English ceramics imported to the United States market, the effect of prices on consumption, and the changes that took place as Americans became the prime market for these wares.

THE CERAMICS INFORMATION EXPLOSION

Museums are filled with objects for which the contexts have been lost. Documents, such as probate inventories, account books, and invoices provide contexts, but the objects they describe are seldom extant. Scholars rarely have surviving assemblages of material culture that would enable them to analyze the objects in conjunction with contemporary documents.

Ceramics are an exception. They occupy a unique position in material culture research because of their intrinsic and extrinsic characteristics. Intrinsic characteristics include the facts that they are easily broken, have almost no recycling value after breaking, and survive well in the ground. Extrinsic characteristics include their prices, which reflect the range from cheap functional household wares to costly items of fashion and style. Ceramic usage was almost universal by the mid eighteenth century; practically every household had some type of ceramics. Because they survive so well, hundreds of excavated assemblages have been accumulated from a variety of households in different areas and time periods. No other type of material culture has the combination of attributes that makes ceramics such a rich source for studying the relationship between people and objects.

Research on ceramics from archaeological assemblages has expanded rapidly over the last few decades. Development of the field of historical archaeology, heightened public interest, and new environmental laws have led to the excavation of many sites. Tools available for this research include published chronologies, a price series for ceramics, and a set of index values that are widely used for the study of expenditure patterns from excavated assemblages. This paper provides a broad overview of changing production, distribution, and consumption patterns as a backdrop for future research.

In the near future the amount of information available will enable scholars to examine expenditure patterns of different economic classes and regional tastes in ceramics as well as questions of social emulation, distribution systems, and changes in dining practices. This intersection of objects, documents, and contexts is the information explosion in ceramic research that will give scholars an unparalleled insight into the material culture of early America.

---

[1] English factories are documented in Bernard Watney, *English Blue and White Porcelain of the Eighteenth Century* (New York: Thomas Yoseloff, 1964). The development of hard-paste porcelain is also discussed in Watney, *English Blue and White Porcelain*, p. 119.

[2] Neil McKendrick, "Josiah Wedgwood and the Commercialization of the Potteries," in Neil McKendrick, John Brewer, and J. H. Plumb, *The Birth of a Consumer Society: The Commercialization of Eighteenth-Century England* (Bloomington: Indiana University Press, 1982), pp. 100–145.

[3] John Thomas, *The Rise of the Staffordshire Potteries* (New York: Augustus M. Kelley, 1971), p. 116; Eliza Meteyard, *The Life of Josiah Wedgwood from His Private Correspondence and Family Papers with an Introductory Sketch of the Art of Pottery in England* (London: Hurst and Blackett, 1866), 2:479–83.

[4] Ann Finer and George Savage, eds., *The Selected Letters of Josiah Wedgwood* (London: Cory, Adams, and MacKay, 1965), p. 58; J. Potter, "Atlantic Economy, 1815–1860: The United States and the Industrial Revolution in Britain," in *Studies in the Industrial Revolution Presented to T. S. Ashton*, ed. L. S. Pressnell (London: University of London, Athlone Press, 1960), p. 58.

[5] Finer and Savage, *Selected Letters*, pp. 75–76, 90, 92.

[6] J. Jefferson Miller II and Lyle Stone, *Eighteenth-Century Ceramics from Fort Michilimackinac: A Study in Historical Archaeology* (Washington, D.C.: Smithsonian Institution Press, 1970), p. 111.

[7] George L. Miller, "Origins of Josiah Wedgwood's Pearlware," *Northeast Historical Archaeology* 16 (1988): 80–92.

[8] Ivor Noël Hume, "Pearlware: Forgotten Milestone of English Ceramic History," *Antiques* 95, no. 3 (March 1969): 390–97.

[9] Geoffrey A. Godden, *Mason's China and Ironstone Wares* (Woodbridge, Eng.: Antique Collectors' Club, 1980), pp. 21–25, 29.

[10] Thomas, *Rise of the Staffordshire Potteries*, pp. 33–34; Miller, "Origins of Josiah Wedgwood's Pearlware." Many early printed patterns are illustrated in Robert Copeland, *Spode's Willow Pattern and Other Designs After the Chinese* (New York: Rizzoli, 1980).

[11] Simeon Shaw, *History of the Staffordshire Potteries and the Rise and Progress of the Manufacture of Pottery and Porcelain with Reference to Genuine Specimens . . .* (1829; reprint, Great Neck, N.Y.: Beatrice Weinstock, 1968), p. 211.

[12] George L. Miller, "Prices and Index Values for English Ceramics from 1787 to 1880" (1988, Department of Archaeological Research, Colonial Williamsburg Foundation).

[13] Shaw, *History of the Staffordshire Potteries*, p. 235.

[14] Thomas, *Rise of the Staffordshire Potteries*, pp. 123–24; David Drakard and Paul Holdway, *Spode Printed Ware* (New York: Longman, 1983), p. 4.

[15] Lorna Weatherill, *The Growth of the Pottery Industry in England, 1660–1815* (New York: Garland Publishers, 1986), p. 450; Josiah Wedgwood, "Remarks upon Mr. Champion's Reply to Mr. Wedgwood's Memorial, in Behalf of Himself and the Potters in Staffordshire," in *Papers Relative to Mr. Champion's Application to Parliament, for the Extension of the Term of a Patent* (London, 1775[?]), p. 11 (Baker Library, Harvard University); Copeland, *Spode's Willow Pattern*, p. 32.

[16] A listing of the Staffordshire price-fixing agreements and the locations of surviving copies are provided in Miller, "Prices and Index Values."

[17] Boyle to Alexander Reed of Philadelphia and D. Isaac of Brooklyn, January 3, 1837, items 14 and 15, box 1169, Minton Archives, Stoke-on-Trent, Eng. Boyle had just become a partner with Thomas Minton and was attempting to bring orders from American importers he had dealt with while working for his father, potter Zachariah Boyle.

[18] George L. Miller, "George M. Coates, Pottery Merchant of Philadelphia, 1817–1831," *Winterthur Portfolio* 19, no. 1 (Spring 1984): 48.

[19] George L. Miller, "A Revised Set of CC Index Values for Classification and Economic Scaling of English Ceramics from 1787 to 1880," *Historical Archaeology* 25, no. 1 (1991): 1–25. Several articles measuring ceramic expenditure patterns from a

number of nineteenth-century sites can be found in Suzanne M. Spencer-Wood, ed., *Consumer Choice in Historical Archaeology* (New York: Plenum Press, 1987).

[20] Ann Smart Martin, " 'Fashionable Sugar Dishes, Newest Fashion Ware': The Creamware Revolution in the Eighteenth-Century Chesapeake," in *The Historic Chesapeake: Archaeological Contributions*, ed. Paul Shackel and Barbara J. Little (Washington, D.C.: Smithsonian Institution Press, 1984); Ralph and James Clews to Ogden, Day, and Company, December 30, 1824, Bowen, Osborne Company Letters, 1824–25, and Ferguson, Day, and Successor Company Papers, New-York Historical Society, New York.

[21] Finer and Savage, *Selected Letters*, pp. 11–12; Drakard and Holdway, *Spode Printed Ware*, p. 7; Reginald Haggar and Elizabeth Adams, *Mason Porcelain and Ironstone, 1796–1853* (London: Faber and Faber, 1977), pp. 27–28; Diana Edwards, *Neale Pottery and Porcelain: Its Predecessors and Successor, 1763–1820* (London: Barrie and Jenkins, 1987), pp. 17–23.

[22] Murry announcement, July 6, 1818, dispatches from the United States Counsels in Liverpool, February 1812 to October 24, 1825, microfilm 1814, roll T3, fr. 14, National Archives, Washington, D.C.

[23] Matthew Smith to James Potts, February 1, 1806, Matthew Smith letterbook, 1803–12, vol. 1, Maryland Historical Society, Baltimore. David Arman and Linda Arman, *Historical Staffordshire: An Illustrated Check-List* (Danville, Va.: Arman Enterprises, 1974).

[24] Matthew Smith to James Potts, February 1, 1806, Matthew Smith letterbook, 1803–12.

[25] Norman Sydney Buck, *The Development of the Organisation of Anglo-American Trade, 1800–1850* (1925; reprint, Newton Abby, Eng.: David and Charles, 1969), p. 136; Miller, "Prices and Index Values," p. 25.

[26] Ogden to Bolton, Ogden and Company, Liverpool, June 29, 1816, Jonathan Ogden letterbook, Ferguson, Day, and Successor Company Papers.

[27] Minutes, October 31, November 24, 1817, Association of Earthen Ware Dealers of Boston, 1817–35, Massachusetts Historical Society, Boston.

[28] Ogden to Bolton, Ogden and Company, Liverpool, September 12, 1816, Ogden letterbook, Ferguson, Day, and Successor Company Papers.

[29] Ralph and James Clews to F. Wilby, December 6 and 16, 1833, Ferguson, Day, and Successor Company Papers.

[30] These invoices and the Staffordshire potters' price-fixing agreements and catalogues are inventoried in the appendixes of Miller, "Prices and Index Values."

[31] John Robinson and Sons, invoice, December 12, 1806, Ferguson, Day, and Successor Company Papers. On the dealings of Coates, see 1789 data in record bk. 13 (May–December 1818), U.S. Circuit Court, Eastern District of Virginia, Richmond, microfilm; the figures for 1825 are found in Miller, "Prices and Index Values," app.

[32] Rodris Roth, *Tea Drinking in Eighteenth-Century America: Its Etiquette and Equipage*, United States Museum Bulletin no. 225 (Washington, D.C.: Smithsonian Institution, 1961), pp. 1–30.

[33] Robert Copeland, "Pottery Trade Sizes" (1983; copy, G. L. Miller Collection).

[34] Arnold R. Mountford, *The Illustrated Guide to Staffordshire Salt-Glazed Stoneware* (New York: Praeger Publishers, 1971), p. 30.

[35] George Savage and Harold Newman, *An Illustrated Dictionary of Ceramics* (New York: Van Nostrand Reinholt Co., 1976), p. 107.

[36] Miller, "Classification and Economic Scaling," p. 14; William H. Adams and Sarah Jane Boling, "Status and Ceramics for Planters and Slaves on Three Georgia Coastal Plantations," *Historical Archaeology* 23, no. 1 (1989): 83–84.

[37] George M. Coates account book, Joseph Downs Collection of Manuscripts and Printed Ephemera, Winterthur Library; Miller, "George M. Coates," p. 47.

[38] George L. Miller, "A Tenant Farmer's Tableware: Nineteenth-Century Ceramics from Tabb's Purchase," *Maryland Historical Magazine* 69, no. 2 (Summer 1974): 197–210; see also William H. Adams, ed., *Historical Archaeology of Plantations at Kings Bay, Camden County, Georgia* (Gainesville: University of Florida, 1987).

[39] McKendrick, Brewer, and Plumb, *Birth of a Consumer Society*.

Family Dinners and Social Teas
Ceramics and Domestic Rituals
Diana diZerega Wall

During the half century that followed the Revolution, middle-class Americans changed their taste in the kinds of ceramics they used to set their tables and serve their teas. These new consumer patterns may have been related to developments in the social contexts of meals, which in turn were related to the changing definition of the family and the roles of its members and ultimately to developments in American society itself. In this paper I use archaeological material from New York City to provide a case study for examining trends in household ceramics and placing them in the social contexts of their use.

CERAMIC TABLEWARE AND TEAWARE

To explore the kinds of ceramic tableware and teaware that were used in New York during the federal period, I examined the ceramic vessels

This paper is dedicated to the memory of Bert Salwen, whose determination, foresight, and imagination helped to shape the discipline of historical archaeology into what it is today. The author gratefully acknowledges the insightful comments of many of the participants in this Winterthur conference, particularly those of Nancy S. Dickinson, J. Ritchie Garrison, and George L. Miller. Finally, the author thanks Winterthur's editors, Catherine E. Hutchins and Onie Rollins, for their insight, patience, and tact in dealing with obstreperous authors.

from several archaeological sites in Manhattan. Such collections are important for studying daily life in the past because information gleaned from them complements what we learn through other sources. The dishes that make up traditional museum collections often include a high proportion of seldom-used pieces that were not subject to the breakage of those in everyday use. Households that had "good" sets of dishes, which survived intact to be donated ultimately to a museum, tended to be those of the elite. The ceramics recorded in merchants' records tell us about the wares that particular merchants had to sell at specific points in time. Archaeological collections, on the other hand, consist of dishes that were subjected to everyday use in individual and often identifiable households and may have been acquired from a number of sources over a long period of time. These dishes were broken in the course of use and then discarded, to become part of the archaeological record.

The ceramic vessels in the samples studied here were used for family dinners and social teas in eleven New York households dating from the 1780s to the 1820s. The households were divided into three chronological groups based on the mean ceramic date of the vessels in each assemblage. These dates are derived from the mean date of popularity or manufacture of the different kinds of vessels for which this information is known. The assumption behind this technique is that new ceramic types (or styles) are first introduced, slowly become popular and replace earlier styles, and then gradually fall into disuse, to be replaced in turn by newer styles. Mean ceramic dates are used here to provide a mean date for when the ceramic vessels in a particular assemblage were acquired by a household.[1]

The three chronological groups date to circa 1790, circa 1805, and circa 1820. The early and middle groups each contain materials from four households; the third has only three. Information on the assemblages, including the sites where they were found, their mean ceramic dates, and the occupations of the heads of the households that used the ceramics, is summarized in table 1.

Most of the motifs used to decorate the teaware and tableware in these assemblages fall into four broad groups: minimally decorated white vessels, shell-edge, Chinese landscapes, and floral motifs. Mean percentages of the tableware and teaware decorated with these different motifs for the assemblages in each of the chronological groups are noted

TABLE 1. A Profile of the New York City Sites

Grouping	Assemblage	Deposit	Mean ceramic date	Site	Occupation head of household
Early	test cut J	privy nightsoil	1783	7 Hanover Sq.[1]	artisan
	cobble floor	basement fill	1787	75 Wall St.[2]	artisan
	feature 51	privy nightsoil	1789	175 Water St.[3]	merchant
	feature 49	wooden box fill	1789	175 Water St.	merchant
Middle	feature 48	privy nightsoil	1803	75 Wall St.	druggist
	test cut AX	wooden box fill	1804	Telco Bk.[4]	grocer
	feature 43	privy fill	1804	175 Water St.	merchant or artisan
	test cut AT	privy fill	1810	Telco Bk.	fur merchant
Late	feature 11	privy fill	1818	Sullivan St.[5]	commission merchant
	component 15	cistern fill	1820	Broad Financial Ctr.[6]	boarding-house-keeper or druggist
	feature 9	privy fill	1823	Sullivan St.	physician

[1] Nan A. Rothschild and Arnold Pickman, "The Archaeological Evaluation of the Seven Hanover Square Block: A Final Report," 1990, New York City Landmarks Preservation Commission files; collection at Duncan Strong Museum, Columbia University.

[2] Louis Berger and Associates, "Druggists, Craftsmen, and Merchants of Pearl and Water Streets," 1987, New York City Landmarks Preservation Commission files, collection at South Street Seaport Museum.

[3] Joan H. Geismar, "The Archaeological Investigation of the 175 Water Street Block," 1983, New York City Landmarks Preservation Commission files, collection at South Street Seaport Museum.

[4] Diana Rockman, Wendy Harris, and Jed Levin, "The Archaeological Investigation of the Telco Block, South Street Seaport Historic District, New York, New York," 1983, National Register of Historic Places files, Washington, D.C., collection at Drew University.

[5] Bert Salwen and Rebecca Yamin, "The Archaeology and History of Six Nineteenth-Century Lots: Sullivan Street, Greenwich Village, New York City," 1990, New York City Landmarks Preservation Commission files, collection at Department of Anthropology, New York University.

[6] Joel Grossman, "The Excavation of Augustine Heerman's Warehouse and Associated Seventeenth-Century Dutch West India Company Deposits," 1986, New York City Landmarks Preservation Commission files, collection at South Street Seaport Museum.

in figure 1. The kinds of motifs on the teaware and the tableware are consistently different from each other within each of the chronological groups; the kinds of motifs that were popular for tableware and teaware changed over time as well.

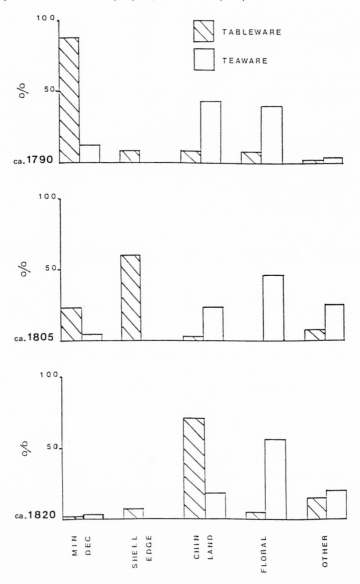

Figure 1.   Mean percentages of tableware and teaware vessels decorated with popular motifs, by chronological group.

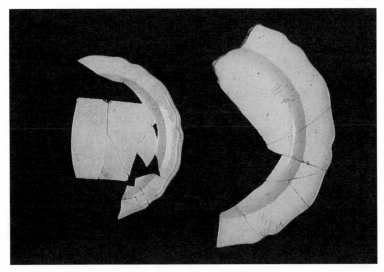

Figure 2. Muffin and twiffler, probably England, 1780s. Creamware, royal pattern; Diam. (muffin) 6⅛″, (twiffler) 8¼″. (South Street Seaport Museum, New York City.)

Most tableware vessels in the early group are minimally decorated. Vessels in the royal pattern predominate in all four households in the early group (fig. 2). The teaware vessels, on the other hand, are evenly represented by those decorated with Chinese landscapes (fig. 3) and floral designs (fig. 4).

For the middle period most tableware vessels in all four assemblages are decorated with blue or green shell-edge motifs (fig. 5). Green predominates in two assemblages and blue in the other two. Each household had minimally decorated vessels as well, but the most popular style was not the royal pattern of the early group but the plain (or Paris) pattern, which is exclusive of any molded decoration at all (fig. 6). The teaware in the households in the middle group shows that floral motifs had become more popular; they predominated over those decorated with Chinese landscapes in three of the four households (figs. 7, 8).

For the later group there is a marked change in the motifs preferred for both tableware and teaware: the majority of the tableware in each assemblage is decorated with Chinese landscapes, whether in hand-

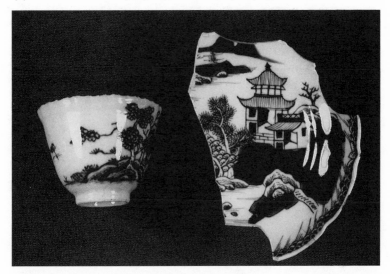

Figure 3.   Teabowl and saucer, probably China, late 18th century. Porcelain, painted; H. (teabowl) 2¼″. (South Street Seaport Museum, New York City.)

Figure 4.   Saucer and teabowl, probably England, late 18th century. Creamware, painted; Diam. (saucer) 5″. (South Street Seaport Museum, New York City.)

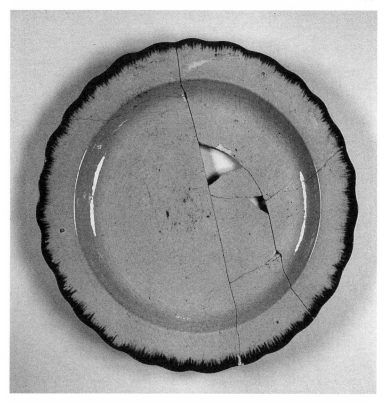

Figure 5.   Muffin, probably England, ca. 1800. Pearlware, shell-edge; Diam. 7¹/₈″. (South Street Seaport Museum, New York City.)

painted Chinese export Canton porcelain or transfer-printed willow-pattern earthenware (figs. 9, 10). The large majority of the teaware is embellished with floral motifs (fig. 11).

STYLE AND SOCIAL CONTEXT

Many archaeologists have studied style as an aid in exploring the definition and maintenance of social boundaries. Considering style as "that part of formal variability in material culture that can be related to the

Figure 6.   Twiffler, probably England, ca. 1810. Creamware, plain (or Paris) pattern; Diam. 8¼". (South Street Seaport Museum, New York City.)

participation of artifacts in processes of information exchange," archaeologists interested in style have focused largely on the study of social boundaries between groups.[2]

Differences in style can also be used to mark various arenas, each with its own social meaning, within the same social group. In addition, changes in style through time can express developments in the social meaning of the context in which an object was used; as the social meaning changes, the style of the object should change as well. Conversely, if we detect differences in style over time, we can infer that the social meaning of the object is changing too.

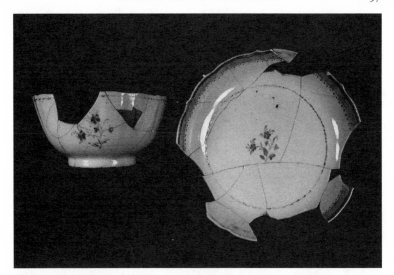

Figure 7. Teabowl and saucer, probably China, ca. 1800. Porcelain, overglaze-painted; H. (teabowl) 2¹/₄″. (South Street Seaport Museum, New York City.)

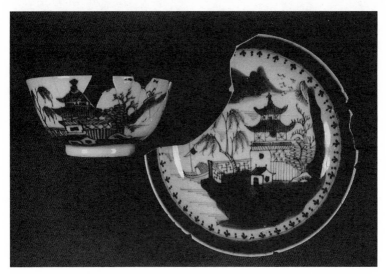

Figure 8. Teabowl and saucer, probably China, ca. 1810. Porcelain, Nanking pattern; Diam. (saucer) 6″. (South Street Seaport Museum, New York City.)

Figure 9.   Plate, probably China, ca. 1820. Porcelain, Canton pattern; Diam. 8½". (South Street Seaport Museum, New York City.)

The kinds of motifs used to embellish the tea- and tableware vessels from the New York City sites suggest that federal New Yorkers used different stylistic motifs to mark the tea ceremony and family meals as social arenas with distinct social meanings. Furthermore, the changes through time in the styles of motifs that were popular for these vessels— from minimally decorated to shell-edge to chinoiserie for tableware, and from chinoiserie to floral motifs for teaware—suggest that the social meaning of each of these meals was changing in the half century after the Revolution. To understand what these changes might mean, we must examine changes in both the social context of ceramic use during

Figure 10. Plate, probably England, ca. 1820. Pearlware, transfer-print, willow pattern; Diam. 9½″. (South Street Seaport Museum, New York City.)

the period of study—changes in family life and the family's place in the larger society—and the contexts of the meals themselves.

NEW YORK CITY AND THE FAMILY

During the federal period New York experienced tremendous physical and economic growth. Its population grew from 33,131 in 1790 to 202,589 in 1830, an increase of more than 600 percent. The city almost tripled in

Figure 11.   Saucer and teacup, England, ca. 1820. Whiteware, transfer-print, geranium pattern; Diam. (saucer) 5 1/2". (Department of Anthropology, New York University.) The pieces are marked "Spode."

size in the same period, with its northern border moving more than two miles to the north, from Chambers Street to 14th Street. This growth was supported by the city's transformation from a provincial colonial city to the economic center of the new nation. In the 1790s New York City became the premier port of the country, and by the mid nineteenth century it was the largest manufacturing center as well.[3]

Most important, the texture of the city's economic life was transformed. Exchange in the colonial period had been dominated by the moral economy, in which transactions, as in Europe in the Middle Ages, were face-to-face between people who knew each other personally. This situation changed during the half century that followed the Revolution; the impersonal relations of the market economy began to prevail in the work lives of most of the city's inhabitants.[4]

The growing dominance of the market economy had ramifications within the city's households as well. For the middle class this period saw the emergence of the form of family that we look on as "traditional" today, with fathers going out to work, older children going off to school, and mothers staying home to run the household and look after younger children.

In the eighteenth century the family life and work life of the city's elite and middle class—its merchants, craftsmen, and shopkeepers— were much more integrated than was the case a century later. Home and workplace were often combined in the same building, under the same roof. Among the middle class, men, women, and children spent much of the day at home, often working together. Men ran their businesses out of their homes, producing goods for market or running their shops in the fronts of their houses. They were also responsible for the moral and physical well-being of family members. Although wives had primary responsibility for running the household and caring for infants, they also helped their husbands in the family trade. When their husbands died, these widows were often able to take over the business. Older children worked at home alongside their parents, with daughters helping mothers with household work and sons helping fathers in the family trade. Boys could live with another family as apprentices, to learn another trade, while girls could also work as household help in other households. Still, the household was a tightly knit corporate unit with most of its members working and living together.

By the middle of the nineteenth century the structure of the elite and middle-class families had changed. There was a stricter division and specialization in the activities of various family members. Home and workplace were no longer combined in the same structure. The men of these families went out to work and were away from home all day. Their primary responsibility was for the economic well-being of the household, a responsibility they fulfilled in the separate, impersonal, morally neutral arena of the marketplace. Older children no longer learned how to be adults solely from their mothers and fathers at home. Rather, they went off to school and were away from home all day as well. Wives and mothers had become the moral, emotional, and physical caretakers of the household, looking after the well-being of household members and society at large. Economically, however, they were totally dependent on their men and stayed at home running the house and looking after small children. This redefinition of the role of middle-class women has been referred to as the "cult of domesticity," and it involved the elaboration of domestic life. The private arena of the home, instead of being a "little commonwealth" (as John Demos called it) or a "microcosm of society" (in Mary Ryan's words) as it had been in the colonial period, had become what Christopher Lasch calls a "haven in [the] heartless world" of the marketplace.[5]

THE SOCIAL CONTEXT OF FAMILY DINNERS AND SOCIAL TEAS

During this period the social contexts of certain meals—particularly the family dinner and the social tea—changed, just as the household was being redefined. Throughout the period, dinner continued to be a relatively private, family meal; it was not an event to which nonfamily members were often invited. Dinner parties were important social events only for elite men.

In the eighteenth century the family dinner both expressed and reinforced the tightly knit, corporate nature of the household. The meal was consumed in the middle of the day and often consisted of a single, one-pot dish, such as soup or stew, which was served with bread. Each family member was served from the communal serving dishes and ate from an individual bowl or plate. More elaborate dinners could consist of a number of dishes served as a single course or as a series of courses.

At this time the table was customarily set in the old English or covered-table plan. The focus was on the food itself rather than on an ornamental centerpiece. The shared serving dishes covered the table in a balanced and symmetrical setting, and none of these served as the visual focal point of the table.[6]

By the mid nineteenth century the new specialization in the roles of family members was expressed in family dinners as well. With most men of the middle class commuting downtown to work, dinner was no longer held in the afternoon but rather was served in the evening. This meal had also gained a new importance. In the eighteenth century, when all family members were together for most of the day, the family dinner had relatively little social significance in daily life. In the nineteenth century, with men and older children away from home all day, the family dinner and other family meals took on a new significance as secular rituals. They had become "constant and familiar reunion[s]" as they were the only daily occasions when all family members were gathered together. They were used to reinforce family ties and the moral values of home life. As Catharine Sedgwick noted in an 1837 novel set in

New York, family meals were "more than the means of sustaining physical wants." They were now "opportunities of improvement and social happiness," as they taught with each enactment the eight lessons of "punctuality, order, neatness, temperance, self-denial, kindness, generosity, and hospitality."[7]

The new importance of family dinner as a secular ritual can be seen in several innovations in the structure and substance of the meal. The meal itself had become more elaborate for most members of the middle class. The one-course, one-dish meals that were popular in the eighteenth century were much less prevalent in the nineteenth century. Nineteenth-century meals were made up of several courses, which were more specialized in their content. Meats and vegetables made up a first main course, pies and puddings a second main course, with dessert forming the last course. The table continued to be set in the old English plan, but an important change was introduced in the 1840s, after the period under discussion here. In the eighteenth century the food itself was the visual focus of the table. The more elaborate the dinner the more completely it covered the table, with no particular dish being selected for special attention. By the middle of the nineteenth century, however, the visual focus of the table was no longer on the food but rather on a functional or ornamental centerpiece. This might be a castor (or condiment stand), a glass dish for serving celery, or even a vase of flowers. The material culture of domesticity had replaced the food as the visual focus of the meal.[8]

By the mid nineteenth century servants were much more common in the homes of the middle class than they had been before, and they did in fact serve at table. The mistress of the house, however, served the soup, the dish that now began the meal, a ceremony that emphasized her role as the family nurturer. Furthermore, the master carved and served what the British anthropologist Mary Douglas has referred to as the "stressed" dish in these dinners—the meat. This act stressed his role as the provider for the family. The servant would hand round only the dishes that were looked upon as relatively unimportant components of the meal—vegetables and starches. That the master and mistress served the most important dishes of the meal underlines the importance of the family ties and family structure that were being reinforced by the meal.[9]

The service that many Americans use today in dinners that celebrate the values of family and community, such as Thanksgiving and Christmas dinners, is still basically the old English plan. On more formal occasions, where ties of association rather than ties of community are stressed, Americans use a different kind of service, called French service, where all the food is impersonally served onto plates by the waiter either at the table or in the kitchen, and food-bearing platters are never placed on the table at all. This kind of service was introduced to the United States in the 1830s but, unlike in England and on the Continent, did not become accepted even for dinner parties until later in the nineteenth century.[10]

The reason behind this elaboration of the family dinner from the eighteenth to the nineteenth centuries lay in its change in social meaning. Although dinner was the main meal of the day in the eighteenth century, in terms of the amount of food consumed, it was not particularly important as a social event because all family members were together for much of the day anyway. By the mid nineteenth century, when husbands and older children were away from home all day, the family dinner had become very important: it was the only time that all of the members of the household were together as a group. It had become a secular ritual and was used to reinforce family ties.

Tea was apparently served in two contexts among the middle class during the period of study: as a beverage that accompanied meals like breakfast and as part of a social ceremony. Throughout the half century following the Revolution the tea ceremony was a social event. Unlike family dinner, it was the meal for which guests were invited into the home. It provided an arena for the display of household status to outsiders.

Among the elite the tea ceremony was generally held after dinner, in the late afternoon, at least during the eighteenth century when dinner took place at noon. It was the focus of parties where a dessert course or possibly even a supper was also served. Even after the family dinner shifted to the evening, these parties continued to take place after dinner. By the 1840s afternoon tea had become a feminine social ritual, indulged in by middle-class and elite women alike.[11]

CERAMICS USED IN FAMILY MEALS AND SOCIAL TEAS

Let us consider once again the ceramics in the archaeological assemblages from the New York City households to see if changes in family life and in the social meaning of dinner and tea can help to explain the changing tastes of the consumers who were buying these wares. New patterns of ceramic use might be related to two different sets of factors: market availability and the social meaning of the ceramics in their context of use.

During the period of study most of the ceramics that were available in New York were imported from England and China. As George Miller, Ann Smart Martin, and Nancy Dickinson have documented elsewhere in this volume, the industrialized Staffordshire potteries produced most of the British wares that were available to American consumers from circa 1770 to the mid nineteenth century. Before the end of the eighteenth century the United States market was relatively unimportant to the potters, but it gained new stature after British manufacturers lost access to markets on the Continent as a result of the Napoleonic wars and European tariffs. From the end of the War of 1812 through the middle of the nineteenth century, the American market absorbed almost half the ceramics exported from England. During this later period the Staffordshire potters were extremely sensitive to what they thought they could sell in the United States.[12]

Porcelains from China were available for purchase throughout this period. Direct trade between the new nation and China was begun almost immediately after the Revolution. Both tableware and teaware were produced for export by the Chinese. These wares were either decorated to order for wealthy American customers or mass-produced for the lower-income market.[13]

Both the kinds of wares available from these two sources and their prices (discussed below) were important limiting factors in the choices made by consumers. Within these parameters, consumers presumably chose the ceramics that seemed most appropriate to them for the context of use.

We saw in figure 1 that the most popular styles of motifs depicted on vessels used in family meals and social teas changed consistently over the period of study. Dishes used at the table went from the royal pattern (see fig. 2) in the early period (circa 1790) to the shell-edge pattern and the plain (or Paris) patterns (see figs. 5, 6) in the middle period (circa 1805) to chinoiserie (see figs. 9, 10) in the later period (circa 1820). The motifs popular for teawares underwent a more subtle change, from an even division between Chinese landscape and floral patterns in the early period (see figs. 3, 4) to floral motifs in the middle and later periods (see figs. 7, 11). Simple availability was not a factor in these developments, since both minimally decorated tableware and teaware and those decorated with shell-edge, chinoiserie, and floral motifs were all available in New York during or before the 1780s.[14]

Other aspects of these vessels may help us to determine whether these changing consumer patterns can be related to the developments documented for the social contexts of the meals in which the vessels were used. We might expect, for example, that as family meals become more important as a daily ritual, the tableware used in this social context may have become elaborated as well. This elaboration might be expressed by increases in the extent of decoration on the vessels, in their relative cost, and in the use of contrasting sets of dishes to mark the relative importance of each meal. Teaware vessels, on the other hand, were consistently used in displaying household status to outsiders. We therefore might expect a relative consistency in their degree of decoration and in their relative cost.

ELABORATION OF DECORATION

We might expect that as dinner became more important as a secular ritual in the lives of federal New Yorkers in the middle and upper classes, the extent of the decorative treatment accorded each vessel that was used in this ritual might have increased as well in order to focus more attention on the meal. For social teas, on the other hand, we would not necessarily expect an increase in the degree of embellishment because this meal continued to be an arena for displaying household status to outsiders during the period, even though the audience for the display became increasingly feminine as time went on. We would therefore expect the teaware vessels to maintain a relatively high degree of decoration throughout the period.

I devised a measure for determining the degree of decoration on these vessels. I gave each tea- and tableware vessel in each assemblage a score based on the number of locations where colored and/or molded decoration occurred. For purposes of standardization, I divided each score by the maximum number of decorated areas for that particular kind of vessel in all of the assemblages. A teabowl, for example, with

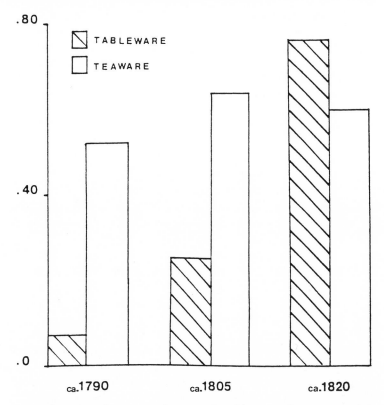

Figure 12.   Mean decorative index scores for tableware and teaware vessels in the assemblages, by chronological group.

decoration on its outer rim, inner rim, and at the center of the bowl was scored 3 because three areas had received decorative treatment. This score of 3 was then divided by 5, which was the maximum number of parts on teabowls that received decorative treatment in all of the assemblages. This resulted in a "decorative index" score of 0.6 for this vessel.[15]

The mean decorative index values for the teaware and tableware vessels in each chronological group are shown in figure 12. Those for the teaware vessels remain roughly the same from period to period; they increase slightly between the early group and the middle group and then decrease slightly between the middle group and the later group.

The scores for the tableware vessels, on the other hand, show a marked increase through time, with a threefold increase between the vessels in the early group and those of the middle group, and between those in the middle group and those of the later group. The indexes for the dinnerware in the later group are considerably higher than those for the teaware in any of the groups, which suggests that by the 1820s decorative embellishment was an important factor in the decision to buy particular kinds of tableware.

RELATIVE COST OF TABLEWARE AND TEAWARE

How much were the women in these households willing to spend on the dishes that were used in presenting dinner and tea? The method I used to explore the relative costs of the vessels is adapted from Miller's research. In studying the Staffordshire potters' price lists for British refined earthenware vessels in the late eighteenth and early nineteenth centuries, he notes that vessels made of plain, undecorated cream-colored ware were cheaper than all of the other wares and that the prices of wares decorated by different production techniques maintained the same ordinal price relationship to each other and to the plain cream-colored wares throughout the first half of the nineteenth century. The prices of British ceramics in general fell during the period, however, both because the prices of the decorated wares declined relative to that of creamware and because the potters increasingly discounted the wholesale prices of their wares—at roughly 10 percent through the War of 1812 and at approximately 28 percent from the end of the war until around 1830. The discounts were partly offset by price increases based on import tariffs during this period. Tariffs were charged at about 5 percent through the War of 1812 and at about 20 percent from the war's end until about 1830.[16]

Miller's work concentrates on the ware made by the Staffordshire potters. It is also possible to estimate the price information on the Chinese export porcelains that formed an important part of the assemblages from the New York City households. It should be noted, however, that information on the price of porcelains is much more tentative than that for the British ware. I have estimated the value of the blue-on-white Chinese export porcelains as three times the value of creamware, and that of the overglaze-decorated porcelains at one and a

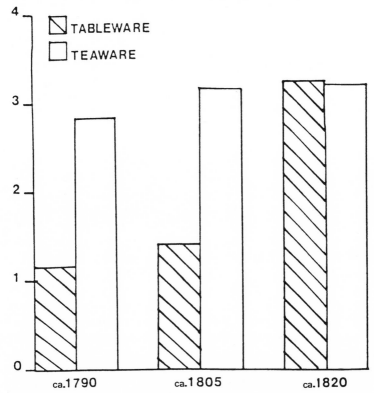

Figure 13. Mean value of tableware and teaware vessels in the assemblages, by chronological group.

half times the value of blue-on-white porcelain, or four and a half times the value of creamware.[17]

The mean values of the tableware and teaware in the archaeological assemblages from the three chronological groups are quite different from each other and also changed through time (fig. 13). Both the discount and tariff rates have been incorporated into the figures. The value of the teaware vessels increases only slightly (12 percent) between the early and middle periods and stays roughly the same between the middle and later periods. In concrete terms this means that the consumers' goal was always to have a flashy tea set and that they were willing to increase this standard slightly as prices came down during the period. This is what we might expect for the vessels used in a social ceremony like tea, which was consistently used to display household status to outsiders.

The value of the vessels used in family meals, on the other hand, shows a marked increase relative to that of teaware during the period of study. Tableware starts out at less than half the value of teaware for the early period and ends up being equal in value to teaware in the later period. The increase is a relatively modest 20 percent between the early and middle period, but there is a leap of 135 percent between the middle and later period. This pattern reveals that during this period New Yorkers were willing to spend ever-increasing amounts of money on the vessels that they used in private family meals, relative to the amount they spent on their teaware.

The increase in the discounting of the prices of Staffordshire wares during this period naturally facilitated these changes in buying patterns by lowering the prices of the vessels, and this price decrease does help to explain consumer practices in buying teaware. All other things being equal, when prices fall, consumers have more choices. They can continue to buy the same product at the new, lower price and spend the difference on either more of the same product or on other items, or they can upgrade their standard of living by buying a higher-quality product for a price close to what they used to spend. When buying teaware, New York consumers apparently chose the second option. They continued to spend approximately the same amount of money on average for each of their teaware vessels as they had in the past (see fig. 13) and presumably were able to buy a slightly better quality of vessels.

The decrease in the price of Staffordshire ware does not explain the changes in buying patterns for tableware vessels. In this case, consumers again chose to upgrade the quality of their ceramics. Instead of continuing to spend the same amount of money on their tableware, however, they chose to buy vessels that were much more expensive than those they had bought in the past. These increases in value more than offset the lowering of the Staffordshire ceramic prices due to discounting. Consumers were willing to spend more and more in absolute terms on these vessels than they had in the past. By the 1820s they were willing to spend as much for their tableware vessels, which were used and seen primarily by household members, as for their teaware vessels, which they used to entertain outsiders. This consumer decision suggests that the social context of family meals and the meaning of family life had changed as well. It supports the interpretation that these New Yorkers were using ceramics to stress the growing importance of family meals and domestic life during the federal period.

USE OF MATCHED DISHES

Finally, let us consider the use of matched dishes for presenting family dinners and social teas in these federal households. If we look on differences in style as expressing social boundaries, the unity of style expressed by the use of matched vessels emphasizes the community of a group rather than the differences among its members. We would therefore expect that matched dishes would be used in family meals throughout the whole period, and that in fact is what we find.[18]

On a larger scale, there is enormous standardization in the tableware patterns that were popular in each of the periods. All of the assemblages in each chronological group contain vessels made of matching wares decorated with matching designs, with relatively little variation in the details of the decoration on even the hand-painted wares. Approximately half the tablewares from each of the households in the early group were made in the royal pattern, half of those from the households in the middle group in the shell-edge pattern, and half those in the later group in Canton-pattern porcelain.

The use of contrasting tableware sets also suggests an elaboration through time. All of the sets from the early group are made up of minimally decorated, plain white vessels. It is hard to imagine how the molded patterns were used to mark the rank of more and less important meals. It is quite possible that contrasting sets of pewter plates were used in conjunction with these minimally decorated ceramic vessels. Pewter plates were very common in homes in rural Virginia during this period. Items made of pewter and other metals rarely appear in the archaeological record, however, as they were recycled rather than thrown away when they were no longer wanted.[19]

The larger assemblages from both the middle and later periods contain contrasting sets of ceramic vessels that could be differentiated on the basis of either their degree of decoration or their relative cost. Sets of decorated shell-edge and plain vessels predominated in the middle period, and highly decorated sets of expensive Canton porcelains and cheaper willow-pattern earthenware were both popular during the later period. This suggests that at least as early as the middle period New Yorkers began to use contrasting sets of ceramic dishes as markers to rank the relative importance of family meals, perhaps to differentiate, for example, Sunday dinner from weekday dinners, or to mark the importance of family dinner as opposed to other meals of the day.

What is less clear is the significance of blue or green trim on the shell-edge vessels in the middle period. While dishes with each color of trim appear in the same assemblage, those with blue trim are more frequent in two of the assemblages, and those with green are more frequent in the other two. Were they used interchangeably in the same course of the same meal? Were they used to mark different courses in a meal? Was one color more popular first and then the other (with green being replaced by blue, as the latter continued to be popular later in the nineteenth century)? Or was one color ranked more highly than the other?

The standardization among the tablewares from all of the households for the later period is particularly striking when we take into account the efforts of the Staffordshire potters to compete for the American market after the War of 1812. The potters began to produce large numbers of vessels decorated with American views and national heroes that (as noted by Miller, Martin, and Dickinson) were apparently not very popular, as they almost never turn up in archaeological assemblages dating from this period. The consistency of the tableware patterns from the New York City households indicates that these consumers had precise ideas about what was suitable when they went shopping for these dishes.[20]

The matched teaware cups and saucers are quite different in this regard, for they are not standardized at all. The most popular pattern in tewares in each of the households was depicted on average on only about a third of the tea vessels in the assemblage, and very few of these patterns were used in more than one of the households.

I believe the standardization of the styles of the tableware vessels used during each period served to emphasize to the members of these households the importance and universality of the community values and social relations that were becoming an important part of home life, as opposed to those that prevailed in the public world of the marketplace.

The social meaning of family dinner and home life was rapidly changing, so the standardization of these wares was important in communicating their message. Their patterned change through time marks the change in the meaning of this meal as it was ritualized. This standardization is particularly striking when we remember that these objects were seen regularly primarily by household members and kin and not by strangers and guests.

The teaware vessels, on the other hand, were used both in a social arena where people of the same class but from outside the household were regularly present as well as at other, more private meals. The diversity of these patterns expresses the variety of messages these households were sending out about their position in this highly diversified society. In the case of the teawares, a much larger sample of households might be required to demonstrate regular standardized patterns in homes dating from each chronological period.

The changes in the ceramic vessels used in these New York City households in the half century following the Revolution can best be understood within the changing social context of the meals in which the vessels were used. The social context, in turn, is closely related to developments in family life and, by extension, in society at large.

The teaware vessels used to present tea to outsiders and to family members alike are relatively constant in their degree of decoration and in their relative cost from circa 1790 to circa 1820. The most obvious change in these vessels during this period, in terms of the variables examined here, is a gradual stylistic shift from a preference for vessels decorated with Chinese landscapes to those decorated with floral motifs. This stylistic change may mark the feminization of afternoon tea.

The ceramic vessels used to present family dinner and other private meals show a consistent elaboration through time, from circa 1790 until at least circa 1820. This elaboration is expressed in changes in the style of decorative motif (from minimally decorated vessels to shell-edge vessels to vessels decorated with Chinese landscapes), in the degree of decorative treatment, in the increased cost of the vessels, and in the introduction of the use of contrasting sets of china to rank the importance of different meals. The elaboration of tableware vessels suggests that these dishes were used to enhance the meals in which they were used and to emphasize the growing importance of domestic life inside these homes.

[1] Stanley South, *Method and Theory in Historical Archaeology* (New York: Academic Press, 1977), p. 217.

[2] H. Martin Wobst, "Stylistic Behavior and Information Exchange," in *For the Director: Research Essays in Honor of James B. Griffin*, ed. Charles E. Cleland, Michigan Anthropological Papers, no. 61 (1977): 321; Margaret W. Conkey, "Style and Information in Cultural Evolution: Toward a Predictive Model for the Paleolithic," in *Social Archaeology: Beyond Subsistence and Dating*, ed. Charles L. Redman et al. (New York: Academic Press, 1978), pp. 61–85; Ian Hodder, "Economic and Social Stress and Material Culture Patterning," *American Antiquity* 44, no. 3 (July 1979): 446–54; and Stephen Plog, "Analysis of Style in Artifacts," *Annual Review of Anthropology* 12 (1983): 125–42.

[3] Ira Rosenwaike, *Population History of New York City* (Syracuse: Syracuse University Press, 1972); Sean Wilentz, *Chants Democratic: New York City and the Rise of the American Working Class, 1788–1850* (New York: Oxford University Press, 1984).

[4] Wilentz, *Chants Democratic*; Betsy Blackmar, "Rewalking the 'Walking City': Housing and Property Relations in New York City," *Radical History Review*, no. 21 (Fall 1979): 131–48.

[5] Aileen S. Kraditor, *Up from the Pedestal: Selected Writings in the History of American Feminism* (Chicago: Quadrangle Books, 1968); John Demos, *A Little Commonwealth: Family Life in Plymouth Colony* (New York: Oxford University Press, 1970); Mary P. Ryan, *Cradle of the Middle Class: The Family in Oneida County, New York, 1790–1865* (New York: Cambridge University Press, 1981); Christopher Lasch, *Haven in a Heartless World: The Family Besieged* (New York: Basic Books, 1977).

[6] Nancy S. Dickinson, "The Iconography of the Dinner Table: Upper and Middling Customs, 1760s to 1860s" (1985, Nancy S. Dickinson Collection) provides much of the background for this discussion; Louise Conway Belden, *The Festive Tradition: Table Decoration and Desserts in America, 1650–1900* (New York: W. W. Norton, 1983), p. 20; Susannah Carter, *The Frugal Housewife* (Philadelphia: Mathew Carey, 1802), pp. 257–60; Margaret Hall, in Una Pope-Hennessy, ed., *The Aristocratic Journey, Being the Outspoken Letters of Mrs. Basil Hall Written during a Fourteen Months' Sojourn in America, 1827–1828* (New York: G. P. Putnam's Sons, 1931); Maria Eliza Rundell, *The Experienced American Housekeeper; or, Domestic Cookery: Formed on Principles of Economy for the Use of Private Families* (New York: Johnstone and Van Norden, 1823), facing p. 8.

[7] Calvert Vaux as quoted in Clifford Edward Clark, Jr., *The American Family Home, 1800–1960* (Chapel Hill: University of North Carolina Press, 1986), p. 42; Catharine Maria Sedgwick, *Home* (Boston: James Munroe, 1837), p. 28, originally cited by Dickinson, "Iconography," p. 21.

[8] Dickinson, "Iconography," pp. 13–14; Belden, *Festive Tradition*, pp. 28–29; Eliza Leslie, *The House Book; or, A Manual of Domestic Economy for Town and Country* (Philadelphia: Carey and Hart, 1844), p. 257; Catharine Beecher, *A Treatise on Domestic Economy, for the Use of Young Ladies at Home and at School* (New York: Harper and Brothers, 1855), p. 309.

[9] Leslie, *House Book*, p. 263; Robert Roberts, *The House Servant's Directory* (Boston: Munroe and Francis, 1827); Mary Douglas, "Deciphering a Meal," in *Implicit Meanings: Essays in Anthropology* (London: Routledge and Kegan Paul, 1979), pp. 249–75.

[10] Belden, *Festive Tradition*, p. 35; Susan Williams, *Savory Suppers and Fashionable Feasts: Dining in Victorian America* (New York: Pantheon Books, 1985). For opposition to *service à la française*, see Allan Nevins, ed., *The Diary of Philip Hone, 1828–1851* (New York: Dodd, Mead, 1927), pp. 299–300.

[11] Rodris Roth, *Tea Drinking in Eighteenth-Century America: Its Etiquette and Equipage*, U.S. National Museum Bulletin 225, Contributions from the Museum of History and Technology, paper 14 (Washington, D.C.: Smithsonian Institution, 1961), pp. 63–91; Brissot de Warville, quoted in Thomas E. V. Smith, *The City of New York in the Year of Washington's Inauguration, 1789* (Riverside, Conn.: Chatham Press, 1972), pp. 116–17; Bradford Perkins, ed., *Henry Unwin Addington's Residence in the United States of America, 1822–1825*, University of California, Publications in History, no. 65 (Berkeley: University of California Press, 1960); Franklin D. Scott, ed. and trans., *Baron Klinkowstrom's America, 1818–1820*, Northwestern University Studies, Special Science Series, no. 8 (Evanston, Ill.: Northwestern University Press, 1952), p. 124.

[12] See George L. Miller, Ann Smart Martin, and Nancy S. Dickinson, "Changing Consumption Patterns: English Ceramics and the American Market from 1770 to 1840," elsewhere in this volume.

[13] Jean McClure Mudge, *Chinese Export Porcelain for the American Trade, 1785–1835* (Newark: University of Delaware Press, 1981), p. 65.

[14] Ivor Noël Hume, *A Guide to Artifacts of Colonial America* (New York: Alfred A. Knopf, 1969), pp. 116, 127, 129, 131, 260; Donald Towner, *Creamware* (London: Faber and Faber, 1978), pp. 19, 48, 57, 68, 93, 95, 98, 99, 107, 123, 144, 145, 175; David Sanctuary Howard, *New York and the China Trade* (New York: New-York Historical Society, 1984), pp. 64, 68.

[15] Documented in Diana diZerega Wall, "At Home in New York: Changing Family Life among the Propertied in the Late Eighteenth and Early Nineteenth Centuries" (Ph.D. diss., New York University, 1987), pp. 378–89.

[16] George L. Miller, "Classification and Economic Scaling of Nineteenth-Century Ceramics," *Historical Archaeology* 14 (1980): 1–40; George L. Miller, "Prices and Index Values for English Ceramics from 1787 to 1880" (1988, Department of Archaeology, Colonial Williamsburg); George L. Miller to author, 1989.

[17] Mudge, *Chinese Export Porcelain*, pp. 100, 166–67; George L. Miller to author, 1986.

[18] "Matched dishes" are defined in this study by the presence of more than one vessel in the same pattern in a particular assemblage; see appendix.

[19] See Ann Smart Martin, "The Role of Pewter as Missing Artifact: Consumer Attitudes Toward Tablewares in Late Eighteenth-Century Virginia," *Historical Archaeology* 23, no. 2 (1989): 1–27.

[20] Miller, Martin, and Dickinson, "Changing Consumption Patterns."

[21] Miller, "Prices and Index Values for English Ceramics"; George L. Miller to author. The features in the sites are interpreted in Wall, "At Home in New York."

APPENDIX

The following tables present the data on the styles, vessel forms, and price index values of the teaware and tableware vessels in the assemblages, by chronological group. All vessels, unless otherwise noted, are made of earthenware; CEP indicates Chinese export porcelain; cc indicates cream-colored earthenware. The index values of serving vessels are not computed because they were often made of sterling or silver plate in wealthier households, and the presence of only the ceramic serving vessels in the archaeological record skews the figures.[21]

TABLE 2. Ceramics in the Early Group Sites

Site	Category ware	Decorative type/style[1]	Vessel form	No.	Index value[2]
Test cut J	table	cc-royal pattern*	table plate	4	1.00
			platter (12″)	1	n/c
		cc-plain*	table plate	1	1.00
			muffin (6″)	1	1.00
		edged*	table plate	2	1.67
		blue CEP-	table plate	1	3.00
		Chinese landscape	soup plate	1	3.00
		blue CEP-floral	table plate	1	3.00
			soup plate	1	3.00
	tea	cc-fluted, scalloped	teabowl	1	2.60[3]
		painted-	teapot lid	1	n/c
		Chinese landscape			
		painted-floral, fluted, scalloped	teabowl	1	3.40[3]
		painted-floral	teabowl	1	2.50
		blue CEP-	teabowl	1	3.00
		Chinese landscape			
		overglaze CEP-floral*	teabowl	2	4.50
			saucer	1	n/c
		European porcelain-floral	teabowl	1	4.00[4]
Cobble floor	table	cc-royal pattern*	table plate	9	1.00
			soup plate	3	1.00
			muffin (7″)	1	1.00
			boat	1	n/c
			dish (16″)	1	n/c
		cc-diamond/beaded*	table plate	2	1.00
		cc-feather*	table plate	5	1.00
			soup plate	1	1.00
			boat	1	n/c
		cc-unidentified	drainer	1	n/c
	tea	painted-floral	teapot lid	1	n/c
		overglaze CEP-Chinese landscape	saucer	1	4.50
		blue CEP-Chinese landscape*	teabowl	2	3.00

TABLE 2. Ceramics in the Early Group Sites (cont.)

Site	Category ware	Decorative type/style[1]	Vessel form	No.	Index value
			teabowl	1	3.00
			saucer	1	3.00
			teabowl	1	3.00
		blue CEP-floral	saucer	1	3.00
			teabowl	1	3.00
			saucer	1	3.00
		European	teabowl	2	4.00[4]
		porcelain-floral*Feature	table		cc-royal
pattern*	table plate	1		1.00	
51			twiffler	1	1.00
		cc-diamond/banded	table plate	1	1.00
		cc-feather	table plate	1	1.00
		white stoneware-barley	table plate	1	n/c
	tea	cc-plain	saucer	1	1.00
		painted–			
		Chinese landscape*	saucer	2	2.50
		painted-floral*	saucer	2	2.50
		blue CEP-			
		Chinese landscape	teabowl	1	3.00
Feature	table	cc-royal pattern*	table plate	5	1.00
49			soup plate	2	1.00
			twiffler	1	1.00
			muffin (6″, 7″)	2	1.00
		cc-plain*	muffin (6″, 7″)	2	1.00
		cc-plain-molded	boat	1	n/c
	tea	cc-plain*	teabowl	2	1.00
			saucer	2	n/c
			teapot	2	n/c
		painted-			
		Chinese landscape*	teabowl	3	n/c
			saucer	6	2.50
		painted-			
		Chinese landscape*	teabowl	5	2.50
		painted-floral*	saucer	2	2.50
		painted-floral	coffeepot	1	n/c
		dipt	teabowl	1	n/c
			saucer	3	1.50[5]
		blue CEP-floral	teabowl	1	3.00

* Matched dishes.

[1] All vessels are earthenware unless European porcelain, Chinese export porcelain (CEP), or stoneware is specified; cc = cream colored.

[2] Indexed to the 1787 price list.

[3] Index value based on the 1796 price list.

[4] Value based on 1824 price list (see Miller, "Classification and Economic Scaling," p. 30).

[5] Index value based on 1825 price list.

TABLE 3. Ceramics in the Middle Group Sites

Site	Category ware	Decorative type/style[1]	Vessel form	No.	Index value[2]
Feature 48	table	cc-plain*	table plate	2	1.00
			soup plate	3	1.00
			twiffler	1	1.00
			platter (12″)	1	n/c
		edged*	table plate	6	1.33
			twiffler	3	1.50
			muffin (7″)	4	1.51
			tureen (5″, 11″)	2	n/c
			boat (6″)	1	n/c
			platter (12″),—	3	3 n/c
			dish (—)	1	n/c
		painted willow*	muffin (6″)	2	3.01[3]
	tea	painted-floral	teabowl	1	1.71
			teabowl	2	1.71
			sugar bowl	1	n/c
		blue CEP-unidentified	teabowl	1	3.00
		blue CEP-Chinese landscape	sugar bowl	1	n/c
		overglaze CEP-floral*	teabowl	1	4.50
			saucer	1	n/c
		overglaze CEP-floral*	teabowl	1	4.50
			saucer	1	n/c
		overglaze CEP-floral*	saucer	3	4.50
		overglaze CEP-floral	teabowl	1	4.50
			saucer	1	n/c
		overglaze CEP-other, "lovebirds"*	teabowl	2	n/c
			saucer	3	4.50
		overglaze CEP other, "sawtooth"*-	teabowl	3	4.50
			saucer	2	n/c
			coffee cup	1	4.50
			caddy	1	n/c
		overglaze CEP-other, pseudoarmorial	teabowl	1	4.50
Test cut AX	table	cc-royal pattern*	table plate	1	1.00
			soup plate	2	1.00
			platter (7″)	1	n/c
		cc-plain*	table plate	2	1.00
			soup plate	1	1.00

TABLE 3. Ceramics in the Middle Group Sites (cont.)

Site	Category ware	Decorative type/style[1]	Vessel form	No.	Index value[2]
Test	table	cc-plain* (cont)	dish (10″)	2	n/c
cut AX			platter (11″)	1	n/c
(cont)		edged*	table plate	3	1.33
			soup plate	3	1.33
			twiffler	2	1.50
			muffin (6″)	1	1.49
			platter (—)	1	n/c
		underglazed-lined blue CEP-	platter (16″)	1	n/c
		Chinese landscape	platter (18″)	1	n/c
	tea-	cc-plain	coffee pot	1	n/c
	ware	painted-floral*	teabowl	2	1.71
		painted-unidentified printed-floral*,	teabowl	1	1.71
		scalloped	saucer	1	4.29
			slop bowl	1	n/c
		printed-floral	saucer	1	3.42
		overglaze CEP- floral*	teabowl	1	4.50
			saucer	1	n/c
		overglaze CEP-floral*	teabowl	1	4.50
			saucer	1	n/c
		overglaze CEP- Chinese landscape	teabowl	1	4.50
		overglaze CEP- other, pseudoarmorial	teapot	1	n/c
Feature	table	cc-royal pattern*	table plate	1	1.00
43			soup plate	3	1.00
		edged*	table plate	10	1.33
			soup plate	1	1.33
			twiffler	1	1.50
			muffin (6″)	1	1.49
			muffin (7″)	1	1.51
			dish (10″, —)	3	n/c
			platter (12″)	1	n/c
	tea	cc-plain	saucer	1	1.00
		painted-floral	teabowl	1	1.71
		painted-floral	teabowl	1	1.71
		painted-floral	teabowl	1	1.71
		painted-floral	teabowl	1	1.71
		painted-floral	saucer	1	1.71
		painted-floral*	saucer	2	1.71

TABLE 3. Ceramics in the Middle Group Sites (cont.)

Site	Category ware	Decorative type/style[1]	Vessel form	No.	Index value[2]
Feature 43 (cont)	tea	painted-floral*	slop bowl	1	n/c
			saucer	1	1.71
		painted-other, "star"*	teabowl	1	1.71
			saucer	1	n/c
		printed– Chinese landscape	teabowl	1	3.42
		printed- Chinese landscape	saucer	1	3.42
		printed- western landscape	saucer	1	3.42
		overglaze CEP- floral	saucer	1	4.50
		overglaze CEP- unidentified	teabowl	1	4.50
Test cut AT	table	cc-royal pattern*	table plate	1	1.00
			muffin (7″)	1	1.00
		cc-plain	table plate	1	1.00
			muffin (7″)	1	1.00
		edged*	table plate	2	1.33
			twiffler	3	1.28
			muffin (7″)	1	1.33
			dish (12″)	1	n/c
			tureen	1	n/c
		printed- western landscape	table plate	3	3.33
			muffin (6″)	1	3.61
		printed- western landscape	muffin (7″)	1	3.50
	tea	red earthenware-plain	teapot	1	n/c
		painted-floral	teabowl	1	2.17
		painted-floral, fluted, scalloped	saucer	1	1.50
		printed- western landscape*	saucer	2	3.00
		blue CEP- Chinese landscape	teabowl	3	n/c
		blue CEP-Nanking*	saucer	9	3.00

* Matched dishes.

[1] All vessels are earthenware unless European porcelain, Chinese export porcelain (CEP), or stoneware is specified; cc = cream colored.

[2] Indexed to the 1804 price list.

[3] Index value based on the 1814 price list.

TABLE 4.(1) Ceramics in the Later Group Sites

Site	Category ware	Decorative type/style[1]	Vessel form	No.	Index value[2]
Feature 11	table	printed- western landscape	muffin (5″)	1	3.01
		blue CEP- Chinese landscape	table plate	1	3.00
		blue CEP- Canton	dish (12″)	1	n/c
		blue CEP- Chinese landscape	table plate	1	3.00
		overglaze CEP- pseudoarmorial	muffin (6″)	1	4.50
	tea- ware	printed- western landscape	saucer	1	2.25
		blue CEP- Chinese landscape	teabowl	1	3.00
		soft paste-floral	teabowl	1	4.20[3]
			coffee cup	2	4.20[3]
			saucer	1	n/c
Compo- nent 15	table	printed- western landscape	muffin (6″)	1	3.61
		printed-Chinese landscape-willow*	table plate	3	2.67
		printed-flown	table plate	1	4.17[4]
		blue CEP– Chinese landscape- Canton*	table plate	5	3.00
			twiffler	2	3.00
			platter (—)	1	n/c
	tea	painted-floral*	saucer	1	1.50
			slop bowl	1	n/c
		printed- western landscape	saucer	1	3.00
		blue CEP-Chinese- landscape	saucer	1	3.00
		blue CEP-Chinese landscape-Nanking	teabowl	2	3.00
			saucer	1	n/c
		overglaze CEP-floral	teabowl	1	4.50
		European porcelain-floral	saucer	1	4.20[3]
		European porcelain-molded	teacup	1	4.20[3]
		European porcelain-floral	teacup	1	4.20[3]

TABLE 4(2). Ceramics in the Later Group Sites (cont)

Site	Category ware	Decorative type/style[1]	Vessel form	No.	Index value[2]
Feature	table	cc-plain*	soup plate	2	1.00
9		edged*	table plate	3	1.33
			twiffler	1	1.28
			platter (16″)	2	n/c
		edged and embossed printed-Chinese	muffin (6″)	4	n/c
		landscape-willow*	table plate	9	2.67
			soup plate	1	2.67
			muffin (7″)	2	3.00
			unid. plate	1	n/c
			tureen (6″)	1	n/c
		printed-western landscape	table plate	1	3.33
			platter (—)	1	n/c
		printed-western landscape	table plate	1	3.33
		printed-other	table plate	1	3.33
		blue CEP- Chinese landscape-	table plate	2	3.00
		Canton*	soup plate	3	3.00
			twiffler	2	3.00
			muffin (6″)	4	3.00
			boat (6″)	1	n/c
		blue CEP- Chinese landscape*	table plate	2	3.00
		blue CEP- Chinese landscape*	twiffler	2	3.00
		blue CEP- Chinese landscape*	muffin (7″)	3	3.00
		blue CEP- floral-Fitzhugh*	muffin (6″)	4	3.00
	tea	painted-floral*	teabowl-Irish	3	n/c
			saucer	5	1.38
		painted-floral*	saucer	3	1.50
		painted-floral*	teacup	2	3.67
			saucer	2	n/c
		painted-floral- geranium*	teacup	3	3.67
			saucer	3	n/c
		painted-floral*	saucer	4	3.00
		painted-floral*	teabowl	1	3.00
			saucer	1	n/c
		painted-western landscape-Lafayette*	saucer	2	n/c
			teabowl	1	3.00

TABLE 4(3). Ceramics in the Later Group Sites (cont.)

Site	Category ware	Decorative type/style[1]	Vessel form	No.	Index value[2]
Feature 9 (cont)	tea (cont)	painted-western landscape	teacup	1	3.67
			saucer	1	3.00
		painted-western landscape*	teabowl-Irish	4	2.75
		painted-western landscape	teabowl-Irish	1	2.75
		European porcelain-Chinese landscape*	saucer	1	n/c
			teacup	2	4.20[5]
		European porcelain-floral	teacup	1	4.20[5]
		blue CEP–Chinese landscape-Fitzhugh*	saucer	3	3.00
			teapot	1	n/c
		overglaze CEP-western landscape	teacup	1	4.50
			coffee cup	3	4.50
			saucer	1	n/c
		overglaze CEP-western landscape	teabowl	1	4.50
		overglaze CEP-floral	teabowl	1	4.50
		caneware-floral	teapot	1	n/c

*Matched dishes.

[1] All vessels are earthenware unless European porcelain, Chinese export porcelain (CEP), or stoneware is specified; cc = cream colored.

[2] Indexed to the 1823 price list.

[3] Index value based on 1836 price list.

[4] Index value based on the relationship between flown and printed wares in the 1846 price list.

TABLE 5. Index Values of Ceramics

Site	Category wares	Index value, European ceramics	Adjusted index value[1]	Index value, Chinese export porcelain	Total index value	Adjusted total index value[2]	Mean index value
Test cut J	table	9.34	8.41	12.0	20.41	21.43	1.79
	tea	12.50	11.25	12.0	23.25	24.41	3.49
Cobble floor	table	21.00	18.90	0.0	18.90	19.85	0.95
	tea	8.00	7.20	28.5	35.70	37.49	3.41
Feature 51	table	4.00	3.60	0.0	3.60	3.78	0.95
	tea	11.00	9.90	3.0	12.90	13.55	2.26
Feature 49	table	12.00	10.80	0.0	10.80	11.34	0.95
	tea	39.00	35.10	3.0	38.10	40.01	2.11
Feature 48	table	30.54	27.49	0.0	27.49	28.86	1.37
	tea	5.13	4.62	66.0	70.62	74.15	4.12
Test cut AX	table	18.47	16.62	0.0	16.62	17.45	1.16
	tea	12.84	11.56	13.5	25.06	26.31	3.29
Feature 43	table	23.13	20.82	0.0	20.82	21.86	1.21
	tea	26.65	23.99	9.0	32.99	34.63	2.31
Test cut AT	table	28.93	26.04	0.0	26.04	27.34	1.82
	tea	9.67	8.70	27.0	35.70	37.49	2.88
Feature 11	table	3.01	2.14	[12.5?]	14.64	18.77	3.75
	tea	14.85	10.57	3.0	13.57	16.28	3.26
Component 15	table	15.79	11.24	21.0	32.24	38.69	3.22
	tea	17.10	12.18	13.5	25.68	30.82	3.42
Feature 9	table	49.96	35.57	66.0	101.57	121.88	2.83
	tea	84.97	60.50	36.0	96.50	115.80	2.97

Source: The index values of European ceramics and Chinese export porcelain are derived from tables 2, 3, 4.

[1] The adjusted index value of European ceramics is computed by deducting 10% from the index value in early and middle periods and 28.8% in the late period; these reflect the discount practices of the Staffordshire potters.

[2] The adjusted total index value is computed by adding 5% to the total index value of all ceramics in the early and middle periods and 20% in the late period; these reflect the prevailing tariff rates.

Manufacturing and Selling
the American Revolution
Ann Fairfax Withington

The American people brought the Revolution to a successful military conclusion with the Treaty of Paris in 1783. During the political crisis that preceded the Revolution and during the Revolution itself, Americans clarified and refined their political beliefs—positive beliefs about how government should be constituted and what kind of relationship should exist between government and the governed; and negative beliefs about the restrictions under which government should operate. Once independence had been declared, the various states all established republican governments and joined in a confederation. The Treaty of Paris marked the end of the war, but even before then the American people had had to define for themselves as well as for the rest of the world the significance of independence and republican governments. After winning the war, they had to incorporate their achievement, brought about through the cooperation of all the states, into a national consciousness.

The achievement lay partly in winning the war against the British Empire and partly in establishing republican governments and producing a society virtuous enough to sustain them. Americans from all states, despite cultural and religious differences; from all classes and occupations, despite different economic interests; and from all parts of the political spectrum, despite different views of the proper relation between state and federal government—all shared the triumph of military victory and approved of republican governments. Whatever their differences, the American people wanted to define and dramatize their military and political success. To do so, they needed visual symbols of their achievement.

In the twenty years following the Declaration of Independence, American political leaders made iconographic decisions. They decided how to represent, in visual symbols, icons, and designs, the thirteen separate republics, the confederation, and, after 1787, the federal republic. The Second Continental Congress made most of the lasting national iconographic decisions; its members ordered commemorative medals, had the flag and the great seal designed, chose the eagle as the national emblem, and issued continental currency with various designs. The Continental Congress did not, however, establish a mint or design a national currency that would supplant state currency, the one important task with iconographic significance that was left to Congress under the federal constitution.

The public soon took cognizance of the new designs. Craftsmen, printers, manufacturers, and private citizens adopted them for their own purposes and modified them to make statements about the Revolution, about republican government and society, and about the United States. Visual representation shaped the revolutionary experience for public consumption, made the past usable for the present, and transformed republican ideology from an ideology locked into a political crisis to one malleable enough to operate in changing economic and social conditions, to operate not only in adversity but in prosperity as well.

Iconography—both official and popular—publicized and defined the Revolution. Editors designed new mastheads for newspapers, and almanacs bore patriotic title pages. Artists and engravers depicted battles, famous places, and famous military events and portrayed heroes in popular prints. Iconography changed the landscape. Monuments and monumental buildings were constructed and identified with the republic by eagle plaques or statues of American heroes placed in niches. Patriots renamed streets, colleges, towns, and taverns. If the local tavern was named the King's Tavern, the owner might rebaptize it and give it a new sign, perhaps featuring George Washington on one side and a Native American on the other. Even ships floating in the harbors sported names of appropriate patriotism: *President, The Constitution, The United States, Congress, Liberty.*

Visual representations of and references to the Revolution facilitated its intellectual incorporation into the public consciousness and made visible the political and psychological consequences of victory. Cartographers drew new maps in which colonies became states, and Liberty took possession of the cartouches. Mapmaking thus verified the possession of territory. American artists also set out to improve the image of America quite literally. In seventeenth- and eighteenth-century Europe, engravers and potters were fond of representing the four continents allegorically as women. In these images, books, scientific instruments, globes, lyres, paintbrushes, and statues littered the ground around the figure of Europe, signifying that her glory rested on cultural achievements, while the figure of America—her nakedness covered to a greater or lesser extent with feathers—was often shown with an alligator or pineapple. Later, European engravers sometimes did identify America with Liberty, but they still refrained from portraying her as civilized and educated. American engravers not only clothed America—the first step toward civilizing her—but also identified her with education and culture by cluttering the landscape around her with the accoutrements of the arts and sciences. Engravers emphasized the importance of knowledge for republicans (in prints, Minerva leads little American boys up the winding path to the Temple of Wisdom) as well as their role in spreading knowledge (in library plates, Minerva gives books to Native Americans).

Myths glorified the revolutionary achievement. George Washington, Paul Revere, Valley Forge, the yeoman-soldier—all became subjects of myth. Old myths were refashioned to make them more indigenous. One engraver Americanized the "Fall from Grace" by adding rattles to the serpent shown in a European print. The rattlesnake, clearly American, showed that the culture inherited from the Old World would be transformed by the New.

Americans took cognizance of the Revolution both at home and at work. At home they pasted patriotic bookplates into their volumes, hung medallions or engravings of American heroes on their walls, painted their overmantels with patriotic themes, poured tea and coffee out of patriotic pots, ate off patriotic plates, and pinched snuff from patriotic boxes. At work both merchants and craftsmen displayed their identity with the new republic. Silversmiths designed eagle hallmarks; papermakers used eagle watermarks. Craftsmen fashioned their trade cards to make references to the republic, appealing to the patriotism of their fellow countrymen: "Americans, encourage the manufactures in your country if you wish for its prosperity."

Membership certificates to societies for promoting agriculture or manufacturing, like trade cards, processed the historical events and endowed them with meaning. Beehives, ploughs, sheep, and sheaves of wheat all suggested an idyllic agrarian landscape of tranquility and productivity—the landscape highly touted by Jefferson and Crèvecœur, which nourished independent and virtuous farmers capable of sustaining a republican government.[1] Ships, bales, wharves, cargo, anchors, scales–these icons on membership certificates depicted the buzz of economic activity, the commerce and manufacturing that Hamilton advocated. Membership certificates, whether for agricultural or manufacturing societies, drew on icons from both groups. They did not divide the world into two ideological camps; instead, they identified their society with everything that benefited a republic.

Objects bedecked with revolutionary symbols appear in increasing numbers in the 1790s. Trade in these objects was already brisk by the time the War of 1812 catapulted English exploitation of United States nationalism to new heights. Some patriotic objects were made in America; many were not (fig. 1). American production stayed within a traditional economic framework; foreign producers turned patriotism into a marketable commodity and, while contributing to an American sense of identity, also challenged principles that had bolstered the Revolution. Americans turned a variety of objects into displays of patriotism: ironware (andirons, flatirons, trivets, firebacks), wax medallions, embroidered samplers, shell pictures, paintings, signs, wooden carvings, woodcuts, prints, wallpaper, redware pottery, and buttons (fig. 2). None of these was produced in any quantity (except prints, to some extent), and none was very expensive. With the exception of prints, none had a wide distribution; most were available only locally. The inlay eagles that cabinetmakers put on furniture, however, did contrast with the other American objects in that they were produced in quantity and appeared on expensive objects.

In using objects as historical evidence it is possible to focus on the object, its producer, or its owner, who may or may not also have been the buyer. Focusing on the object is for the most part the domain of art historians and curators, but historians can use material objects to plumb human psychology: the motivation of the producer or buyer, and the attitude of the owner toward possession. In the case of early American objects, samplers and prints represent the extremes of the producer-

Figure 1.   Box, England, 1790–1810. Brass; H. ¹⁵/₁₆″, Diam. 2¹/₂″. (Winterthur.)

consumer spectrum. Samplers were not made for the purpose of selling. Instead, they served as a "voice" for the maker. Usually bearing the maker's name, samplers were often put on display to demonstrate her skill, moral sentiments, and perhaps knowledge. For example, a young New Englander of the late eighteenth century, Lydia Withington, stitched her name into the lower right-hand corner of her sampler of Boston Harbor. She claimed an association with Boston; she showed a knowledge of geography and cartography; and she identified herself and her work with the new republic by having an *E Pluribus Unum* eagle alight on the cartouche and another eagle soar above the compass

Figure 2.   Commemorative buttons, Philadelphia, 1789. *Top*, brass; Diam. 1⁵/₁₆″; *bottom*, copper. (Winterthur.) The oval links on the top button enclose state initials.

east-northeast of Hogg Island. The sampler itself shows how cultural norms were inculcated. Lydia not only learned to sew, she also displayed her patriotism.

Many girls produced mourning pictures for Washington. These glorified a hero of the republic and also made visible the act of remembering. In stitching a picture, the girl would have internalized a patriotism enhanced by sentimentality. In several such samplers the tomb says "sacred to the memory of George Washington," but what is sacred is not the tomb but the memory. The underlying message proclaimed that a republic drew strength from keeping alive its dead hero. And from a sacred memory it was a small step to a sacred George Washington. John James Barralet, in his engraving *The Apotheosis of Washington*, depicted Washington, arms outstretched, wafting on celestial currents up to paradise.

The new sentimental attitude toward death seen in stitched mourning pictures contrasted with the prerevolutionary Puritan attitude. Puritans believed they should be joyful at funerals because death released the soul for salvation. The mourning samplers that became popular after the Revolution, however, showed that people were now allowed to grieve and were even expected to do so. Grief put on display showed a person's capacity to feel. At the death of Washington, mourning became a national act, a quasi-communion at the altar of patriotism. Death became sentimentalized, and with the death of Washington so did patriotism. Weeping figures drooping over the tomb beneath willow or palm trees showed personal and emotional attachment to the republic, which, in the twenty years following the Revolution, had come to be personified by Washington.

Unlike the case of samplers, where the producer was also the consumer, prints were created in quantity for sale to a broad public. Printers, as entrepreneurs, advertised in newspapers to get customers to subscribe in advance and finance an engraved plate from which multiple prints could be run. Some printers and engravers sought to increase their sales by offering reductions in price to wholesalers who bought prints in bulk for resale to the public.

Most American objects glorifying the Revolution fell somewhere between the privacy of samplers and the broad market of prints. They emerged from a direct personal relationship between producer and consumer. Usually a customer ordered a particular object from a craftsman. Limners, for example, like engravers, produced images of George Washington; unlike engravers, however, they sold their skill rather than a stock of objects. They might produce a Washington medallion for a client, but they did not put Washington's image on objects in order to sell them. They made their living by teaching and by executing portraits on canvas, on ivory, or in wax. Itinerants for the most part, they established personal relationships with their customers, whose particular demands they sought to satisfy. Similarly, sign painters did not try to sell their products by painting George Washington on them. If they painted his image, they did so at the desire of a customer.

The trade in American-made objects that referred to the Revolution or to republican society was characterized by a common feeling between producer and consumer. The objects with their messages and iconography testify to a pride in the American achievement and a desire to publicize both the achievement and the pride. United States producers did not in general use American iconography to increase sales by creating new desires. Figureheads did not sell ships, and Washington's image did not sell signs, andirons, or firebacks. If a shopkeeper needed a sign, he might be pleased to have Washington's image on it, but he would not buy the sign unless he needed it. Similarly, the inlay eagles that were offered as an option on furniture were more a decorative motif than a marketing device.

There are indications, however, that the American market was changing. Although objects were not mass-produced and advertisements continued to inform prospective buyers of the availability of goods without trying to create a desire for them, the image of George Washington in various poses and manifestations was mass-produced, and clearly Americans felt a new need to have a national hero and to possess him. The figure of Washington became a commodity and, although multiplied rather than dismembered, was distributed among the people in a process analogous to the old trade in saints' relics. Craftsmen, painters, limners, engravers, and sculptors who produced his image catered to this need. Even though many people made small amounts of money from their ability to reproduce Washington's image, no large-scale venture arose in the United States to exploit this taste.

Although Americans did not mass-produce objects glorifying the Revolution, the Chinese and English did. These foreign producers did not hesitate to make use of the American Revolution and republican sentiment to sell their products. Their motivation differed from that of American producers, and their mode of production helped to stimulate American appetites and turn Americans into consumers of souvenirs.

On February 22, 1784, the *Empress of China* raised sail in New York harbor and headed for China with cotton, wool, fur, and ginseng root. When the ship returned fifteen months later with a cargo that netted a 25 percent return on the investment, merchants in New York, Salem, Boston, and Philadelphia hastened to outfit their own ships. The China trade had begun, and by the 1790s it was flourishing. At first tea and silk were considered the important cargo, and china served as ballast. But soon china became popular and assumed greater prominence in the trade.

Unlike American objects, Chinese porcelain was mass-produced and exported to various foreign markets by a highly organized and efficient system. Porcelain is a fine-grained, translucent, white ceramic ware made from kaolin and petuntse (a mixture of feldspar, white clay, and silica). Its production was broken down into many processes, and workers specialized in different tasks: mining the kaolin and petuntse, driving the buffalo that crushed the material, transporting the crushed material to warehouses, mixing the clay with water, putting the clay in the sun to dry, beating the baked clay, transporting it to the pottery, raising the object on a wheel or throwing the clay over a mold, putting the objects in the sun to dry, painting underglaze patterns (each painter specialized in a particular pattern), applying the glaze, packing the objects in saggers (boxes made of fire clay), stacking the saggers in kilns, stoking the fires of the kilns, decorating the porcelain after firing (sometimes overglaze decoration was put on at Canton to fill special orders), firing the pieces a second time, packing the pieces into barrels with straw, and transporting the porcelain to Canton. As many as seventy workers might contribute to the production of a piece for export (figs. 3, 4, 5, 6).[2]

In the China trade, the producer and consumer had no direct contact. They were separated by distance and even more by culture. The Chinese knew little about the West and cared to know nothing at all about the United States. They saw contact with foreigners as contami-

Figure 3.   *Carrying It [Clay] Home in Boats*, China, 1800–1810. Watercolor; H. 9³⁄₈″, W. 9⁵⁄₈″. (Winterthur.) The fifth in a series of twenty-three paintings depicting the various processes in the mass production of Chinese porcelain.

nation and took measures to prevent it. Chinese were not allowed to teach their language to foreigners, and foreigners were confined to restricted areas and not allowed into Canton.

Nevertheless, the Chinese did produce porcelain especially for the American market—porcelain bearing the emblem of the Society of the Cincinnati, eagles (scrawny eagles, eagles dressed in American chevrons, and Rhode Island eagles placing their hope in God), and the tomb of Washington. The initiative for such designs, however, came not from the producers but from American merchants. In placing a spe-

Figure 4.   [*Turning Clay into Dishes*], China, 1800–1810. Watercolor; H. 9⅛″, W. 9⅞″. (Winterthur.) The tenth in a series of twenty-three paintings depicting the various processes in the mass production of Chinese porcelain.

cial order, a merchant would send the painters something to copy. Each painter would reproduce the foreign designs as faithfully as possible considering his complete ignorance of the significance of the designs. In one case an artist, given a print of George Washington to copy, reproduced it stipple and all (fig. 7). In another case the porcelain came back decorated with both the picture and the instructions, "This is the drawing to copy."³ In still another case a painter peopled the Continental Congress with a cast of Chinese patriots solemnly signing the Declaration of Independence. Once the American trade was well established, however, an American design such as the eagle became standard—even

Figure 5.   *Taking Out, Packing, and Weighing*, China, 1800–1810. Watercolor; H. 9¼″, W. 10″. (Winterthur.) The fifteenth in a series of twenty-three paintings depicting the various processes in the mass production of Chinese porcelain.

though the Chinese taxonomy of the eagle included several unorthodox aviary specimens.

The Chinese trade in objects glorifying the Revolution differed from the internal American trade in two ways: the producers did not share the same culture as the consumers, and the objects were mass-produced. Thanks to its system of mass production, China shipped large quantities of fairly standardized wares to America. But for whom were the imported wares destined? Chinese porcelain came in large sets: services for breakfast, dinner, and tea. A tea service would have 50 pieces; a dinner set had from 170 to 300 and would typically include dinner, soup, and dessert plates, salad bowls, oblong and round platters of various sizes,

Figure 6.   *Loading Boats for Canton*, China, 1800–1810. Watercolor; H. 9⁷/₁₆″, W. 10″. (Winterthur.) The twenty-second in a series of twenty-three paintings depicting the various processes in the mass production of Chinese porcelain.

insets or drainers for the larger platters, tureens of two heights (12 ³/₄″ and 5″), and sauce boats. American merchants dealing in Chinese porcelain were serving an elite market—people who had grand parties and put their food on display. Cookbooks of the period suggested menus, illustrated the arrangement of the courses on the table, and provided recipes.[4] Symmetrical placement of dishes on the table meant that serving pieces had to come in even-numbered multiples. The Chinese also produced exotic pieces of porcelain that conferred status on the owner: large urns; three-, five-, or seven-piece garnitures for the mantel; and fruit compotes. Given the elitist character of these imports, it is quite appro-

Figure 7.   Flagon, China, 1810–20. Porcelain, H. 11 1/8″. From an engraving by David Edwin after Gilbert Stuart. (Winterthur.)

priate that the first American iconography on Chinese porcelain was the badge of the Society of the Cincinnati, a recently established hereditary order for officers of the American and French armies who had fought in the American Revolution (fig. 8).

Figure 8.   Teapot, China, 1800–1815. Porcelain, hand painted; H. 4⅝″.
(Winterthur.) The gilt initials "ES" indicate that the piece was ordered for an
individual.

As soon as America emerged from the depression of the mid 1780s
and Americans once again had money to spend, English manufacturers, like the Chinese, began to produce objects with iconography
that celebrated the Revolution and the new republic: prints and
maps, buttons, snuffboxes, enamel mirror knobs and curtain tiebacks,
textiles, handkerchiefs, wallpaper, plaques, Staffordshire statuettes, and
creamware. The British launched the trade in American souvenirs,
producing a wide range of objects (figs. 9, 10). The best-organized of
these manufacturing ventures was the production of creamware in
the Midlands. English creamware, like Chinese porcelain, was mass-
produced, and English producers, like their Chinese counterparts, did
not identify with the sentiments or ideology of Americans although, of
course, they were much better acquainted with American culture than
were the Chinese.

Figure 9.   Brush, England, 1789–97. Beech, polychrome; H. 2¹/₄″, L. 9¹/₄″. (Winterthur.)

Just before the American Revolution, English potters developed the technique of transferring engraved prints onto creamware, allowing them rapidly to turn out objects bearing detailed images. English creamware, like Chinese porcelain, displayed eagles: *E Pluribus Unum* eagles, militaristic swan-eagles, and turkey-eagles (fig. 11). The British eagles, however, were bigger and busier than the hand-painted Chinese variety. They might spread over the whole belly of a pitcher. Often they were part of an allegorical print and might bear a message such as MAY SUCCESS ATTEND OUR AGRICULTURE TRADE AND MANUFACTURES. The word *our* dissociated the object from the producer, who subsided into anonymity, and identified the object with the consumer, who was glorified together with the republic. The verbal message was reinforced by a picture—perhaps of a particular ship or person—on the other side of the object. The general and the specific, the abstract and the personal, and the message

Figure 10.   Razor, England, 1800–1825. Horn, steel; L. 5¹⁵/₁₆″. (Winterthur.) The handle is decorated with the figure of Washington; a beehive, symbolizing industry; and a cornucopia, symbolizing plenty. On the reverse of the handle is a bust of Liberty.

and the agent worked together. Pitchers, bowls, and mugs commemorated patriots (Washington, Benjamin Franklin, John Adams) who had brought the republic into existence and abstractions (Liberty, Commerce, Agriculture) that sustained it. The English potters, sublimely indifferent to the propaganda and ideology of their wares, produced American eagles tearing apart British lions. They bore no grudge against George Washington, a marketable commodity who filled their coffers, although they did not much care how accurately they represented him. Washington decorated English wares as a military hero, a president, a corpse, and an airborne seraph (fig. 12). English potters thought Americans might also appreciate creamware that showed Gen. Charles Cornwallis's surrender. (In the War of 1812, even while cannonballs were flying, English potters churned out transfer-printed wares

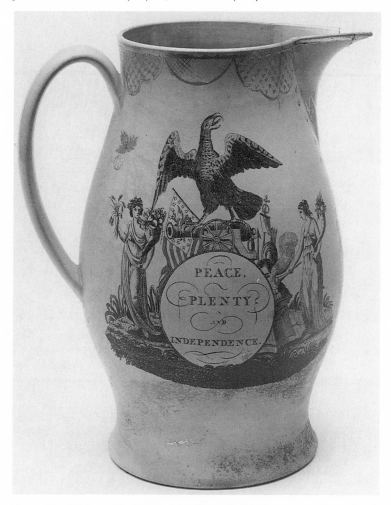

Figure 11. Pitcher, England, 1792–1825. Earthenware, transfer printed; H. 10½″. (Winterthur.)

celebrating American victories for Americans and British victories for the British.)[5]

The large quantities of creamware that survive and their explicit iconography allow us to draw certain inferences and conclusions about

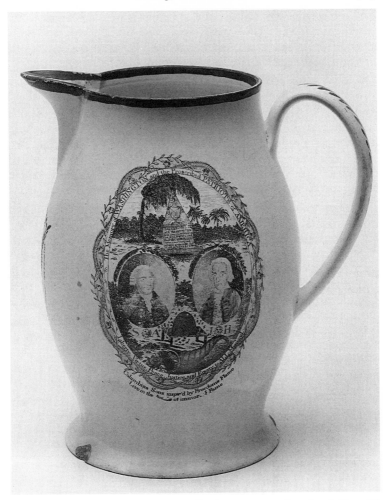

Figure 12. Pitcher, England, 1804–25. Earthenware, transfer printed; H. 10³/₈″. (Winterthur.) The floral border encloses a memorial print, *The Memory of Washington and Proscribed Patriots of America*. Washington's tomb is flanked by portrait busts of Samuel Adams and John Hancock.

the British trade. First of all, English producers were not aiming at an elite market. They sought to make money by selling in volume at a price that even tradespeople and sailors could afford. In general the objects were sold singly as souvenirs rather than as dinner sets or tea services.

While the English producers, like the Chinese, identified an American market and catered to it, they were also geared to specialized markets. For example, pitchers with Masonic signs on one side and patriotic symbols on the other represented a union between the Masons and the new republic (fig. 13). Similarly, English producers emphasized the patriotism of individual states by associating the state symbol with an eagle representing the nation. Sailors could buy a pitcher expressing their sentiments and displaying their patriotism. Craftsmen could buy mugs glorifying the association of their craft with the new nation.

The most popular forms of transfer-printed creamware—pitchers, mugs, and bowls—suggest the social function of these objects glimmering with visual messages. They would be used in a convivial gathering in which people expressed their sentiments publicly, affirmed their relationship with others, and sealed both sentiments and relationship with a toast. The pitcher with "Success to the Sailor" or "Success to the Trade of Vermont" emblazoned under the snout in effect toasted the group that was using it. The pitchers scripted the activity in which they were used and commented on its validity. Toasting enhanced patriotism by encouraging people to voice their sentiments in public.

Why did English potters make pitchers for sailors, Masons, or cordwainers? There were sound reasons in each case. Sailors as a group offered a promising target in the souvenir trade because they were numerous, traveled, and were exposed to the objects. Also, a shipping boom that lasted from 1793 to 1808 inflated their wages from $8 to $30 a month, giving them money to spend on souvenirs.[6] Societies like the Masons could be represented emblematically and therefore offered an easy marketing target. Craftsmen in the United States did not form guilds, but they do seem to have inherited the coats of arms of the British guilds. These symbols gave them a corporate identity psychologically and visually, although not legally. The coat of arms expressed the idea of a corporation with a will of its own, and the national emblems— the eagle, the flag, Liberty—juxtaposed with the coat of arms indicated

Figure 13. Pitcher, England, 1800–1825. Earthenware, transfer printed; H. 7¹/₂″. (Winterthur.)

the disposition of this corporate will toward the republic or toward the Constitution.

In the English trade, the consumer and the producer did not share the same sentiments. English producers were interested in the consumer only as consumer. Their strategy was to produce cheap wares that spoke to different nonelite segments of society. The pictures and messages used were chosen to entice Americans in general or specific groups of Americans to buy the product. The British producer was not trying to fill a need; he was trying to create a desire. And he succeeded.

Various relationships between consumers and producers characterized the American, Chinese, and British trade in objects that referred to the Revolution and the new republic. The mass production of souvenirs of the Revolution encouraged American buying, but the trade also put American buyers in a somewhat anomalous position. The buying spree of the 1790s took place in a political and historical context. How Americans responded to, interpreted, and reflected on their consumption bore reference to the events and political ideology that the material objects glorified. The way in which the Revolution was conducted and the development of an ideology that defined certain acts as political and certain behavior as appropriate had grown out of patterns of consumption that preceded the Revolution.

Historians John McCusker and Russell Menard have demonstrated that during the eighteenth century demands for goods rose in the colonies for a variety of reasons, such as growing population, improved transportation, and rising levels of personal income and wealth. Under these conditions, the import trade increased dramatically. Between 1720 and 1770 per capita imports rose by about 50 percent. The increase was sharper during the end of the period, between 1750 and 1770. Most of these imports were manufactured goods rather than raw materials, food, or semimanufactured goods.[7]

The political crisis between the American colonies and Great Britain that began in 1764 took place in an environment of rising consumption of British goods. Although the primary issue in contest was not economic, still economic conditions colored the colonists' response to the political crisis. Colonists were engaged in a buying spree when parliamentary taxes brought them up short. More people had more money than they had ever had before, and many of them were spending it in much the same way as the English spent theirs. They bought expensive imports, such as porcelain and fabrics; they gambled; they attended the theater; and they engaged in activities like horse racing and cockfighting.

Americans responded to the political crisis by resolving to change the way they lived. Many of the changes grew out of economic boycotts designed to put pressure on English exporters in the hope that they would lobby in Parliament for the repeal of repressive legislation. The nonimportation, nonexportation, and nonconsumption agreements, while pragmatic, also fit in with the colonial ethic of frugality. Extravagance meant spending money on luxuries, and luxury led to corruption. As it happened, luxury items, as opposed to necessities, almost all came from England. Therefore, the boycott of English imports had moral as well as pragmatic connotations. But colonists also reformed their lives in ways that had no economic bearing on England and were exclusively moral. They resolved not to hold horse races or cockfights, not to play cards, and not to go to the theater. The revolutionary atmosphere had called forth an ethic of asceticism that was linked to the political ideology evolving at the same time. This political, republican ideology was also formulated in moral terms. Reformers wanted to cleanse government of corruption by having proportionate representation, frequent elections, and residency requirements and by eliminating sinecures, patronage, plural office holding, and standing armies. A virtuous citizenry would participate actively in government.[8]

According to the accepted political theory of the day, grounded in the ideas of Charles-Louis Montesquieu, the character of a people determined the form of government they could sustain. Monarchies depended on a people motivated by honor; tyrannies, on a people motivated by fear; republics, on a people motivated by virtue. Without a virtuous citizenry, republics would collapse. Americans had established thirteen republics and one confederated republic, so virtue for them had a certain urgency; the survival of their government depended on it. They defined virtue as industry and frugality.

What happened to the prewar morality of asceticism after the Revolution? A brief postwar economic boom swamped frugality, but in 1784 when the boom collapsed and an economic depression hit the country, the rhetoric of asceticism once again resounded in the newspapers. Luxuries were again condemned as the cause of corruption and imports from England as a form of enslavement. "After all the blood and treasure we have expended," complained one editor, "we are actually taxed by Great Britain. Our imports help to fill her revenue, and to pay the interest of a debt contracted to enslave us." Another wrote, "Let us examine the dress of a fine gentleman, or even of the plainest citizen, who walks the streets of Philadelphia; and upon a calculation, we will probably find, that he pays a much higher yearly tax to the King of

Great-Britain, than to the Congress of the United States."[9] Americans interpreted in political terms the economic depression brought about by their own irresponsible willingness to contract debts. Having transformed an economic crisis into a constitutional grievance, Americans resurrected the ascetic rhetoric of the early days of the imperial crisis. Consumption, associated with British imports, resumed its politically suspect position as a cause of economic and moral enslavement that endangered the survival of the confederation.

In the late 1780s Americans, prosperous once again, increased consumption. Most of the objects they bought were foreign—Chinese, British, or French—and many, especially those with revolutionary iconography, would have been classified as luxuries rather than necessities (fig. 14). In the 1790s Americans abandoned the revolutionary ethic of frugality. They did so just at the time they had established a new federal republic, when they must have been concerned about its success. Virtue was now valued for political as well as moral reasons. This new slant on virtue is reflected in Americans' changing aesthetic taste. After the Revolution, allegory supplanted satire as the most popular aesthetic style. While satire was grounded in visible virtue, allegory was grounded in visible vice. This shift in taste can be seen in the political prints of the day.

Before the Revolution, English political prints served both the British and American markets. Highly satirical, these prints laid bare the vices and follies of society by ridiculing those who held political power. Who was ridiculed depended on the political bent of the satirist, but in the scramble and shuffle in England from 1762 through 1783, when ministries toppled and factions coalesced and dissolved, the opportunities for capturing an enemy in an act of corruption or folly seemed limitless.

After the Revolution, a different sort of print found a vogue in America. The grotesque world of homo-unsapiens sprouting tails, horns, hooves, or feathers; of devils; pissing dogs; and waddling-geese politicians gave way to a world populated by divine women: America, Liberty, Peace, Plenty, Wisdom, Learning, Agriculture, and Commerce (fig. 15). The eighteenth-century taste for allegory is not one we share today. When confronted with a gallery of languid goddesses displaying their name tags and emblems, draped over steps that lead nowhere, leaning against Doric columns that support nothing, or twiddling a globe amid a throng of docile obese cherubs, our attention flags. But people in the

Figure 14.   Mantel clock, Arsand, Paris, 1780–1800. Ormolu, marble; H. 20″, W. 14⅛″. (Winterthur.) A banner below the clock face bears the inscription "Washington/First in War, First in Peace/First in the Hearts of His Countrymen."

Figure 15. Memorial to George Washington, China, 1800–1815. Painting on glass; H. 28⅝″, W. 21″. (Winterthur.) The medallion of Washington is surrounded by Love, embracing the medallion; Honor, looking on; and Justice, holding scales and a sword and wearing a Masonic apron.

eighteenth century loved this means of communicating—and it *is* a means of communication, for allegory always bears a message.

What does the taste for allegorical presentation tell us about early Americans? First, allegories replaced satire in the 1780s and 1790s. Political satires appeared occasionally, but they were far outnumbered by allegories. Satire exposes vice by making people realize the difference between what is and what ought to be. Americans in the confederation and early national periods felt particularly threatened by vice. According to accepted political theory, vice among citizens would topple republics. It was not only evil but also politically subversive. Americans wanted to prevent vice, but they could not bear to admit its existence.

Allegory, not satire, best suited their needs. Allegory portrays the world as it ought to be, an idealized world. Unity of purpose replaces the tension of satire. Interlocking images reinforce each other: Concord, Productivity, Abundance, Commerce, Learning, and Industry all contribute to the meaning of the whole, a republic. Personifications such as Liberty, Wisdom, or Agriculture replace the real people of the satires who had been ridiculed with unreal names, such as Jeremy Twitcher, Lord Gawkee, or His Grace of Spital Fields (fig. 16). Allegorical prints, purged of nasty particulars, expressed a wish fulfilled through visual abstraction.

Morality flows through allegories and sustains them. Allegories express a moral message that depends on analogy. However tedious we may find the morality, and however inane we may find the method of proceeding by rote correspondences, we should not lose sight of the prominence of morality in the social and political order of the new republic. A well-ordered republic was an expression of virtue, and virtue sustained the republic and kept it in order.

Allegories balanced abstractions with hagiolatry, the idealization of heroes. Virtuous people who had served the republic were put on display in prints, statues, statuettes, and plaques. When Washington or Franklin mingled with female abstractions in an allegory, the juxtaposition reinforced the moral message. Women stood for republican virtues; men, singled out because of their deeds, were associated with female virtues, and the print itself glorified the republic by fixing it in the very act of honoring its virtuous leaders. Unlike the identifiable people in satiric prints, individuals shown in allegories were the heroes of the print and not its victims, and the allegories, by their inclusion of heroes,

Figure 16.   John Christian Ranshner, *In Memory of Washington*, United States, 1800. Wax, pearwood, shell; H. 26³/₄″, W. 22¹/₂″. (Winterthur.) The base of the obelisk is covered with various trophies. To the left are Charity, holding a baby, and Liberty, holding a liberty pole; to the right are Minerva, wearing a helmet, and Plenty, holding a cornucopia.

showed that republics prized gratitude. Revolutionary iconography, pregnant with morality and packaged in allegory and hagiolatry, glorified and commemorated the Revolution and idealized the virtuous republics that issued from it.

How did the souvenir trade fare in the 1790s, a decade in which the new federal republic was buoyed by prosperity? Objects with revolutionary iconography proliferated, many of them imported from England or China. Americans, newly prosperous because of their shipping, bought these objects: creamware from the English Midlands, Chinese porcelain, ormolu and gilt-bronze clocks from France, hardly necessities or conveniences but thoroughbred luxuries made enticing to the consumer with emblems of the republic. With frugality an acknowledged moral norm of republican ideology, how could the virtuous republican citizen justify buying a two-hundred-piece dinner set of porcelain bearing the federal eagle? Surely he would have been struck by the oxymoron of republican extravagance. But the republican iconography in reality may have provided a rationale for consumption. A cordwainer buying a pitcher with his craft's coat of arms juxtaposed with the federal eagle, or a merchant buying a dinner set of federal-emblem china, was pledging allegiance to the new nation. They were not buying luxuries but chunks of patriotism.

Eighteenth-century critics defined allegory as saying one thing and meaning another. It is possible to see republican allegories as a kind of duplicity that eased the conscience of the consumer. The goddesses with their emblems preached virtue, which in republican terms meant industry and frugality. Industry and frugality would produce plenty, and plenty was associated with peace and independence. But the iconography was deceptive. The cornucopia (Plenty) bursting with fruit and grain should have been shown disgorging porcelain tea services, Liverpool pitchers, ormolu clocks, enamel snuffboxes, French and British wallpaper, and printed handkerchiefs. Plenty is represented in the prints as productivity in the necessities of life, not as consumption of luxuries. The allegories cleaned up the economic activity and, by filtering it through a republican and patriotic screen, legitimized it. The iconography on the objects may have operated as a substitute morality. Americans buying luxuries with patriotic iconography and messages could leave behind the austerity of revolutionary morality at the same time that they glorified the Revolution and idealized the republic.

With the help of iconography, the Revolution entered the American consciousness. As Americans brought objects decorated with patriotic motifs into their houses, the violent Revolution became domesticated. People established an intimacy with revolutionary heroes by adorning themselves with revolutionary accoutrements: George Washington gleamed from shoe buckles and flashed from rings; Washington buttons fastened clothing; and his memorial lockets dangled from female bosoms. The death of Washington hastened the sentimentalizing of the Revolution. Meanwhile, highly visible objects such as weathervanes, signs, ship figureheads, currency, and flags as well as more ephemeral expressions of patriotism such as parades, toasts, and fireworks made the Revolution visible and public, portraying it as a legacy shared by all.

Domesticated, personalized, sentimentalized, and democratized, the Revolution was also adulterated. The process of manufacturing the Revolution logically entailed selling it. At first revolutionary iconography served as a decorative motif expressing the sentiments of the maker or the client. But with the influx of mass-produced objects from China and England, it became a marketing device. Producers did not share the sentiments of the consumers; they wanted only to make money. George Washington, who had spent years begging Congress for clothes and food for his troops and who served without pay as head of the American army, became both an object of consumption and an implicit salesman—a falsity that subsequent generations have embraced and embellished. Republican leaders stressed frugality and abhorred extravagance, which they defined as spending money on luxuries, unnecessary objects. Today, Americans glorify consumption. Stores celebrate the birthday of the first president with seductive sales, and Americans rush out to gratify their appetites and buy, buy, buy—happy in the belief that George Washington would have wanted it that way.

---

[1] For the relationship between agrarian iconography and republican ideology, see Ann Fairfax Withington, "Republican Bees: The Political Economy of the Beehive in Eighteenth-Century America," in *Studies in Eighteenth-Century Culture*, vol. 18, ed. John W. Yolton and Leslie E. Brown (East Lansing, Mich.: Colleagues Press, 1988), pp. 39–77.

[2] Alfred Tamarin and Shirley Glubok, *Voyaging to Cathay: Americans in the China Trade* (New York: Viking Press, 1976), pp. 71–84. The authors have reproduced a series of watercolors on porcelain produced by an unknown Chinese artist, 1800–1810. The watercolors are at Winterthur.

[3] Tamarin and Glubok, *Voyaging to Cathay*, p. 87.

[4] Susan Grey Detweiler, *George Washington's Chinaware* (New York: Harry N. Abrams, 1982), p. 133. Detweiler reproduces a suggested arrangement for two courses of a dinner presented by John Farley in *The London Art of Cookery and Housekeeper's Complete Assistant* (London, 1785).

[5] Christina H. Nelson, "Transfer-printed Creamware and Pearlware for the American Market," *Winterthur Portfolio* 15, no. 2 (Summer 1980): 93–115.

[6] Curtis P. Nettels, *The Emergence of a National Economy, 1775–1815* (New York: Holt, Rinehart, and Winston, 1962), pp. 233–35.

[7] John J. McCusker and Russell R. Menard, *The Economy of British North America, 1607–1789* (Chapel Hill: University of North Carolina Press, 1985), pp. 277–87. McCusker and Menard use the data to show that imports from Great Britain were not expanding as fast as the British-American economy. They therefore postulate the demand for goods exceeded the supply, a situation that encouraged domestic manufacturing. For my purpose, the significance of their data lies simply in the dramatic increase in British exports.

[8] For a discussion of ascetic morality as a political strategy, see Ann Fairfax Withington, *Toward a More Perfect Union: Virtue and the Formation of American Republics* (New York: Oxford University Press, 1991).

[9] *Pennsylvania Mercury*, August 10, 1787; *Dunlap's American Daily Advertiser*, August 23, 1791.

Habit and Habitat at Peale's Philadelphia Museum

Charlotte M. Porter

In the United States, Thomas Jefferson's study of large fossil remains (paleontology) and Alexander Wilson's study of birds (ornithology) marked out different paths for American science during the early republic. Jefferson's approach led to the federally funded scientific surveys characteristic of the nineteenth century, while Wilson's methods attracted private enterprise and publication. Since both types of study involved collections, museums were essential to their advancement. One of the first natural history museums in the United States was Charles Willson Peale's Philadelphia Museum, established in 1786.[1]

Located in Philosophical Hall of the American Philosophical Society from 1794 to 1802, Peale's museum eventually exhibited more than 243 birds and 212 mounted quadrupeds as well as fish, shells, rocks, insects, and various ethnographic artifacts. During the early republic it served the United States government as a repository for the finds of major exploring expeditions—those of Lewis and Clark, Stephen H. Long, and Charles Wilkes. These collections, which included many new species, brought scientific renown to Peale's museum, but they were not the first of their kind. The Charleston Library Society had opened a natural history museum in 1773, and collections of curiosities—some more scientific than others—were to be found in other cities.

In Peale's museum, science, technology, and education came together under one roof.[2] Although Peale himself did not write a major technical work, his collections popularized the scientific ideas of others.

The collections demonstrated the close link between artistic statement and scientific novelty in those years. Peale enjoyed his museum's fame, and he masterfully used the appeal of natural history in the United States to promote graphic arts, engraving, and early experiments with lithography.

The museum also supplied materials for illustrators and models for painters. Equally important, it cultivated an audience willing to buy their works. Peale's exhibits included a portrait gallery of famous Americans. On the museum walls, natural and human history were to be viewed together. A British tourist preferred the collection of artifacts, complaining, "The proprietor unfortunately happens to be a painter and has disfigured it with some wretched specimens of his art, most of which are pretended portraits of worthies, born only to be forgotten."[3] Benjamin Franklin, Nathanael Greene, and David Rittenhouse, to mention a few, were not to be forgotten.

The idea of a museum was novel to many Americans, but Peale, who had studied in London, was aware of precedents. European "cabinets," or assemblages of curiosities, that were open to the public typically included biological specimens, Native American novelties, Chinese porcelain, and Roman coins—the objects people, then and now, most like to see. These collections were products of exploration and colonial expansion. During the eighteenth century British patrons fostered a pattern of correspondence and exchange with American naturalists. Since biological specimens were often new species unknown to science, agriculture, and horticulture, they traveled in one direction, to Europe. Thus, economic interests combined with natural history pursuits to establish great collections, including Britain's Royal Botanic Gardens (Kew).[4] Even after the American Revolution, affluent London amateurs continued to spend a great deal to import species of plants and animals.

Charles Willson Peale was unusual among his contemporaries because he recognized that American species should be housed in the United States. Then as now, stable, permanent collections required money for acquisitions and maintenance, and Peale lacked funds. In February 1790 he circulated among "the great Public of the American States" a long printed broadside seeking financial support. He hoped to have a building designed by Benjamin Henry Latrobe for the south side of the State House garden in Philadelphia: "The Public are therefore the more cheerfully solicited to help forward this tender plant, while it is yet under the nurturing care and anxious attention of its present possessor, and until it shall have grown into maturity." He indicated the significance of his project, noting that "much might be said of the importance that such a collection and arrangement would be of to society."[5]

On a more practical level, Peale had a large family to feed. It was his intention "to get the Museum on a public Establishment." Peale wanted permanence, preservation, and position. After the federal government moved to Philadelphia in 1790, he asked President Washington to aid his enterprise by appointing him postmaster general. Peale needed a way to give his museum "a National Magnitude" and to assure financial security for his extended family, which it supported. He was unsuccessful, but he was not easily discouraged. Two years later he brought together a twenty-seven-member museum board of "Inspectors or Visitors," with Jefferson as its president.[6] Despite the existence of this board, the General Assembly of Pennsylvania was not moved to fund Peale's museum. German-speaking and Quaker representatives objected to state interference in education and opposed the type of legislation Peale needed. In January 1802, Peale wrote Jefferson to appeal for the nationalization of his museum: "Things huddeled togather as I am now obliged to put them, loose much of their beauty and usefulness, they cannot be seen to advantage for study."[7] He argued that government subsidy was essential for the lasting purpose of any museum, the safekeeping of collections. His plea was unsuccessful.

Funding and permanent storage for collections proved to be a formidable challenge in the new nation. Peale had to mark time before the Pennsylvania legislature agreed to allow him to use the State House free of rent. In the interim several other planned museums failed. In New York the Tammany Society established the American Museum in 1790; five years later the society relinquished its collections to the keeper, Gardiner Baker. Baker died soon afterward, and the collections were dispersed. In Peale's own city of Philadelphia the contents of the equally short-lived American Museum of Pierre Eugène Du Simitière were auctioned in 1785. One man could not hold together a museum, and Peale repeatedly reminded those he petitioned for funds that his museum reflected the industry of one enthusiastic man — himself. Peale and other American naturalists such as Alexander Wilson and Thomas Say observed foreign patronage of science with mixed emotions. The French government, for example, set aside Fr 20,000 a year to train and equip collectors. The results were an increased empirical base and multiple specimens, some reserved for study, others for display.[8] In 1803 the ornithological holdings of the Natural History Museum in Paris numbered 3,411 specimens. By contrast, ten years of unpaid effort by Peale, with the help of his children and Wilson, yielded only one-third of that number.

Lacking funds for a museum building, Peale kept his collections from 1802 until 1827 on the upper level of the Pennsylvania State House (now Independence Hall). This was the building in which the Constitutional Convention sat, and the continuing civic functions in rooms upstairs led to interesting juxtapositions for Peale's displays. One end of the main gallery, the Long Room, abutted the Negro witness room of the Guardians of the Poor. By 1812 the Long Room displayed 1,240 birds, 6,000 insects, 1,920 minerals and fossils, and other "miscellaneous curiosities." It also contained an organ with 85 stops. Leaving the Long Room, the visitor took the stairs to the Marine Room, which contained 121 fish, 148 snakes, 112 lizards, and 40 tortoises and turtles. Lower animals on the Great Chain of Being were also represented, and not all of them were small: among 1,044 shells and corals were several giant Indian Ocean bivalves weighing 150 pounds. Other rooms featured costumed wax figures with artifacts and a series of dressed-up "anthromorphs" (monkeys) "employed in the occupations of men." A private apartment discreetly displayed potentially offensive "anatomical preparations."[9]

The "mammoth," Peale's greatest treasure, created his reputation at home and abroad. The "antique wonder" was reconstructed from remains exhumed from marl pits near Newburgh, New York. Peale financed the dig with an interest-free loan from the American Philosophical Society and enlisted the help of Caspar Wistar, a knowledgeable anatomist and influential member of the society. The result of this collaborative effort was a giant skeleton, 11' 5" high and 18' long. At the museum the monster required its own exhibition space. Peale opened the Mammoth Room on December 24, 1801, and kept it open until 10 P.M. every day except Sunday. Having incurred a debt of $2,000 during the dig, Peale was compelled to charge a separate admission fee of 50¢ to enter the room; this was twice the price of general admission. A second skeleton was taken abroad by his oldest sons and correctly classified by George Cuvier in 1806 as an American "mastodonte."[10] Special attractions with separate fees, such as the mammoth or the "Famous Grisly

Bear" of 1803, supplemented general admission fees, but the amounts were insufficient to finance daily operations of the museum.

Peale initiated special events in part to raise money. These Tuesday and Thursday evening programs, enlivened by music, were social gatherings. They provided participants, he said, with "an agreeable and fashionable lounge." In 1800 he advertised a "Course of Lectures on the Science of Nature with Original Music." This program combined the "Beauties of Creation" with a dirge for his first son, Titian, who died in his youth. Peale's approach was sentimental but sophisticated. In 1816 he pioneered the installation of gaslights in the galleries. This step was part of his imitation of exterior space and permitted visitors to enjoy the museum after dark. Ignoring a common stricture, Peale did not segregate visitors with separate viewing times for men and women. In fact, many of Peale's practices violated museum etiquette of the day. Situated on the upper story above street noise and dust kicked up by horses, the Long Room appears to have been refreshingly airy, thanks to its high ceilings and tall windows. Peale's exhibits attracted local and national dignitaries, Native American delegations, and foreign travelers. Even in their first location on Lombard Street, the collections were a marvelous sight.[11]

Peale's museum expanded beyond collections. The Lecture Room in the State House became a site of scientific instruction, an important part of Peale's designs. Later, lectures were also delivered in the hall of the University of Pennsylvania as Peale strengthened his institutional ties and academic credentials. The *Philadelphia Medical and Physical Journal* announced in 1805 a series of natural history lectures divided into nomenclatural and philosophical discussions of zoology. The latter included physiology, manners, instincts, and uses of animal species. These lectures in the "valuable MUSEUM of Mr. Peale" were informal counterparts to instruction offered by Benjamin Smith Barton, the first professor of natural history at the University of Pennsylvania. Following Barton's unexpected death in 1815 and the demise of the natural history department at the University of Pennsylvania, Peale created a museum faculty of naturalists consisting of Gerard Troost, Richard Harlan, Thomas Say, and John Davidson Godman.[12]

While collections and lectures reflected the museum's content, another side of Peale's educational approach was behavioral. A visit to the museum complemented a local custom, the evening stroll. In 1796 a tourist described the hot, muggy Philadelphia summer: "During these days no one stirred out of doors that was not compelled to do so. . . . A very different scene was presented in the city as soon as the sun was set; every house was then thrown open, and the inhabitants all crowded into the streets, to take their evening walks, and visit their acquaintance." Peale managed to convert the fashionable circuit walk into an indoor experience. The promenade became "A Walk with a Friend to the Museum," and Peale used this phrase as the title of a guidebook he published for visitors. In its earliest conception, Peale's museum walk brought together the physical elements of an eighteenth-century garden. The Reverend Manasseh Cutler recalled "a mound of earth, considerably raised, & covered with green turf from which a number of trees ascended & branched out in different directions. . . . In the pond was a collection of fish with their skins stuffed."[13]

Like picturesque gardens, Peale's exhibits were intended to be viewed in succession. He even constructed a grotto, the prototype for the walk-through caves of many modern museums. In the rooms he integrated collections of curios and examples of technology and arranged them "in a most romantic & amusing manner." With the popular "magic lanthorn," Peale created outdoor transparent paintings of historical subjects and expensive mobile montages or moving pictures. He also exploited theatrical effects inside the museum with carved, wooden waves moved by cranks with real spray spurting from hidden pipes. Waxworks heightened the dramatic appeal of 800 ethnographic artifacts. Among these Peale placed a wax figure of himself, realistic in every detail except that it did not "take a part in ye. conversation."[14] In the end, Peale's museum visitor became both observer and participant, actor and audience.

Not everyone enjoyed these artificial effects. Early feminist Frances Wright was "a little offended": "It had been in better taste, perhaps, to turn the upper rooms of this empty sanctuary into a library, instead of a museum of natural curiosities or a maesoleum of dead monsters." Other visitors identified with Peale's taste and enjoyed seeing their own likenesses in this unusual setting. For 8¢, Moses Williams, Peale's freed slave, created profiles with a "physiognotrace." Wright had missed the point altogether. Peale's 130 portraits of revolutionary heroes were intended as intellectual role models, and to these worthies Peale added notable men of science such as David Rittenhouse, William Maclure, and

William Bartram. His museum was a kind of library in which objects played the role of books. The "Book of Nature" was the emblem he preferred, and it was printed for all to see on the museum's admission ticket. Peale consistently associated natural history with books and literacy. That he routinely published donations to the museum in local newspapers suggests that his target was the reading public. His museum needed and supported the publishing arts, and Peale explored many facets of printing in his uneven efforts to promote intellectual culture among his fellow citizens.[15]

In 1808 Peale took on an additional responsibility, one that became central to his museum's purpose. He began to amass and illustrate the natural history findings of government expeditions to the Far West. The museum served as a repository for collections made during expeditions and surveys, establishing both a purpose and a pathway of growth for other scientific institutions during the nineteenth century. Procedures for proper handling and accession of federal collections were poorly defined, however. Neither Meriwether Lewis nor George Clark was trained in the rudiments of collecting, and although the zoological objects they and Zebulon Pike sent back to President Jefferson were scientifically exciting, not all were suitable for exhibition. Jefferson retained the best specimens at his Poplar Forest estate. Things he could not keep, or did not care for, he forwarded to Peale, who drew pictures of a few of them. Other materials arrived in Philadelphia inadequately preserved for public exhibition. The frail remains of several damaged Louisiana tanagers had to be pieced together in order to complete one exhibit mount.[16]

The museum and the public were better served by the next federally sponsored scientific expedition to the trans-Mississippi West, the Stephen H. Long expedition of 1819. Peale secured his own interests by arranging a place for his youngest son, a second boy named Titian. The teenager, an enthusiastic marksman, was to bag specimens and prepare skins for the museum. Knowledge that Titian was retracing parts of the Lewis and Clark route seems to have rekindled the aging artist's enthusiasm. During the expedition's first season Peale began work on an oil composition, *Noah and His Ark* (Pennsylvania Academy of the Fine Arts, Philadelphia). As he wrote Titian, he planned to incorporate a bison into the traditional biblical format. Peale had once hoped to domesticate bison for their wool. Titian did his part to fulfill his father's expectations. He dutifully prepared almost 200 drawings of western subjects, including studies of bison, which Long later deposited at the museum.[17]

Charles Willson Peale relied heavily upon his children's talents to further his museum idea. He and son Rembrandt eventually produced a gallery of more than 270 historical pictures and portraits. The extent of their industry was surprising. Traveling with the naturalist Thomas Say in 1817, young Titian saw a copy of one of his father's portraits on Cumberland Island, Georgia. On the Long expedition in the rough town of St. Louis, Titian observed several Osage Indians who had come to trade; he recognized "among them an old chief whose portrait Rembrandt painted in Philadelphia some years since." The man was apparently a member of a delegation that had come to the museum as part of Jefferson's western diplomacy. These visits often had unintended consequences. In 1824 another Native American delegation stopped at the museum en route to the nation's capital. The sight of "these lords of the forest" in such surroundings inspired George Catlin to create his traveling gallery.[18]

The museum exerted considerable and diverse influence upon artists in the early republic. Thomas Sully and John and Thomas Doughty were frequent visitors as young artists. Sharing an interest in aboriginal armament, they and Titian Peale were members of the United Bowmen. In 1825 portrait painter John Neagle endorsed Rembrandt Peale's recipe for "drying oil paintings without damaging their colors." Neagle rented a studio in the Peales' short-lived New York City museum and was able to follow the family's accomplishments. Ten years later he noted that James Peale, Jr., used "*Light red & Indigo* for many studies of landscape from nature," but warned that "*oil studies* have turned brown, while his water coloured drawings are fresh & distinct." Neagle also praised the "Swiss method" of museum-based artist Alexander Rider.[19] Rider colored engravings of birds for later volumes of Alexander Wilson's 9-volume *American Ornithology* and prepared illustrations for John Godman's work on mammals.

The museum offered artists more than examples of technique. John Trumbull planned a series of paintings around Peale's collection of military costumes; Sully made copies of the gallery portraits; the Doughty brothers and Titian Peale founded a periodical called the *Cabinet*. Devoted to rural sports and the art of lithography, the magazine frequently discussed or illustrated objects from Peale's collections and reflected the editors' shared interests in outdoor life.[20] The *Cabinet* colorfully demonstrated that museum collections provided unique models for athletes, artists, illustrators, and naturalists.

Peale's museum was a model for other institutions. In 1814 his sons founded a Baltimore museum, the first in the United States to be housed in a building intended as a museum. Peale was by this time a seasoned advocate of the fine arts and artistic taste, and he copied his own ideas. In 1794 he had organized twenty-nine other artists to form a short-lived Columbianum. Ten years later he joined a larger group of the city's prominent citizens to establish the Pennsylvania Academy of the Fine Arts. In many ways this academy for the visual arts anticipated its scientific counterpart, the Academy of Natural Sciences, founded eight years later in Philadelphia for the promotion of natural history.[21] Peale's son Titian was one of the first curators, and the early scientific leaders—Say, Harlan, Troost, and Charles-Alexandre LeSueur—were all involved with the museum at various points in their careers. In fact, Peale's collections had stimulated the American development of zoology, followed by the formation of professional groups in Philadelphia and later in New York, Ohio, and Indiana.

Peale's influence was also informal and collegial, with the loan of study specimens. In 1792 naturalist William Bartram drew a black squirrel, "the property of Mr. Peale, who kindly *lent* it." Bartram was probably working from a mount or skin, although a number of Peale's specimens were living. A few years later Palisot de Beauvois published an illustrated account of a siren, based upon a living amphibian Peale had maintained for him. Peale had a knack with animals, and de Beauvois described other experiments with live rattlesnakes, adding "the tribute which every lover of this beautiful and useful science owes to his [Peale's] zeal, his courage, and his constancy."[22]

Published from 1826 to 1828, John Godman's *American Natural History* is another instructive example of this debt. Godman was a museum faculty member who had married Angelica Peale, Rembrandt's daughter. Every aspect of his book's success reflected the museum. In the popular work he discussed his own research conducted at the museum as well as the mammals Titian collected on the Long expedition. The plates of animals described in Godman's volumes were drawn by museum artists, LeSueur, or Rider, using museum mounts and Titian's western studies. The publisher, Mathew Carey, also included Titian's engraved plate of the museum mastodon and Charles Willson Peale's comparative studies of skulls of the common ox and bison.[23]

In 1810 Peale turned over the museum's management to his son Rubens, who instituted some changes to his father's plan. The elder Peale took special pride in the fact that his exhibits were systematically arranged according to the leading European authorities of the day, Carolus Linnaeus, Jean-Baptiste Lamarck, and Georges-Louis Buffon. Rubens, however, replaced his father's scientific catalogue with texts from the Bible. His action may have been a response to the charges of atheism directed toward natural science in some quarters; the tendency of science toward dangerous ideas had been an undercurrent in the rhetoric of Jefferson's political detractors. Charles Willson Peale supported Jefferson, but he had never intended the exhibitions at his institution to be controversial. Family values were basic to his promulgation of science. A lively oil portrait shows a woman with three plump youngsters. As they turn the pages of an illustrated natural history book, they enjoy the benefits of a republican government—education and public health.[24]

Peale, who was also the author of *An Essay to Promote Domestic Happiness*, advocated natural history as an integral part of the American domestic scene. His portrait of the woman with young children looking at a plant book illustrated only the earliest step in the introduction of American youth to natural history: "Parents may regard MR. PEALE'S Museum as a school of education for their children: A young gentleman who does not know the natural riches of his country is indeed very deficient: a young lady, with all her taste in finery, is wanting in *fine taste*, if she has no desire to be acquainted with the sweet little humming-bird, the gay paradise-bird, the golden pheasant, the beauteous ring-dove, and many other lovely fellow beings."[25] Peale's famous 1821 painting *The Artist in His Museum* (see Elizabeth Johns, "Science, Art, and Literature in Federal America," fig. 1, elsewhere in this volume) clearly shows this museum public. In the background, youths of both sexes and a father with his small son study the exhibitions. Natural history in Peale's view promoted civility by underpinning the social graces. The museum experience, as interpreted by Peale, provided an important step in the maturation of the nation's youth and social improvement.

Peale practiced what he preached. His many children and grand-children grew up in the museum: they cared for various animals in the menagerie; they helped prepare exhibits; and they colored natural history plates. The museum experience, for better or worse, guided their careers.[26] Even the names Peale gave them were words of encourage-ment and direction—Raphaelle, Titian, Rembrandt, Rubens, Franklin, Angelica Kauffman, and Sophonisba.

Peale's collections of science and art substantiated his larger view of the world as a great book or chain of animals, plants, and minerals. He organized his museum around this principle of natural connections, but unlike Jefferson, he accepted the possibility of breaks or extinction.[27] Outside the museum a number of Peale's paintings refer to these natural connections by using objects as links to bind together different genera-tions of people and different forms of being. Some of the objects are nat-ural history items; others are books or articles of clothing. All are carefully painted, and all convey some sense of learning from objects, one of the fundamental principles of the Philadelphia museum. As sym-bols these objects give important information about the people Peale has portrayed. The sitters are prosperous citizens of a new nation; they are the sort of people Peale wanted to encourage to visit and support his mu-seum. In a word, they are the literate public Frances Wright felt he should address.

In contrast to his museum portraits, these pictures were intended to be hung in the houses of the sitters or their relatives, becoming domes-tic objects, daily companions that provide lessons to viewers by virtue of the values they impart.[28] Indeed, many of the sitters are shown in their homes with books. Peale's portrait of James Gittings presents the wheat farmer in a room of his house (fig. 1). Prosperous and sedate, Gittings holds hands with his wife, demonstrating the affection that binds the family. Elizabeth Buchanan Gittings holds their granddaughter, Louisa, who playfully scratches a pet chipmunk. Peale's museum experience qualified him to observe interactions between children and animals. This little girl is the caretaker of an energetic captive. Less docile than the popular flying squirrel, the chipmunk was not the species preferred as a household pet.

Except for this little distraction in the picture's center, the canvas shows an ordered interior, the result of family industry and commitment. In the upper corner a window gives a glimpse of the labor that has made

Figure 1.   Charles Willson Peale, *Mr. and Mrs. James Gittings and Grand-daughter*, Baltimore, 1791. Oil on canvas; H. 40″, W. 64″. (Peale Museum, City Life Museums, Baltimore.)

Gittings's stability possible. In the exterior world a boss works the slaves; the slaves work the oxen; the oxen work the land; the land yields the wheat. In the fields outside the binding links of domestication is the yoke of oppression. Almost an afterthought, the view is distant and somewhat displaced. Like the chipmunk's chain, another link to nature, the details of captivity are real but small. These bonds do not perturb the overall composition; they make the group portrait possible.

In contrast to the connections among living things of the plant and animal kingdoms, crystals—members of the mineral kingdom—epitomized solitude and repose for Peale. These qualities rather than physical beauty characterize his portrait of Mrs. James Smith (fig. 2). Mrs. Smith is shown as a stolid matron with her elegantly dressed grandson. Using the book in her lap, she is coaching the boy in Hamlet's soliloquy "To be or not to be." Young Campbell Smith is shown as a little man, but this text is no easy task for an eight-year-old boy. His struggle with the difficult lesson in identity parallels the new nation's search for identity. The picture also reminds us that most education occurred in the home.[29]

Figure 2.   Charles Willson Peale, *Mrs. James Smith and Grandson*, Philadelphia, 1776. Oil on canvas; H. 36⅜″, W. 29¼″. (National Museum of American Art, Smithsonian Institution, gift of Mr. and Mrs. Wilson L. Smith, Jr., and museum purchase.)

More lessons in taste and comportment are shown in Peale's 1790 studio piece of Hannah Duncan Nicholson and her bright-eyed son (fig. 3). An obviously affluent but refreshingly unaffected mother, she presents her well-maintained offspring for the viewer's admiration. The child touches his mother for reassurance and holds up a spray of wild yellow snapdragons, a nonnative species called butter-and-eggs. This is a playful, almost flirtatious, double portrait. Much of its verve derives from the painter's canny mixture of objects, natural and artificial. True innocence finds an almost comical contrast in the baby's oversized hat, an exemplar of worldly fashion. Perhaps the hat is his mother's or one of Peale's studio props. Divorced from a specific domestic setting, these sitters are energetic and mobile. Like the roadside wildflowers, they flourish at home anywhere, at ease in a hospitable world. They are prepared for adversity with very good looks, but like flowers, they will fade.

Generation and posterity are again related to qualities of action and repose in Peale's portrait of William Smith and his grandson Robert (fig. 4) Smith proudly places his right hand on the lad's head. In a refined gesture he supports a peach twig between two fingers of his left hand; the little boy cheerfully holds up a peach. At Smith's elbow are books and a pruning knife. This is a man of both thought and action. Smith, pictured as extremely tall, was influential in drafting the constitution of the state of Maryland. Robert, another "fruit" of his considerable endeavors, is an assurance of their posterity. It is a triumph of the good republican government and public welfare he helped create that Smith has lived to enjoy his grandson. His consciousness of this fact is evidenced by his request to be painted with the child.

Technology, another peacetime benefit, informs Peale's lamplight portrait of his brother James (fig. 5). Peale returned to a theme explored in an earlier oil portrait of James, who was also an artist. This is a double picture. James Peale examines a miniature, a likeness of one of Rembrandt Peale's daughters, that is itself the work of James's daughter Anna. James proudly studies both female attributes—the subject's beauty and Anna's skill. James admires his daughter's miniature; the viewer admires his brother's painting of a painting. The object of their admiration, a likeness of Rosalba Peale, is the link between the generations. The link, a small work of art, is artificial rather than natural. Viewing is made possible by the light, also artificial, of the argand lamp (recently invented by

Figure 3.   Charles Willson Peale, *Mrs. John Nicholson and John Nicholson, Jr.*, Philadelphia, 1790. Oil on canvas; H. 36″, W. 27⁵/₁₆″. (Art Institute of Chicago, gift of Mr. and Mrs. Carter H. Harrison.)

Figure 4. Charles Willson Peale, *William Smith and His Grandson*, Baltimore, 1788. Oil on canvas; H. 51³/₄″, W. 40¹/₄″. (Virginia Museum of Fine Arts, Richmond, Robert G. Cabell III and Maude Morgan Cabell Foundation and Arthur and Margaret Glasgow Fund.)

Figure 5.   Charles Willson Peale, *James Peale*, Philadelphia, 1822. Oil on canvas; H. 24¹/₂″, W. 36″. (Detroit Institute of Arts, gift of Dexter M. Ferry, Jr.)

Aimé Argand).[30] Art and technology are brought together as the lamplight unites the viewer and the viewed in a circle of illumination.

Peale's portrait of viewing or method of seeing was not a casually selected approach. Admiration of nature's connections was an essential component of eighteenth-century scientific behavior. Natural history illustrations shared with portraiture a focus on identification (or likeness) and generation. The best natural history plates, like the best family portraits, included both the male and female, and often the juvenile, forms of the species represented. In the case of invertebrates, different stages of maturation were commonly referred to as degrees of perfection, an Aristotelian concept. The sexually active adult is the perfect insect; the caterpillar, by contrast, is regarded as imperfect because it cannot reproduce its own kind or species. The nocturnal portrait of James Peale offers an interesting parallel to such illustrations. The faithful likenesses attract viewers as night lamps attract moths; the small cased portrait encapsulates its subject as a cocoon contains a caterpillar, the link to the next generation.

Botanical plates similarly showed life stages of the species, representing and emphasizing their reproductive potential through seeds, fruits, or roots. Like portraits, these scientific illustrations had a definite purpose. They were, in Peale's words, a guide to the new nation's natural resources. Rembrandt's canvas *Rubens Peale with a Geranium* is, in this sense, a portrait incorporated into a botanical illustration (fig. 6). Rubens's two pairs of glasses draw attention to the functions of vision—seeing, reading, and admiration—essential to understanding both art and science. Their reflection on his downy cheeks invites reflection or introspection, a link, to use another scholar's phrase, "between observation and intelligence."[31] The optical properties of the corrective lenses and the reduction of human flesh to a reflecting surface also link the earthly world of biology and the larger world of natural philosophy.

Like the museum exhibits, this portrait uses a living species as a model. Rembrandt has painted the geranium, an introduced African species, in the format of a taxonomic illustration. He has shown the various stages of fructification regardless of visual appeal. Does nearsighted Rubens notice the same details the viewer discerns? Rubens and the geranium, with its long nodding seed pods, both verge on realization. Like Rubens's second set of glasses, the plant's curling leaves are part of a cycle of growth and exchange. The composition implies that young Rubens has nurtured this plant as part of a project or lesson. The boy's expression suggests the plant is a source of pride in a job well done. Native soil has allowed this exotic species to thrive, just as a nation in peacetime has a place for this weak-eyed boy to succeed. The portrait attests to the republican triumph of child care, optics, and diet, or medicine, science, and horticulture. Each has its emblem—chubby cheeks, glasses, and potted plant. Like Hannah Nicholson's prize baby, the geranium is an object of admiration and a symbol of posterity. Rubens and his charge need each other for full realization and identity. Both require nurturing, as art and nature meet in this dual coming of age. Unlike the geranium, however, limited in Aristotelian terms by its vegetable soul, Rubens can move on to manhood. The lesson of the plant has become a lesson of life.

This theme was a major message of Peale's approach to nature. A printed ticket to the Philadelphia museum read: "The Birds and Beasts will teach thee! Admit the Bearer to PEALE'S MUSEUM, Containing the Wonderful works of NATURE!" Charles Willson Peale wanted to preserve

Figure 6.   Rembrandt Peale, *Rubens Peale with a Geranium*, Philadelphia, 1801. Oil on canvas; H. 28¼″, W. 24″. (National Gallery of Art, Patrons' Permanent Fund.)

nature's "wonderful works." Illustrations—works of art—could not replace the objects themselves. At his museum the feminine appreciation of "sweet little humming-bird" and "golden pheasant," which Peale cited as exemplars of fine taste, was acquired by looking at stuffed skins. Peale developed methods of taxidermy, and his realistic style of mounting was adopted by other naturalists because it yielded attractive and realistic results. In 1809 Wilson wrote a colleague, "Thanks for your bird, so neatly stuffed, that I was just about to skin it." The next year he published Peale's procedures for preparing bird skins.[32] Lasting collections, Peale's dream, opened the door for artistic accuracy and true scientific research by others.

Mounted specimens served a second function. It is important to remember that illustrations of specimens were not drawn from nature or living creatures, as many published plates of the period claim. Rather, artists drew museum specimens in lifelike poses. Natural history plates by Wilson, Rider, or LeSueur were actually portraits of museum objects. Titian Peale illustrated insects as if they were pinned specimens.[33] Some individuals appear to lie on the page like artifacts of scientific study. They are real examples of the Linnaean taxonomic ideal, the generalized scientific definition of the species. They are also pretty objects of admiration. In their own way these likenesses function like deception pictures, and they often share content with their artistic counterparts— insects, shells, and bird eggs.

The pictorial devices of still lifes and deception pictures appear in paintings by Charles Willson Peale, most interestingly his self-portraits. The unveiling of nature in Peale's famous canvas of 1821 (see Johns, "Science, Art, and Literature," fig. 1, elsewhere in this volume) is largely a deception picture. The curtain is thematically related to the cloths in covered paintings by Raphaelle Peale. Was the father influenced by the son? An earlier use of this motif appears on a museum solicitation in which a putto raises a curtain upon a prehistoric landscape. The image is captioned, "Of grains are Mountains form'd."[34] Lest the viewer miss the lesson, Peale has written the word "nature" across the curtain.

The uncovering of nature is also the theme of the famous *Exhumation of the Mastodon* from the bogs of New York State (fig. 7). The animal itself cannot be seen. Again, lest the viewer miss the message, Peale has shown himself, with the help of son Raphaelle, creating an illusion. They are unrolling a huge drawing of the creature's leg bones. Here are the giant's scapula, tibia, ulna, and humerus for all to see. The canvas again unites a traditional scientific illustration, here anatomical, with portraiture. As in trompe l'oeil, the drawing is a surrogate for the real thing. Like the miniature in Peale's portrait of his

Figure 7.   Charles Willson Peale, *The Exhumation of the Mastodon*, Philadelphia, 1806–8. Oil on canvas; H. 50″, W. 62¹/₂″. (Peale Museum, City Life Museums, Baltimore.)

brother, discussed above, the image of the fossil leg bones is a picture of a picture. The oversized scroll, too, becomes an object of admiration since the real bones, the true wonder, have not yet been uncovered. Like the encased miniature in the portrait of James Peale, the earth contains one of the subjects of this complex tableau.

In the first lesson of nature the viewer joins the onlookers while the excavation is in progress. The mammoth is still in situ, mysteriously there but not yet visible. Discovery is shown literally as an uncovering, but here the veil of nature is swamp muck, not cloth. Other aspects of this picture may have been more startling to contemporary viewers, and they remain so today. The picture documents a new and profound insight—biological extinction. In a heroic effort, Peale's men contend with the same forces of nature that doomed the giant species. Looming thunderheads and distant lightning portend disastrous flooding. The quagmire that brought down the mammoth threatens to wash out the pit and defeat Peale's scientific endeavor.

This dramatic tension between human beings and the elements diverts attention, but does not detract, from the larger republican values of hard work and peace. Peale's workers are hired laborers, not slaves. The tools of war—tents and other equipment borrowed from the army—are shown in the service of science. As the United States Army Corps of Engineers was newly authorized by Congress, Peale emphasized engineering in the painting. The huge waterwheel was essential to the excavation's success. In this picture the moving wheel links various human activities. Peale exhorts the laborers to shovel the pungent muck, fill the buckets, and pump out the water of John Masten's bog. Peale, the builder of the "Draisiana," or velocipede, and other gadgets, loved labor-saving devices.[35] With characteristic fervor for self-improvement, he has offered an emancipatory vision of machinery at work. Like the small window in the Gittings portrait, this canvas records economic dimensions—in this case, those of scientific progress. The waterwheel symbolizes the Great Chain of Being, with one important difference. This picture documents that links in the chain are broken from time to time. Extinction occurs. Change takes place.

Despite the odds, the excavation proved almost completely successful. Missing portions of the mastodon skeletons were recreated at the museum by clever deception, either modeled in papier-mâché or carved in wood by sculptor William Rush.[36] Reconstruction made real the classification of an extinct species for the first time in the history of science. And that is the picture's final lesson of nature. The future value of this scientific discovery rests with the playful children, too young to comprehend the significance of the activities taking place before them. Long afterward, it must have been a special source of joy for this younger generation to see themselves (and others they never knew) associated with this great American event. But viewer beware: Peale's apparent factuality in this painting is deceptive. The artist's infant children, his deceased second wife, and her relatives were not present at the exhumation. The artist has used the great bannerlike drawing of bones to bind kin of all ages. People, plants, animals, the living and dead, and time past and present are brought together with posterity. This is a picture about the process of scientific research.

At the Philadelphia museum the products of research—collections—were made more real by works of art. This juxtaposition is reversed in Peale's famous *Staircase Group*, in which a physical object makes a painting more real (fig. 8). Created in 1795, this clever portrait shows two of Peale's teenage boys as they ascend a stairwell marked at its base by a real wooden step. Originally installed at one end of Peale's museum hall, the portrait reiterates the values of domesticity and child rearing in the museum setting. Viewers found the work to be amusing, and Washington, ever the gentleman, is said to have bowed to the two boys in passing.[37] Again, objects in the museum setting reinforced civility.

Staircase Group served Peale as more than an architectural endpaper. In 1795 the work hung with three trompe l'oeil compositions by Peale's oldest son, Raphaelle, in the first art exhibition held at the city's Columbianum. This association is noteworthy because deception pictures, such as those painted by Raphaelle and other Peale family members, often tell a different story from that of the patriarch's museum although theirs, too, is a message about the economic aspects and aspirations of life in the American republic. Still-life pictures, like museum exhibits, relied upon material culture and the appeal of objects. Imported ceramic baskets, glassware, and delicate cloths represent American taste. Bright piles of fruits and vegetables document the consumerism essential to both horticulture and Peale's collections. Abundance was the emblem of hospitality and hard work. Viewing pictures of foodstuffs was, in part, a moral exercise, an approbation of the public well-being possible through the discipline that successful agriculture requires and the improved diet that results. Peale's museum echoed these values, and he reiterated them in an epistle he printed for Jefferson on the preservation of health and promotion of happiness.[38]

Still-life compositions expressed Jeffersonian agrarian ideals. Trompe-l'oeil artists have also been called "painters of the humble truth," a Franklinian value. Certainly their pictures express the republican veneration of self-improvement, personal industry, and even poverty. Expert practitioners, unfortunately, were frequently too poor to enjoy the "Boards of Plate" and "costly piles," objects they so carefully delineated. Despite acclaim for natural history books that bore the museum's imprint, the expense of illustration proved limiting. American publishers were unable to employ the pool of artists capable of producing plates,

Figure 8.   Charles Willson Peale, *Staircase Group*, Philadelphia, 1795. Oil on canvas; H. 89″, W. 39½″. (George W. Elkins Collection, Philadelphia Museum of Art.)

and too many remained underemployed. Samuel Lewis, for example, prepared faculty diplomas at the museum for Say, Godman, Harlan, and Troost. An accomplished drawing attributed to him shows a card rack with a prospectus from the leading seller of natural history books, Mathew Carey, and a ticket to Peale's museum.[39] These printed ephemera were well-chosen companions, but the lesson for artists was not encouraging.

Deception pictures, like natural history plates, deal with different degrees of perfection. Even in a democratic republic some things are forever concealed; others are exposed to public view. Literate viewers— and they must be literate—are tempted to snoop through the old notes and chipped envelopes, details of the artist's precarious existence. Deception artists probed the reality of objects to uncover values in an increasingly technological society. Like Peale's displays, their little pictures are didactic. The nails, tacks, and hanging racks, which Peale had taken every effort to hide in his museum dioramas, pay homage to the workmanship fundamental to successful trompe l'oeil pictures. Like painted flies, they are also deliberately distracting. Beguiling, witty, and boldly painted, they challenge the senses to question the reality of objects and any message they might impart.

Peale used natural history objects as models. He designed exhibits to develop intellectual skills he deemed essential to republican life. Objects and their handling were in his view primary. The value of knowledge of the natural world, however, changed for a younger generation of urban viewers, those children he showed frolicking at the great dig. Life based upon Peale's reading of nature and classical authors was losing its motivating appeal in an increasingly acquisitive mercantile society. A student of the museum's bird collections, Wilson begged his readers to go beyond admiration of stuffed mounts and their workmanship: "Let us examine better into the operations of nature, and many of our mistaken opinions, and groundless prejudices will be abandoned for more just, enlarged and humane modes of thinking."[40] Wilson's bird books bravely addressed humane issues—class structure, bigotry, and wildlife management—among discussions of nesting habits, plumage, and nomenclature. His remarks in one of the finest natural history publications of the early republic might easily have been a caption to a still-life painting. Uncovering self-deception through close observation of objects was the challenge basic to both endeavors.

Natural history and deception pictures required a dual public, thinking viewers and patrons. Peale attempted to cultivate both. To Peale's mind, the grand lesson of nature was the Great Chain of Being, which united persons with their accomplishments. His private portraits of patrons repeated the message of the museum gallery of heroes. Despite Wright's complaint, Peale's displays were intended as full visions of the human place in nature. They reflected Peale's image of his own role as a social and civilized being in a natural world he both admired and sought to improve. His self-portraits depict his endeavors as part of the public good. Peale was not a great scientist. He was neither a mathematician nor an anatomist of note, and he relied heavily on the knowledge of others for his natural history displays. Still, his museum was the best-known public place of science in its day. As Wilson's work demonstrated, it was a repository for collections, a center for publication, a training ground for artists, and a forum for new ideas.

----

[1] Sally Gregory Kohlstedt, "International Exchange and National Style: A View of Natural History Museums in the United States, 1850–1900," in *Scientific Colonialism: A Cross-Cultural Comparison*, ed. Nathan Reingold and Marc Rothenberg (Washington, D.C.: Smithsonian Institution Press, 1986), pp. 169, 171; Charlotte M. Porter, "Natural History Museums," in *The Museum: A Reference Guide*, ed. Michael Shapiro and Louis Ward Kemp (Westport, Conn.: Greenwood Press, 1990), pp. 1–6.

[2] Harold Sellers Colton, "Peale's Museum," *Popular Science Monthly* (1909): 221–38; Brooke Hindle, *The Pursuit of Science in Revolutionary America, 1735–1789* (Chapel Hill: University of North Carolina Press, 1956), pp. 128–31, 138; and Charles Coleman Sellers, "Peale's Museum," *Transactions of the American Philosophical Society*, n.s., 43 (1953): 253–59.

[3] As quoted in Russell Lynes, *The Art Makers: An Informal History of Painting, Sculpture, and Architecture in Nineteenth-Century America* (New York: Dover, 1970), p. 88. Many of these portraits are in the Independence National Historical Park collection, Philadelphia.

[4] Hugh Honour, *The New Golden Land: European Images of America from the Discoveries to the Present Time* (New York: Pantheon Books, 1975), pp. 32–34; Oliver Impey and Arthur MacGregor, eds., *The Origins of Museums: The Cabinet of Curiosities in Sixteenth- and Seventeenth-Century Europe* (Oxford: Clarendon Press, 1985); Raymond Phineas Stearn, *Science in the British Colonies of America* (Urbana: University of Illinois Press, 1970), p. 516; Ray Desmond, "The Historical Setting of Kew," in *Kew: Gardens for Science and Pleasure*, ed. F. Nigel Hepper (Owings Mills, Md.: Stemmer House, 1982), pp. 7–20.

[5] Peale as quoted in Charles Coleman Sellers, *Mr. Peale's Museum: Charles Willson Peale and the First Popular Museum of Natural Science and Art* (New York: W. W. Norton, 1980), p. 148; see also Charles Coleman Sellers, *Charles Willson*

Peale, memoirs of the American Philosophical Society, vol. 23 (Philadelphia: By the society, 1947).

⁶ Peale to Washington, October 30, 1791, June 27, 1790, in Lillian B. Miller, Sidney Hart, and Toby Appel, eds., *The Selected Papers of Charles Willson Peale and His Family*, vol. 1: *Charles Willson Peale: Artist in Revolutionary America, 1735–1791* (New Haven: Yale University Press, 1983), pp. 627, 589; Sellers, *Mr. Peale's Museum*, pp. 56, 40.

⁷ Peale to Jefferson, January 12, 1802, in Lillian B. Miller, Sidney Hart, and David Ward, eds., *The Selected Papers of Charles Willson Peale and His Family*, vol. 2: *Charles Willson Peale: The Artist as Museum Keeper, 1791–1810* (New Haven: Yale University Press, 1988), p. 386.

⁸ John C. Greene, "The Founding of Peale's Museum," in *Bibliography and Natural History . . .*, ed. Thomas R. Buckman (Lawrence: University of Kansas Press, 1966), p. 70; Robert I. Goler, " 'Here the Book of Nature Is Unfolded': The American Museum and the Diffusion of Scientific Knowledge in the Early Republic," *Museum Studies Journal* 2, no. 2 (Spring 1986): 18; Joel J. Orosz, "Pierre Eugène Simitière: Museum Pioneer in America," *Museum Studies Journal* 1, no. 5 (Spring 1985): 15. Paul L. Farber, "Discussion Paper: The Transformation of Natural History in the Nineteenth Century," *Journal for the History of Biology* 15 (Spring 1982): 148–49; and Paul L. Farber, "Development of Taxidermy and the History of Ornithology," *Isis* 68 (December 1977): 550–66. Farber does not develop the importance of taxidermic mounts as models for ornithological illustrations.

⁹ For the museum's floor plan and contents, see *Historical Catalogue of Paintings Attached to the Philadelphia Museum* (Philadelphia, 1813), which sold for 25¢.

¹⁰ Sellers, *Mr. Peale's Museum*, p. 146; Charles Willson Peale, *Skeleton of the Mammoth Is Now to Be Seen at the Museum, in a Separate Room* ([Philadelphia]: John Ormond, [ca. 1801]), Broadside Collection, American Philosophical Society, Philadelphia; Peter J. Whybraw, "A History of Fossil Collecting and Preparation Techniques," *Curator* 28, no. 1 (March 1985): 12.

¹¹ Manasseh Cutler, journal extract, July 13, 1787, as quoted in Miller, Hart, and Appel, *Peale: Revolutionary America*, p. 485.

¹² [Benjamin Smith Barton], announcements in *Philadelphia Medical and Physical Journal* 2 (1805): 205; see also Charles W. Peale, *Discourse Introductory to a Course of Lectures on the Science of Nature with Original Music* (Philadelphia: Zachariah Poulson, 1800). In 1795 Barton succeeded to the professorship of *materia medica*; Francis W. Pennell, "Benjamin Smith Barton," *Proceedings of the American Philosophical Society* 86 (September 1942): 110. Sellers, *Mr. Peale's Museum*, p. 239.

¹³ As quoted in Elisabeth Donaghy Garrett, "The American Home, Part V: Venetian Shutters and Blinds," *Antiques* 128, no. 2 (August 1985): 260; Sellers, *Mr. Peale's Museum*, p. 239; Manassah Cutler, journal extract, Miller, Hart, and Appel, *Peale: Revolutionary America*, p. 484. An excellent general bibliography on the circuit walk can be found in Robert P. Maccubbin and Peter Martin, eds., *British and American Gardens in the Eighteenth Century . . .* (Williamsburg, Va.: Colonial Williamsburg Foundation, 1984), pp. 16–18, 84–92, 136–47.

¹⁴ [W. N. Blane], *Travels through the United States and Canada . . .* (London: Baldwin, 1828), p. 22; Manassah Cutler, journal extract, Miller, Hart, and Appel, *Peale: Revolutionary America*, pp. 484, 483. Peale's debt to the American stage has been explored by James Sims, "Space, Light, and the Word: Charles Willson Peale as Performance Artist" (Paper presented at "Charles Willson Peale: An Interdiscipli-

nary Study of His Work," October 23, 1981, National Portrait Gallery, Smithsonian Institution, Washington, D.C.) Peale's museum innovations are discussed in James Thomas Flexner, *History of American Painting, 1760–1835: The Light of Distant Skies* (New York: Dover, 1969), pp. 97–99; Kenneth Silverman, *A Cultural History of the American Revolution: Painting, Music, Literature, Science* (New York: Columbia University Press, 1987), pp. 452–53.

[15] [Frances Wright], *Views of Society and Manners in America,* ed. Paul R. Baker (Cambridge: Harvard University Press, Belknap Press, 1963), p. 48; Edgar P. Richardson, Brooke Hindle, and Lillian B. Miller, *Charles Willson Peale and His World* (New York: Harry N. Abrams, 1982), p. 153; *National Gazette,* September 4, 1793; "Additions and Donations to Peale's Museum," miscellaneous newspaper clippings, Academy of Natural Sciences, Philadelphia; Edgar P. Richardson, "Charles Willson Peale's Engravings in the Year of National Crisis, 1787," in *Winterthur Portfolio 1,* ed. Edgar P. Richardson et al. (Winterthur, Del.: Henry Francis du Pont Winterthur Museum, 1964), pp. 166–81.

[16] A. Hunter Dupree, *Science in the Federal Government: A History of Policies and Activities* (Cambridge: Harvard University Press, Belknap Press, 1957), p. 22; Donald Jackson, ed., *Letters of the Lewis and Clark Expedition with Related Documents, 1783–1854* (Urbana: University of Illinois Press, 1962), pp. 135, 241, 261, 263–64, 267–68, 272, 373, 410; Donald Jackson, *Thomas Jefferson and the Stony Mountains: Exploring the West from Monticello* (Urbana: University of Illinois Press, 1981), pp. 188, 274–75. Peale's drawings and engravings of the expedition specimens are among the Charles Willson Peale Papers, American Philosophical Society, Philadelphia. Alexander Wilson to Alexander Lawson, April 6, 1810, XMCZ Collection, Houghton Library, Harvard University; Alexander Wilson, *American Ornithology; or, The Natural History of the Birds of the United States,* 9 vols. (Philadelphia: Bradford and Inskeep, 1808–14), 3:27, pl. 20.

[17] Roger L. Nichols, "Stephen Long and Scientific Explorations on the Plains," *Nebraska History* 52, no. 1 (Spring 1971): 51–64; Jessie Poesch, *Titian Ramsay Peale, 1799–1885, and His Journals of the Wilkes Expedition,* memoirs of the American Philosophical Society, vol. 52 (Philadelphia: By the society, 1961), pp. 22–35; C. W. Peale to T. Peale, December 25, 1819, as cited in Charles Coleman Sellers, "Art of Charles Willson Peale," *Transactions of the American Philosophical Society,* n.s., 59 (1969): 44. Most of Titian's drawings are owned by the American Philosophical Society.

[18] A. O. Weese, ed., "The Journal of Titian Ramsay Peale," *Missouri Historical Review* 41, no. 2 (January 1947): 160. Catlin as quoted in George M. Cohen, "George Catlin: Indian Painter with a Noble Mission," *Art and Antiques* 4 (January–February 1981): 53. The museum paintings were auctioned in 1854 for a total of $11,700; see Moses Thomas and Sons, *Peale's Museum Gallery of Oil Paintings* (Philadelphia: Wm. Y. Owens, 1854); *Catalogue of an Exhibition of Portraits by Charles Willson Peale and James Peale and Rembrandt Peale* (Philadelphia: Pennsylvania Academy of the Fine Arts, 1923), p. 61. Charlotte M. Porter, "Following 'Bartram's Track': Titian Ramsay Peale's Florida Journey," *Florida Historical Quarterly* 61, no. 4 (April 1983): 436. The copy Titian saw was *General Nathanael Greene,* painted by Thomas Sully; see Miller, Hart, and Appel, *Peale: Revolutionary America,* p. 405n.

[19] John Neagle, "Receipts for Making Megellup, Varnish, and Drying Oil," 1825, American Philosophical Society, Philadelphia; John Neagle, "Lessons in Landscape Painting," 1827, American Philosophical Society.

20 Only two volumes of *The Cabinet of Natural History and Rural American Sports* were issued from 1832 to 1834 before the editors went broke.

21 Sally Gregory Kohlstedt, "Institutional History," *Osiris*, 2d ser., 1 (1985): 26–27; Lillian B. Miller, *Patrons and Patriotism: The Encouragement of the Fine Arts in the United States* (Chicago: University of Chicago Press, 1966), p. 110; Maurice E. Phillips, "The Academy of Natural Sciences of Philadelphia," *Transactions of the American Philosophical Society*, n.s., 43 (1953): 266–72.

22 Bartram to Benjamin Smith Barton, December 31, 1792, Bartram Papers, Historical Society of Pennsylvania, Philadelphia; A.M.T.J.P. de Beauvois, "On a New Species of Siren," *Transactions of the American Philosophical Society* 4 (1799): 280; A.M.T.J.P. de Beauvois, "Memoir on Amphibia," *Transactions of the American Philosophical Society* 4 (1799): 365.

23 John Godman, *American Natural History . . .*, 3 vols. (3d ed.; Philadelphia: Hogan and Thompson, 1836), 2: facing pp. 52, 131.

24 Regarding Rubens Peale, see Edward P. Alexander, *Museum Masters: Their Museums and Their Influence* (Nashville: American Association for State and Local History, 1983), p. 64; Patsy A. Gerstner, "The Academy of Natural Sciences, 1812–1850," in *The Pursuit of Knowledge in the Early American Republic*, ed. Alexander Oleson and Sanborn C. Brown (Baltimore: Johns Hopkins University Press, 1976), p. 177. The Hannah Peale portrait is in a private collection.

25 "A Lover of Nature" to the *Pennsylvania Packet*, March 27, 1790, cited in Miller, Hart, and Appel, *Peale: Revolutionary America*, p. 583.

26 Poesch, *Titian Ramsay Peale*, pp. 13–16.

27 Lester P. Coonen and Charlotte M. Porter, "Thomas Jefferson and American Biology," *BioScience* 26, no. 12 (December 1976): 745–50; and Charles A. Miller, *Jefferson and Nature: An Interpretation* (Baltimore: Johns Hopkins University Press, 1988), pp. 27, 50–53.

28 Margaretta M. Lovell, "Reading Eighteenth-Century American Family Portraits," *Winterthur Portfolio* 22, no. 4 (Winter 1987): 243–64.

29 Charles Willson Peale, *Scientific and Descriptive Catalogue of Peale's Museum* (Philadelphia: Samuel H. Smith, 1796), p. viii; Gretchen Townsend, *Education in the Young Republic* (New York: Fraunces Tavern Museum, 1988), pp. 8–11.

30 Peale, December 19, 1822, as cited in Richardson, Hindle, and Miller, *Charles Willson Peale*, p. 104.

31 John Wilmerding, "America's Young Masters: Raphaelle, Rembrandt, and Rubens," in *Raphaelle Peale Still Lifes*, ed. Nicolai Cikovsky, Jr., Linda Bantel, and John Wilmerding (New York: Harry N. Abrams, 1988), p. 86.

32 Wilson to William Bartram, October 11, 1809, as quoted in Clark Hunter, ed., *The Life and Letters of Alexander Wilson*, memoirs of the American Philosophical Society, vol. 154 (Philadelphia: By the society, 1983), p. 317; Wilson, *American Ornithology*, 2:ix.

33 See plates drawn by Titian Peale for the first volume of Thomas Say, *American Entomology; or, Descriptions of the Insects of North America*, 3 vols. (Philadelphia: Samuel Augustus Mitchell, 1824–28), 1: n.p.

34 William H. Gerdts, "A Covered Painting or Fruit Piece," in *A Gallery Collects Peales*, ed. Robert Devlin Schwarz (Philadelphia: Frank S. Schwarz and Sons, 1987), p. 20; Sellers, *Mr. Peale's Museum*, p. 155.

35 Richardson, Hindle, and Miller, *Charles Willson Peale*, pp. 147–51; Silvio A. Bedini, *Thinkers and Tinkers: Early American Men of Science* (New York: Charles Scribner's Sons, 1975), pp. 364–65.

[36] Sellers, *Charles Willson Peale*, 2:141.

[37] Lillian B. Miller, "The Peale Family: A Lively Mixture of Art and Science," *Smithsonian* 10, no. 1 (April 1979): 70.

[38] Phoebe Lloyd has helped me to reevaluate Charles Willson Peale's role as a father; see also Lloyd, "The Unpeeling of Raphaelle Peale" (Paper presented at "Making History at the Brooklyn Museum," April 16, 1988), and Phoebe Lloyd, "Philadelphia Story," *Art in America* 76, no. 11 (November 1988): 157–58, 167–68. Regarding aspirations of life, see John Wilmerding, "The American Object: Still-Life Paintings," in John Wilmerding, Linda Ayres, and Earl A. Powell, *An American Perspective: Nineteenth-Century Art from the Collection of Jo Ann and Julian Ganz* (Washington, D.C.: National Gallery of Art, 1981), pp. 88–89; and Nicolai Cikovsky, Jr., "Democratic Illusions," in Cikovsky, *Raphaelle Peale*, p. 33; Charles Willson Peale, *An Epistle to a Friend, on the Means of Preserving Health* . . . (Philadelphia: Jane Aitken, 1803).

[39] William H. Gerdts, *Painters of the Humble Truth: Masterpieces of American Still Life, 1801–1939* (Columbia: University of Missouri Press, 1982); David E. Shi, *The Simple Life: Plain Living and High Thinking in American Culture* (New York: Oxford University Press, 1985), pp. 61, 85, 99. William H. Gerdts, "A Deception Unmasked; An Artist Uncovered," *American Art Journal* 18, no. 2 (1986): 13. Lewis's drawing was formerly attributed to Raphaelle Peale; Linda Crocker Simmons to C. M. Porter.

[40] Wilson, *American Ornithology*, 1:157.

Science, Art, and Literature in Federal America
Their Prospects in the Republic
Elizabeth Johns

Science, art, and literature took an uncertain place in federal America. Although traditionally considered to be evidence of a highly developed intellectual culture, in the early republic they had no self-evident roles. More than a few citizens of educated background yearned for the kind of hierarchical society in which such pursuits would be carried out by individuals of privileged position. Yet the evolving social structure of the new nation permitted, indeed encouraged, mobility and diversity in all areas of life—even in intellectual endeavors. Thus, ambitious and talented citizens from a variety of economic and social levels found themselves drawn to scientific, artistic, or literary activities as avenues for self-development. They variously explored, practiced, and advocated these disciplines as interesting activities, as means for making money, and as patriotic advancements of the national interest.

Many studies have probed the separate development in early America of each of these disciplines.[1] Yet in every field, and especially in the history of art, a great deal has still to be determined about the class interests, regional differences, audiences, and broadly ideological positions involved in this development. To help call attention to the pertinence of some of these perspectives, especially as they bear on the history of art, this essay briefly examines the prospects for all three of these disciplines as the early practitioners saw them.

In the late eighteenth century, scientific, artistic, and literary areas of creativity—so distinct in their intellectual and social function today—were understood as constituting one kind of enterprise, and a questionable one at that. This enterprise was the "cream" on top of the political and economic goals of ideal and everyday republican life. Early Americans variously identified the pursuit of literature and science with the gentleman class, with leisure, and with utility; they saw the pursuit of painting as the task of artisans working for the benefit of the privileged. These inherited, usually explicit, assumptions needed to be rethought.

In the broadest terms, energetic would-be scientists, artists, and writers shared three kinds of problems. First, they were remote from European urban and intellectual centers. How could their pursuit in distant America relate to the conception and practice of their discipline in Europe? Second, republican ideals were admirable, even glorious, but untried. Were expensive, potentially class-reinforcing, and not clearly utilitarian pursuits compatible with republicanism? And third, the American citizenry on all levels was clearly diverse and competitive; many of the audiences were uneducated, and the average citizen seemed bent on economic success. What pertinence could the sciences and the arts claim for citizens so singlemindedly devoted to their own interests?

For a sense of how shocking these prospects appeared after the dust had cleared in 1789, let us first look to circumstances that prevailed earlier. In the colonial era, scientific investigation, visual imagemaking, and literary composition were carried out on relatively clear terms. They were tied to the values and practices of England and, to a lesser extent, Continental Europe. In Philadelphia Benjamin Franklin conducted his scientific experiments in the context of the activities of scientists and societies in England and Scotland. Artists like John Singleton Copley in Boston and innumerable itinerant painters up and down the Atlantic seaboard created virtually nothing but portraits, their audience being an extension of an English society that trusted words more than images and used portraiture as a sign of individual status. And writers, like New Englanders Cotton Mather and Jonathan Edwards, were typically clergymen who wrote in the great English Puritan tradition of the cleric-poet using moral authority to promote public virtue.

The Revolution changed the terms of these symbolic pursuits dramatically. Leaders of the new nation were confident that this society, with so superior a type of government, was also one in which superior intellectual achievements could flourish. And yet the ideals of the new republic—freedom, equality, and virtuous self-discipline—raised questions about the precise role of intellectual and imaginative achievements in such a body politic. Scientific, artistic, and literary activities seemed always to have been the products of hierarchial societies, which sanctioned privilege, luxury, and even despotism. How and by whom were such pursuits to be conceived afresh and carried out in a republican framework?

There were not only ideological problems but also practical difficulties, which in many instances were so great that they obscured all other considerations. One was that the nation was dispersed over a vast territory in which the center of government was not the center of culture. Further, the cities that dominated the different regions, such as Boston, Philadelphia, Charleston, and Cincinnati, were relatively small, which meant that few resources were available to the scientist, artist, or writer. Another major problem was that across the nation citizens of all levels of education and wealth were engaged in an intensifying struggle to define equality in terms of their own stake in society. The evolving market system made it possible, indeed irresistible, for them to concentrate their drive for status on material achievement rather than on intellectual or artistic ground. And finally, the moral dominance that the clergy had earlier exercised in some regions was lost with the Revolution, resulting in a secular society where members denied the authority of any voice or pursuit but their own. Scientists, artists, and writers had to be, first and foremost, powerful advocates for their own perceptions of their discipline and for their own—often purely economic—interests.

In its largest outline, the story of these pursuits over the federal period is one of aspiring practitioners trying to define their mission against conditions that ranged from the uncertain to the downright discouraging. Would-be scientists had arguably the easiest task, but they still faced difficulties. During a period in which European scientists were making one theoretical breakthrough after another in such fields as astronomy, physics, and geology, their counterparts in federal America—like artists and writers, as we will see—had no institutional support or community of audiences that would make possible such conceptual achievements. Working generally in urban centers, they carried out their more empirical studies as a sideline to such primary roles as physician, professor, surveyor, instrument maker, and even, in the case of Thomas Jefferson, president of the United States. Detracting from the claims of scientists that the discipline deserved special recognition and support was the notion that anyone could learn science, as Yale president Timothy Dwight assured the young divinity student Benjamin Silliman when he recruited him to teach science at the college in 1802.[2]

Another potentially detrimental factor in the development of science was the influence of the commercial spirit—something that was to undermine the arts as well. Citizens' desire to turn every moment of their time into cash was often, when the talk turned to science, subsumed in rhetoric about the "utility" of scientific pursuits. Thus it was commonplace to argue that the best service science could render to the new republic was to contribute to the great march of material "progress" in agriculture, manufacturing, and engineering. Even an intellectual like Thomas Jefferson endorsed this conception of science, commenting, for instance, that geology was a pursuit "too idle to be worth an hour of any man's life."[3] Europeans, fascinated with American inventions such as the steamboat, began to dub the new republic the "practical" nation. Not all scientists, especially during that later part of the federal period, agreed with this utilitarian view of their goals, but they were not so impolitic as to say so.

Discouraging as were these elements, however, the positive aspect of science in the new republic was exhilarating. Certain scientific opportunities in the United States were absolutely compatible with features of the discipline at large, as defined in western Europe. This aspect was to set off the sciences from the arts completely. Americans occupied the eastern rim of a continent that offered untold quantities of raw data to be recorded, described, analyzed, and classified. If they could not enjoy the ivory tower of theory, they had a more exciting field of evidence, a greater potential laboratory, than did their European counterparts. During the federal period the country fairly hummed with notetakers. Scientists— or at least men of scientific leanings—discovered, described, and classified plants and animals, geological formations, Indians and Indian dialects, and "antiquities." Innumerable energetic collectors, recordkeepers, and correspondents both promoted and practiced science. Science as conceived in these terms not only did not threaten republican values but actually helped advance them. The tasks of describing the natural world, of bringing it into intellectual order through classification, and of diffusing this knowledge clarified the dimensions of the physical reality in which all citizens lived. Moveover, such scientific work did not challenge traditional beliefs in God and in God's presence in creation. Scientists could say, as did the ornithologist Alexander Wilson in 1808, that their studies would lead citizens to "the contemplation and worship of the *Great First Cause* . . . [a task] worthy of rational beings, and doubtless agreeable to the Deity."[4]

This mixture of elements favorable and unfavorable to the pursuit of science led in two successive directions. First, scientists attempted to integrate science into the self-consciously republican enterprise. Charles Willson Peale provides the best example of this effort.[5] Early in the period, inspired by a deep belief in the relationship of science to national progress, intellectual advancement, and religious piety, Peale conceived in Philadelphia that remarkable phenomenon, his museum. Its displays included stuffed fish, birds, and land animals; minerals and soils; insects and plants; fossils; the skeleton of a mastodon; and living animals. With his museum, Peale effectively tested in the 1780s and 1790s whether science could appeal to a broad spectrum of the republican audience. Not precisely a popularizer, especially in the early days, Peale wanted to put on common footing in his museum both the privileged and the ordinary citizen: to educate them both and, in turn, to link that education to piety. His museum was a great "school of nature," he claimed, and nature herself revealed the order and glory of God. Peale believed himself to have founded the ideal scientific institution for a republic, and in his self-portrait painted in 1822 he situated this accomplishment as definitive of his life (fig. 1).

As compatible with publicly expressed national values as were Peale's goals, he engaged in a constant struggle almost from the beginning to keep his project afloat financially. He had to lure audiences into the museum with events and exhibits that were less and less scientific, such as concerts, theatrical spectacles, and odd inventions. Eventually his enterprise faltered. After Peale, few entrepreneurs even attempted to popularize science until considerably later, and the field in the 1820s took its second direction. A reversal of its earlier relationship to the social constituency, this direction was also a contrast to those of art and literature.

Science in America became, if not hermetic, at least its own point of reference. During the 1820s and 1830s, scientific men set the pattern for this development by establishing increasing numbers of societies and journals, garnering university teaching positions, and attracting

Figure 1.   Charles Willson Peale, *The Artist in His Museum*, Philadelphia, 1822. Oil on canvas; H. 103 3/4″, W. 79 7/8″. (Joseph Harrison, Jr., Collection, Pennsylvania Academy of the Fine Arts, Philadelphia, gift of Mrs. Sarah Harrison.)

government support. In pulling away from the early faith that science would be accessible to all of "the sovereigns," they laid the foundations of subsequent impressive achievements in such fields as astronomy, botany, geology, and meteorology. As they withdrew from the larger social sphere of the American public, they joined the mainstream of the transatlantic disciplines. The raw material on the North American continent enabled them to do so.

Artists and writers, however, found their raw material unpromising. While the relationship of science to a reasoned, ordered republican ideal was easily argued, especially if science had practical benefits, painting and literature, which aimed at a moral interpretation of humanity, could not be so benignly packaged. The American constituency, patrons, and subjects of the artistic and literary enterprises presented enormous problems, which had to be addressed by the painters and writers of the young republic.

Unlike scientists, who in gathering the bones and plants of the New World could take pride in their ongoing work for the discipline, artists felt little kinship to the great artistic tradition. There were no art institutions or artistic communities, and few citizens knew anything about art. In 1790 in fact, there were almost no collections of painting, sculpture, or even prints; history painting attracted neither practitioners nor audience; and even well-educated citizens like John Adams suspected that art might be connected necessarily with very unrepublican luxury and glitter. Only the portrait enjoyed any status. Even more than scientists, early painters had to be jacks-of-all-trades.

By hard work and persistence, however, in the first twenty years of the republic artists slowly brought painting to the attention of more and more citizens. Proud owners of estates and mills commissioned topographical landscapes, and city leaders craved artistic commemoration of building projects, such as Philadelphia's new waterworks (fig. 2). The Peale family, prolific and indefatigable, stimulated the domestic market for still lifes (fig. 3), and a few artists succeeded in arousing public interest in simple genre scenes. Laymen and artists in New York, Philadelphia, and Boston formed fledgling academies for exhibitions and instruction, and young well-born painters, such as Washington Allston and John Vanderlyn, even found patrons to finance ambitious programs of study in Europe. Once they returned to the United States, however, Allston, Vanderlyn, and other artists who aimed for the "higher" spheres

Figure 2.   Thomas Birch, *Fairmount Waterworks*, Philadelphia, 1821. Oil on canvas; H. 20⅛", W. 30¹/₁₆". (Pennsylvania Academy of the Fine Arts, Philadelphia, bequest of the Charles Graff Estate.)

found little or no community of support. History painting, which across the Atlantic was the great vehicle for expression of political, social, and intellectual aspirations, could secure no foothold in the republic, and portraiture continued to dominate artistic expression. Even in this endeavor United States audiences and patrons, unchastened by much experience with actual art, set themselves up as experts on what and how artists should paint. Charles Bird King, who painted the genre scene *The Itinerant Artist* in obvious resentment of family members who meddled with the portraitist, was only one of many artists to complain (fig. 4). Focused on their own lives and ambitions, most patrons and audiences saw no relationship whatsoever between painting and the national political enterprise. While orderly topographical landscapes testified to the practical capabilities of settlers and communities, in all other respects painting seemed to be an activity pursued by and for the entrepreneurially ambitious.

There was one prominent exception to this state of affairs, seen in the work of two artists. Scientists had argued for a clear republican

Figure 3.   James Peale, *Still Life No. 2*, Philadelphia, 1821. Oil on wood; H. 18″, W. 26⁷/₁₆″. (Pennsylvania Academy of the Fine Arts, Philadelphia, Henry D. Gilpin Fund.)

ideology for their discipline, and these artists were to do so as well, in the domain of the portrait.

Traditionally, the apparatus of the portrait—costume, setting, and pose—had been used to assert individual status. Especially when undertaken for public display, however, the portrait could also be a major vehicle for communicating to the viewer the sitter's virtue, achievement, and responsibility to the community. Both Gilbert Stuart and Peale, artists of modest social background but of tremendous intelligence, wit, and drive, worked from the early 1790s through the late 1810s to create images of individuals that were also statements of republican values. They promoted themselves as portraitists not of the commercially successful—merchants or bankers—but of the socially and morally responsible—the statesmen, scientists, and political leaders of the new nation. Stuart, working in Philadelphia, Washington, and Boston, and Peale, working in Philadelphia, self-consciously created a body of republican portraiture in two forms: the individual portrait and the portrait gallery.

Figure 4.   Charles Bird King, *The Itinerant Artist*, Washington, D.C., ca. 1825. Oil on canvas; H. 44¾″, W. 57″. (New York State Historical Association, Cooperstown.)

In the individual portrait they followed two guidelines. First, they stripped the background of all the conventions associated with social status, using only props that had intellectual and moral associations, such as the desk, books, and the column. Second, they focused on the moral vision of the sitter as conveyed in a particularly earnest look. Stuart claimed specifically that he tried to evoke the interior "character" of his sitters.[6] His portraits of James Madison (fig. 5) and Thomas Jefferson (fig. 6) are excellent examples, particularly that of Jefferson. In the portrait of Madison the books and the sitter's intense gaze convey his long intellectual leadership of the nation. The portrait of Thomas Jefferson, in which Stuart placed the column, a traditional symbol of virtue, prominently behind the sitter, memorably presents the author of the Declaration of Independence, the leader of the republicans, and the third president as a figure of unique integrity. In Stuart's zeal to present the radiant interior character of his sitters, he often eliminated

Figure 5.   Gilbert Stuart, *James Madison*, Boston, 1805–7. Oil on canvas; H. 48¹/₄″, W. 39³/₄″. (Bowdoin College Museum of Art, Brunswick, Maine, bequest of James Bowdoin III.)

even the trappings of costume, as in his late portrait of John Adams (National Museum of American Art). In at least one portrait Stuart's ideals are evoked by inversion. In his *Lansdowne* portrait of George Washington he was so uncomfortable with a commission that called

Figure 6. Gilbert Stuart, *Thomas Jefferson*, Boston, 1805–7. Oil on canvas; H. 48³/₈″, W. 39³/₄″. (Bowdoin College Museum of Art, Brunswick, Maine, bequest of James Bowdoin III.)

specifically for the conventions of furniture, symbols of wealth, and significant stance that he produced a stilted, unconvincing image (fig. 7). The Washington that Stuart preferred was the man he presented in the *Vaughan* portrait, an early construction of the character of the revered national leader (fig. 8).

Figure 7.   Gilbert Stuart, *George Washington (The Lansdowne Portrait)*, Boston, 1796. Oil on canvas mounted on wood; H. 96″, W. 60″. (Pennsylvania Academy of the Fine Arts, Philadelphia, bequest of William Bingham.)

Figure 8.   Gilbert Stuart, *George Washington (Vaughn Portrait)*, Boston, 1795. Oil on canvas; H. 29″, W. 23¾″. (Andrew W. Mellon Collection, National Gallery of Art.)

In Philadelphia Peale followed a similar strategy. Whether his sitter was an astronomer, a statesman, or an explorer, Peale presented him in the simplest possible format. In his portrait of Benjamin Franklin, for instance, Peale depicted the early political leader, scientist, and

Figure 9.   Charles Willson Peale, *Benjamin Franklin*, Philadelphia, 1785. Oil on canvas; H. 23⅛″, W. 19¹/₁₆″. (The Joseph Harrison, Jr., Collection, Pennsylvania Academy of the Fine Arts, Philadelphia, bequest of Mrs. Sarah Harrison.)

diplomat with a plainness and intensity that are unforgettable—and also precise embodiments of Franklin's own presentation of himself (fig. 9). In his portrait of William Bartram, Peale presented the botanist as a gen-

Figure 10.   Charles Willson Peale, *William Bartram*, Philadelphia, 1808. Oil on canvas; H. 23″, W. 19″. (Independence National Historical Park Collection, Philadelphia.)

tle and thoughtful lover of even the simplest natural specimen, qualities for which he was affectionately known up and down the Atlantic seaboard (fig. 10).

The portrait gallery enabled Peale to make an even more explicit statement of republican ideology. This was his major contribution to art. Conceiving his gallery of portraits of citizens who had made their mark through intellectual achievement to be a fundamental part of his museum, Peale not only recognized the individual sitters with his portraits but also honored, tutored, and argued for the body politic within which these individuals had played significant roles. Peale in effect spoke for the constituency: he became an exponent of what the citizenry aspired to as virtue. Moreover, he placed the portraits above the natural history displays in the highest stratum of his museum exhibits (see fig. 1), clearly conveying the exalted place of man (and by implication man's responsibility) in God's ordered universe. Much like the touring, tabulating scientist, Peale the republican portraitist recorded what was distinctive, and, moreover, what was exemplary in the New World.

Stuart and Peale were the most prominent portraitists and perhaps the best-known painters in the 1790–1825 period. Yet late in their careers their idealism as portraitists had become as old-fashioned as the earlier idealism of scientists who believed that science would be a broadly public pursuit (notable particularly in Peale's museum enterprise). Scientists had turned inward, but artists, who needed patrons and a complex social world to survive, had turned outward for material, literally to the landscape. By 1826 New York City, the new center of American commerce, finance, political manipulation, and social change, had taken the lead in artistic patronage, exhibition, and reception as well, and artistic production changed radically in consequence.

By the late 1820s rampant diversity and economic self-interest in American society had eclipsed the earlier ideal of a republican community. Stuart was finishing his career by making innumerable copies of the one great republican, George Washington, and Peale was concentrating on various inventions. A new generation took over. Portraitists such as Henry Inman in New York and John Neagle in Philadelphia, among others, pursued the portrait as a frank symbol of the material success of the sitter. Neagle's portrait of William Potts Dewees, created only two-and-one-half decades after some of Peale's portraits of ideal leaders, is a telling example (fig. 11). Neagle masked his sitter's plebeian origins and socially disdained medical specialty (obstetrics) by presenting Dewees with the full assistance of costume, pose, and significant furnishings and possessions. The painting constructs the sitter as socially elegant and as

Figure 11. John Neagle, *Dr. William Potts Dewees*, New York City, 1833. Oil on canvas; H. 56 3/4″, W. 44 3/4″. (University of Pennsylvania School of Medicine, Philadelphia.)

a reader, an author, and, perhaps most important, a collector of European art. Only early in national life had art seemed to have a clear relationship to the meaning of the community; only briefly did the community seem to many to have an identifiable collective meaning.

The new nation proved to be a glorious field of exploration for scientists, making possible the participation of American sciences in the discipline at large. In art certain painters were able to turn the portrait to exemplary moral use and thus accommodate imagery to national rhetoric, for a brief period at least. In literature, however, the situation was different. The most salient aspect of American literature during the federal era was writers' struggle for an audience.

This struggle had an important precedent. In eighteenth-century England, which was very much a secular society, writers had had to come to terms with a broader readership across social classes. The period saw the rise of the novel, with its appeal to the authority of the individual reader, the proliferation of poetry for the more ordinary reader, and the struggle of such moralizing authors as Swift and Johnson to market their social and political criticism in persuasive forms.

American eighteenth-century colonial literature, on the other hand, was almost wholly the work of clergymen and aimed toward religious or highly specific moral ends. Few authors—Benjamin Franklin was the most notable exception—acknowledged that readers had their own authority and, what was more, had every right to assert it.

After the Revolution United States writers had to face the lessons that English writers had begun to learn earlier. Enormous practical problems confronted both the would-be writers and their publishers. Like scientists and artists, literary men were confronted with regional dispersion, social anxieties, and the national obsession with commerce. Complicating the situation, publishing was dominated by reprints from British publications in every form, from almanac joke to newspaper column to journal article. Behind this phenomenon was not only the eagerness of American editors to fill up their columns but the entrenched obsequiousness of both publishers and readers, for years after the Revolution, toward what they perceived as British cultural superiority. In the face of so constant a barrage, Americans who tried to make their mark as writers pursued their craft in moments snatched from work as lawyers, editors, and merchants. Like scientists, they were typically more solidly middle class in social identification than artists and thus had a more tendentious relationship with both the "upper classes" and "ordinary" citizens. This strongly affected their flexibility.

To writers the vexing matter of an increasingly democratic audience was even more exasperating than for scientists and artists. Because printed matter, even that purported to be literary, was putatively accessible to everyone, the audience for literature was much larger than that for science. Yet the terms of publication were those of a market economy, an economy not subvertible by promises of utility (as in the sciences) or by the currying of individual patronage (as in the arts). Those who chose to write and publish were responsible to, and tried to gain the response of, a daunting diversity of readers. Who would assume the moral function of the writer—and in the process take the financial risk—for an audience who proclaimed themselves the writer's equals? Thus the most powerful force shaping federal literature was not its field of inquiry (as in the sciences) or its capacity to support an ideology (as in painting) but the author's problematic relationship to his audience.

Just as there were two succeeding directions in the development of science and painting in the period, two basic patterns can be detected in literature as well. Earlier writers assumed a respectful, educated audience who knew the classics; the later ones virtually begged for a hearing from a popular readership that was uneducated and fixed on commercial success. Early writers judged literature to be fundamental to individual moral life; later ones conceived their work as a desperate battle against the degenerating moral life of the entire social constituency of the republic. Two examples of these patterns are Joel Barlow and Hugh Henry Brackenridge, the former well born and working in New England, and the latter of ordinary background and working in Philadelphia and Pittsburgh.[7]

Barlow, a teacher, lawyer, and statesman educated at Yale in the classical tradition, believed that so grand a form of government as a republic deserved a literary epic. He spent almost a decade writing *The Vision of Columbus*, which he published in 1787, an epic poem featuring an angel who unveils to the explorer an inspiring vision of America. Barlow couched his tale in nine books—258 pages—of rhyming iambic pentameter and highly artificial rhetoric. The work attracted virtually no readers beyond the original subscribers, who, one suspects, hardly knew what they were signing up for. Yet in 1807 Barlow decided to try again, this time not to celebrate the republic's glorious future but instead to thunder against what he perceived as the evils encroaching upon it. Insisting that American readers pay attention to an epic of ten books rather than nine, Barlow fulminated against land speculation, corrupt politics, ignorance, religious hypocrisy, and social climbing. This poem was no more popular than its predecessor.[8]

A greater contrast to the (perhaps deliberate) blindness of Barlow to his audience can hardly be imagined than the strategy of Brackenridge several years later. Brackenridge, a "preacher, poet, magazine editor, lawyer, judge, and novelist," also worried about the social uncertainties after the Revolution. But to arouse an audience about his concerns he did not choose the epic form, nor did he rant and rave. In *Modern Chivalry*, which he published in two parts in 1793 and continued to add to over the next twenty years, he devised a novel-like narrative modeled on such comic works as *Don Quixote* and *Tom Jones*. He created a varied cast of characters drawn from the contemporary social constituency rather than that of the past, and from real life rather than from the ethereal realm; he put together a rambling, even haphazard plot; and he employed dialects rather than elevated language. He had learned well the lessons of eighteenth-century English writers. There are no traditional heroes in *Modern Chivalry*. The central character is Captain Farrago, a figure for the declining American aristocracy, who travels around the nation to learn about its citizens. He is accompanied by his Irish servant, Teague O'Regan. Afraid of the democratic tendencies in the new republic, Farrago lies, commits fraud, betrays his friend, and is in other ways as well thoroughly reprehensible. His sidekick Teague is illiterate, foolish, and undisciplined, but through enormous energy he rises above his station, attracts genteel ladies, and gets a government job.[9] Throughout this highly energetic and unpredictable work, Brackenridge laughed at New England merchants, scientists of the American Philosophical Society, doctors, clergy, Indian negotiators, speculators, immigrants, duelers—in short, every element of the democracy.

Brackenridge wrote out of an anxiety about the future of the republic that seems to have been no less intense than that of Barlow, but he chose different strategies to attract his busy, unintellectual, money-making readers. At the top of his list was humor. "We mean [our preaching] for the coming generation, as well as the present," he admitted, "and intending solid observations, *we interlard pleasantry to make the boys read*." He denied that his work was satire, claiming with obvious tongue-in-cheek that after all there was "nothing [in American society] to be ironical about." He simply intended, he joked, to provide the reader with "something to read without the trouble of thinking." When it was not clear that his audience was even reading (much less thinking), Brackenridge affected insouciance about their lack of interest. "I wish I could get this work to make a little more noise. Will nobody attack it and prove that it is insipid, libellous, treasonable, immoral, or irreligious? If they will not do this, let them do something else, praise it, call it excellent, say it contains wit, erudition, genius, and the Lord knows what! Will nobody speak? . . . are yooooe all asleep in the hold there?"[10]

It was Brackenridge's stance—amused, critical, both a part of and separate from the readership—that would be adopted by future writers. The new generation of poets and novelists who came to the fore in the 1820s and who persisted in their careers until midcentury, including such men as William Cullen Bryant and James Fenimore Cooper, and Yankee playwrights (and, slightly earlier, writer Washington Irving), variously enthralled, soothed, and delighted readers by enabling them to identify *other* members of the body politic as causing disorder. Unlike scientists, who increasingly claimed private expertise, and artists, who learned to please ambitious but inexperienced patrons, writers had to imagine a common reader whom they could neither identify precisely nor dislike too much.

It may well have been that the most demanding task that scientists, artists, and writers faced in the early republic was not developing skill in their discipline but judging the appropriate relationship of that discipline to an increasingly democratic society. Whether the botanist who tabulated the flora of the new world, the portraitist who held up community achievement for admiration, or the writer who railed against the flaws in republican society, the scientist, the artist, and author all made the difficult journey from self-conscious interpreters of the new republic to roles as private citizens in a society of competing interests. By 1830 scientists were establishing bases of institutional support and banding into professional organizations that would stand apart from the general public. Painters had begun to carry out the exaltation of the landscape, finally having found an artistic subject that audiences could delight in as both national and virtuous. Writers had learned to cloak their moral exhortations to a democratic citizenry in the rhetoric of sentiment and light comedy.

It is on this larger social world, especially as it affected art, that future study could most profitably focus. In this world the European art-historical tradition was not nearly so important to artists as the social makeup of their constituency, the demands of national ideology, and the claims of a market economy. The struggle of scientists and writers against the same forces, and the distinct directions that they took, provide crucial points of comparison.

[1] John C. Greene, *American Science in the Age of Jefferson* (Ames: Iowa State University Press, 1984); Nathan Reingold, *Science in Nineteenth-Century America: A Documentary History* (New York: Hill and Wang, 1964); George H. Daniels, *American Science in the Age of Jackson* (New York: Columbia University Press, 1968); Emory Elliott, *Revolutionary Writers: Literature and Authority in the New Republic, 1725–1810* (New York: Oxford University Press, 1982); Joseph J. Ellis, *After the Revolution: Profiles of Early American Culture* (New York: W. W. Norton, 1979); and Gordon S. Wood, ed., *The Rising Glory of America, 1760–1820* (New York: Braziller, 1971). Significantly, there is no art-historical study that focuses on the period as a political and social unity; instead, one needs to consult surveys, such as Matthew Baigell, *A Concise History of American Painting and Sculpture* (New York: Harper and Row, 1984), and studies of patronage (including issues of ideology) such as Neil Harris, *The Artist in American Society: The Formative Years, 1790–1860* (New York: Braziller, 1966); Lillian B. Miller, *Patron and Patriotism: The Encouragement of the Fine Arts in the United States, 1790–1860* (Chicago: University of Chicago Press, 1966). For a recent study of the ideological struggles of the first decade of the republic, see Joyce Appleby, *Capitalism and a New Social Order: The Republican Vision of the 1790s* (New York: New York University Press, 1984). In discussing art I will frequently use the word *painting* because there was virtually no sculpture being produced during this era.

[2] Reingold, *Science*, p. 1.

[3] Greene, *American Science*, p. 32.

[4] Alexander Wilson, *American Ornithology; or, The Natural History of the Birds of the United States*, 9 vols. (Philadelphia: Bradford and Inskeep, 1808), 1:3.

[5] For the most recent study of Peale, see Edgar P. Richardson, Brooke Hindle, and Lillian Miller, *Charles Willson Peale and His World* (New York: Harry N. Abrams, 1982).

[6] There is no satisfactory book-length study of Stuart. Dorinda Evans is presently bringing to completion a monograph on the artist that will deal in detail with Stuart and character.

[7] For detailed studies of both Barlow and Brackenridge, see Elliott, *Revolutionary Writers*.

[8] Both works are reprinted in William K. Bottorff and Arthur L. Ford, eds., *The Works of Joel Barlow*, 2 vols. (Gainesville, Fla.: Scholar's Facsimiles and Reprints, 1970).

[9] Elliott, *Revolutionary Writers*, p. 170; Hugh Henry Brackenridge, *Modern Chivalry*, ed. Claude M. Newlin (New York: American Book Co., 1937).

[10] Brackenridge, *Modern Chivalry*, pp. 443–45, 250, as quoted in Elliott, *Revolutionary Writers*, pp. 212, 189, 188, 197